Great Dates in Islamic History

General Editor, Robert Mantran

☑® Facts On File, Inc.

AN INFOBASE HOLDINGS COMPANY

Great Dates in Islamic History

Facts On File, Inc.
11 Penn Plaza
New York NY 10001

Library of Congress Cataloging-in-Publication Data

Great dates in Islamic history / general editor, Robert Mantran.
     p.   cm. — (Great dates)
   Some material in this volume was originally published: Les Grandes dates de l'islam. Paris : Larousse, c1990, in series: Les Grandes dates.
   Includes bibliographical references (p.   ) and index.
   ISBN 0-8160-2935-0 (alk. paper)
   1. Islamic countries — History — Chronology.   2. Islam — History — Chronology.   I. Mantran, Robert.   II. Grandes dates de l'islam. III. Series.
DS35.627.G74   1996
909′.097671 — dc20   95-12883

Facts On File books are available at special discounts when purchased in bulk quantities for businesses, associations, institutions or sales promotions. Please call our Special Sales Department in New York at 212/967-8800 or 800/322-8755.

Text design by Robert Yaffe
Jacket design by Catherine Rincon Hyman
Translation by Richard Watts
Vetting and editing of the whole work, and writing of assorted boxes and chapter 12, by Norbert Scholz
Maps by Florence Neal

This book is printed on acid-free paper.

Printed in the United States of America

MP TT 10 9 8 7 6 5 4 3 2 1

CONTENTS

iii

Contents

LIST OF MAPS

INTRODUCTION

For Europeans, world history has long been equated with the history of Europe or even with the specific national history of each country concerned. This has produced "European History," or national history in which most world events were seen, examined and analyzed from an essentially "Eurocentric" point of view.

Most notably in the 19th century—the century during which Europe affirmed her political and economic superiority—facts and ideas were presented taking neither the origin nor the relevance of these facts into account except in terms of European involvement or influence. From this perspective, the Islamic world was considered unimportant, if not negligible. The history of this part of the world was only partly written—and not with impartiality—at a time when this region had come under the domination of the colonial powers. As to its longevity, expansion, and civilization, few people other than specialists in the field could recall more than a few events or personalities in Islamic history: the battle of Poitiers in 732, Sulayman the Magnificent, etc.

Today, the Muslim world plays an extremely important role. The countries that make up the world of Islam have, since World War II, gained their independence; they have a population of one billion people; several Islamic nations have enormous riches, starting with their income from oil; the Muslim religion seems "unstoppable."

The history of the Muslim world unfolds over the centuries and, as with any other history, knows periods of greatness as well as periods of stagnation or decline. In addition, the Muslim world covers a vast area, stretching from the Atlantic Ocean to the Indian Ocean, and from Morocco to Indonesia. It is therefore impossible to ignore the Muslim world in the study or analysis of the world at large, past and present.

For this reason it is useful to present, by means of this chronology, the stages and the important periods of the history of Islam, as well as the countries in which it established itself and the peoples who have adopted it.

Its history is complex and remarkably different from the history of Christian nations in religious, institutional, cultural and artistic aspects. One should not be surprised, then, to find—in addition to the enumeration of events—these aspects being addressed in this chronology. As it was impossible to provide minute details, we chose to show, in broad strokes, how Islam has played a role in the history of the world.

The number of periods and countries involved necessitated the collaboration of specialists, each covering the area in which they are particularly competent; hence the division of the chronology into sections covering historical periods and geographical regions, with the insertion of additional information where appropriate. Although the presentation of this subject makes such divisions necessary, one should keep in mind the continuity of history, which is only inadequately captured by all the dates and brief introductions.

This work is in no way exhaustive and does not have as its goal the illumination of the entire history of Islam and of all the Muslim nations; omissions and approximations do appear. Nevertheless, one can hope that this book will provide students, colleagues in the discipline of history, and all others who wish to learn about Islam, a practical chronology. Although it is simplified, it can be used as a means of comparison across time of the Muslim and non-Muslim worlds. A great number of events taking place today can be understood with the knowledge of past events; the authors of this book hope to have provided a useful tool for the acquisition of this knowledge.

ROBERT MANTRAN

THE LANGUAGES OF ISLAM

Arabic

Arabic belongs to the Semitic family of languages. As the language of the Qur'an, it gradually became the medium of Islamic politics and culture. In the beginning it was the language only of the army and the small class of officers and governors, but through the administrative reforms of the Umayyad Caliph 'Abd al-Malik (685–705) in the late 7th century, it became the official administrative language of the empire. In the wake of the migration and urbanization of Arab tribes, as well as the Islamization of non-Arab tribes, Arabic spread as the language of the Islamic state and of classical Islamic culture. With the fragmentation of the Islamic empire, Arabic developed into different dialects, none of which became a separate written language. Modern standard Arabic in terms of grammar and vocabulary leans heavily on the classical Arabic of the Qur'an, even though numerous non-Arabic words have entered the language.

The Arabic alphabet consists of 28 signs, written from right to left. Short vowels, the absence of a vowel, or the doubling of a consonant usually are not indicated, but they can be indicated above or below the signs if need be. As in other Semitic languages, most words are derived from three root consonants (radicals) and are modified according to a pattern of more than ten variations.

al- is the Arabic definite article

Consonants that have no equivalent in the English alphabet are:

'	(hamza)	: glottal stop
h		: aspirated h
kh		: like German ch
dh		: voiced th
gh	(ghayn)	: formed in back of the throat
r		: rolled r
s		: palatalized s (will not be indicated here)
d		: palatalized d (will not be indicated here)
t		: palatalized t (will not be indicated here)
z		: palatalized z (will not be indicated here)
'	('ayn)	: formed in lower throat
q		: k formed in back of the throat

(Some of the characters used in the French and German transliteration system are different.)

The Other Languages of Islam

Persian is the successor language of Pahlawi (Middle Persian, as opposed to Old Persian of the Achaemenids), the language of the Sasanid Empire. Around the 11th century, it replaced the dialects of the Persian towns, where it continued to flourish even under outside rule.

Urdu developed under the influence of Persian and spread from India to Indonesia, Malaysia (14th–15th century), and the Sultanate of Atjeh in Sumatra (16th–19th century).

Turkish belongs to the language group of the Turk languages, unrelated to Arabic. It is close to Mongolian and other Central Asian languages. With the expansion of the Ottoman Empire, the Ottoman language became the administrative language of the empire, even though it did not replace Arabic and Persian. In 1928, Atatürk introduced modern Turkish, written in Latin script.

ARABIC NAMES

Arabic names consist of five components: (1) *ism* derived from Islamic or pre-Islamic tradition, e.g., Ibrahim, Dawud, 'Abd Allah (servant of God), Asad (lion); (2) *kunya*, a surname, denoting the father of the oldest son (e.g., Abu Ja'far = father of Ja'far), or an attribute (e.g., Abu al-Atahiya = "father of folly"); (3) *nasab*, the father's/mother's name (e.g., Ibn Rushd = son of Rushd, abbreviated b. Rushd); (4) *nisba*, the place of origin, or residence (e.g., al-Qurashi = from the tribe of Quraysh); (5) *laqab*, one or more surnames (e.g., al-Atrash = "the deaf one," al-Jahiz = "the goggle-eyed")

A typical Arab name would follow the formula: *laqab - kunya - ism - nasab - nisba - laqab*. E.g., 'Izz al-Din (*laqab*) Abu Ja'far (*kunya*) Muhammad (*ism*) ibn Sayf al-Din (father's *laqab*) Abi al-Mansur (father's *kunya*) Muhammad (father's *ism*) ibn 'Izz al-Din (father's *laqab*) Abi al-Qasim (grandfather's *kunya*) Thabit (grandfather's *ism*) ibn Muhammad (great-grandfather) ibn Husayn ibn Hasan ibn Rizq Allah al-Qurashi (*nisba*) al-Tahhan (*laqab* = "the miller").

The Islamic Calendar

The Islamic calendar dates from the Hijra (Hegira) in 622 C.E. It is based on the lunar year and so is shorter than the Western or Gregorian calendar, which is based on the solar year. Islamic festivals are therefore celebrated at different times of the Western year.

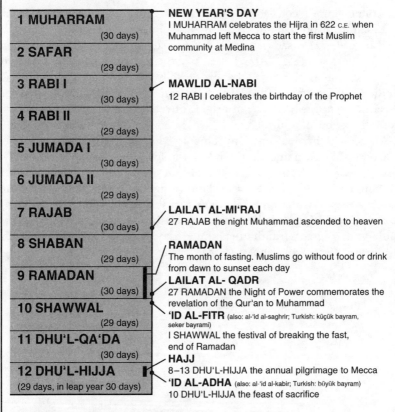

1 MUHARRAM
(30 days)

NEW YEAR'S DAY
I MUHARRAM celebrates the Hijra in 622 C.E. when Muhammad left Mecca to start the first Muslim community at Medina

2 SAFAR
(29 days)

3 RABI I
(30 days)

MAWLID AL-NABI
12 RABI I celebrates the birthday of the Prophet

4 RABI II
(29 days)

5 JUMADA I
(30 days)

6 JUMADA II
(29 days)

7 RAJAB
(30 days)

LAILAT AL-MI'RAJ
27 RAJAB the night Muhammad ascended to heaven

8 SHABAN
(29 days)

RAMADAN
The month of fasting. Muslims go without food or drink from dawn to sunset each day

9 RAMADAN
(30 days)

LAILAT AL- QADR
27 RAMADAN the Night of Power commemorates the revelation of the Qur'an to Muhammad

10 SHAWWAL
(29 days)

'ID AL-FITR (also: al-'id al-saghrir; Turkish: küçük bayram, seker bayrami)
I SHAWWAL the festival of breaking the fast, end of Ramadan

11 DHU'L-QA'DA
(30 days)

HAJJ
8–13 DHU'L-HIJJA the annual pilgrimage to Mecca

12 DHU'L-HIJJA
(29 days, in leap year 30 days)

'ID AL-ADHA (also: al-'id al-kabir; Turkish: büyük bayram)
10 DHU'L-HIJJA the feast of sacrifice

The only reliable way of converting Islamic (Hijri) dates (H) to dates in the Christian era (CE) is by consulting conversion tables. An approximation can be obtained by applying the following formula:

Islamic dates to CE:
$$CE = (H \cdot {}^{32}/_{33}) + 622$$
CE to Islamic dates:
$$H = (CE - 622) \cdot {}^{32}/_{33}$$

- On March 1, 1917, **Turkey** introduced the Gregorian calendar.
- In 1925, **Iran** reintroduced the Persian sun year, which is adjusted to the Gregorian calendar, but begins with the Hijra. The conversion of these "hijra sun years" (*hijri shamsi*, H.Sh.) is easy: HSh + 621 (for dates between March 21 and December 31), and HSh + 622 (for dates between January 1 and March 20).

The days of the week are named by ordinal numbers, except for Friday and Saturday:

yawm al-ahad (the first day) = Sunday
yawm al-ithnayn (the second day) = Monday
yawm al-thulatha' (the third day) = Tuesday
yawm al-arbi'a' (the fourth day) = Wednesday
yawm al-khamis (the fifth day) = Thursday
yawm al-jum'a (the day of congregation) = Friday
yawm al-sabt (the day of rest) = Saturday

Pre-Islamic Arabia
and the Origins of Islam

In the middle of the Arabian Peninsula lies an expansive desert, but it is not a world without inhabitants; in the coastal regions, in the foothills, on the borders of Palestine and Mesopotamia, towns were set up that, for the most part, served as resting points for caravans. Due to the peninsula's location between two oceans and three continents, it had become an important intersection for long-distance trade since antiquity.

In southern Arabia (Yemen) there had been a prosperous kingdom, and, according to tradition, it was the home of the Queen of Saba (Sheba). During the time of the Romans, a number of kingdoms emerged: for example, the Nabatean Petra, east of the Dead Sea; Palmyra, west of the Euphrates; and Himayr in the south. In addition to the cults devoted to the divinities who personify the planets, there were Jewish and Christian communities, which had settled along the trade routes. Central and northern Arabia are the domain of nomadic Bedouins as well as of some more sedentary peoples living in oases or in the towns located mostly in the west. They worship spirits, jinns, and divinities, one of whom, Allat, is superior to all others. Northern and southern Arabs speak dialects that, through the poetry of those regions, evolve into the Arabic language, which finds its most important expression in the Qur'an.

At this time the Byzantine, Persian (Sassanid), and Ethiopian civilizations emerge, competing with each other for supremacy in the region. While these powers exhaust each other's forces, Muhammad receives his revelation and founds a new religion, Islam. Capitalizing on the weakening of the Byzantine and the Sassanid peoples, who had been at war with each other for more than 20 years, his first two successors (caliphs) orchestrate a vast territorial expansion of the Arabs; nevertheless, the conversion of the conquered peoples will take place slowly. With the accession of Muhammad's cousin and son-in-law 'Ali to the caliphate, Muslim unity sustains an irremediable blow that translates into a rupture, leading to conflicts between the partisans of the Sunnis and Shi'is, the two principal groups of Muslims.

Qur'an

The sacred scripture of Islam, revealed to Muhammad directly by God. It contains 114 chapters (*suras*) of differing length. At the death of Muhammad, there was no complete collection of his revelations (which had been written on stones, bones, pieces of leather or wood etc.). His followers unified the Qur'an, as it is known today. It is the basis of Islamic jurisprudence and contributed to the rapid expansion of Islam.

Sunnis — Shi'is

Sunnis: They constitute the majority of Muslims. They accept the authority of the first generation of Muslims and the first four caliphs. Sunnism is also referred to as "Muslim Orthodoxy," since the Sunnis claim to adhere to the words, deeds and scripture of Muhammad.

Shi'is: They consider 'Ali to be the legitimate successor of Muhammad, not the first four caliphs. They competed with the Sunnis for political and doctrinal dominance, but were ultimately pushed back to the area of present-day Iran and Iraq, as well as North Africa. They are divided into numerous subgroups and there are Shi'i minorities in many Muslim countries. The most important Shi'i group is the twelver Shi'a, which accepts a chain of 12 imams as legitimate successors of Muhammad. According to their belief, the 12th imam lives on in occultation and will return to establish the divine kingdom on earth.

The Pre-Islamic Arab World (until the beginning of the 7th century)

9th century B.C.
Mention of the "Aribi" in Assyrian cuneiform script; describes nomads of the steppe as owners of camels, in northern Arabia (including those of Iran).

7th century B.C.
In southern Arabia, the Ma'in, Saba', Qataban, Hadramaut and Qahtan kingdoms develop civilizations based on agriculture. Ma'rib dam built in the Saba' kingdom (Yemen).

2nd century B.C.
Nabateans, of Arabian descent, build the kingdom of Petra east of the Dead Sea.

1st century B.C.
Ma'in and Qataban kingdoms disappear. Domination of southern Arabia by the Himyarites.

105 A.D.
Creation in Arabia of a Roman province (in Nabatean territory).

End of the 3rd century

Lakhmid kingdom founded in north-eastern Arabia by Christianized Arabs; it is a vassal of the Sassanids. Capital: Hira.

288–328

Reign of the Lakhmid Imru al-Qays.

4th–5th century

Kinda kingdom founded in central Arabia, sponsored by Yemeni kingdom in order to balance Romans and Sassanids; breaks apart when Yemen is occupied by the Abyssinians.

5th century

Mecca dominated by the Quraysh tribe, who controlled the caravan trade; becomes an important city for long-distance trade; the city also is a pilgrimage site, due to its possession of the Ka'ba.

Circa 490

In northwestern Arabia, Ghassan tribe settles, becoming vassals of Byzantium to fight against the Sassanids. Members of the tribe are adepts of monophysite Christianity (which emphasizes the unity of human and divine nature in Jesus).

Beginning of 6th century

The Himyarite king, Dhu-Nawas, converts to Judaism; persecution of Christians.

524

Invasion led by Dhu-Nawas against the Christians in Najran.

525

Invasion of Yemen by the Christian Abyssinians in alliance with Romans; end of Jewish kingdom.

542

Ma'rib dam (Yemen) breaks; symbolizes decline of south Arabian agricultural society.

570

The Ethiopian governor Abraha attacks Mecca in order to eliminate the pagan Ka'ba. The attack fails. Since there was an elephant in Abraha's army, this year became known as the "year of the elephant."

609–620

Sassanid conquests in Syria and in Egypt by Khusraw II.

622–629

Byzantine reconquest during the reign of Heraclius; restoration of

---

Ka'ba

The central sanctuary in Islam; a roughly cube-shaped building in Mecca that houses a black stone. According to tradition, Abraham and Ismael laid its foundation. It had been a pilgrimage site in pre-Islamic times. The fact that it was filled with pagan idols made the Muslims forbid the participation of polytheists after they entered Mecca in 630 and made the Ka'ba their central sanctuary.

status quo, but forces of Romans and Sassanids are depleted.

Muhammad (571–632)

570 or 571

Birth of Muhammad (in Mecca) soon after the death of his father.

577

Death of Amina b. Wahb, Muhammad's mother. He is raised first by his grandfather 'Abd al-Muttalib, then by his uncle Abu Talib.

Circa 590–595

Muhammad travels to Syria: supposedly meets the monk Bahira in Basra. Bahira allegedly recognizes him as the future prophet of the Arabs and teaches him faith in one God.

Circa 591

Muhammad begins work for Khadija, a rich widow caravan owner. He marries her in 596; she is much older than he.

Circa 610

First visions: first revelations received from the angel Gabriel.

613

Muhammad transmits the revelation to the Meccans. First followers; first persecutions by the Qurayshites, who feared he would undermine the commercial and religious order.

615

Exodus of some of Muhammad's followers into Ethiopia because of the persecutions. Muhammad stays in Mecca.

619

Death first of Khadija, then of Abu Talib.

620–621

The Khazraj and Awz tribes, from the town of Yathrib (approx. 200 miles north of Mecca) convert to Islam.

622

June. The Aqaba Pact: some of the recently converted of Yathrib promise loyalty to Muhammad and promise him and his followers protection if they come to Yathrib.

Summer. Muslims from Mecca leave for Yathrib.

Sept. 24/12 Rabi I, year 1 of the Islamic calendar. The Hijra: Muhammad responds to the call of enemy Jewish and Arab tribes to serve as a mediator, and flees to Yathrib, since he fears for his life in Mecca. Yathrib later becomes Madina al-Nabi (in abbreviated form, Madina or Medina), "the city of the prophet."

623/1

February. Muhammad marries 'A'isha, daughter of Abu Bakr, his companion. "Constitution of Year I": Muhammad settles conflicts in Medina, laying the foundation of the Muslim community (*umma*). Marriage of Fatima, daughter of Muhammad, to Ali b. Abu Talib, Muhammad's cousin. Muhammad continues fight against the pagan Mecca.

624/2

January/Rajab. Attack on a Meccan caravan at Nakhla (near Mecca).

March/Ramadan. Muslims raid Qurayshit' caravan in Badr; first significant victory of Islam.

April/Shawwal. Jewish tribe of the Banu Qaynuqa expelled from Medina, since Jews do not accept Muhammad's teachings.

625/3-4

March 23/7 Shawwal. Muslims defeated by Quraysh in Uhud; Quraysh fail to suppress Medina.

August/Rabi I 4. The Jewish sect of the Banu Nadir expelled from Medina.

627/5-6

March/Dhu'l-Qa'da. Meccans fail to conquer Medina, which is protected by a ditch ("Campaign of al-Khandaq" = the ditch).

May/Muharram. The Jewish sect of the Banu Qurayza from Medina massacred.

628/6-7

March–April/Dhu'l-Hijja–Muharram. Meccans oppose Muhammad's pilgrimage to Mecca. Negotiations and truce of Hudaybiyya (named after a tree at the city boundaries of Mecca, where the negotiations took place). Muhammad offers a 10-year truce to the Quraysh in exchange for allowing the Muslims a peaceful pilgrimage to Mecca.

May–June/Muharram. Muhammad conquers the Khaybar and Fadak oases.

629/7-8

March/Dhu'l-Qa'da. Peaceful pilgrimage of Muslims to Mecca.

September/Jumada I. Muslims defeated by the Byzantines at Mu'ta, near the Dead Sea.

December/Shawwal. Truce of Hudaybiyya broken by some Bedouin allies of the Quraysh.

630/8-9

January 11/20 Ramadan. Muhammad accompanied by about 10,000 men enters Mecca without a fight. Destruction of the Ka'ba idols. Interior of the sanctuary declared sacred (haram). Unification of the Hawazins of Taif and of the Bedouin tribes under the banner of Islam. Treaty signed with the Christians from Najran (Yemen) to accept Muhammad's political control while maintaining their allegiance to Jesus.

631/9

March/Dhu'l-Hijja. Abu Bakr put in charge of the pilgrimage (hajj).

632/10-11

March/Dhu'l-Hijja. Pilgrimage to Mecca by Muhammad (later called the Farewell Pilgrimage).

June 8/13 Rabi I. Death of Muhammad in Medina. Turns the duty of leading the prayer over to Abu Bakr.

The First Four Caliphs (632–657)
Military Expeditions and Conquests
632–634/11–13: Caliphate of Abu Bakr

633/12-13

End of the secession by the competing prophet Maslama (called Musaylima) among the Banu Hanifa in central Arabia. Hira occupied by Khalid b.

al-Walid, a convert from the Quraysh, and a distinguished commander. Victory of Kharizma in Mesopotamia. The Ghassanids defeated in Marj Rahit.

634/13

July 30/28 Jumada I—Victory of Ajnadayn over the Byzantines. Occupation of all of Palestine, except Jerusalem and Caesarea.

August 23/22 Jumada II—Death of Abu Bakr.

634–644/13–23: Caliphate of 'Umar b. al-Khattab (companion of Muhammad)

'Umar is designated by Abu Bakr.

634–642/13–21

Campaign against the Sassanids.

635/14

October/Sha'ban. Muslim victory in Buwayb.

637/16

June/Jumada I. Sassanids crushed in Qadisiyya (Iraq).

August/Ramadan. Fall of Ctesiphon (Mada'in), the Sassanid capital. Basra founded as a garrison town in southern Iraq.

638/17

Kufa founded as a garrison town on a branch of the Euphrates.

639/18

Occupation of Ahwaz and Khuzistan.

642/21

Sassanids defeated in Jalula and Nihavand. The Arabs rule Mesopotamia and western and central Persia.

635–641/14–20: Syrian and Palestinian Campaigns

635/14

February 25/1 Muharram. Victory of Khalid b. al-Walid in Marj al-Suffar, near Damascus.

September/Rajab. First occupation of Damascus.

636/15

August 20/12 Rajab. Battle of Yarmuk (near the Jordan River). Byzantines abandon Syria. Permanent occupation of Damascus.

637/16

Ba'lbek, Homs and Hama taken.

638/17

Jerusalem taken; Jews expelled, but not Christians.

639/18

Mu'awiya, a former leader of the Quraysh, becomes governor of Syria.

641/20

Caesarea taken.

639–646/18–25: The Egyptian Campaigns

639/18

December/Dhu'l-Hijja. First raid by 'Amr b. al-'As into Egypt.

640/19

January/Muharram. Faramiya and the Bilbays taken.

July/Rajab. Victory over the Byzantines at Ayn Shams.

641/20

April 9/21 Rabi II. Surrender of the Egyptian citadel of Babylon.

642/21

September 29/28 Shawwal. Alexandria occupied. Barka taken. Occupation of Cyrenaica.

643/22

Fustat founded.

643/22

November 3/26 Dhu'l-Hijja. Assassination of the caliph 'Umar by a dissatisfied slave.

644–656/23–35: Caliphate of 'Uthman b. 'Affan

'Uthman, a rich merchant and son-in-law of the Prophet, who had participated in the immigration to Ethiopia, is elected shortly before 'Umar's death.

645/24

Alexandria retaken by the Byzantines.

645–646/25

Armenia under Muslim suzerainty.

646/25

Summer. Alexandria permanently occupied by the Muslims.

647/26

Raids into Cappadocia, Phrygia, and Ifriqiyya.

649/28

First Arab maritime expeditions; occupation of Cyprus.

651/30

Eastern Persia occupied.

655/34

Defeat of the Byzantine fleet off Lycia (Battle of the Masts).

656/35

June 17/18 Dhu'l-Hijja. Assassination of 'Uthman after increasing dissatisfaction in the provinces with his handling of finances and accusations of nepotism. 'Ali b. 'Ali Talib, Muhammad's cousin and son-in-law, is proclaimed caliph.

The Muslim Community

632/11

After the death of Muhammad, rivalry develops between the *Ansars* (auxiliaries of the Prophet and the converts from Medina) and the *Muhajirun* (emigrés from Mecca to Medina). The latter group conquers with the choice of Abu Bakr as Muhammad's successor (*khalifa:* caliph).

632–633/11–12

Political and religious secession (*ridda,* "apostasy") of diverse tribes who reaffirm traditional tribal peculiarism; renewal of Judaism and Christianity. Secessionists vanquished by Khalid b. al-Walid's army.

634–636/13–15

Progressive unification of Arabia by the caliph 'Umar. Jews from Khaybar are forced to immigrate to Jericho and Christians from Najran immigrate to Syria. The Arabian peninsula is the only territory containing exclusively Muslims (*dar al-Islam*).

638/17

Organization of the conquered territories in Syria (the *jund*); military bases established (*amsar*).

Caliph

(*khalifa* = successor): Since Muhammad did not decide on his successor, the Muslim community soon split over the problem of who was his legitimate heir. After the secession of the Shi'is under 'Ali, the Sunnis maintained their caliphate in the Arab East until the Mongol invasion of 1258. One of the centerpieces of Islamic philosophy is the question of the characteristics of the right caliph. A politically insignificant shadow-caliphate continued until 1924, when it was formally abolished by the Turks.

Dar al-Islam:

Lands under Muslim rule as opposed to *dar al-harb* (the lands of war). It is every Muslim's duty to help extend the dar al-Islam by violent or peaceful means (*jihad*).

People of the Book

(*ahl al-kitab*): All members of the monotheistic religions, especially Christians and Jews. They enjoy special protection by Muslims (*dhimma* = protection; *dhimmi* = the protected), although they do not have the same rights as Muslims.

641/20

Institution of the first *diwan*, office of financial and military affairs. Landholders required to pay property taxes (*kharaj*): the Christians, the Jews and the Zoroastrians (*ahl al-kitab*— "People of the Book") pay a poll tax (*jizya*) in exchange for protection (*dhimma*).

651–652/30–32

Soldiers' rebellion in Iraq; factional strife in Kufa and Khurasan, which refuse 'Uthman's governor.

656/35–36

Egyptian troops march on Medina and assassinate the caliph 'Uthman.

June 17/18 Dhu'l-Hijja. Ali elected thanks to the *Ansar*. His adversaries rally around 'A'isha (Muhammad's widow), Talha and Zubayr, two of her most loyal associates among the Muhajirun.

December 9/16 Jumada II 36. "Battle of the Camel" near Basra ('A'isha observed the battle on camelback). 'Ali's adversaries defeated, allowing 'Ali to move his capital from Medina to Kufa.

657/36-37

Spring. Mu'awiya, governor of Syria, declares blood revenge against 'Ali. Beginning of rupture (*fitna*) of the Muslim community.

July 26/8 Safar 37. Battle of Siffin (east of Aleppo) between Mu'awiya and 'Ali ends in a stalemate. Arbitration accepted. Some of 'Ali's followers, the Kharijis, reject arbitration and leave his army (from Arabic: *kharaja* = to leave). They later engage the caliphs in numerous battles, and form their own sect with puritan tendencies. By the 8th century, most of them have been eliminated.

658/38

July 17/9 Safar. The Kharijis conquered by 'Ali at Nahrawan.

659/38

January/Sha'ban. In Adhruh, arbitration rejects claims of both Ali and Mu'awiya.

660/40

May/Muharram. Mu'awiya proclaimed caliph by his troops, and his new title is recognized in Syria, Palestine, Egypt and Hejaz. 'Ali recognized as caliph in Iraq and Iran.

661/40

January/Ramadan. 'Ali assassinated in Kufa by a Khariji in revenge for the massacre of Nahrawan.

Religion

610

March/26-27 Ramadan. The night during which Muhammad has his first revelation. Known as "The Night of Destiny" (*layla al-qadar*), it is commemorated every year.

610-632

Muhammad has the revelations that will become the text of the Qur'an.

615

Ascent of Muhammad to the seventh heaven (according to Muslim legend).

622/1

July 16/1 Muharram. Start of the Muslim calendar, beginning with the Hijra.

April 622

Duties of the believers delineated ("five pillars of Islam"): recognition of the unity of God and Muhammad's status as the prophet (*shahada*), prayer five times a day (*salat*), giving of alms (*zakat*), fasting during the month of Ramadan (*sawm*), pilgrimage (*hajj*) to Mecca. Designation of a specific site for prayer, the mosque (*masjid*).

623/1

Constitution of the community of believers (*umma*) proclaimed in Medina (Yathrib).

624/2

February/Ramadan. Month of Ramadan designated period of fasting; Mecca designated in place of Jerusalem as site for the geographical orientation of prayer.

632/10

The process and rituals of the pilgrimage (*hajj*) to Mecca fixed.

Circa 653/32

Text of the Qur'an, or Vulgate, established by Zayd b. Thabit; it contains 114 Suras (chapters) further broken down into verses (*ayat*).

657/37

Following the Battle of Siffin, Muslim community divided into three groups: the Sunnis (*ahl al-sunna*), the orthodox majority who follow Mu'awiya; the Shi'is (*shi'a 'Ali* = 'Ali's partisans); and the Kharijis (*khawarij*), who refuse to recognize the authority of either the Mu'awiya or 'Ali.

The Umayyads:
The Arabo-Muslim Expansion

The first rupture (*fitna*) among the Muslims was followed by the recognition of Mu'awiya as caliph, which did not imply the creation of a dynasty. Bit by bit, however, thanks to the political astuteness of its founder, a dynastic power was established based on a close relationship with the Arab tribal army (*muqatila*), military expansion, and the taxes paid by the protected non-Muslims. Expansion, the creation of new military bases (*amsar*) in Ifriqiyya and in Transoxiana, along with the forced submission of the Berbers, Sogdians and Bactrians, filled the treasury and would ultimately lead to the emergence of a hierarchical power structure. The Muslim state adopted the symbols of power: money, *tiraz*, and the seal of the caliph on official documents on papyrus. In the meantime, the legitimacy of the ruling Umayyad dynasty was called into question by the Companions of the Prophet (the Muhajirun) and their heirs, defenders of the Meccan aristocracy, and by the Kharijites, whose incessant revolts point to their weakness.

Although complete tolerance existed in the religious sphere, the dissatisfaction of different groups within the empire became more and more acute. On one hand, the Iranian *mawali*, non-Arab converts to Islam, demanded participation in the political and social power structure from which they had been excluded under Umayyad rule. On the other hand, tribal rivalries among the Arabs themselves added to the tensions. In addition, the expanding empire demanded more and more funds both for a centralizing state apparatus and to support ever-growing specialization in the army. Whereas before, Islamic expansion was encouraged by all strata of society, now a professional army came into existence, demanding regular wages, and alienating those no longer involved in military conquest.

The Umayyad Dynasty and the Problem of Legitimacy

661/41

August 28/25 Rabi II. Mu'awiya accepted as caliph in the empire, in particular by Hasan and Husayn, 'Ali's sons.

661–680/41–60

Government based on "wisdom" and the loyalty of the tribes: as "first among his peers," Mu'awiya avoids all pretense that his authority is religiously derived; as tribal chief, he receives support of the Syrian army.

678/58

Mu'awiya insists that his oldest son be recognized as his successor.

680/61

Yazid becomes caliph.

680/61

October 10/10 Muharram. 'Ali's son Husayn is killed in the battle of Karbala' (near Kufa) after he revolts against Yazid. His "martyrdom" gives birth to the idea of vengeance and mourning among the Shi'is.

683–692/64–73

Second *fitna:* Ibn al-Zubayr, son of a Companion, is recognized as the anti-Umayyad caliph in Mecca and supported by his brother in Iraq: Meccan aristocracy opposed to the dynastic principle. But tribal rivalries in some provinces undermine his authority. In Syria, the Qays and Mudar (Tamim and Azd) follow Ibn al-Zubayr; Kalb and Rabia follow Marwan, a cousin of Mu'awiya's (and the chief advisor of 'Uthman). Marwan I and Kalb triumph over the Qays in the battle of Marj Rahit, 684/65 (east of Damascus).

684–685/65

Schism between Kharijis, quietist 'Ibadis and radical Azraqis, due to lack of formalized theology and the contact with different peoples throughout the empire. Khariji rebellions in Najd, Iraq and Iran.

685/65

January 4/22 Jumada I. March of the Shi'is (*tawwabbun* = repentants) to Kufa; they offer themselves to the Syrians for slaughter in penance for their abandonment of Husayn.

685–687/65–67

Shi'i revolt led by Mukhtar in the name of Muhammad b. al-Hanafiyya, one of Ali's sons, and the prospective caliph. Mukhtar attempts to set up an egalitarian state with equal rights for the *mawali*. The old Kufan aristocracy turns against him, and defeats him with the help of the governor of Basra (687).

685–705/65–86: Caliphate of 'Abd al-Malik

Arabic adopted as the administrative language; first Muslim gold money minted; construction of a network of strategic roads marked by stones.

692/73

Al-Hajjaj, commander of 'Abd al-Malik's forces, conquers Mecca and kills Ibn al-Zubayr; elimination of second caliph, and end of the second *fitna.*

694–714/75–95

Al-Hajjaj is installed as governor of the Sassanid provinces. Assumes dictatorial powers, imposes centralization and Arabization. Severe fiscal policy for the *mawali*.

696/77

Monetary reform: First coins of the Islamic state are minted, replacing

MONEY AFTER THE REFORM OF 696			
Coins	Weight	Title	Type
Gold Dinar	4.25 g	96/98%	After the money showing the caliph
Silver Dirham	2.97 g		standing, purely epigraphic types: Date and place of minting, political and religious themes: *kalima* "prophetic mission," "Umayyad symbol" and the seals of the caliph and governor.
Brass Fals	variable		Epigraphic: name of governor, eulogies, distinctive mark of the mint.

previous Byzantine coins, thus asserting the power of the Islamic state.

700/81

In Kufa and Basra, revolt led by the "nobles," descendants of the Prophet (*ashraf*), against the plebeian Hajjaj, a movement tainted by Kharijism.

707–715/88–96: Caliphate of Walid I
Walid I founds the mosque in Damascus.

715–717/96–99: Caliphate of Sulayman
Break with Hajjaj's policies; the *mawali* accepted as volunteers in the army.

717–720: Caliphate of 'Umar II
Conciliation of Shi'is and Kharijis through his piety; encourages ascent to ruling class by conversion to Islam.

720–724/102–105: Caliphate of Yazid II
Debauched sovereign isolated in his palace. Khariji revolts among the Arabs from Kirman and Sijistan.

724–743/105–125: Caliphate of Hisham
The last great Umayyad Caliph. Makes the administration more effective.

743–744/125–126: Caliphate of Walid II
Struggles between factions at the heart of the Umayyad court and army; the caliph attempts to substitute primogeniture for seniority within the clan. The caliph is killed in a Marwanid plot.

744/126: Caliphate of Yazid III
"Yemeni" policy (end to the distribution of lands, end of expansionism, moderate fiscal policy, adoption of the theology of free will, *qadariyya*).

13

Religious Movements and the 'Abbasid Revolution

684–692/65–72

Great Khariji revolts fomented by the ancient readers of the Qur'an over right interpretation of Islam; Arab oligarchy rules the empire. Despite an egalitarian program, Muslims pay only the *zakat* and the State survives on the *jizya* from the *dhimmi*, which they had to pay in return for their special protection (*dhimma*).

701/81–82

Khariji revolt led by Ibn al-Ash'ath, a chief of the Qahtan tribe, in Iran and Iraq against al-Hajjaj, who crushed the Khariji movement.

716/98

'Abbasid movement (*da'wa*) based on the testament of the 'Alite al-'Abbas b. 'Abd al-Muttalib b. Hisham, an uncle of the Prophet. Initially, the movement had sympathies for Shi-'ism, but later persecuted that sect. Its goal was to depose the Umayyad usurpers and reinstate the family of the Prophet.

736/119

Success of the *da'wa* in Khurasan (Iran).

740/122

Revolt led by the Zayd, the imam of a Shi'i sect, in Kufa against the Umayyads. Zayd dies in the attack.

744/127

Abu Salama, head of the 'Abbasid movement in Iraq, holds the position of *wazir al-Muhammad*, "representative of the Family."

745/128

Abu Muslim ("The Muslim"), a freed and recently converted Iranian slave, is given the position of military leader in Khurasan: *amir al-Muhammad*, "Commander for the Family."

747/129

The imam Ibrahim, the spiritual leader of the movement, is arrested; he dies in an Umayyad prison.

June 9/25 Ramadan. The revolt in Khurasan set in motion: a black flag is flown, and a *khutba* (Friday session) begun in the name of the imam they await.

748/131

Medina taken by 'Ibadi Kharijis, defeated by Marwanis.

749/132

Kufa (Iraq) taken and Abu al-'Abbas, the brother of Ibrahim, proclaimed caliph.

750/132

Battle of the Greater Zab: defeat and death of Marwan II in Egypt; the Umayyads massacred. Execution of Abu Salama. Beginning of the 'Abbasid era.

755/137

Execution of Abu Muslim by the caliph al-Mansur: elimination of the leading figures of the 'Abbasid Revolution; a Marwanid regime reestablished; former Umayyad insurgents and a selection of the faithful from the participants (*da'i*) in the *da'wa* granted pardons (*aman*).

755/137

In Khurasan, revolt led by Sunbadh in the name of Abu Muslim, presently "occulted" and soon to be *mahdi*, who will return and erect the divine kingdom on earth.

Conquest and Islamization

648–649/28

Organization of the Muslim navy.

653/33

Naval attack against Cyprus (Byzantines) and the surrounding archipelago.

654–655/34

"Battle of the Masts": naval victory over the Byzantines.

668–673/47–53

First siege of Constantinople fails.

670/50

Kairuan, base for the conquest of the Ifriqiya, founded by 'Uqba b. Nafi.

679/58

Carthage taken.

683/63

'Uqba b. Nafi killed by the Berber Kusayla in a revolt; the Arabs retreat to Cyrenaica (in modern Libya).

695–698/76–79

Reconquest of the Maghrib; defeat of the revolt led by the Berber "Prophetess" Kahina, by Hasan b. al-Nu'man.

710–713/91–94

Expansion, in the east, to the Indus delta.

711/92

Tariq b. Ziyad, the Berber governor of Tangier under Musa b. Nusayr, the governor of Ifriqiya, passes through the Strait of Gibraltar. (Hence the name "Gibraltar": *Jabl al-Tariq* = Tariq's mountain). In Spain, defeat of King Roderic and the Visigothic state. With the help of a large Arab army, the Muslims invade Spain.

712/93

Establishment of the Malatya/Melitene province, on the border with Cappadocia; peopled by Aramaean peasants fleeing the Byzantines.

717–718/98–100

Unsuccessful siege of Constantinople under the Caliph Sulayman.

718/100

Battle of Covadonga (Spain): unsuccessful attempt by the Muslims to suppress the resistance by the Asturians. Beginning of the Christian Reconquista (reconquest) of Spain.

721/102

Narbonne (France) taken.

731/113

Derbend founded, near the mouth of the Volga.

732/114

Defeat of the Andalusian governor in the battle of Tours and Poitiers (France) by Charles Martel, the founder of the Carolingian dynasty. Although this battle was hardly more than a border skirmish, Christian historiography sees it as the key event in the containment of Islam in Europe.

740/123

Berber revolt in North Africa, especially in Morocco; the Berbers of Spain also rebel against the Arabs.

742/125

Nine provinces in Andalusia conceded to the Syrian contingent of the invading army (*jund*) after they had been called to help defeat the rebellious Berbers in Spain. The Syrians remain in Spain and settle in the plains. This establishes their antagonism toward the Arabs who had come earlier.

747/129

Byzantine naval defeat of the 'Abbasids off Cyprus ensures Christian dominance of the Mediterranean for another century.

The Iranian Provinces

665/45

Ziyad b. Abu Sufyan becomes governor of Basra and the Iranian provinces. Settlement of 50,000 Arab families in Khurasan.

706–715/87–96

Conquest of Transoxiana, starting with the Merv oasis, by Qutayba b. Muslim.

712/93

Muslim conquest of Samarkand and Khwarizm.

714/95

Conquest of Ferghana: submission of the prince = *ikhshid*.

722/104

The governor 'Umar b. Hubayra resumes Hajjaj's policy and limits the granting of *'ata* pensions.

733/115

Number of enlisted and pensioned soldiers limited to 15,000, leading to the revolts of the Arabs from Khurasan.

738/120

Fiscal reform by governor Nasr b. Sayyar in order to contain social unrest: *mawali* pay fewer taxes.

Religious Life

Circa 674–circa 706/54–87

John the Damascene, tax collector for the caliph, then Melkite monk, starts the "Damascus polemic" against Islam, continued by the Melkite bishop of Harran, Theodora Abu Qurra (740–820).

685–705/65–86

'Abd al-Malik imposes 'Uthman's style of organization for the Qur'an as opposed to the one used by Ibn Mas'ud (used in *kufa*).

699–700/80

Death of Ma'bad al-Juhani, founder of Murjism.

Circa 700/circa 80

Karaite movement, composed of Iraqi Jews (Abu 'Isa 'Ubayda and Anan b. David), opposed to rabbinical Judaism. Ideas of "occultation" (*ghayba*) and return (*raj'a*) gain popularity in Muslim eschatology, based

Murji'a:

(from Arabic *irja'*, postponement, deferment). A quietist sect of early Islam. In their opinion, sinners should not be condemned, because faith can offset sins. They were politically uninvolved and believed that outward confession of faith was sufficient for a good Muslim. The sect emerged mainly in reaction to the Kharijis, who saw sin in more absolute terms.

Mahdi

(Arabic = the one who is under divine guidance). Especially among the Shi'is, an occultized imam who will return at the end of time and liberate mankind from all sin, evil and injustice.

on the notion of *mahdi*. Parallel development of the notion of transmigration of the soul among Shi'i *ghulat* (extremists), who attribute divine qualities to 'Ali and other imams.

708/89

Death of the monophysite bishop, Jacob of Edessa, founder of the Syrian liturgy, who invented a grammar for the Syrian language.

716/97

The Parsis (Zoroastrians) emigrate from Kuhistan to Gujerat (northern India).

728/110

Death of Hasan al-Basri, preacher, heir to the asceticism (*zuhd*) of Abu Dharr al-Ghifari, master of the Sufis. Wasil b. 'Ata (699–748) and 'Amr b. 'Ubayd (699–761), his students, are the prime movers in the *mu'tazila*

school, focusing on divine unity, free will of man and the justice of God, the eternity of Hell, the obligation to fight for good against evil; in their doctrine the Muslim sinner is neither believing nor unbelieving, and rationality is considered the basis of theology. This emphasis on rationality contributed to the adoption of Greek philosophy and other sciences by Muslim scholars.

735/118

Coptic riots (Egypt) in reaction to the prohibition of the construction of new churches.

742/125

Persecution of the *zindiq*, all those religious who believed in the dual co-existence of good and evil in the world and who did not follow the orthodox interpretation of the Qur'an. They were located mainly in Iran and Iraq.

743/125

Secretary Ghaylan, master of the *qadariyya* school, executed: upholds free will of man, as opposed to predestination (*jahmiyya*). Allegedly the 'Abbasids were Qadaris.

746/128

Jahm b. Safwan, founder of the *jahmiyyah* school, executed. According to the *jahmiyyah*, man has no influence on his own salvation; instead its adherents believed in predestination and the predetermination of salvation.

Society, Civilization and Culture

691/72

Dome of the Rock is built in Jerusalem. Census: heavy taxation, according to *The Chronicle*, written by the Jacobite patriarch Denis of Tall-Mahr; lands abandoned, increase in the number of migrants, growth in wealth of notables (in Iran, *dihqans*), peasant disturbances.

705–715/86–89

The great Umayyad mosque in Damascus is built; town of 'Anjar in the Bekaa using a grid pattern is built in honor of Walid I. In the Syrian desert, many princely residences, oases and hunting lodges are built.

707–709/88–90

Reconstruction of the mosque of Medina after the city had been sacked in 603/63 by the Umayyads because of rebellions.

709–717/90–98

al-Aqsa mosque of Jerusalem built.

728/109

Qasr al-Hayr al-Gharbi in the Syrian steppe built; becomes a model for Umayyad princely residences.

Chapter 3   750–905

The 'Abbasids, the Muslim Empire and Hegemony

The establishment of an "Islamic monarchy" based on the *imamat* and on wide-reaching delegation of power to the confederates of the 'Abbasid *da'wa* makes it possible to maintain the unity of the Empire, since Umayyad Spain and Khariji North Africa had already gained autonomy. With military expansion halted and the Byzantine front stabilized, the dynasty, established by the energetic al-Mansur, faces virulent opposition from a rejuvenated and spiritualized Shi'ism. The 'Abbasids vaccilate between brutal repression of Zaydi devotees and an agreement with the Imamis who adhere, as do the 'Abbasids, to Mu'tazili moral philosophy. Shaken by the war of secession between Amin and Ma'mun and then by the fourth *fitna*, the dynasty radically transforms, in two separate stages, its military machinery; then, in order to escape the effects of the religious quarrels in Baghdad, it establishes a new capital, Samarra. There the 'Abbasids will eventually fall into the hands of Turkish generals.

The cultural domain feels the greatest effect of the accumulation of capital by the prebendaries, civilian officials, military officers and scholars. The Empire's capital in Iraq sets the tone for the regional capitals by establishing extensive trade relations from India to China, by developing a taste for the consumption of luxury products and by engendering a refined culture, while the literature, law and classical theology of Islam flourish. However, tensions increase between autonomous provinces as well as between the prebendary state and the exploited peasant class. Toward the end of the 9th century, the latter support the gnostic Isma'ili movement and its military branch, the Qarmates, who threaten the heart of the Empire.

Political Life

750–754: Caliphate of Saffah
Extermination of the Umayyads and their high officials.

19

ISLAM'S MAIN DYNASTIES 749–1990

West	Center	East
Spain and Africa	Arabia, Syria, Iraq, Anatolia, Azerbaijan	Iran, Afghanistan, India, Central Asia
● Umayyads 756–1031 (Spain) Reclaimed title of caliph after fleeing west from 'Abbasids	● 'Abbasids 749–1258 (Islam) Caliphs in Baghdad who lost power	● Samanids 819–1005 (Khurasan, Turkestan) Revived Iranian culture at Samarkand and Bukhara
○ Idrisids 789–926 (Morocco) Founded Fez	○ Zaidi Imams 860–c. 1281 & 1592–1962 (Yemen) Led own sect of Shi'ism	● Saffarids 867–1495 (Khurasan, India) Eastern Iranian dynasty
● Aghlabids 800–909 (Tunisia, Libya, Sicily)	● Tulunids 868–905 (Egypt, Syria) Nominally 'Abbasid Turk governors	○ Buwayhids 932–1062 (Iran, Iraq) Ruled from Baghdad for 'Abbasids
○ Fatimids 909–1171 (N. Africa, Egypt) Isma'ilis, claimed title of caliph	○ Qarmatians 894–990 (Arabia) Isma'ilis in N.E. Arabia	● Ghaznavids 977–1186 (Afghanistan, N. India) Expanded Islam into India
Zirids 972–1148 (Tunisia, E. Algeria) Of Berber origin, under Fatimids initially; capital Kairuan	● Seljuqs 1038–1194 (Iraq, Iran) First Turk dynasty, reunited central lands	● Karakhanids 992–1211 (Turkestan) Turk dynasty in Bukhara
Hammadids 1015–1152 (Algeria) Zirid branch, founded trading state	● Seljuqs of Rum 1077–1397 (Anatolia) Rulers in conquered Asia Minor	● Khwarizm Shahs 1077–1231 (Turkestan) Seljuq governors founded empire destroyed by Genghis Khan
● Almoravids 1056–1147 (Morocco, Spain) Saharan Berber religious movement, founded Marrakesh	● Zangids 1127–1222 (Syria) Seljuq governors, began holy war against Crusaders	○ Isma'ilis (Assassins) of Alamut 1090–1256 (N. Iran, Syria) "Terrorists" destroyed by Mongols
	● Ayyubids 1169–1260 (Egypt, Syria) Founded by Saladin	
	● Rasulids 1229–1454 (Yemen) Turk rulers	

- Almohads 1130–1269 (N. Africa, Spain) Berber religious movement
- Marinids 1196–1465 (Morocco)
- Hafsids 1228–1574 (Tunisia) Berbers finally overthrown by Ottomans
- Nasrids 1230–1492 (Spain) Kingdom of Granada, last Muslim state in Spain
- Sa'dids 1511–1659 (Morocco) Claimed descent from Prophet
- Alaouites 1668– (Morocco) King Hassan II is this dynasty's 17th monarch
- Fulani 1804–1903 (N. Nigeria) Religious revival founds Sultanate of Sokoto

- Mamlukes 1250–1517 (Egypt, Syria, Arabia) Slave-soldier sultanate ousted by Ottomans
- Ottomans 1281–1924 (Islam) Turks from N.W. Anatolia; imperial capital Constantinople; held caliphate from 1517
- Aq-Qoyunlu 1378–1508 (E. Anatolia, Azerbaijan) Turkoman "white sheep" dynasty
- kara-Qoyunlu 1380–1468 (Azerbaijan, Iraq) Turkoman "black sheep" dynasty
- Wahhabis 1746– (Arabian Peninsula) Militant spread of Puritan Islam
- Saids c. 1749– (Oman, Zanzibar) Sultans of Zanzibar till 1964
- Hashemites 1916– (Arabia, Iraq, Jordan) Descended from Prophet, still rule Jordan
- Saudis 1924– (Saudi Arabia) Guardians of Mecca and Medina

- Golden Horde 1226–1502 (S. Russia) Islamized Mongol successor state
- ○ Ilkhanids 1256–1353 (Iran) Islamized but divided Mongol successor state
- Timurids 1370–1506 (Turkestan, Iran) Tamerlane the Great and successors
- Shaybanids 1500–1598 (Turkestan) Capital Bukhara
- ○ Safavids 1501–1732 (Iran) Made Shi'ism official
- Moghuls 1526–1858 (N. India) Emperors until deposed by British

- Sunni
- ○ Shi'i

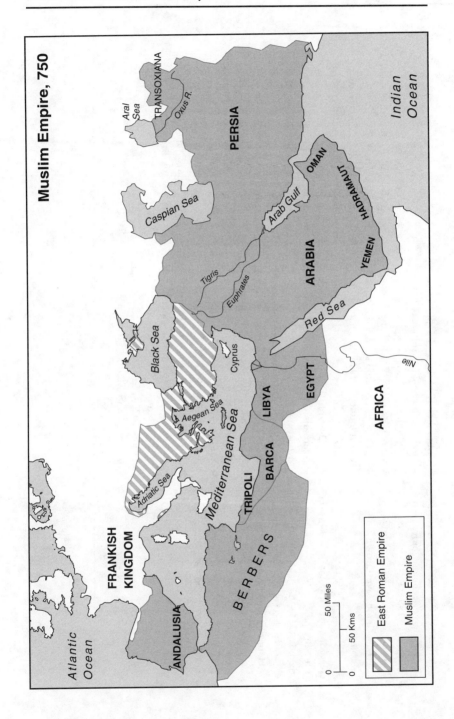

Muslim Empire, 750

East Roman Empire

Muslim Empire

754–775/138–158: Caliphate of al-Mansur

al-Mansur, the brother of Abu al-'Abbas, becomes caliph at the expense of their uncle 'Abd Allah. The question of succession remains unsettled under the 'Abbasids.

762/144–145

Revolt led by the 'Alid mahdi Muhammad b. 'Abdallah, in Mecca; defeat and death. Baghdad founded, capital of the caliphate.

775–785/158–169: Caliphate of al-Mahdi

Strong influence of the Shi'i minister Ya'qub b. Dawud. Persecution of the Manicheans consolidates al-Mahdi's legitimacy; 'Alid unrest subsides.

785–786/169–170 Caliphate of Musa al-Hadi

Musa's brother Harun is designated as his successor. Musa incarcerates Harun to promote his own son as caliph after his death, but Khayzuran, Harun's and Musa's mother, speeds up the succession by murdering the caliph; renewed outbreaks of 'Alid unrest.

786–809/170–193: Caliphate of Harun al-Rashid

Until 803/187, government led by the Persian Barmakids, a family of scribes of Bactrian and Buddhist descent: Yahya is secretary and tutor to the caliph; Fadl is Harun's head of affairs and Amin's (Harun's son) tutor; Ja'far, Fadl's brother, is Ma'mun's tutor.

802/186

The Meccan Decrees: Harun appoints his sons Amin and Ma'mun to the positions of caliph and successor to the caliph, respectively.

803/187

Al-Harun executes Ja'far and imprisons Yahya and al-Fadl; both die soon thereafter. Reason = growing wealth and influence of the Barmakids; government led by Fadl b. al-Rabi, a member of the Barmakid family, who assumes the title wazir, but is soon deposed.

809–813/193–198: Caliphate of Amin

Al-Amin designates his son as his successor; Ma'mun, governor of Khurasan, leads a revolt. Al-Ma'mun's army under Tahir b. al-Husayn conquers Baghdad; assassination of al-Amin.

813–833: Caliphate of Ma'mun

816–838/201–223

In Azerbaijan, revolts led by Babak, head of the Mazdakite sect of the Khurramiyya (*khurramiyya*).

832/217

Revolt by the Bashmurite Copts (Egypt) put down by al-Ma'mun.

833–842/218–227: Caliphate of al-Mu'tasim

Mu'tazilite government led by Ibn Abi Du'ad; Umayyad revolt led by Abu Harb, the "veiled one."

839–840/224–225
Revolt led by the Iranian prince, Mazyar, who converted to Islam; persecutes Arab immigrants and Muslim Iranians; defeated in 840.

842–847: Caliphate of Wathiq

844/229
'Abbasid authority only formally recognized in Iran, where the Tahirid family rules.

847–861/232–247: Caliphate of Mutawakkil
Mu'tazilism abandoned; Turkish officers hold power in Samarra.

861/247
Assassination of the caliph by Turkish officers. Anarchy.

861–862: Caliphate of Muntasir
Turkish soldiers rule for one decade.

862–866: Caliphate of Musta'in
The caliph flees from Samarra to Baghdad to seek protection from the army.

866–869: Caliphate of Mu'tazz
Army proclaims Mu'tazz caliph; siege of Baghdad; execution of Musta'in; army executes Mu'tazz.

869–883/255–270
Insurrection by black slaves (the Zanj) in the swamplands of lower Iraq. An 'Alite caliph and a warrior state established.

869–70: Caliphate of Muhtadi

869–892/255–279: Caliphate of Mu'tamid
Regency of his dynamic brother Muwaffaq, who battles the Saffarids and the Zanj and reestablishes caliphal power.

873/259
Ya'qub al-Saffar, governor of Sistan, puts an end to the Tahirid governorship. He conquers Nishapur. Conquered in 876/262 by Muwaffaq, he bequeaths the Iranian provinces to his brother 'Amr.

877–899/264–286
In Iraq, revolt by the Qarmates (Isma'ili splinter group), led by Hamdan Qarmat. In 894, founding of a Qarmate state in the eastern part of the Arabian peninsula.

892–902/279–289: Caliphate of Mu'tadid
The Saffarids are overcome while the struggle against the Qarmates continues.

Institutions

750/132
'Abassid caliphate: adherence to the imamat, titles and surnames of rulers have a religious character, as opposed to the tribal simplicity of the Umayyads. For example, al-Mansur means "the triumphant one," al-Mahdi = "the rightly guided one," al-Rashid = "the rightly guided one," al-Mutawakkil = "the one who is trusted upon." Development of administrative services: *diwan* (administrative body) for the army (*jund*), the

land tax (*kharaj*), private estates (*diya*), the Treasury (*bayt al-mal*), an administrative language (*insha*) and the postal service (*barid*). Conflict over succession — seniority or primogeniture — remains unsolved.

775/158

During the caliphate of Mahdi, the role of the *wazir* is developed; part prime minister, part all-powerful vice emperor, and part confidant of the caliph.

798/184

Death of Abu Yusuf Ya'qub, a Hanafi lawyer, author of the *Book of Land Taxes* (*Kitab al-Kharaj*), promoter of the *kharaj* reform — regressive taxation that favors increasing the value of land through irrigation and that creates a tax exemption for "new agricultural products."

800/184

In North Africa, autonomy proposed for the provinces governed by Ibn Aghlab and his descendants, in return for tribute; the Aghlabids' participation in the *da'wa hashimiyya* guarantees their loyalty.

820/205

Autonomy for the Iranian provinces entrusted to military commander Tahir, then to his sons, until 862/248.

867/253

With the Saffarides of Iran, a new type of autonomous emirate rises; it is insurrectional and plebeian, based on the *'ayyarun* and pride in Persian roots.

868/254

Government of Egypt entrusted to Ibn Tulun. His son, Khumarawayh,

seeks to dominate the caliphate by large-scale building activities and expansion of the army.

Circa 885/272

Growing autonomy of provincial governors; rise of emirates with governments and administrative services similar to those in Baghdad; prestige and cultural flourishing of the princely courts (especially Samanids in Nishapur), and awakening of Iranian national consciousness.

The Border and the Dar al-Harb

751/133

Battle of Talas (central Asia): the Chinese pull back. Arabs learn about paper from Chinese prisoners of war, and start manufacturing paper in Samarkand.

754/136

A new Khurasanian army: 100,000 men.

778/162

Border raids and border fortifications (*thughur* and *'awasim*) organized by the Harun.

782/165

Expedition across Byzantine Asia Minor to the Bosphorus.

813/198

The *Abna'* army, which supported Amin, replaced by a so-called *'abbasiyya* army, recruited by Tahir in Khurasan.

826–902/212–289
In Sicily, revolt led by the Byzantine governor Euphemius; conquest of the island by Muslim volunteers driven by the jurist Asad b. al-Furat.

827/212
Conquest of Crete by the Cordobans who had been expelled from Alexandria.

830–833/215–218
Ma'mun on the Byzantine front in Tarsus—repeated offensives; exchange of prisoners.

838/223
Amorium (Asia Minor), cradle of the Byzantine dynasty, taken.

841–871/226–257
Muslim emirate in Bari in the Puglia province.

842/227
Naval attack on Constantinople led by Abu Dinar is dispersed by a storm.

852/238
Byzantines land on the Egyptian coast; Mutawakkil fortifies the ports on the Mediterranean.

Circa 866/252
The Khurasanian army is replaced by the *shaqiriyya*, an army composed of *ghulam*, Turkish slaves, obeying the orders of Turkish officers. Originally designed as a counterweight to the Khurasanian army by Musta'in, the Turkish army eventually dominates the caliph.

870
Conquest of Malta.

879/265
Fall of Syracuse; Sicily taken from the Byzantines. The important Islamic trade post in the Chinese port of Canton is destroyed.

882–915/269–302
Bridgehead south of Rome, on the Garigliano, established by the Muslims of Sicily.

904/291
Naval expedition by Leon of Tripoli (Rashid al-Wardami); devastation of Thessalonica.

Africa and Spain

Circa 744/129
In the Barghawata principality (on the Atlantic coast of Morocco), Berbers practice a particular form of Islam: prophecy, the Qur'an with 80 *suras* in Berber language, *shari'a* based on custom.

756/138
Umayyad Emirate of 'Abd al-Rahman I (survivor of the massacre) in Andalusia; founder of the Umayyad dynasty of Spain (755–1031).

758/141
Ibadite emirate of 'Abd al-Rahman b. Rustum, in Orania (Tahert)—hereditary regime (lasts until 908).

788/172
Zaydite emirate of 'Alide Idris in Walila (Volubilis).

795/180
Ibn Aghlab founds a new Kairuan, 'Abbasiyya, where he stations a troop

of 5,000 black soldiers. Founder of the Aghlabid dynasty.

816/202

Introduction in Spain of the Malikite school of legal interpretation of the Qur'an.

817/202

Revolt in the town of Cordoba; 20,000 families are expelled — some emigrate to Fes, ca. 15,000 toward the east; some make their livelihood as pirates; others conquer Byzantine Crete (827-961); others occupy Alexandria.

821/206

A chain of fortified monasteries (ribat) protects the Tunisian coast (Sus, Monastir).

851-859/237-245

Religious crisis in Cordoba: after public slander of Islam and the Prophet by local Christians, 45 death sentences, among them the historian and priest Eulogius, who was decapitated in 859.

854/240

Death of Sahnun b. Sa'id, Malikite lawyer from Kairuan, who had established his *madhhab* (law school) in Ifriqiyya; his writings advocated a Puritan opposition to the ruling classes and were well known in the Emirate of Cordoba.

856-863/242-249

During the reign of the Aghlabid Abu Ibrahim Ahmad, large-scale water projects and the construction of the "10,000 castles," or fortified villages, undertaken.

879/266

Beginning of the revolt by the newly converted Muslims (*muwalladun*) from the mountain provinces of southern Spain, led by 'Umar b. Hafsun, against discrimination by "established" Muslims. 'Umar b. Hafsun builds the gigantic fortification Bobastro and successfully defends it until his death in 918.

Religious Life

765/148

After the death of the imam Ja'far al-Sadiq, the Shi'i divide into three major movements: *Isma'ilism*, activist and philosophical; *Zaydism*, activist and militant; *Imamism*, pietist.

776-780/159-163

Revolt of the "Whites" in Iran against Muslims, led by Muqanna, known as "the veiled one" and thought to be the reincarnation of Abu Muslim; after his defeat, he committed suicide.

779/163

Persecution of the "Manicheans," the *zindiq*, accused of being too free thinking.

827

al-Ma'mun adopts Mu'tazili doctrine.

864/250

Spread of Zaydi doctrine in Iran: first Zaydi emirate on the Caspian coast.

869/255

Order given to remove the pictorial representations on the walls of the 'Abassid palace. This action reveals

Shi'ism

Isma'ilism: Shi'i sect that believes that Isma'il, the son of the sixth imam Ja'far al-Sadiq, is the seventh imam, who lives on in occultation. Their religion is based on a symbolism of Semite and non-Semite religions, mixed with neo-Platonist elements. There were various subgroups that composed an insurrectional movement against the caliphate; the most important ones were (1) the *Qaramita* (Qarmatians) (in East Arabia and Bahrain), and (2) the *Fatimids* who founded their own caliphate (909–1171) and ruled in Egypt, North Africa, Palestine and parts of Syria. Today there are various Isma'ili factions in Yemen, Syria, Iran, India, Afghanistan and Turkestan.

Zaydism: considers Zayd, the son of the fourth imam, as the legitimate imam, who lives on in occultation. Their doctrine is relatively close to Sunnism, and has Mu'tazili features. There were repeated uprisings against Sunni rule; in 897 an independent Zaydi state came into existence in Yemen, and from 864 to 1126 a Zaydi dynasty ruled in Iran south of the Caspian Sea.

Imanism: twelver Shi'is, consider the 12th imam, Muhammad b. Hasan al-Mahdi, to be the legitimate imam. In Iran this group is the dominant religion, and in 1979 it became the state religion (before that the twelver Shi'is had not been able to build their own state). Other Imami minorities live in Iraq, Syria, Lebanon, Turkey, Afghanistan, India and Pakistan.

pietist tensions and the influence of the Hanbalis.

873/259

Disappearance of the 12th 'Alite imam marks the beginning of the "Lesser Occultation" (*ghayba*, which lasts until 940) during which he is represented by deputies. After that the "Greater Occultation" begins until the Mahdi reappears.

890/277

Qarmatians rise in southern Iraq.

897/284

Zaydi state in Yemen.

Urban Society

757/140

Sijilmasa founded in Tafilalt, a caravan center in the Sahara.

762/145

Baghdad founded (*Madinat al-Salam* = city of peace) by Mansur as the capital of the 'Abbasid empire; indicates the shift away from Byzantium toward Persia. The city lay on important trade routes with Persia and India.

786/170

Cordoba mosque built.

794/178

Use of paper, acquired from the Chinese, becomes more widespread.

End of 8th century/2nd half of 2nd century

Rapid expansion of Islamic urban civilization: clothing styles, cooking, lifestyles, games, consumption of luxury goods follow the example set by Baghdad. Importance of music, singing and poetry.

Beginning of 9th century/1st half of 3rd century

Shu'ubiyya literary movement among educated people of Iranian origin: reflects growing sense of national consciousness among Iranian converts; directed against Arab domination, not against Islam.

808/192

Fes founded.

822/206

The famous musician Ziryab arrives in Cordoba from Baghdad. Al-Andalus absorbs elements of Eastern art with the influx of other artists.

830/215

al-Ma'mun builds the Bayt al-Hikma (house of wisdom) university in Baghdad.

836/221

Colossal new capital of Samarra founded by Mu'tasim: 35 km wide. Mosque in Kairuan built.

838/223

Samarran palace of the Jawsaq al-Khaqani.

849/234

New town, Ja'fariyya, founded by Mutawakkil in Samarra, with the Great Mosque, allegedly built by Abu Dulaf (860/245).

879/266

Construction of Fustat (old Cairo) for Ibn Tulun, governor of Egypt, and his officers, the Qata'i'; mosque of Ibn Tulun, modeled after the one in Samarra, is built.

892/279

Under the caliph al-Mu'tadid, Baghdad reaches its cultural zenith (despite religious and political unrest elsewhere); the Crown (Taj) and the Pleiades palaces built. One source mentions over 2,000 baths.

The Economy

2nd half of 8th century/2nd half of 2nd century

Distribution of "new agricultural products" from India and Iran in the Mediterranean region: rice, sugar cane, cotton, silk and legumes modify agriculture, taxation and consumption patterns. Urban centers rely heavily on the trade of precious goods, financed by property taxes.

758/141

The Canton fire: break in the relations between Iraq and China, which eventually leads to the arrival (circa 825/211) of Tang junks in the Persian Gulf.

Circa 780/164

Trade between the Maghrib and Europe, but weak circulation of Muslim money (primarily linked to the slave trade) in Europe.

800/184

Paper factory in Baghdad founded.

Circa 840/225

According to geographer Ibn Khurdadhbih, development of trade with Byzantium, arrival in Iraq of Russian merchants and link with the Carolingian world through Jewish merchants (*Radhanites* = itinerant merchants).

875–878/261–265

Second break in relations with China: Arab merchants massacred in Canton; henceforth, stable trade in Kalah (the Malacca peninsula).

Philosophical and Doctrinal Trends

Circa 713–805/95–189

Rabi'a al-'Adawiyya, poetess of divine love, leads the Sufi communities of Iraq.

747–815/130–200

Abu Nuwwas, Bacchic poet and libertine.

Circa 750/132

First appearance of romance literature (*adab*) translated from Persian. Khalil (died c. 786/170) and Sibawayhi (died 793/177) establish Arabic grammar and lexicography.

Circa 776–868/160–255

Jahiz, *adab* encyclopedist and Mu'tazilite. Supported by caliph, writes a book about superiority of blacks over whites; praises character of Turks.

Circa 788–886/172–272

Abu Ma'shar, known as Albumasar, astronomer from Baghdad.

Circa 800–847/184–232

al-Khwarizmi, astronomer of the Bayt al-Hikma academy, father of algebra.

Circa 801–866/185–252

al-Kindi, astronomer and optician, first of the great Islamic-Arab philosophers; influenced by Greek philosophy.

808–873/192–260

Hunayn, Nestorian doctor, translates Hippocrates.

810–870/194–256

al-Bukhari, traditionalist, author of the most famous canonical collection of *hadith*.

Circa 815–883/200–270

Dawud b. Khalaf, founder of the literalist school of law and *hadith*, known as *zahiri*, which rejects analogy.

828–889/213–276

Ibn Qutayba, encyclopedist, historian and theologian.

844/229

Ibn Khurdadhbih, geographer and postmaster (*barid*) of Baghdad: *Book of Itineraries and Kingdoms*.

857/243

Death of Ibn Masawayh, translator of Greek authors who wrote on medicine, astrology and pharmacy.

869/255

In Jerusalem, death of Ibn Karram, Sufi founder of the Karramiyya brotherhood.

891/278

Ya'qubi, geographer: the *Book of Countries*.

892/279

Death of al-Baladhuri, historian: *A Genealogy of Nobles*; the *Book of Conquests of Countries*.

The 'Abbasids:
The Era of Schisms

A fter the 'Abbasid dynasty overcame the Qarmatian threat and to re-established order in Iraq, the beginning of the 10th century witnessed the unthinkable: the split of Islam into two, and eventually three, rival caliphates.

The formidable Messianic movement of Isma'ili gnosis, which seeks to re-establish—in the neo-Platonic spirit—the unity between encylopedic knowledge, individual salvation and the political duty of insurrection in the name of the long-awaited *Mahdi* prolongs the effort begun by militants in the 8th century (Murjites, Mu'tazilites, Zaydites) to create a new *da'wa*. One branch, led by the madhi 'Ubaydallah, establishes a stronghold in Ifriqiyya in a Berber region devoted to the radical and fervent practice of Islam. His triumph in Kairuan presages total victory in the future. The split among Isma'ilis—between Qarmates, soldiers, gnostic philosophers (the Pure Brothers) and political movements—does not allow the new Fatimid dynasty to capture Baghdad after the conquest of Egypt and the establishment of Cairo, nor are they able to re-establish an Islamic unity. On the contrary, the Fatimids' progress in Africa liberates Umayyad Spain from the fear of 'Abbasid reprisals and allows the restoration of the Umayyad caliphate, whose authority remains limited to Andalusia. Instead of a unified Islamic *umma*, there are three competing caliphates.

The division of the Muslim world into three empires allows for a Christian counteroffensive, which leads to a triumph over Syria and the reconquest of Antioch, and provides a threat to the Spanish Marches (the northern provinces bordering on Christian territory and Sicily). However, the rapid cultural, literary and doctrinal growth of the *Dar al-Islam* is not compromised; it remains easy to travel and communicate in this area kept together by a common civilization. The reawakening of Mediterranean trade, after a long period of war and insecurity for merchant vessels, contributes to this cultural unity. And while Isma'ilism enters into a crisis under the Fatimid caliph Hakim and subsequently explodes into rival movements, the empire, which had been united under the Umayyads, deprived of all ideological support, breaks into a number of rival kingdoms.

The 'Abbasid caliphs, on the contrary, rely on a version of *Sunnism*, which assembles the pietism of traditionalists and the anti-Mu'tazilite affirmations of new Ash'arite and Maturidite theological schools to form a new political bond.

The Near and Middle East

After having triumphed over their mortal enemies, the Zanj, the Saffarids and Qarmatians, the 'Abbasid caliphate enters a period of lethargy. The caliph, isolated in his palace, becomes henceforth the puppet of the emirs.

The conquest of the capital and the appointment of the caliph are from this point forth the military's goals: the position of the chief of the emirs (*amir al-umara*) and the revenues of the state and the Iraqi provinces, impoverished by the devastation of war, fall successively into the hands of Arab Hamdanids and Iranian Buyids, then of the Turkish sultans of the Seljuq clan.

Nevertheless, the caliphate lives on on the spiritual front, in the hope that this will lead to a political resurgence. It obtains the tacit support of the Imami Shi'is in their fight against the Isma'ilis, and launches its own Sunni *da'wa*, inspired by Hanbali pietism.

In the border regions, expansion is resumed by religious conversion toward central Asia, and by military conquest toward India, while the entry of Oghuz Turks into Iran and Iraq is a harbinger of new turbulence.

The 'Abbasid Near East

908–932/295–320:
Reign of Muqtadir

Domination by the eunuch Mu'nis, the commander-in-chief: alternation in the vizierate between Ibn al-Furat, Shi'i, and 'Ali b. 'Isa, of Nestorian origin. Intrigue and conflict: Muqtadir killed by order of Mu'nis.

908/296

The Hanbali reformers' attempt to bring Ibn al-Mu'tazz (a cousin of Muqtadir) to power fails.

930–935/319–323

Iranian revolt led by Mardawij b. Ziyar; the "golden throne" and the title of *shahanshah* reestablished; attempt to merge Zarathustrian and Isma'ili doctrine. His military leaders were the three brothers Ali, Hasan and Ahmad, sons of Buyeh (Arabic: Buwayh, hence Buyids). Mardawij is assassinated by one of his Turkish slaves in 935.

923–934: Caliphate of Qahir
933/321

Execution of Mu'nids by order of the caliph Qahir. Different army factions

Arabic Surnames:

The Hamdanite Hasan initiated a tradition according to which the *amir al-umara'* assumed an honorary surname (*laqab*) under which he would be known to posterity. He himself adopted the *laqab Nasir al-Dawla* (supporter of the state). Others are *Mu'izz al-Dawla* (the one who increases the glory of the state), *'Imad al-Dawla* (the pillar of the state), or *Rukn al-Dawla* (the support of the state), etc.

fight for leadership during the next 12 years; the result is anarchy.

934/322
Qahir, blinded and deposed; a Hamdanid emirate in Jazira, led by Nasir al-Dawla.

934–936: Caliphate of Radi
936/324
Muhammad Ibn Raiq, of Khazar descent, prefect of police, first *amir al-umara*, unites supreme command of the army and administrative and financial control of the empire.

940–944: Caliphate of Muttaqi
944/333
Muttaqi, blinded and deposed; violent conflict between Nasir al-Dawla, Ibn Raiq, the Turk Kurtegin and the amir al-Baridi.

944–946: Caliphate of Mustakfi
945/334
Triumph of the three Shi'i Buyid brothers, 'Ali Imad al-Dawla, Hasan Rukn al-Dawla and Abu al-Husayn Mu'izz al-Dawla, who become the rulers of the Persian provinces with an army of Daylamite followers. Mu'izz al-Dawla, great emir of Baghdad until his death in 967/356.

946–974: Caliphate of Muti'
949–983
The Buyid Adud al-Dawla rules Iran (from 977 also Iraq); renews Iranian royal rule.

957/356
The Buyid Bakhtiyar dominates the caliphate; eliminated in 978/367 by 'Adud al-Dawla who unifies the Buyid domains of Fars, Kirman, Iraq and Oman; proclaimed king by the caliph.

974–991: Caliphate of Ta'r
983/372
After 'Adud al-Dawla's death, conflict among his sons; Baha' al-Dawla triumphs and reaffirms the unity of the Buyid provinces.

991–1031: Caliphate of Qadir
1012/403
Death of Baha' al-Dawla; Buyid decadence.

1031–1075: Caliphate of Qa'im
1034/425
Oghuz Turks led by the Seljuqs (Toġrïl-Beg and Caġrï-Beg), penetrate into Iran.

1055/447

Arrival of Toġrïl-Beg in Baghdad; proclaimed "Sultan of the East and the West" by the caliph; elimination of the Buyids. Toġrïl-Beg will marry the daughter of the caliph in 1062/454. This marks the beginning of the Seljuq sultanate that controls the caliphate.

The Byzantine Front

Beginning of 10th century/end of 3rd century

Autonomy of the Armenian-Arab emirates, the Armenian states (Bagratids and Ardzruni) and the Sajite governors in Azerbaijan.

912/299

Progression of Armenians from Vashpurakan toward Malatya.

914/302

The Hamdanid Abu al-Hayja', governor of Mosul.

934/322

Byzantine offensive mounted against Malatya and the Marches: Diyar Bakr, Diyar Rabi'a and Diyar Mudar.

935/324

The Banu Habib tribes settle among the Byzantines.

942/330

The *mandil* of Edessa (Christian relic) relinquished to the Byzantines.

947/336

The Hamdanid Sayf al-Dawla (945-967) establishes the emirate of Aleppo, which stretches from Syria to Armenia, and leads the "Sayfite" war, an annual attack on the Byzantines, until his death in 967/356. Strong support from Bedouin warriors.

953/342

Sayf victorious over Bardas Skleros in Mar'ash.

958-969/347-359

The triumphs of emperor Nicephoros Phocas: Antioch, Cilicia, Tarsos taken, border repopulated by Jacobite peasants.

970/359

Aleppo pays a tribute to the Byzantines, becomes a vassal state.

977/366

Revolt led by Bardas Skleros, supported by the Muslims.

977-1002/367-392

Reconstitution of the Hamdanid emirate, vassal of Byzantium.

1045-1055

Seljuq campaigns against Armenia and eastern Anatolia pose threat to eastern borders of Byzantium.

Institutions

10th century/4th century

Distribution of plots of land (*iqta'*) to the military, instead of wages. The owner had the right of usufruct for a certain period of time, after which the *iqta'* was redistributed. Later on, these lands became hereditary, but officers often demanded the allocation of more profitable *iqta's* when the revenue they derived from their old ones became too low. This prevented the rise of a hereditary aristocracy. The absence of strong state power and economic hardships lead young men to establish associations, known as the *fityan* or *ahdath* ("good-for-nothing"); militias, sports, "chivalrous" ideology (*futuwwa*). Some rely on petty theft, others form organized gangs of criminals (*ayyarun*). Development of "protection taxes" (*talji'a, himaya*) whose payment is brutally imposed by military officers.

969/358

Followers of the *ahdath* in Syrian towns (Damascus, Harran, Aleppo in 1002/413).

980/370

The Buyid 'Adud al-Dawla restores Sassanid customs — the title *shahanshah*, Pahlavi inscriptions, the *taj* crown. Theory of double power: prophecy and caliphate for the Arabs, royalty for the Persians.

Circa 1000/end of 4th century

Establishment of the hereditary *riyasa* (office of *ra'is*, "mayor" and administrator) in cities in an atmosphere of conflict between factions.

1058/450

Death of Mawardi, pro-caliphian lawyer, theoretician of the *Foundations of Sovereignty*; justifies the legitimization of usurpers by the caliph as long as the former declares his adherence to Islam and vows to defend the *shari'a*. This serves to maintain the unity of the empire despite continuous changes in rulership.

The Eastern Front

961-963/350-352

Alptigin, a Turkish general of the Samanids, establishes autonomy of Ghazna (Afghanistan), first in the name of the Samanids.

977-997/367-387

Sabüktigin, (Sebüiktigin) slave governor of the Samanids in Ghazna: frequent campaigns against pagans and Isma'ilis in India; founder of the Ghaznavid dynasty in Afghanistan, northern India and Khurasan; autonomy.

992/382

Occupation of Bukhara by Islamicized Turkish emirs: the Qarakhanids replace the Samanids in Central Asia.

999/389

The caliph Qadir first recognizes Mahmud (Sabüktigin's son) of Ghazna's conquests, then recognizes his independence. Mahmud's campaigns lead him to northwest India; conquest of Khurasan, Khwarazm and western Persia. Mahmud formally establishes Islamic rule in the name of the 'Abbasid caliph in the conquered territories.

1008/398

Introduction of elephants by Mahmud. Expansion into India (army made up of Turkish *ghulam* and *ghazi* garrisons) for spoils. On the political front, local accords with the Rajput warrior nobility.

1025/416

The Seljuqs, at the head of the Oghuz Turks, pass the Oxus River.

1030/421
The authority of Mas'ud of Ghazna, Mahmud's son and successor (after interregnum of his brother Muhammad), recognized by the caliph Qa'im.

1036-1037/428
Seljuqs conquer Khurasan, led by Toġrïl-Beg and Caġrï-Beg.

1040/431
The battle of Dandanqan: the Seljuqs defeat Mas'ud; the battle opens Persia to Seljuq invasion.

1041/432
The Seljuqs occupy Khwarazm.

1043/435
Toġrïl conquers Tabaristan and the Persian city Raiy; proclaims himself "protector of the leader of the believers" after negotiations with the Caliph Qa'im.

1051/443
Intrusion of Turkish tribes into Azerbaijan and upper Mesopotamia.

Urban Civilization

10th century/4th century
Development of the economic autonomy of towns, which depend less on property taxes: Baghdad becomes an artisans' metropolis (immigration of tradesmen: weavers and embroiderers from Tustar, blacksmiths from Mossul); in certain industrial towns (Tinnis, Damiette, Dabiq, Shata, Tuna, Bahnasa), Egyptian weaving of linen and silk.

904-954/291-343
Nishapur, the Samanid capital, and Bukhara at their zeniths.

961/350
In Baghdad, palace of the Buyid Mu'izz al-Dawla is built. In the cities in Syria and Iraq, rapid increase in number of *ayyarun* groups, helping the factions; an ideology close to that of the *futuwwa*.

980/370
In Baghdad, palace of 'Adud al-Dawla, the *Dar al-Mamlaka*, is built.

999-1020/389-421
Construction of Ghazna, Mahmud's capital, and the palace of Lashkari Bazar.

Beginning of 11th century/5th century
In Iraq and Iran, pilgrims' obsession with the tombs of the "twelver" Shi'i imams: creation of new towns, Karbala, Mashhad (built on 'Ali Rida's tomb), Qumm and Samarra (where the 12th imam went into occultation in 876/260).

1st half of 11th century/5th century
Frequent urban uprisings: clans, weavers' movements against the high cost of living, conflict between Shi'is and Sunnis and between different schools of legal interpretation of the Qur'an (*madhhab*).

Religious Life: Isma'ilism

873-935/260-324
Abu al-Hasan al-Ash'ari, who continued the Mu'tazili tradition (non-created Qur'an, but divine attributes

explained symbolically). Absolute opposition of the Hanbalis and Zahiris to Ash'arism.

882–942/268–330
Saadiah Gaon, president of the Rabbinical Academy of Sura.

10th century/4th century
Nusayris settle around Aleppo.

900/287
Rupture between Qarmatians and Fatimids.

902/289
The Qarmatians attack Salamiyya, residence of the Fatimid imam, who flees to the Maghrib.

907/294
The Qarmatians from Iraq squashed. Death of Zikrawayh. The Qarmatians retreat to Bahrain where they found a Hegirian state in Ahsa (al-Hasa).

930/317
The Qarmatians from Bahrain attack Mecca and take the Black Stone; they conquer Oman.

940/329
The fourth representative of the imam who had been hidden from the "twelvers" dies without having appointed a successor; beginning of the "Grand Occultation."

945/334
Death of Abu Mansur al-Maturidi, from Samarkand; integrates into Islamic orthodoxy elements of Mu'tazilism; radius of activity limited to Central Asia.

Circa 945–1022/333–413
Shaykh al-Mufid, theoretician of depoliticized and philosophical "twelver" Shi'ism, but critic of the powerful.

959/348
Spread of Isma'ilism in India; an Isma'ili state is established in Multan, located in the Sind region.

963/352
The Buyid ruler Mu'izz al-Dawla establishes the Shi'i holidays of 'ashura' (10 Muharram) and 'Id al-Ghadir (18 Dhu'l-Hijja). 'Ashura' commemorates the murder of Husayn by the Caliph

Nusayris:

Also called Alawis; an ethnic group situated mainly in Syria, with some in Lebanon and Turkey. In Syria, they constitute approximately 6 percent of the population, and with Hafez al-Assad they rule the country today. They are closely related to the revolutionary Qarmatians of the 10th/4th century. Although they are often called Shi'is, their doctrine resembles Isma'ilism, and their practices include pre-Islamic elements of astral religion, divine emanation, and Christianity. Their practices do not include Islamic rites, but they have been sanctioned as a branch of Islam by the Lebanese Shi'i leader Musa al-Sadr.

Yazid; in order to show their grief, Shi'is fast during the ninth day of Muharram, and on the tenth certain groups publicly injure themselves. On *'Id al-Ghadir*, according to Shi'i interpretation, Muhammad designated 'Ali as his successor in the oasis Ghadir al-Khumm (between Mecca and Medina).

989/378
Yemen adheres to Isma'ilism.

991–1031/381–422
Sunni *da'wa* of the caliph Qadir; of a pietist and puritan Sunni orthodoxy.

991/381
Foundation in Baghdad, by the vizier Sabur b. Ardashir, of the *Dar al-'ilm*, ("house of knowledge"), a Shi'i library containing 10,000 volumes.

995–1055/334–447
Development of Hanbalism in Baghdad: movement condemns the *kalam*, *mu'tazila* and mendicant Sufism, emphasizes doctrine of the uncreated Qur'an.

997/387
Ghaznavits rally around the Hanafi-Mu'tazili credo; they support on a local basis the *karramiyya* Sufi order.

1003/394
The Buyid Baha' al-Din pursues an active Imami Shi'i policy; he names the 'Alid Abu Ahmad al-Musawi president of the *mazalim* tribunal, emir of the pilgrimage, prosecutor of the 'Alids and chief *qadi*. The caliph refuses this latter nomination.

1011/402
Joint condemnation of the Fatimids by the Sunnis and the Imami Shi'is.

1018/409
Profession of faith by Qadir; he defines Sunnism in opposition to Mu'tazilism; the Mu'tazilis retract; prohibition of the *kalam*.

1020/411
The Kirmani *da'i* lays out the Isma'ili cosmological doctrine.

1042/433
New reading of the Qadiri profession of faith: individuals possess free will but nevertheless fulfill outside destiny; free will thus lies in the ability to choose or to deny the absolute.

1050/441
Shi'is and Sunnis of Baghdad reconcile after years of civil war.

1058/450
Failure of Basasiri's (leader of Turkish mercenaries) Isma'ili movement in Baghdad; defeat by the Seljuq Togril-Beg.

Philosophical and Doctrinal Trends

10th and 11th centuries/4th and 5th centuries
After the failure of the Mu'tazili *kalam*, development of the *falsafa*.

1st half of the 10th century/4th century
The neo-Persian language established: heavy Arab lexicographical content, poetry (syllabic meter) abandoned in favor of Arab quantitative prosody.

839–923/225–310

Tabari, historian and theologian; author of the *History of the Prophets and the Kings*, a universal history of the world, and *The Full Exposition of the Qur'anic Commentary*.

Circa 864–935/250–323

Razi, physician and philosopher; author of the *Hawi* (*Continens*) and the *Mansuri* (*Liber Almansoris*). His works had a strong influence in medieval Europe, and were translated into Latin, Greek and other European languages.

Circa 874–950/260–339

al-Farabi, neo-Platonic philosopher, exercised great influence on European thought. His works include *Statecraft*, *The Virtuous City*, and *The Book on Music*.

910/298

Death of the Sufi Junayd, al-Hallaj's teacher; wrote no books, but was famous for his teachings.

915–965/303–354

Mutannabi, poet of the court and Hamdanid war. Often celebrated Bedouin lore in his poetry. His real name was Abu al-Tayyib Ahmad b. al-Husayn al-Ju'fi, "Mutanabi" meaning "the would-be prophet."

921–922/309–310

Ibn Fadlan's delegation to the land of the Bulgars from the Volga, of which he left a famous travel account.

Circa 932–after 1009/320–400

Miskawayh, humanist in the service of the Buyids.

946/336

Death of Suli, the 'Abassids' courtier and historian.

956–957/345–346

Death of Mas'udi, historian, geographer, philosopher, scientist, author of the *Meadows of Gold* and 33 other works, most of which are lost.

969/358

Publication of the *Treatises of the Brotherhood of Purity* (consisting of 51 tracts) (*Rasa'il*), scientific encyclopedia put together by neo-Platonic philosophers of Isma'ili faith, known as the "Brotherhood of Purity" (*Ikhwan al-Safa*). The *Rasa'il* was influential in medieval Europe.

976–997/366–387

Publication of *View of the World* from the explorer and geographer Ibn Hawqal.

980–1037/307–428

Abu 'Ali Husayn b. Sina (Avicenna), physician and philosopher, one of the most famous intellectuals of the Middle Ages, author of the *Qanun*, a medical encyclopedia, which was a basic text for the teaching of medicine in Europe until the 17th century.

982/372

Baghdad: a large hospital founded by the Buyid 'Adud al-Dawla.

985/375

Publication of *The Best Itinerary for Acquiring Knowledge of the Provinces* by Muqaddasi, explorer and geographer.

1003–1061/394–453

Nasir-i Khusraw, poet, philosopher, explorer and militant Isma'ili, author of the *Sefer-nama*, an account of his travels.

1004–1005/395

Firdawsi, in the Ghaznian court, dedicates the neo-Persian epic *Shah-nama* (Book of Kings) to Mahmud. The work consists of 60,000 verses and became the Persian national epic.

The Economy

10th century/4th century

Continuous relations with China and India; Iran copies Chinese models, in particular speckled Tang ceramic goods (splashware), celadon and, later, Song porcelain.

Beginning of the 10th century/beginning of the 4th century

Development of deposit and exchange banks, linked to the collection of taxes: the office of *jahbadh* (money changer and controller; a state official) filled by the Jews Yusuf b. Fin'as and Harun b. Imran.

904–954/291–343

During the Samanid reign, massive trade in furs imported from the Taiga (Russian, Finnish and Scandinavian). Trafficking in Turkish slaves in Transoxania and Khurasan, evident from the abundance of Samanid dirhams on the upper Volga, near Novogorod, on the Baltic and Scandinavian coasts and on the roads along the Carpates in the north.

2nd half of 10th century/4th century

Muslim trade in India, particularly in Saymur, near Bombay.

End of 10th century/end of 4th century

Gold content in coins lowered: the Buyid dinar falls from 20 to 12 and then to 10 carats.

Circa 1000/390

Gulf crisis. Insecurity created by Qarmatians and pirates. Siraf, port of Fars, is abandoned. Withdrawal of merchants from Hormuz.

Circa 1015/405

Crisis on the "fur route," under pressure from the Turks. Recruitment of Turkish slaves decreases due to Islamization. Decrease in the circulation of Muslim currency in the Russian, Baltic and Scandinavian regions.

Taxes

The total revenue collected by the central *diwan* of the 'Abbasid Empire approached 400 million dirhams at around 750. The decentralization of authority and of administration reduced this sum to 300 million around 850 and to 210 million in 919.

The Fatimids

Heirs to an activist Zaydism, the Fatimid *imams* integrated, during their exile in Syria, neo-Platonic gnostic principles into their doctrine: they present themselves as *mahdi* and maintain a *da'wa* for the purposes of initiation and secrecy. Their ascent to power in North Africa rapidly brings with it the disenchantment of a population that is not invited to join the ranks of the Isma'ili faithful. Their conquests of Egypt and most of Syria do not necessarily imply the subsequent conquest of Baghdad.

In fact, the dynasty is in the grips of internal difficulties brought on by the adaptation of the millenarin message to the daily realities of governing, coupled with the difficult problem of succession. Under Hakim, the dynasty loses its center, while the *da'wa* explodes (incited by the Druzes who await the return of Hakim). The Fatimids lose control over North Africa and Sicily, and limit themselves to governing an eastern domain enriched by the resurgence of the important Mediterranean spice trade.

North Africa: The Arrival of the Fatimids

903/291
The Fatimid Mahdi in the Maghrib, 'Ubaydallah, taken prisoner in Sijilmasa. Before his capture he was in the service of his *dai* Abu 'Abdallah, who converts the Kutama Berbers to Isma'ilism.

905–935/292–323
Egypt governed by the 'Abbasids.

909/297
Abu 'Abdallah takes Kairuan, then liberates the Mahdi.

910/297
January 15/29 Rabi II — Triumphal and messianic entrance into Kairuan.

911/298
Execution of Abu 'Abdallah; 'Ubaydallah ruler of Fatimid empire; builds Mahdiyya (Tunisia) as his capital; assumes title of caliph, claiming to be the sole ruler of the *umma*.

919–921/307–309
The Fatimids attack Egypt.

920/308
Conquest of Fez.

921/309
Sijilmasa taken.

934–945/322–334
Caliphate-Imamate of Muhammad al-Qa'im, son of the Mahdi. Established in Mahdiyya, the Imami dynasty continues the traditions of secrecy, initiative hierarchy and messianic tensions that date from their clandestine period in Syria.

935–946/323–334
Egypt governed by the *ikhshid* Muhammad b. Tughj.

943–947/332–336
Formidable Khariji revolt of North African Berbers against the Fatimids

led by Abu Yazid, the "man on the donkey," put down by Isma'il al-Mansur, the third Fatimid caliph.

953/341
Death of al-Mansur in Mansuriyya, a garrison town he had built close to Kairuan.

958/346
The Slav general Jawhar leads an expedition to the Atlantic.

961-968/349-357
Egypt governed by the black eunuch Kafur, tutor of the sons of the *Ikhshids*.

968/357
Jawhar's second expedition solidifies Fatimid control over North Africa.

969/358
Conquest of Egypt by the Fatimid army led by Jawhar; Cairo and the al-Azhar mosque founded.

973-362
The caliph Mu'izz settles in Cairo; vizierate of the Jew Ja'qub b. Killis; the Jewish convert al-Fadl b. Salih becomes commander-in-chief.

975/364
'Aziz proclaimed caliph by the *da'wa*'s dignitaries, against the wishes of his father.

926-1021/387-411: The Reign of Hakim
1006/396
Umayyad anti-caliphate in Upper Egypt led by Abu Rakwa with the support of Berber tribes; defeat by

Fatimids and execution of Abu Rakwa.

1011-1013/402-403
Palestine: an 'Alid anti-caliphate is established, led by al-Hasan b. Ja'far; Bedouin, bribed by al-Hakim, oust b. Ja'far, ending the caliphate.

1020/410
Large fire in Fustat.

1021/411
al-Hakim is assassinated during a ride in the desert, only his donkey and clothes reappear. His older sister, Sitt al-Mulk, assumes responsibility for the government until al-Zahir becomes caliph.

1030/421
Byzantine attack on Jerusalem fails.

Institutions

910-973/297-362
Fatimid caliphate in Ifriqiyya: the imamate is transmitted from father to son, by secret designation (*nass*), which necessitates that the choice be made by an initiate who is close to the family as "proof" (*hujja*), without regard for primogeniture; the vizierate appears after the Fatimids settle in Cairo, first with Ya'qub b. Killis, a converted Jew, then with the Christian 'Isa b. Nasturus.

973/362
After the conquest of Egypt, a more complex and less family-based Fatimid administration: principle of the concession of land (*iqta'*), allocated by the administration (*diwan al-majlis*);

growing complexity of the financial branch of the administration (*diwan al-amwal*); important role of the Chancellory's foreign policy (*diwan al-insha'*) as well as that of his *sahib*.

991/380
"Office of Embroidery" (*dar al-dibaj*) set up in Cairo.

997–1000/387–390
Duties of the prime minister (*masita*) established, granting more vizieral functions, first for the Berber Ibn 'Ammar, then for the eunuch Barjawan.

The Maghrib and Sicily

947/336
Revolt in Palermo, led by the Banu Tabari oligarchy, put down by Hasan b. 'Ali, the first Kalbite emir.

965/354
Byzantine menace in Sicily. Kalbite victory in Rometta and Caliphal decision to assemble all the population groups in fortified towns with *khutba* mosques. Generalized "incastellamento" of the island.

996–1016/386–406
In Mahdiyya, government led by the Sanhaji Berber Badis in the name of the Fatimids; he is supported by his uncle Hammad b. Buluqqin.

1007/398
Rupture between Badis and Hammad. Two dynasties founded: Zirites in Mahdiyya, and Hammadids in

Qal'a (from the Banu Hammad tribe in Hodna).

1019/410
In Palermo, an attempt at fiscal reform by the Kalbite Ja'far. He attempts to substitute the tithe with a plow tax; Ja'far expelled to Egypt.

1027/418
The Zirids lose Tripolitani to the Zanata Berbers.

1035/427
The Zirid Mu'izz b. Badis threatens Sicily; the attempt fails.

1051/443
Mu'izz b. Badis breaks with Isma'ili Shi'ism and the Fatimid dynasty, an event he prepares for by coining money with Maliki inscriptions.

1052/445
Fall of the Kalbite emir Simsam. Sicily divided: Ibn Thimna al-Qadir in Syracuse, Ibn Maklati in Catana, Ibn Hawwas in Castrogiovanni (Enna). Autonomous power of the *shaykhs* in Palermo. Ifriqiyya invaded by the Banu Hilal tribes, causes major destruction.

The Italian Front

902/289
Aghlabite offensive in Calabria; establishment of an autonomous province in North Africa.

951/340
Fatimid victory over the Byzantines in southern Italy.

962/351

Fatimids retake Taormina, known as Mu'izziyya, in honor of the caliph.

965/354

Byzantines conquer Cyprus. Byzantines attack Sicily and are defeated in the battle of the Trench, in Rometta.

982/372

Naval victory by the Kalbite 'Ali over Emperor Otto II's navy near Crotona.

986-1002/376-392

Kalbite victories in Calabria and Basilicata.

1015/405

Rupture between Hakim and Emperor Basileios II.

1026-1035/417-426

Combined incursions by the Zirid and Kalbite navies into the Illyrian and Greek coastal region.

1038-1041/429-432

Devastating Byzantine attack on Sicily led by Georges Maniakes; reconquest of the northeastern section of the island. Maniakes called back and the Kalbite Simsam reunifies the island. Peace treaties between Fatimid Egypt and Byzantium ensure lasting peace.

Civilization and Culture

921/308

Mahdiyya, the Fatimid capital, founded on a Tunisian peninsula. Model of the palace-city designed for the Isma'ili elite.

932/326

Khalisa, Isma'ili palace-city that is residence for the emirs near old Palermo, founded.

940/329

Death of Eutychius (Sa'id b. al-Batriq), Melkite patriarch from Alexandria, author of the *Annals* of world history.

969/358

Jawhar, the general of al-Mu'izz, founds Cairo (al-Qahira), a heavily fortified palace-city erected while the planet Mars (al-Qahir) is ascendant. Initially called al-Mansuriyyah, after the entry of al-Mu'izz in 973 it is renamed Qahria al-Mu'izziyyah ("The victorious [city] of Mu'izz").

974/363

Death of the *qadi* Nu'man, Mu'izz's collaborator and *da'wa* dignitary, author of *The Pillars of Islam*.

End of 10th century/end of 4th century

Sawiris b. al-Muqaffa, bishop of Ashmunayn, continues his *History of the Patriarchs*.

988/378

Ibn Killis establishes 35 teaching positions in the Azhar mosque in Cairo.

998-1019/388-410

Palermo erupts during the Kalbite Ja'far's rule: the Maredolce castle; poetry flourishes; its main proponent is Ibn Hani (d. 973).

1006–1007/396

Yahya, Melkite doctor who emigrated to Antioch. *History of the Alexandrian Patriarchs*.

1007/398

Qal'a, the Banu Hammad tribe's capital in which the Manar and Lac palaces are constructed.

1033–1034/424–425

Jerusalem surrounded by a wall as protection against Byzantine incursion.

1046–1077/438–470

Christodulos, Coptic patriarch, settles in Fustat.

The Economy

10th century/4th century

Development of maritime commerce in the Mediterranean, on the Damietta-Mazara-Tunis-Almeria axis. Spanish and Sicilian silk are traded for Egyptian linen and Syrian spices and sugar.

959/348

The "Greek market" in Fustat; sign of a slowdown in military operations and of a rebirth of the north–south maritime routes.

969/359

Fatimids increase value of money with the help of gold from Africa; gold content of the dinar at 98–100%.

996/386

The dinar quarter (*rub'a*, then *tari*) minted by the Fatimids, mostly in Sicily; distribution of gold money among the middle and lower classes. Local economy improves. Incident in Fustat: 160 Amalfi merchants, Byzantine subjects, killed by a crowd run wild as a result of a fire at the arsenal; Fatimid policy attracts Italian merchants and the systematic transit of spices, pepper, lacquer, musk, brazil wood and mirobalan from the Indian Ocean through the Red Sea and Aden.

1030–1040/421–432

Development of trade in Tyre, Sayda and Tripoli, based on the export of sugar and the transport of spices. In Egypt (as evident from the documents from the Geniza in Fustat), Jews participate in the traffic of goods to Mazara and Kairuan, and the progressive re-emergence of Alexandria.

1054/447

Byzantium delivers grain when Egypt is struck by famine.

The Umayyads of Spain and the Kings of the Ta'ifas

The proclamation of the Fatimid caliphate allows the emirial dynasty of al-Andalus, who consolidated his border with the Christian kingdoms in the north of Spain, to restore the Umayyad caliphate in 929/316.

After the suppression of the revolts by recent converts (*muwalladun*), Cordoba's power finally rivals Baghdad's and the city begins to find its past glory as it is reflected in the material wealth and prestige of architectural projects.

With armies made up of *saqaliba* (Slavs), the military authorizes, from 976/366 to 1008/399, the "dictatorship" of the *hajib* (treasurer) al-Mansur, following the example of the eastern emirs. The weakness of the dynasty, isolated in its palace, incites the Hammudis, a branch of the 'Alid family of the Idrisids, to attempt an overthrow of the caliphate. At the same time, many new principalities are being formed by high-ranking military and civil officers. As *ta'ifas*, kingdoms (from the expression *muluk al-tawa'if*, "king of factions" or "regional rulers"), they tend to create caliphate legitimacy. The anarchy that results does not immediately weaken Muslim Andalusia as regards Castile and Leon and does not take anything away from the brilliance of Andalusia's civilization.

Political Life

918/305
Death of rebel Ibn Hafsun; his capital, Bobastro, will be taken in 928/315. At the height of his power, Ibn Hafsun had ruled over Malaga (Rayyo), Grenada (Ilbira), and had an ally in the province of Jaen.

929/316
'Abd al-Rahman III assumes the title of *amir al-mu'minin* and the surname Nasir li din Allah (protector of God's religion). By doing so, he emphasized the Umayyads' claim to the caliphate against the 'Abbasids, and tried to counter the heterodox Fatimids.

931/319
Occupation of Ceuta by the Umayyads.

955/344
Naval war against the Fatimids. Establishment of Almeria.

961–976/350–366:
Reign of al-Hakam II ('Abd al-Rahman's son)
The Marches are placed under the central government secure from neighboring Christian kingdoms, and the Idrisites from North Africa remain subjugated. Norman attack on the Atlantic coast of al-Andalus.

976/366:
Caliphate of Hisham II
Muhammad b. Abi 'Amir al-Mansur runs the state; ruthless elimination of all competition.

1002/392
After the death of al-Mansur, regency of his son 'Abd al-Malik al-Muzaffar.

1008/399
After the death of Muzaffar, his brother 'Abd al-Rahman "Sanchuelo" (after his Basque grandfather, Sancho Garces I, king of Pamplona) serves as regent; abdication of Hisham II; short-lived caliphates of Muhammad al-Mahdi and Sulayman al-Muast'in.

1010–1013/400–403:
Second Reign of Hisham II
Agony of the Umayyad caliphate; conflicts between the freed slaves of al-Mansur, who founded the 'Amirite principality of Valencia, and the Slavs from the army.

1016–1018/407–408:
Caliphates of ʿAli b. Hammud
and al-Qasim
1017/408
Restoration of the Umayyads; several puppet caliphates until 1030/420.

1022/413
The Aftasi dynasty (Arabized Berbers) founded, in Badajoz, by the minister Ibn al-Aftas.

1023/414
The *qadi* of Seville, Ibn ʿAbbad, takes power as Arabs, the Abbadis, fight the Berbers, conquering a large part of al-Andalus. After Ibn ʿAbbad's death, his son proclaims himself *hajib*, then assumes the caliphate name of Muʿtadid (1041/433).

1030–1039/420–431
The splintering of al-Andalus: the Dhu al-Nunid dynasty in Toledo, the Jawhari dynasty in Cordoba, the Hudid dynasty in Saragossa and the Zirid dynasty in Grenada all demand control of the caliphate. Warrior principalities include the Slavs and the Mujahid in Denia. They constitute the kings of the *tawaʾif.* Conflicts between groups of Arab descent and those of Berber descent.

Culture and Civilization in al-Andalus

913/301
Construction of the Alcazar of Seville.

931/319
Umayyad residence built in Bilyunaysh, near Ceuta.

936/325
Palace-city of Madinat al-Zahra' built near Cordoba.

956/345
Construction of the Mosque of Tortosa.

970/359
Death of the Jewish scholar and diplomat Hasday b. Shaprut, adviser to ʿAbd al-Rahman III. Translations from Greek into Arabic.

977/367
Death of the chronicler Ibn al-Qutiya, the "son of the Visigoth."

978/368
Amirid residence of Madinat al-Zahira established; becomes seat of Ibn ʿAmir al-Mansur's administration.

987–988/377
The Great Mosque of Cordoba expanded by al-Mansur.

987–1076/377–369
Ibn Hayyan, historian of al-Andalus, author of the *Muktabis.*

1007–1066/398–459
Ibn Sida of Murcia, philologist, author of two extensive dictionaries.

1008–1010/399–401
Madinat al-Zahira and the Rusafa palace sacked.

1009/399

Death of Abu al-Qasim al-Zahrawi (Abulcasis), doctor from Cordoba; translation of his work into Latin.

994-1064/385-455

Ibn Hazm, author of the *abab* and Zahirite theologian, writes the *Necklace of the Dove* and a history of the monotheistic religions.

The Eastern Front

939/327

Defeat of the Umayyad army in Simancas by Ramire II of Leon; parts of his army desert 'Abd al-Rahman, who is almost taken prisoner.

980-1002/370-392

Al-Mansur reforms military and gains victories. More than 50 military campaigns.

985/375

Conquest of Barcelona.

988/377

Conquest of Leon.

997/388

Conquest of Santiago de Compostela.

1003-1007/393-398

Victorious incursions of the 'Amirids into Catalonia, Galicia, Navarre and Castile.

1015-1016/406

Mujahid of Denia attacks Sardinia.

1017/407

Start of the Burgundian crusades against Spain.

1037/429

Bermudo III of Leon killed in the battle of Tamaron.

1053/445

Ferdinand I of Castile's campaign against Toledo.

Non-Arab Dynasties

From the 11th to the 13th century, power, both in the Muslim East and West, is in the hands of non-Arab rulers: Berbers in the West, Turks and Kurds in the East. The Muslims must also face enemies from the outside: the beginning of the Christian "Reconquista" of Spain, and the arrival of the Crusades in the Near East; further to the east, in the 13th century, the Mongol invasion by Genghis Khan, which then only disrupts the borders of the Muslim world, but later, under his successors, penetrates deeply into the territories of Islam. In 1258, Baghdad, capital of the 'Abbasid caliphate, is conquered and destroyed by the Mongol Hülegü. In the Maghrib and in Spain, the Almoravid dynasty appears, followed by the Almohad dynasty. These dynasties concentrate on religious rigor and the struggle with the Christian rulers in Spain. In the center of the Muslim world, Salah al-Din (Saladin), after his victory over the Crusaders in the kingdom of Jerusalem, manages to restore unity, which subsequently breaks down after his death. In Iraq but mostly in Asia Minor, the Seljuqs add a certain dynamism that is directed most notably against the Byzantines. In Iran, in Afghanistan and in central Asia, the Turks and Mongols contribute to the splintering of the Muslim world.

Just as the 10th and beginning of the 11th century witnessed the rise of Shi'ism among the Fatimids of Ifriqiyya and then of Egypt, the period that follows sees a renewal of Sunnism, as becomes evident by the construction of mosques and, most notably in the Near East, of the *madrasa*. Also, the growth in numbers of religious and secular authors such as Ibn Tufayl, Ibn Rushd, Idrisi, Mawardi, Yaqut, Ibn al-Athir and Ibn 'Arabi is a reflection of this phenomenon. This period, rich in historical events, is also marked by a phenomenal intellectual and artistic flowering.

The Almoravids and Almohads

The Almoravids, followed by the Almohads, successively succeed in reuniting under their authority a large part or all of the Maghrib and Muslim Andalusia.

Each time, the conquest is done in the name of Islam; the original unity of each movement is cemented by the doctrine of a religious leader who reproduces, along with his companions in life as well as in war, the model of the Prophet of Islam and of his primitive community.

Nevertheless, each movement has the tendency to lose its coherence. Unitary ideology becomes, through its exclusivity, a source of weakness and is not enough to maintain cohesion among the tribal groups.

Wars exhaust the supply of soldiers and strengthen the opposition. The rulers call on foreign elements to be employed as soldiers: Christian mercenaries and Bedouin Arab tribes previously driven out of the East by the Fatimids. This produces political instability and demographic and economic changes.

The Andalusian cities begin to resent the presence of these outside powers that they had employed to stop the Christian Reconquista. The Reconquista continues despite the temporary relief afforded by the intervention of the Maghribi forces. Moreover, the economic situation of the Mediterranean basin changes in favor of the Italian merchant cities.

The Almoravid Conquest

1046/338

Yahya b. Ibrahim, the leader of the Sahanja Berbers of the western Sahara, returns from a pilgrimage to Mecca with the religious scholar and missionary 'Abd Allah b. Yasin. Ibn Yasin wins followers among several Berber tribes (Lamtuna, Masufa, Gudala) who join forces, calling themselves al-murabitun (Almoravids). They form an exclusive group and do not allow members of other tribes to join the inner circle of the murabitun. The word murabitun probably derives from the monastery (ribat or rabita) of Ibn Yasin's teacher, Wagag b. Zaluy.

1054/446

Conquest of the city of Awdaghust by the Murabitun from the black kingdom of Ghana. Yayha Ibn 'Umar,

head of the Lamtuna, attacks the north.

1055-1056/447

Conquest of Sijilmasa; expulsion of the Zanata emirs. Expeditions into Adrar; death of Yahya Ibn 'Umar in combat during his siege of Azuggi. Murabitun conquer the Sous (Sus) from the Masmuda.

1056/448

Abu Bakr b. 'Umar replaces his deceased brother Yahya.

1057-1058/449

Conquest of the Upper Atlas by the Murabitun; the Masmuda surrender. Conquest of Aghmat from the Maghrawa. Abu Bakr marries the widow of the vanquished emir, the influential Zaynab al-Nafzawiyya.

1058-1059/450-451

The Zanata Banu Ifran in Tadla and the Atlantic plains are attacked.

51

Struggle with the heterodox confederation of the Barghwata in Tamesna (between Asfi and Salé).

1059/451

Death of 'Abd Allah Ibn Yasin in combat.

1060/452

Beginning with Aghmat, Abu Bakr extends his conquests to the north. Meknes (Miknas) taken.

1061/453

Return of Abu Bakr to the Sahara, where he extends the Almoravid domination into the black kingdom of Ghana. He leaves his wife Zaynab and abandons the leadership of the North to his cousin Yusuf b. Tashfin.

1061/454

According to legend, Yusuf b. Tashfin establishes the town of Marrakesh.

1063-1072/455-465

Almoravid conquest of Fez and its region from the Maghrawa, and of the plateau of Fazaz from the Banu Ifran. Fez taken definitively in 1070/462, as is Fazaz in 1072/465. Penetration into the Rif.

1070/463

Abu Bakr founds Marrakesh as his capital; returns to the Sahara to quell a rebellion; makes Yusuf b. Tashfin his deputy.

1072/465

Yusuf b. Tashfin prevents Abu Bakr from returning to Marrakesh.

1077/470

Conquest of Ceuta and Tangier from the Barghwata.

1079-1082/472-475

Almoravid conquest of the central Maghrib from the Zanata Marghrawa. Oudja, Tlemcen, Tenes and Algiers taken.

1080-1081/473

Yusuf b. Tashfin mints money in his name.

1085/478

Toledo taken by the forces of the Reconquista under Alfonso VI of Castile. The kings of Seville, Badajoz and Malaga, call on Yusuf b. Tashfin to intervene in Andalusia.

1086/479

The Almoravids land in Algeciras. Almoravid and Andalusian victory over the Castilians in Sagrajas (al-Zallaqa), close to Badajoz. Yusuf b. Tashfin assumes the title of "emir of the Muslims," which is acknowledged by the 'Abbasid caliph.

1088-1100/481-493

New Almoravid interventions in Spain. Yusuf b. Tashfin insures his power over all the ta'ifa kingdoms by exerting military pressure.

1090/483

Third intervention of Yusuf b. Tashfin in Andalusia; elimination of all kings of the ta'ifa by 1092 with the exception of Valencia and Zaragoza.

1102/495

Valencia taken.

1106/500

Death of Yusuf b. Tashfin.

The Almoravid State and the Almohad Conquest

1106–1143/500–537: Reign of 'Ali b. Yusuf b. Tashfin

Domestic politics characterized by balance of power among the Almoravid governors. Struggle against the Almohad threat. Wars in Spain against Castile and Aragon.

1106–1116/500–510

The Berber legal scholar Ibn Tumart travels in the East; legal and theological education in Iraq; he is influenced by al-Ghazali's reconciliation of Orthodoxy and Islamic mysticism.

1109/503

Almoravid power is based on Maliki ideology of strict observance of religious precepts, and on the decrees of its lawyers; burning of the works of al-Ghazali (in Cordoba) and censorship of intellectuals with Ghazalian leanings.

1110/504

Zaragoza taken.

1116–1121/510–515

Ibn Tumart returns to the Maghrib. Preaching against and censorship of the standards of behavior in Tunis, Constantine and Bijaya (Bougie). 'Abd al-Mu'min, a Berber from northwest Algeria, becomes the disciple of Ibn Tumart. Return to Morocco. Theological controversies with Almoravid legal scholars in Marrakesh. Ibn Tumart, in danger of imprisonment, escapes to his tribe.

1118/512

Zaragoza taken by the king of Aragon.

A Call to the Almoravids

"Bits of news had been coming rapidly reporting that the emir Yusuf b. Tashfin had suddenly appeared out of the Sahara leading a new, vigorous and determined Islamic community, proclaiming his determination to see that truth triumph and to fight those who deviated from religious law; that he had just conquered the Maghrib and had unified most of it. Weighing matters, al-Mu'tamid (king of Seville) thought he might have to summon his help. . . . He consulted with his aides on the subject. His son al-Rashid told him the following: 'Try to work things out with the Christian using your own means, and do not rush to bring in someone who will rob us of our royalty and will divide us: you know who these people are.' Al-Mu'tamid responded: 'My son, it is better in my mind to die a shepherd in the Maghrib than to render Andalusia a land of infidelity, for if I do that, the Muslims will curse my name until the end of time!' His son then told him, 'Father, do what God has told you to do!'

Ibn al-Khatib, A'mal al-a'lam, ed. E. Lévi-Provençal, Beirut, 1956
translated by A. L. de Prémare

1121/515

Ibn Tumart proclaimed *mahdi* in the Lower Atlas and the Sus.

1123–1130/517–524

The "Unitarian" community (*al-Muwahhidun*, Almohads) in Tinmall, in the Upper Atlas (ca. 75 km southwest of Marrakesh). Rigor in social, religious, political and military organizations. The Almohads comprised 8 Masmuda tribes, or factions of tribes. They formed an exclusive and strictly hierarchical society.

1125–1126/519–520

Alfonso I of Aragon invades eastern Andalusia, settles 14,000 Mozarabs.

1130/524

Death of the *mahdi* Ibn Tumart after a defeat at al-Buhaysa, and a failed siege of Marrakesh. His death is announced only once 'Abd al-Mu'min has a firm hold of power three years later.

1132/527

'Abd al-Mu'min proclaimed successor to the *mahdi* in Tinmall, assumes the caliphal title *amir al-mu'minin*.

1132–1141/527–535

Progressive conquest by 'Abd al-Mu'min of the Sus, Dra, Upper and Middle Atlas, Tafilalet, Rif and Northern Orania.

1143/537

Death of the Almoravid sovereign 'Ali b. Yusuf. His son Tashfin follows him. Rivalries between Almoravid clans. Secession of local Andalusian dynasties.

1145/539

Reverter (Ruburtayr), leader of the Christian militias in the service of the Almoravids, dies in combat. Tlemcen taken by 'Abd al-Mu'min. Death of Tashfin.

1146/540

The Almohads take Oujda, Guercif, Fez, Miknas and Sale. Expeditions by Almohad generals into Spain; Cadiz taken.

1147/541

Almohad triumph in Marrakesh. 'Abd al-Mu'min proclaimed "emir of the believers." Marrakesh becomes Almohad capital (execution of Almoravids). Power taken by the Almohads in Seville. Muhammad Ibn Ghaniyya, Almoravid governor in Majorca, declares his independence. A combined force of Castile, Aragon, Pisa and Genoa under the leadership of Alfonso VII of Castile takes Almeria.

The Almohad Empire

1150/545

A delegation of Andalusian notables recognizes 'Abd al-Mu'min as their ruler.

1151/546

Conquest of central Morocco. Elimination of the Hammadid dynasty in the Bougie (Bijaya) region. Victory over the Banu Hilal Arabs in Setif. The Banu Hilal tribes are deported to the Atlantic regions of northern Morocco, where they are settled.

1157/552

The Almohads take power in Almeria and Grenada.

A Predestined Meeting

"Know, my brother, that 'Abd al-Mu'min, endeavoring to meet the imam [Ibn Tumart, in Bougie], mixed with students who lined his route and went with them to the door of the mosque. The Impeccable One, lifting his head, stopped before him and said: 'Come in, young man!' He entered and wished to sit in the middle of the crowd. The imam, the impeccable Mahdi, said this: 'Approach, young man!' . . . Then he said to him: 'Where are you going, brave boy?' — 'Sayyidi, to the East, to learn science.' The Impeccable One declared: 'The science that you want to discover in the East you have just found in the West!' Then, once the crowd had left, . . . the [future] caliph wanted to leave. The Impeccable One then said: 'You will spend the night with us, young man!' . . . And he spent the night with us. . . . And the Impeccable One read his book to the one who would be his successor. And I, that night, holding a torch, heard him declare: 'Religion will only triumph with 'Abd al-Mu'min, son of 'Ali, torchlight of the Almohads!' "

al-Baydhaq, *Akhbar al-Mahdi Ibn Tumart*, ed. Rabat.
translation by A. L. de Prémare

1159–1162/554–558

Conquest of the eastern Maghrib. End of Roger II of Sicily's power in Mahdiyya. 'Abd al-Mu'min structures the Almohad state. Rigorous fiscal organization of all of the Maghrib. Direct administration of two-thirds of the land; subject to taxation; certain Berber and Bedouin tribes follow the central government.

1163/558

Illness and death of 'Abd al-Mu'min in Rabat.

1163–1184/558–580: *Reign of Abu Ya'qub Yusuf, son of 'Abd al-Mu'min*
1165/560

The Portuguese take Evora.

1167/562

Repression of rebellions in the Rif.

1171–1172/567

Seville becomes second capital of the Empire and seat of Andalusian administration.

1172/567

Abu Ya'qub ends the secession of Ibn Mardanish ("Rey Lobo" in Spanish chronicles) in Murcia. The Armenian Qaraqush controls Tripoli.

1173–1174/569

Truce between Castile and Aragon after a series of struggles.

1174/569

Devastating plague in North Africa.

1177/573

Cuenca taken by Alfonso VIII of Castile.

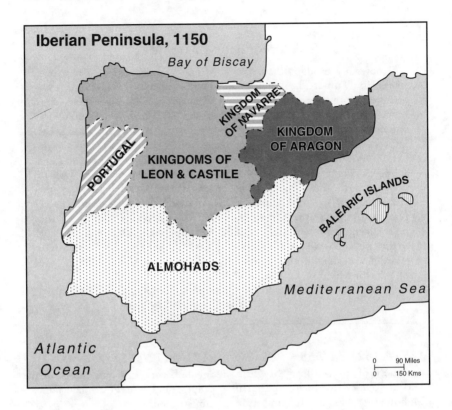

Iberian Peninsula, 1150

Bay of Biscay

KINGDOM OF NAVARRE

KINGDOM OF ARAGON

PORTUGAL

KINGDOMS OF LEON & CASTILE

BALEARIC ISLANDS

ALMOHADS

Mediterranean Sea

Atlantic Ocean

0   90 Miles
0   150 Kms

1180–1181/576

Repression of dissidence among Arab tribes in Gafsa.

1184/580

War against the Portuguese. Siege on Santarem fails. Death of Ya'qub Yusuf.

1184–1199/580–595: Reign of 'Abu Yusuf Ya'qub al-Mansur
1184/580

Abu Yusuf proclaimed "emir of the believers." Defense of strict orthodoxy; censorship of Malikism. Jews forced to wear distinguishing emblems.

1185/581

The Banu Ghaniyya Almoravids from Majorca land in central Maghrib: Bougie (Bijaya), Algiers, Miliana, Ashir and the Qal'a taken from the Bani Hammad. Until 1237/633, the Banu Ghaniyya, along with their Arab allies and the Armenian mercenary leader Qaraqush, maintain, by attempting to restore the Almoravids, a state of permanent dissidence in central and eastern Maghrib, which precipitates the decline of the Almohads.

1189–1192/585–587

War against Sancho I, the king of Portugal.

1195/591
Victory of Alarcos (al-Arak) over the Castilians. Abu Yusuf Ya'qub assumes the title of *al-Mansur bi Allah*, "The Victorious One with the help of God."

1199/595
Death of Ya'qub al-Mansur. Succeeded by his son al-Nasir li Din Allah.

1203/600
al-Nasir reconquers al-Mahdiyya, previously controlled by the Banu Ghaniyya. He establishes Abu Muhammad, son of the Almohad shaykh Abu Hafs as quasi-autonomous governor of the eastern Maghrib.

1209/606
Defeat of the Banu Ghaniyya in the Nefusa mountains.

1212/609
In Spain, decisive defeat of the Almohads at Las Navas de Tolosa (al-'Uqab) by the united troops of Castile, Aragon, Leon and Navarre. This leads to the retreat of the Almohads from al-Andalus in 1225.

1214–1269/610–668
Decline of the central power of the Almohads. Intra-dynastic rivalries, quarrels over secession.

1213/610
Death of al-Nasir li Din Allah.

1215–1217/612–614
Dissidence of the Zanata Banu Marin in the central Maghrib and northern Morocco, led by 'Abd al-Haqq.

1224–1229/620–626
Andalusia secedes. Ibn Hud, king of Murcia first, then of all of Andalusia.

1226/622
The Pope establishes the bishopric of Marrakesh.

1228/625
Independence of Ifriqiyya.

1230/627
The Almohad al-Ma'mun conquers his rival in Marrakesh, with the support of the king of Castile. He repudiates Almohad doctrine.

1235/633
Independence of the Zanata Banu 'Abd al-Wad in Tlemcen (led by Yaghmurasan b. Zayyan).

1236/634
Hafsid independence in Tunis (led by Abu Zakariyya' Yahya); economic treaties with Venice, Pisa, Genoa.

1237/634
Nasrid independence in Grenada.

1245/642
Jaen taken by Ferdinand III of Castile.

1246/643
Nasrid emirate of Grenada pays tribute to Castile.

1248/646
The Banu Marin rule over eastern Morocco first, then over northern Morocco. Creation of the Marinid kingdom under Abu Yahya Abu Bakr.

1253/651
The Hafsid al-Mustansir bi-Allah proclaims himself caliph; recognized

by the sharifs of Mecca, and possibly by the Mamluks.

1269/668
The Marinids take Marrakesh (under Abu Yusuf Ya'qub).

Civilization and Culture
Almoravid Art

11th century/5th century
Canals built for water transport to palm groves and Marrakesh.

12th century/6th century
The ramparts of Marrakesh built.

12th century/6th century
Ancient mosque of the Kairuan in Fez enlarged.

Beginning of 12th century/6th century
Great Mosque of Algiers built.

1135/529
Great Mosque of Tlemcen built.

Almohad Art

1153–1154/548
Mosque of Tinmall built.

1158/553
Mosque of the Kutubiyya built in Marrakesh.

1171–1176/566–571
Great Mosque of Seville built.

1193/589
The Giralda, the minaret of the Great Mosque of Seville, completed. The ramparts of Rabat built. Hassan mosque and the minaret of Rabat built.

Islamic Science

1076–1158/468–543
Abu Bakr Ibn al-Arabi of Seville, traditionalist and lawyer; ex-disciple of al-Ghazali in the East.

1083–119/476–544
The *qadi* of Ceuta, 'Iyadh Ibn Musa al-Yahsubi, traditionalist and lawyer; author of the *Kitab al-shifa'*, "Book of Healing."

Spiritual Life

Ribat of the Banu Amghar of Tit, near Azemmour (Azammur).

1164/559
Death of Ibn Hirzihim (Sidi Harazem), of Fez, ascetic.

1177/572
Death of Abu Ya'azza Yalennur (Moulay Bou'azza), ascetic, from Middle Atlas.

1197/594
Death of Abu Madyan, of Seville, ascetic, who had settled in Bougie (Bijaya).

Theology, Philosophy, Medicine

1126–1198/520–595
Ibn Rushd (Averroes), of Cordoba; jurist and philosopher. Emphasizes the autonomy of philosophical knowledge from religion. His commentary on Aristotle is translated into Latin,

and is widely read in the Christian Occident. Refutation of al-Ghazali's work on the "self-destruction of the philosopher."

1135-1204/529-601

Ibn Maymun (Maimonides), of Cordoba, Jewish theologian and doctor, author of the *Guide for the Lost*; greatest and last philosopher of Jewish rationalism in the Mediterranean tradition.

1139/533

Death of Ibn Bajja (Avempace) of Saragossa, philosopher, author of the *Tadbir al-mutawahhid*, "Regime of the Solitary Man." Theoretician of Islamic music.

1161/557

Death of Ibn Zuhr (Avenzoar) of Seville, doctor.

1185-1186/581

Death of Ibn Tufayl (Abubacer, Albubather) of Guadix, philosopher, author of the philosophical novel *Hayy Ibn Yaqazan*, "The Living Son of the Vigilant."

Historiography

Around middle of 12th century/6th century—al-Baydhaq, companion of the *mahdi* Ibn Tumart, and chronicler of the beginnings of the Almohad movement.

987-1076/377-469

Ibn Hayyan, of Cordoba, historian of Andalusia.

1090/483

'Abd Allah Ibn Buluggin, ancient Sanhajan king of Grenada, exiled by Yusuf Ibn Tashfin to Aghmat, author of historico-political memories, the *Kitab al-tibyan.*

1224/621

'Abd al-Wahid al-Marrakushi of Marrakesh: *Kitab al-muʾjib*, a history of the Almohads.

Geographers and Explorers

1080-1169/473-565

Abu Hamid al-Gharnati, of Grenada; travels to the Middle East, Iran, central Asia and central Europe, writes accounts of his travels.

1094/487

Death of al-Bakri, from Huelva, botanist and geographer, author of the *Kitab al-masalik wa al-mamalik.*

1145-1217/540-614

Ibn Jubayr of Valencia. Voyage to the East while on pilgrimage to Mecca; writes accounts of his travels.

1154/548

al-Idrisi (death in 1165/560) writes a work of descriptive geography, *Nuzhat al-mushtaq fi ikhtiraq al-afaq* ("Joy of the one who wants to travel the horizons"), or *Kitab Rujar*, after a request from Roger II of Sicily: contains 70 maps, and for the first time conveys to the Arabs knowledge about western and northern Europe.

Literature

1058-1139/450-533

Ibn Khafaja of Alcira, classical poet, nicknamed "The Gardener," minstrel of nature.

1101–1183/494–578

Ibn Bashkuwal (region around Valencia), author of a collection of biographies of men of letters from the 11th and 12th centuries/5th and 6th centuries.

Circa 1105/498

al-Dhakhira, anthology of Andalusian poetry from the 11th century/5th century, written by Ibn Bassam of Santarem.

Circa 1134/529

Death of al-Fath b. Khaqan, author of an anthology of Andalusian poetry, *Qala'id al-'iqyan*, "The Golden Necklaces."

1160/555

Death of Ibn Quzman of Cordoba, the most famous poet writing in the *zajal* stanza; poetry in the Andalusian dialect of Arabic.

The Great Seljuqs, the Fatimids and the Crusades

Coming in stages from central Asia to Iraq around 1050, the Turkish tribe of the Seljuqs plays a fundamental role in safeguarding the 'Abassid caliphate of Baghdad, which was threatened by an attack of the Egyptian Fatimids. Having become for all intents and purposes the holders of power in Iran and Iraq, the Seljuqs extend their domination to Syria, but are stopped by the Fatimids in Palestine. The Crusaders, who succeeded in creating states in the Near East, benefit from the internal struggles among Muslims until Nur al-Din (the emir of Aleppo and Damascus) and more importantly Salah al-Din (Saladin) manage to achieve unity once again and to retake the greatest part of their domains from the Latins. After the death of Saladin, Syria and Egypt subdivide into several states, rival or allied depending on the circumstances, which favors, in the middle of the 13th century, the appropriation of power by soldiers recruited from the Caucasus or from Turkish regions (the Mamluks), while the Middle East witnesses the invasion of the Mongols.

Political Life

1055/447

Seljuq Turks, led by Toğrïl-Beg, overthrow the Buwayhids in Baghdad. The caliph al-Qa'im recognizes him as the "Sultan of the East and the West."

1056/448

The Seljuqs take Mosul from the 'Uqaylids.

1058/449

Turkish mercenaries paid by the Fatimids and led by al-Basasiri (the Turkish general of the Buyids) capture Baghdad and the caliph.

1060/452

Toğrïl-Beg retakes Baghdad and, in addition, takes Aleppo; al-Basasiri is killed. The Seljuqs are the uncontested rulers of the eastern and central Islamic world.

1063/455
Death of Toğhrïl-Beg, who is succeeded by his nephew Alp Arslan; military expeditions against Byzantium and the Fatimids.

1065/457
The Persian Nizam al-Mulk in the service of the Ghaznavids becomes the vizier of Alp Arslan and Malik Shah. Centralization of the empire; consolidation of rural and urban economy; expansion of the *iqta'*—system of military fiefs.

1067-1068/459-460
Alp Arslan attacks Armenia and central Anatolia.

1071/463
August/Dhu'l-Qa'da. Seljuq victory over the Byzantines in Manzikert (Malazgird): after Byzantines invade Armenia, Romanos IV Diogenes taken prisoner. Result: Anatolia is open for Turkish conquest.

1072/464 or 465
Death of Alp Arslan I on an expedition to Transoxania; succeeded by Malik Shah.

1074/466
The Armenian convert Badr al-Jamali (in Cairo) combines the posts of vizier and military commander-in-chief of the Fatimid empire.

1076/468
The Seljuqs take Damascus from the Fatimids; the general Atsiz takes Jerusalem.

1077/469
Atsiz invades Egypt and is vanquished by Badr al-Jamali near Cairo.

1078-1095/471-488
Tutush, brother of Malik Shah, emir of Syria and Palestine, replaces Atsiz; his two sons, Duqaq and Ridwan, will be the rulers of Damascus and Aleppo, respectively.

1084/477
Antioch taken by the Seljuqs.

1090/483
Seljuq power contested for the first time. Beginning of a revolt by Hasan al-Sabbah, who takes over al-Alamut in Iran. The Qarmatians sack Basra.

1092/485
October/Ramadan. Murder of Nizam al-Mulk by the "Assassins." Death of Malik Shah; succeeded by his son Barkyaruq.

1094/487
March/Rabi I. Death of Badr al-Jamali in Cairo.

1095/487
January/Dhu'l-Hijja. Death of the Fatimid al-Mustansir bi-Allah.

1095/488
The Armenians retake Edessa (al-Ruha) from the Seljuqs.

1096/489
Pope Urban II starts the First Crusade with the goal of conquering Jerusalem.

1097/490
Baldwin of Boulogne takes Tell Bashir in northern Syria.

1098/491
Edessa, ancient Byzantine possession, becomes for a half-century the capital

Assassins

An Isma'ili sect that supports the imamate of Nizar, the successor of Badr al-Din al-Jamali, the emir and vizier of the Fatimid empire. When Nizar is defeated in battle and killed in prison, some Isma'ilis claim that Nizar has only gone into occultation. In the Persian fortress Alamut, Hasan al-Sabbah predicts the return of Nizar, and instigates attacks on Sunni, Fatimid and Christian leaders. Allegedly the members of this sect (who called themselves *fida'iyyun* — "those who sacrifice themselves") were prone to take hashish, hence their name "Hishishiyyun," or the European version, "Assassins."

of the Count of Edessa, Baldwin replacing the Armenian prince Thoros.
June 2/Jumada II. Antioch taken by the Crusaders. The Frankish principality of Antioch founded.
July/Shawwal. Jerusalem besieged by the Fatimid vizier al-Afdal, son of Badr.

1099/492
July 15/22 Shawwal. The Crusaders conquer Jerusalem; they make life difficult for Jews and Muslims. The Franks face the Fatimids near the border fortress of Ascalon ('Asqalan), henceforth a key strategic concern for the Muslims and the Crusaders. The Muslim troops are dispersed by the Franks before they start fighting.

1100/494
December 25/Safar. Baldwin I proclaimed "King of Jerusalem."

1102/495
Baldwin I beats the Fatimids in Ramla and takes Qaysariyya (Caesarea). Tartus taken by Raymond of Toulouse.

1103/496
Tancred of Normandy regent of Antioch.

1104/497
On the coast, the Crusaders take 'Akka (Acre) and Jubayl (Byblos).
May/Jumada I. Bohemond and Baldwin I of Edessa defeated in Harran by the *atabeg* of Mosul who is supported by the Artuqites of Diyar Bakr. Tughtakin (Tughtigin), *atabeg* of the Seljuq Duqaq, becomes ruler of Damascus after Duqaq's death.

1105/498
Seljuq Turks beaten by Tancred in Tizin, near Aleppo. Death of the Seljuq sultan Barkyaruq. Victory in Harran for Mawdud, *atabeg* of Mosul in the name of the Seljuq sultan.

1105-1113/499-507
Upsurge in the terrorist activities of the Assassins of Syria.

1106/500
Khalaf b. Mula'ib, representative of the Fatimids, executed by the Assassins; Afamiya (Apameia) taken by Tancred.

1108/501
Ladhiqiya (Latakia) taken by Tancred.

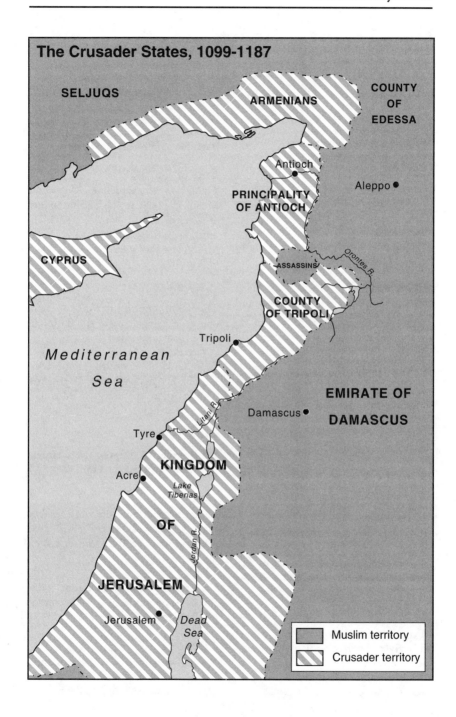

The Crusader States, 1099-1187

SELJUQS

ARMENIANS

COUNTY OF EDESSA

Antioch

Aleppo

PRINCIPALITY OF ANTIOCH

CYPRUS

ASSASSINS

Orontes R.

COUNTY OF TRIPOLI

Tripoli

Mediterranean Sea

EMIRATE OF DAMASCUS

Damascus

Litani R.

Tyre

KINGDOM

Acre

Lake Tiberias

OF

Jordan R.

JERUSALEM

Jerusalem

Dead Sea

Muslim territory

Crusader territory

1109/502

The Crusaders take Tripoli and Beirut. The county of Tripoli founded.

1110/503

Baldwin I takes Sayda (Sidon). Mawdud attempts to take control of al-Ruha (Edessa).

1113/507

October/Rabi II. After the failure of his campaign against Jerusalem, Mawdud comes to Damascus at the invitation of the Seljuq *atabeg* Tughtakin; there, he is assassinated, according to public rumor, by Tughtigin.

1115/509

Alliance between the Crusaders and Tughtakin against the *atabeg* of Mosul, whose army is decimated in Tell Danith by Roger of Antioch.

1116–1118/510–512

Baldwin I leads an attack on Egypt: occupies the port of Ayla and incorporates it into the kingdom of Jerusalem, thus severing the land route of the pilgrimage from Cairo to Mecca.

1118–1131/512–525

Reign of Baldwin II in Jerusalem.

1119/513

Il Ghazi, the Artuqid from Mosul, makes himself ruler of Aleppo; he defeats the Franks of Antioch in Tell Aqibrin near Antioch (battle of the "*Ager sanguinis*").

1125/519

Tyre (Sur) taken by the Crusaders; this gives them control of the coast. Ascalon is the sole port available to the Muslims. Aq-Sunqur al-Bursuqi, *atabeg* of Mosul, takes Aleppo.

1126/520

April/Rabi I. The caliph grants the position of *shihna* of Baghdad and Iraq to Zangi (Zengi) b. Aqsunqur, who preserves control of the fiefs of Wasit and Basra received from the Sultan. He is the de facto ruler of Baghdad and of lower Iraq.

End of 1126/520

'Izz al-Din Mas'ud leaves Aleppo for Mosul and Isfahan; he is granted post of *atabeg* of Mosul by the sultan Mahmud. He wishes to maintain a Syrian-Mesopotamian state under the aegis of Mosul.

1127/521

Tughtakin, opposed to Mas'ud's plan, obtains the departure of the Batinians settled in Damascus.

July/Rajab. Mas'ud dies during a siege on Rahba on the Euphrates. Part of his troops rejoin Tughtakin. The position of *atabeg* of Mosul is given to Zangi.

1128/522

Zangi, ruler of Aleppo, takes Hama; he attacks Antioch in 1130/524.

1140/534

Zangi forced to lift the siege on Damascus. Two years later, he will crush the Crusaders on the Orontes river.

1144/539

December/Jumada II. Zangi takes Edessa (al-Ruha). This is the reason for the Second Crusade (1147–1149).

1146/541

Nur al-Din succeeds Zangi, his father, who is assassinated during the siege on Qal'at Ja'bar, as emir of Aleppo.

1147/541

Second Crusade to Damascus led by the German Conrad III and the French Louis VII.

1148/543

July/10 Rabi I. Definitive defeat of the Second Crusade.

1149/544

Nur al-Din defeats Raymond of Poitiers at Inab (Hisn Innib) and takes Afamiya (Apamia), al-Bara and Artah. The Franks are pushed back west of the Orontes.

1150/545

July/Rabi I. Frankish garrison of 'Azaz capitulates.

1153/548

August/Jumada I. Baldwin III, king of Jerusalem, takes Ascalon, the last Fatimid base on the Syrian-Palestinian coast.

1154/549

Nur al-Din annexes Damascus.

1158/553

February/Muharram. Baldwin III recaptures Harim.

July/Jumada I. Nur al-Din beaten northeast of Tiberias.

1159/554

Manuel Comnenos imposes his suzerainty over Antioch. Siege of Aleppo by the Franks and Byzantines, who make peace with Nur al-Din.

1160/553

Majd al-Din, governor of Aleppo, takes Renaud of Chatillon prisoner.

1161/556

Egypt prevents invasion by pledging an annual payment of 160,000 dinar to Jerusalem; the money is never paid.

1162/557

Baldwin III succeeded by Amalric I in Jerusalem.

1163/558

Turmoil in Egypt. Amalric I attempts to intervene.

March/Jumada I. Defeat of Nur al-Din in al-Buqay'a.

1164/559

Nur al-Din occupies Egypt with his Kurdish general Shirkuh, who, along with his nephew Saladin (Salah al-Din b. Ayyub) is besieged by Amalric I in Bilbao. Having obtained the provisional retreat of Shirkuh, Amalric I pulls out. Harim taken by Nur al-Din; the counts of Antioch and Tripoli taken prisoner.

1167/563

Shirkuh returns to Egypt. Amalric I forces Shirkuh and Saladin to leave Egypt, which becomes a de facto protectorate of Jerusalem.

1168/563

Amalric I tries to conquer Egypt and suffers a defeat near Damietta; the Fatimids call on Nur al-Din for help. Nur al-Din takes Cairo. After the assassination of the Fatimid vizier Shawas, Shirkuh is appointed vizier.

1169/564

Death of Shirkuh; Saladin (age 31) becomes vizier of the last Fatimid caliph. Joint expedition of the Franks and Byzantines, who besiege Damietta in vain.

1169–1193/564–589
Saladin controls Egypt; he reestablishes the 'Abassid *khutba* in Cairo.

1169/564
Saladin eliminates the rebellious Armenian and Negro regiments of the Fatimid caliph in a street battle.

1170/565
Amalric I forces Nur al-Din to lift the siege on Kerak and drives Saladin back into Gaza.

1171/569
Saladin abolishes the Fatimid caliphate of Egypt; replacement of Isma'ili *qadis* by Sunni *qadis*; death of al-'Adid, the 19-year-old last Fatimid caliph; coins minted in the name of the 'Abbasid caliph and Nur al-Din. Saladin establishes the dynasty of the Ayyubids (which continues until 1250).

1173–1174/569
The Ayyubids take Aden. Deaths of Nur al-Din and Amalric I. Baldwin IV proclaimed king of Jerusalem. Saladin takes Damascus, Hims, Hama.

1175/570
Saladin granted the sultanate of Egypt, Syria, Palestine; truce with Jerúsalem.

1177/573
Baldwin IV defeats Saladin at Tell al-Safiya (Mont Giscard) near Ramla.

1179/575
Saladin raids Tyre (Sur). Defeat of Baldwin IV's army at Marj'uyun. Egyptian navy attacks Acre.

1180/576
Truce between Saladin and Baldwin IV.

1180–1225/575–622:
The Reign of the 'Abassid Caliph al-Nasir in Baghdad
With the help of the *futuwwa* movement, he leads Baghdad's caliphate to new cultural heights.

1182/578
Saladin raids Nazareth, Tiberias and Beirut; offensive against Mosul.

1183/579
Saladin takes Aleppo; he supplants Nur al-Din's son, al-Salih. All of Mesopotamia (including the cities Edessa, Harran, Mardin, Sinjar, Nasibin and Amid [Diarbakis]) come into his possession. Reginald of Chatillon is defeated by Egyptian fleet after attack on Mecca and Red Sea ports.

1184/580
Saladin ravages Galilee.

1185/581
Truce between Saladin and Raymond III of St. Gilles (Tripoli and Tiberias).

1187/583
July 4/25 Rabi II. Crushing victory by Saladin over the Crusaders in the battle of Hattin (west of Lake Tiberias). Reginald of Chatillon is taken prisoner and executed; King Guy of Jerusalem is taken prisoner.

November/Shawwal. Saladin takes Jerusalem back from the Crusaders, thus provoking the Third Crusade.

1188/584

Saladin conquers all the Frankish states in the East except Tyre, Tripoli and Antioch.

1190–1192/585–588

Third Crusade undertaken by Frederick Barbarossa (who dies on his way to Asia Minor), Philip II Augustus and Richard Lionheart.

1191/587

July/Jumada II. Acre ('Akka) taken by the Crusaders after a two-year siege. During the next 100 years the city becomes the de facto capital of the kingdom of Jerusalem.

September/Shawwal. Saladin defeated in Arsuf.

1192/588

August/Shawwal. Richard Lionheart defeats Saladin in Jaffa; falters in Jerusalem and returns to the West.

September/Shawwal. Three-year truce between Saladin and the Franks.

1193/589

Death of Saladin. Egypt and Syria (Bilad al-Sham) divided among his successors.

1197/593

Beirut retaken by Crusaders. John I of Ibillin becomes lord of Beirut.

1200–1218/596–615: Reign of al-Malik al-'Adil

Restores unity to the Ayyubid empire. His sons rule various cities and countries: al-Malik al-Kamil in Cairo, al-Malik al-Ashraf in the Jazira, and al-Malik al-Mu'azzam in Syria.

1200/597

Bohemond IV brings Antioch and Tripoli together.

1201–1202/598–599

The plague causes sharp decrease of population in Egypt.

1208/604

Commercial treaty between the Ayyubids of Aleppo and Venice.

1210/606–607

al-'Adil has a fortress built on Mount Thabor that dominates the Acre plain; impetus for the Fifth Crusade.

1217/614

Defeat of the Fifth Crusade at Mount Thabor.

1218/615

Death of the Ayyubid al-Malik al-'Adil; al-Malik al-Kamil (1218–1238/615–635) becomes sultan of Egypt. The Fifth Crusade lands in Damietta.

1219/616

November 5/5 Shawwal. The Crusaders take Damietta, soon reconquered by al-Kamil (1221); eight-year truce signed.

1228/625

Sixth Crusade. Frederick II in Syria; negotiations with al-Kamil.

1229/626

Peace treaty ("Treaty of Jaffa") between Frederick II, leader of the Sixth Crusade, and the Ayyubid al-Malik al-Kamil. Frederick enters Jerusalem; re-establishment of the Frankish kingdom of Jerusalem.

1232/629

al-Kamil eliminates the rulers of Amid (Diyarbakir) and Hisn Kayfa.

1238/635

Al-Kamil takes Damascus. Death of al-Malik al-Kamil results in fragmentation of the Ayyubid empire, due to struggles among the different parts of the empire.

1239/636

Defeat of the Sixth Crusade in Gaza. Attempt to renew the treaty of 1229 fails; al-Salih Ayyub, al-Kamil's son, wins the struggle of succession, and with the help of the military becomes sultan of Egypt (1240–1249).

1240/637

Isma'il, al-Salih's uncle and sultan of Damascus, surrenders Galilee to the Crusaders. Al-Salih cedes Jaffa, Ascalon, and Tiberias to Richard, Earl of Cornwall. Al-Salih retakes Galilee and Ascalon (1247), becomes ruler of Damascus, establishes his suzerainty over Hims, and challenges al-Nasir Yusuf, his cousin in Aleppo.

1242–1258: Reign of al-Musta'sim, last 'Abbasid Caliph of Baghdad
1244/642

Jerusalem taken by Khwarizmi Turkish troops, whom al-Salih had enlisted after their defeat by the Mongols; worst defeat for the Crusaders since the Battle of Hattin.

1245/643

Capitulation of Damascus.

1247/645

Al-Salih takes Tiberias and Ascalon.

1249/647

The Seventh Crusade, led by Louis IX (Saint Louis) lands in Damietta and takes the town.

1250/648

Battle of al-Mansura. Louis IX capitulates; the Crusaders are weakened by hunger and sickness. Louis IX has to buy his freedom for 800,000 dinar. The Mamluks control Egypt. The Ayyubid of Aleppo, al-Malik al-Nasir, takes Damascus from Egypt. In Cairo, power passes into the hands of the Mamluks (Aybak and Baybars). Death of al-Salih; his son and successor Turanshah is assassinated by Turkish soldiers; al-Salih's widow Shajar al-Durr is the formal ruler (*malikah al-Muslimin* = queen of the Muslims) for a short time.

1250–1254/648–652

Louis IX held captive in Syria.

1252/650

Aybak deposes the 6-year-old sultan Ashraf Musa and proclaims himself sultan.

Religion and Society

1058/449

Shi'i revolt in Iraq.

1067/459

The Nizamiya *madrasa* founded in Baghdad by the Seljuq vizier Nizam al-Mulk.

1173/569

Saladin founds a *khanaqah* (institution of higher learning attached to a mosque) in Cairo.

1213/610

Appearance of the Qalandar order (wandering dervishes who lived on alms) in Damascus.

1234/631

Inauguration in Baghdad of the Mustansiriyya *madrasa,* in which the four Sunni "schools" or *madhhab* (Shafi'i, Hanafi, Hanbali, Maliki) are taught on equal footing.

Art, Architecture

11th century/5th century

Cairo under the vizier Badr al-Jamali; second wall with three gates, Bab Zuwayla, Bab al-Nasr and Bab al-Futuh, built; on the Muqattam, which overlooks Cairo, the al-Juyushi mosque is built.

1076/468

Beginning of the reconstruction of the citadel of Damascus.

1176/572

Saladin undertakes the reconstruction of the Great Citadel of Cairo.

1183/579

Qaraqush builds the Citadel of Cairo on the Muqattam.

1209/606

Al-Malik al-Zahir refurbishes the citadel of Aleppo.

1243/641

Inauguration in Cairo of the Salihiyya *madrasa.*

Civilization and Culture

1058/449

Death of the blind poet Abu al-Ala'al-Ma'arri, author of the *Risalat al-ghufran,* "The Letter of Pardon" (1033/424), the action of which takes place in Heaven and Hell.

May/Rabi I. Death of Al-Mawardi, Shafi'i *qadi* in Basra and Baghdad, author of *Kitab al-Ahkam al-Sultaniyya,* ("The Ordinances of Government") on governmental institutions and legal theory of Sunni Islam.

1122/516

Death of al-Hariri, author of the celebrated "Sessions" (*Maqamat*) in Arabic rhymed prose.

1165/560

March/Jumada I. Death of the vizier of the 'Abbasids Ibn Hubayra al-Baghdadi (born December 1105/Rajab 499), author of a "general survey" of Sunnism and its doctrinal divergences.

Circa 1170/565

Growth of a medical school and hospital (Bimaristan) in Damascus, founded by Nur al-Din.

1188/584

Death of Usama b. Mundiqh, Syrian prince and man of letters (born in 1095/488), author of *Kitab al-I'tibar,* a book of memories that describes relations between Franks and Muslims.

1201/597

Death of 'Imad al-Din al-Isfahani, historian (born in 1125/519), author of *al-Fath al-qussi fi al-fath al-qudsi,* on the conquest of Jerusalem.

Fiscal Resources

Islamic law permits some fundamental taxes that constitute the basis for a fiscal system; in addition there are taxes and rights that are not mentioned in Islamic law (for example, tariffs on merchandise). Among the canonical taxes:

a) the *jizya*, a tax levied on the *dhimmis*, non-Muslim adherents to the monotheistic Abrahamic religions, especially Christians and Jews, also called *ahl al-kitab* (People of the Book), and collected after the end of the lunar year. The *dhimmis* received a receipt, *bara'a* which allowed them to travel during the year without being harassed by collectors from other regions.

b) the *zakat*, or legal almsgiving, one of the five obligations of Islam, a tax of solidarity to which free Muslims are subject. Non-Muslims pay it in certain cases. The *zakat* applies to land and personal property; it is levied based on wealth—livestock and agricultural production. In practice, the *zakat* on agricultural products became a tithe (*'ushr*); collection times were based on the solar calendar. For animals, the rate varied according to species: camels, cattle, goats or sheep. There was also a *zakat al-fitr*, which one paid on the occasion of the breaking of the fast by giving out food, lodging and clothing to the needy.

c) the *kharaj*, the fundamental tax of the treasury of a Muslim state. It implies a service of surveying and registering landowners and their parcels, noting the boundaries, the type of soil and the local flora. It is the major and most regular resource of the administration since it is attached to the property tax. It is an ancient tariff and has two incarnations: Egyptian-Nilotic, based on the Nile floods, and Syrian-Iraqi, based on irrigation.

1215/611

Death of al-Harawi al-Mawsili, Syrian, teacher at the Shati'i *madrasa* in Aleppo and author of a *Kitab al-Ziyarat*.

1216/613

The geographer Yaqut (a freed slave of Greek origin) (1179–1229/575–626) reunites the material of his principal works: *Mu'djam al-Buldan* (geographical dictionary which describes all real and literary locations in the Islamic world), *Kitab al-Muqtadad fi al-Ansab* (on genealogy) and *Mu'jam al-Udaba'* (encyclopedia of biographies of Muslim philologists and writers).

1233/630

Death of Ibn al-Athir, historian (born in 1160/555), author of *al-Kamil*, a historical annal covering the beginning of the world until 1228/625.

1235/632

Death of the Egyptian Ibn al-Farid (born in 1181/576), the most significant Sufi poet who wrote in Arabic, author of a *Diwan* composed, most notably, of the *Khamriyya* ("ode to wine" describing divine love) and the *Nazm al-Suluk* (poem of progress).

1240/648

Death of Ibn 'Arabi, native of Spain (born in 1665/560), one of the greatest Sufis of Islam. He makes clear his Sufi doctrine in *al-Futahat al-Makkiyyah*.

1248/646

Death of Ibn al-Baytar, native of Malaga; named chief of the botanists by al-Malik al-Kamil. Author of *Mughni fi al Adwiyya* and of the *Jami' fi Mufradat al-Adwiyya*.

The Seljuqs of Rum

After having established their domination over Iran and Iraq, the Seljuq Turks pursued the advance toward the Caucasus and Asia Minor. In the latter region, their defeat of the Byzantine emperor Romanos Diogenes, in 1071, near the Lake of Van, allows for the penetration into Byzantine territory of a branch of the Seljuqs, and also other Turkish tribes. The Anatolian central plateau little by little becomes their domain, and the dynasty of the Seljuqs of Rum (Asia Minor) imposes itself by the end of the 12th century. During the first half of the 13th century, the dynasty dominates this region politically, economically and intellectually; the region's political center, Konya, is very prosperous. There as well, the Mongol invasion in the middle of the 13th century brings the fall and disappearance of this sultanate by the end of the 13th century.

Wars and Foreign Relations

1071/463

August 26/Dhu'l-Qa'da. Victory of the Seljuq sultan Alp Arslan over the Byzantine emperor Romanos Diogenes in Mantzikert (Malazgird), near the Lake of Van. Asia Minor opens up to Turkish tribes.

1074/466

Sulayman b. Qutlumush, leader of the Seljuqs of Rum (Asia Minor), brings his court to the Byzantine Emperor Michael VII.

1077/470

Iconium (Konya) taken.

1078/471

The Seljuqs on the shores of the Marmara Sea and in Nicaea (Iznik).

1086/479

June 5/18 Safar. Death of Sulayman Shah near Aleppo. His son Qïlïsh Arslan I is taken prisoner.

1092/485

Qïlïsh Arslan I takes power in Nicaea.

1095/488

Alexius, the Emperor of Byzantium, asks the Pope for help against the Seljuqs.

71

1097/490

June–August/Rajab–Ramadan. Nicaea taken, then Konya, by the First Crusaders.

1098/491

June/Jumada II. Antioch taken by Crusaders. Bohemond of Tarentum becomes its prince.

1101/494

August–September/Shawwal–Dhu'l-Qa'da. Reinforcements of the Crusaders defeated in Asia Minor by the allied forces of the Seljuqs and the Danishmendids of Northern Anatolia.

1107/500

Qïlïsh Arslan I dies in Upper Mesopotamia in a battle with the Seljuqs of Iraq.

1119–1120/513–514

Reconquest of several towns in Asia Minor by the Byzantine emperor, John II Comnenos.

1119/514

John II Comnenos retakes Trapezond.

1144/539

December 27/28 Jumada II. Edessa (Urfa) taken from the Crusaders by Imad al-Din Zangi (Zanki), which prompts the Second Crusade.

1147–1148/542

October–January/Jumada I–Shawwal. Series of defeats inflicted by Mas'ud I on the armies of the German Emperor Conrad III (at Dorylaeum) and the King of France Louis VII (at Laodicaea).

1162/557

Peace treaty between Qïlïsh Arslan II and Manuel I Comnenos.

1175/571

War declared by the Byzantine emperor against the sultan.

1176/572

September/Rabi I. Byzantine army under Manuel I Comnenos crushed by Qïlïsh Arslan in Myriocephalon.

1190/586

April–May/Rabi I and Rabi II. Frederick Barbarossa, emperor of Germany, invades the sultanate and takes Konya. He drowns in the Calycadnos (Gök Su) in Cilicia (June).

1204/600

The Crusaders conquer Constantinople; division of the Empire into feudal Crusader states; Nicaea, Trapezond (Trebizond), and Greek empires.

1207/603

March/Shawwal. Port of Antalya taken. Trade advantages granted to the Venetians.

1214/611

November 3/27 Jumada II. Sinope taken from the emperor of Trapezond.

1216/613

The fortresses of the Cilician passes are taken from the Armenians.

1221/618

Kalonoros taken (renamed 'Ala'iya/ Alanya); conquest of eastern Pamphylia.

1225/622

Attack on the Crimea. Sudaq becomes a Seljuq protectorate until 1239/637.

1226-1231/623-638
Annexation of Erzinjan, Erzerum and Ahlat. First Mongol raids into eastern Asia Minor.

1239/636-637
Occupation of Georgia, Kars and Ani, all taken by the Mongols.

1240/637
Diyarbakir taken by the Seljuqs. Kiev taken by the Mongols.

1241/638
Mongol army defeats an army of Poles and Teutonic knights at Liegnitz (Silesia); devastates Hungary. Recalled home because of the death of Ögödey, the Great Khan.

1243/641
June 26/6 Muharram. The Seljuq army crushed by the Mongols in Köse Dagh.

1256/654
October 15/23 Ramadan. Second Mongol victory at Aksaray.

1277/675
April 16/10 Dhu'l-Qa'da. Invasion of Asia Minor by the Mamluk Baybars: the Mongol-Seljuq army conquered at Elbistan, captures Caesarea (Cappadocia).

Internal Events

1078/471
Seljuq sultanate founded.

1095/488
First mention of the Danishmendid tribe, rivals of the Seljuqs, established in the Sivas-Kayseri-Ankara region.

1100/493
August/Shawwal. Siege on Malatya by the Danishmendids. Bohemond of Antioch taken prisoner.

1104/497
August/Dhu'l-Qa'da Death of Qïlïsh Arslan I, Sulayman Shah's son.

1107/500
Qïlïsh Arslan I dies in a battle with the Seljuqs of Iraq.

1116/510
Shahanshah stripped of his power by his brother Mas'ud I.

1143/538
December 6/26 Jumada I. Death of the Danishmendid Muhammad and dissolution of his emirate; Ankara and other towns taken by the Seljuq Sultan Mas'ud.

1152/547
Death of Sultan Mas'ud.

1185-1187/581-583
Unrest in Anatolia due to Turcoman groups.

1186-1187/582-583
Qïlïsh Arslan II divides his territory among his sons, brother and nephew; he keeps Konya; recognized as sultan.

1192-1194/588-590
War between several sons of Qïlïsh Arslan II.

1194-1204/590-600
Rukn al-Din Sulayman Shah II usurps (and re-establishes the unity of) the sultanate.

1220–1237/617–634: Reign of 'Ala al-Din Kay Kubad I

Zenith of the Seljuq sultanate.

1240–1242/638–640

Turkoman popular uprising led by the populist preacher, Baba Ishaq, with aid of Iranian and Turkish urban refugees from the East; suppression of uprising with the help of Frankish mercenaries.

1245–1249/643–646

Vizier Shams al-Din Isfahani in power.

1249–1254/647–652

After death of Shams al-Din Isfahani, the *atabeg* Jalal al-Din Karatay maintains unity of the sultanate.

1257/655

Rukn al-Din Qïlïsh Arslan IV proclaimed sultan. Pre-eminent role of the vizier Mu'in al-Din Pervane. At the end of year, the Mongols force the division of the sultanate: the west (Konya) to 'Izz al-Din Kay Ka'us II; the east (Sivas-Kayseri) to Qïlïsh Arslan IV.

1261/659

Kay Ka'us II flees to Constantinople. Qïlïsh Arslan IV now sole sultan.

1262/660

Turkoman revolts in Asia Minor, crushed by Mu'in al-Din.

1277/676

August 21/1st Rabi I. Execution of Mu'in al-Din Pervane. Direct administration by the Mongols.

1277–1297/676–696

Revolt by the Turkomans. Decline of the sultanate.

1286–1298/685–697 and 1303–1310/702–710: Reigns of Mas'ud II, the last Seljuq sultan

Power exercised de facto by the Mongols.

The Economy and Society

End of 11th century–12th century/end of 5th–6th century

The Anatolian plateau domain of the Turkoman tribes. In the towns, Greeks, Armenians (the original population), Turks (soldiers, civil servants), Iranians (civil servants, artisans, merchants, religious dignitaries).

Circa 1130/524

First minting of Danishmendid money, in copper.

Circa 1140/534

First minting of Seljuq money, in copper.

12th century/6th century

Establishment of the *iqta'* system, which granted revenue from lands to soldiers or civil servants in return for services. This system relieves the treasury from having to pay the soldiers, but at the same time it reduces the empire's tax revenues. The *iqta'* system is adapted by the Ayyubids, the Mamluks and the Ottomans.

Middle of 12th century/6th century

Mention of the term *uj* (border soldier), comparable to the Byzantine *akritai* or the Arab *ghazi*.

1175/570

First Seljuq money made of silver.

2nd half of 12th century/6th century

First caravanserais in Asia Minor.

After 1210/607

First mention of the *akhi* guilds, the successors of the *futuwwa* associations in a Turkish town (Antalya).

Beginning of 13th century/7th century

Sivas, important commercial center.

1216/613

Trade agreement between Seljuqs and Cyprus.

1220/617

Trade opportunities granted to Venetians in Antalya.

1233/630

First Seljuq money made of gold.

Before 1243/640

More than 30 inns for caravans (*khan*) built in Anatolia. Principal routes: Antalya-Konya-Kayseri-Sivas-Tokat-Black Sea, Trapezond-Erzerum-Iran, Konya-Aleppo.

Middle of 13th century/7th century

Turkoman tribes established on the perimeter of the sultanate. Arrival of Haji Bektash, possibly related to the Baba'is (followers of Baba Ishaq, the leader of the popular revolts in 1240). The Bektashi order developed mythical and epic literature in Turkish.

After 1260/658

The Mongols apply increased fiscal pressure on the Seljuqs (tributes, taxes).

2nd half of 13th century/7th century

Progression of the *akhi* in the social and political life of towns. Baba'i movement in Turkoman popular circles.

1300/700

Permanent representation of the Genoans in Sivas.

Civilization and Culture

End of 12th century/6th century

Sharaf al-Din al-Tiflisai, author of works on medicine, astrology and literature.

Beginning of 13th century/7th century

Arrival in Anatolia of Baha al-Din Veled, father of Jalal al-Din Rumi. Rumi founds the "Order of the Transcendental Dervishes," and writes some of the most important pieces of world literature in Persian. His masterpiece, the *Mathnavi*, contains more than 47,000 verses, and emphasizes the search for the love of God.

1215/612

The mystic Ibn 'Arabi in Anatolia.

1241-1242/639

Munyat al-mufti, legal treatise by Yusuf b. Sa'id al-Sijistani.

1244/642

Arrival in Konya of the Persian mystic Shams al-Din Tabrizi.

Circa 1245/643

Jalal al-Din Rumi under the sway of Shams al-Din Tabrizi.

1264/622

Tshelebi Husam al-Din Hasan, *akhi* of Konya, first leader of the disciples of Mevlana Jalal al-Din Rumi.

1273/672

December 17/5 Jumada II. Death of Mevlana Jalal al-Din Rumi.

1274-1275/673

Death in Konya of Sadr al-Din Qonewi, who inspired many mystics.

1280/679

Completion of the *Chronicle of the Seljuqs* by Ibn Bibi.

1284/683

Sultan Veled, son of Jalal al-Din Rumi, founder of the order of Mevlani dervishes.

Circa 1294/693

The *Seljuqname* written anonymously.

End of 13th century–beginning of 14th century/7th century

Yunus Emre, the most important popular mystical poet of the beginnings of Turkish literature.

1323/723

Completion of the *Historical Chronicle of Aksarayi*.

Turkia — Land of the Turks

Having penetrated into Byzantine Asia Minor following the victory of Alp Arslan at Mantzikert in 1071, the Seljuqs, followed by other Turkish tribes (Danishmendids, Saltuqids, Mengujekids, Artuqids), benefit from the ongoing power struggle in Byzantium. Little by little, they establish their authority over the central Anatolian plateau, where their presence inspires a chronicler of the Third Crusade to give this region the name "Turkia." They eliminate their Turkish and Turkoman rivals, make Konya their capital and, at the beginning of the 13th century, enter into a period of prosperity and prestige. But the arrival of the Mongols, which led to severe military defeats, had as its consequence the destabilization, followed by the division and finally the disappearance of the Seljuq sultanate. Nonetheless, it did establish the starting point of the Turkish occupation of a region that they would not relinquish and that becomes the base for all their future activities.

Art, Architecture

1140/535

Great Mosque of Danishmend in Kayseri.

1146/541

Tomb (*türbe*) of Halife Gazi in Amasya.

1179/575

Great Mosque (Ulu Jami') of Erzerum.

1180/576

Great Mosque of Sivas.

1201/576

Caravanserai (*khan*) of Altinapa (on the Konya-Beyshehir route).

1205/601

Shifa'iye hospital in Kayseri.

1217/614

Hospital in Sivas.

1220/617

Mosque of 'Ala al-Din in Konya.

1227–1237/624–634

The Kubadabad palace in Beyshehir.

1229/626

"Sultan Han" caravanserais (on the Konya-Aksaray and Kayseri-Sivas routes).

1236–1246/633–644

Susuz Han caravanserai in Burdur.

1238/635

Tomb of Huvand Hatun in Kayseri.

Circa 1241/638

Kubadiye palace in Kayseri.

1243/640

Sirtshali *madrasa* in Konya.

1251/649

Karatay's *madrasa* in Konya.

1253/651

Çifte *madrasa* — minaret and tomb of Hundi Hatun, in Erzerum.

1254/652

Inje Minareli *madrasa* in Konya.

1271/669

Gök *madrasa* in Sivas.

1272/670

Great Mosque of Afyon Karahisar.

1276/674

Döner Kümbet in Kayseri.

Turks and Mongols in the Middle East

The Samanid state, to ensure its control over eastern Iran and central Asia, recruited troops from Turkish tribes who converted to Islam. The chieftains of these tribes assumed an increasingly important role in the army and eventually in the administration of the state. One among them, Alptigin, became governor of Khurasan. In 961/350, he rebelled, gaining independence, and established himself in Ghazna, southwest of Kabul. Nevertheless, his chosen successors were forced to recognize Samanid suzerainty until Sebüktigin, in 977/367, imposed his authority over the last of the Samanids and founded the Ghaznavid dynasty prior to engaging himself in incursions into India.

His son Mahmud (997–1030/387–421), the most famous of the dynasty's sovereigns, continued the expansion in India, conquering the Punjab and Kashmir. He made his court in Ghazna a center of culture and art where the poet Firdawsi and the encyclopedist al-Biruni lived. However, the dynasty was supplanted by another Turkish tribe, the Seljuqs.

In concert with the Qarakhanids, the Ghaznavids created one of the first Turko-Muslim dynasties. For a time, it was supported by a fundamentally Turkish element while governed by an administration that remained principally Arab and Iranian. As a confirmed Sunni, Mahmud recognized the sovereignty of the ʿAbbasid caliph and engaged in vigorous action against the neighboring Shiʿis. Most important, he initiated the Islamization of a region of India that has been a part of the Islamic world ever since.

Politics

962–1186/351–582: Ghaznavid Dynasty
977–997/366–386
Sebüktigin, Alptigin's slave general, founds the Ghaznavid dynasty in Khurasan, Afghanistan and north India.

1039/430 or 1040/431
The Ghaznavid Masʿud, crushed by the Seljuqs at Dandanaqan, loses Khurasan and West Persia; the Ghaznavids survive in Ghazna (Sistan) and northwest India.

1064/456
Seljuqs destroy Ani and take Kars.

1st half of 12th century/6th century
Founding of Firuzkuh (Jam) first capital of the Ghurids, a mountain people of eastern Iran.

1118/512
The Ghaznavid Arslan overthrown by the Seljuq sultan, Sanjar. The Ghaznavids become tributaries of the Seljuqs.

1118–1159/512–544: Reign of the Seljuq Sultan Sanjar
1120–1150/514–554
The Qara Khitay, who had been expelled from northern China, rulers of the two Turkestans. Their loose administration does not alter the social conditions significantly.

1124/518
Death of Hasan-i Sabbah, leader of the Assassins (see box on page 62).

1124–1138/518–532
Kiya Buzurg Ummid, Hasan-i Sabbah's lieutenant, becomes second daʾi (missionary) of the Nizari Ismaʿilis in Alamut; resists Muhammad Tapar's troops. Hasan-i Sabbah chose him as his successor.

1125/519
The Qara Khitay begin their migration, penetrate into Turkestan and

fight the Turkish Qarakhanids, settled in Kashghari at that time.

1128/522

The Qara Khitay attempt an invasion of Transoxiana.

1141/536

Qatwan plain — defeat of the organized army of Muslims under Sanjar, beaten by nomadic tribes of the Qara Khitay. The Qara Khitay in Samarkand and Bukhara.

1148/543

The Khwarizmi Atsiz b. Anushtigin achieves independence from the Seljuqs.

June/Muharram. Atsiz surrenders to Sanjar; he remains faithful to Sanjar after his capture by the Oghuz. He dies July 30 1156/9 Jumada 551. He built the foundations for a great state that would last until the Mongol invasion.

1148–1215/543–612

Ghurid dynasty in Afghanistan.

1151/546

The Ghurids under 'Ala' al-Din Husayn pillage Ghazna; this limits the power of the Ghaznavids to the Punjab.

1153/548

Sanjar, the Seljuq sultan from Persia, vanquished and taken prisoner by the Uyghurs, who pillage Khurasan.

1167/562

Birth of Temujin, the future Genghis Khan.

1172–1200/567–596: Reign of 'Ala' al-Din Tekish in Khwarizm
1172/568

Sultan Shah, chased from Khwarizm by his brother, 'Ala' al-Din Tekish, delineates his own principality in Khurasan with the help of the Qara Khitay.

1173/569

Khusraw Malik, the last Ghaznavid, leaves Ghazna for Lahore.

1186/582

Mu'izz al-Din Muhammad b. Sam (Muhammad Ghuri) dispossesses the Ghaznavids of the Punjab and Lahore.

1188/584

Temujin unifies his empire.

1190/586

Sultan Shah taken prisoner near Marw by Mu'izz al-Din of Ghazna. His territories fall into Ghurid hands.

1192/588

Delhi and Ajmer become part of the sultan of Ghazna's territories.

1193/589

Conquest of Khurasan by the Khwarizmi 'Ala' al-Din. Ikhtiyar al-Din Muhammad Bakhtiyar Khalji attacks the Bihar province, in India.

1194/590

'Ala' al-Din chases the Seljuqs out of Persia.

1198/595

Conquest of Kanawj by the Ghurid sultan Shilab al-Din Muhammad b.

Sam. War between the Ghurids, who are supported by the caliph and the Qara Khitay. Baha' al-Din Sam, the Ghurid from Bamiyan, occupies Balkh.

1198–1200/594–596
Temujin takes control of the Nayman, a group of Mongol nomads pushed to the west by the Qara Khitay.

End of the 12th–beginning of the 13th century/5th–7th century
A flood of Turks from Khwarizm into Iranian states.

1202/598
Temujin exterminates the Tatars and, the following year, assumes control over the Karaites.

1203–1204/600–601
Muhammad Bakhtiyar Khalji, native of Ghur, takes Nadya, capital of the kingdom of Sena in Bengal. He falters in Bhutan and in Tibet.

1206/602
Death of Muhammad Bakhtiyar Khalji. Temujin assumes the title of Genghis Khan and has himself recognized as "universal emperor" by the Turks and Mongols.

1208/604
Genghis Khan completes his subjugation of Turkestan. Muhammad of Khwarizm takes Transoxiana from the Qara Khitay.

1209–1214/606–611
Muhammad of Khwarizm takes Afghanistan from the Ghurids.

1211/608
Accession of the Turk Shams al-Din Iltutmish, founder of the independent sultanate of Delhi. The Naymans destroy the empire of the Qara Khitay.

1218/615
The Mongols invade Turkestan. The Khwarizm shah 'Ala' al-Din Muhammad kills Genghis Khan's envoys in Otrar on the Jaxartes River. The Mongols retaliate; beginning of the Mongol invasion of the Middle East.

1219/616
Genghis Khan's first raid on Islamic states. He defeats the Khwarizm shah.

1220/617
The Mongols take Balkh and Nishapur, invade Persia and launch a raid across the Caucasus.

1221–1222/618
The Mongols take Kabul.

1221/618
Death of the Khwarizm shah 'Ala' al-Din b. Muhammad.

1223/620
Khwarizm shah Jalal al-Din b. Muhammad (reigns from 1220–1231/617–628) retakes Persia from the Mongols.

1227/624
Death of Genghis Khan; empire divided among his four sons: Jötshi, Jaghatay, Ögödey and Tuluy.

1230/627
August/Ramadan. Vanquished in Erzinjan, the Khwarizm shah Jalal al-

Din Manguberti is repulsed by the Seljuqs of Rum and pulls back to Azerbaijan.

1231/628

August/Shawwal. Attack on Jalal al-Din's camp in Ahlat at night; he is assassinated while attempting to flee. End of the Khwarizm shah dynasty.

1235–1239/632–637

Mongols complete the conquest of Iran.

1251–1257/649–655

Hülegü, a grandson of Genghis Khan, leads an offensive against western Asia.

1256–1259/654–657

Hülegü conquers Iran, Iraq and Transoxania. Destroys Alamut, the fortress of the Assassins (1256). In Iran: Mongol dynasty of the Ilkhans.

Religion and Society

1127/521

The theologian Shahrastani writes the *Kitab al-Milal wa al-Nihal*, treatise on religion and sects.

1166/561

Death of the Sufi preacher 'Abd al-Qadir al-Jilani in Baghdad, founder and most famous leader of the order of the Qadiris (named after him) in Iraq, Turkey, India, central Asia and China. He reconciled Hanbali legal thought with the ecstatic individualism of the mystics. Death of Ahmad Yesevi, mystic from Turkestan, one of the first popular Turkish poets, influenced by Iranian mysticism.

1191/587

Death of Yahya al-Suhrawardi, Sufi mystic and proponent of a philosophy of illumination. Saladin accuses him of heresy and has him executed.

1209/606

Death of Fakhr al-Din al-Razi, historian and theologian in Herat, who continued the orthodox view of Islam in *Kitab al-muhassal*.

1230/627

Death of Farid al-Din 'Attar, Persian mystical poet, pharmacologist and doctor; author of the *Tadhkirat al-Awliya* ("Recollections of the Saints"), a collection of anecdotes and biographies about well-known Sufis, and of *Mantiq al-Ta'ir* ("The Language of the Birds").

Civilization and Culture

1045/436

Nasir-i Khusraw on a pilgrimage to Mecca.

1066/458

Literary activity on the part of the Persian philosopher 'Ali b. Ahmad Asadi, author of the oldest epic complementary to the *Shahname* by Firdawsi.

1111/505

Death of Ghazali.

1126/520

Death of 'Umar al-Khayyam, Khurasani poet and sage from Nishapur. In science, a discipline of Ibn Sina (Avicenna); reform of the Persian calendar (*jalali,* named after the Seljuq sultan Jalal al-Dawla Malik Shah), which (although it was not used) is more accurate than the Gregorian calendar; work on geometry and algebra. Among his best-known works, the *Nawruz-name,* known as "Quatrains of 'Umar Khayyam." His poetry became famous in the west due to the English translation by Edward Fitzgerald in the 19th century.

1144/538

Death of al-Zamakhshari, Persian philosopher, Mu'tazili Qur'an commentator and philologist born in Khwarizm (1075/467). Author of *Mufassal,* a book on grammar. Major work: the commentary on the Qur'an *al-kashshaf 'an haqa'iq al-tanzil* ("The Unveiler of the Truths of Revelation").

1182/578

Death of Rashid al-Din Watwat, native poet of Balkh. His *Diwan* contains 7,000 verses.

1190/586

Death of al-Anwari, astrologist and poet of Sanjar's court, born in Khurasan. Caustic satirist.

1199/595

Death of Khaqani, Persian poet, author of the *Tufhat al-'Iraqayn* and a *diwan.*

1203/599

Death of Nizami, Persian poet and mystic (born in 1140/535 in Ganja), author of the *Khamsa,* a collection of five epic poems that includes a rendition of the Arabic love story, "Layla and Majnun," and the "Seven Princesses."

Art and Architecture

End of 10th century/4th century

Architectural work of Lashkar-i Bazar, started by Sebüktigin.

After 1018/409

In Ghazna, Great Mosque with a *madrasa* and a library (Mahmud).

1088/481

Great Mosque of Isfahan, during the reign of Malik Shah.

1099–1115/492–509

Minarets of Ghazna built (Mahmud III).

End of 12th century/6th century

Ghurid minaret of Jam, in Afghanistan built.

End of 12th–beginning of 13th century/6th–7th century

Zenith of Persian pottery.

Sub-Saharan Africa

Between 800 and 1000, Arab authors begin to mention the lands of black sub-Saharan Africa. Starting in 1000, their knowledge of the *Bilad al-Sudan* (the land of the blacks) becomes more substantial.

On the Atlantic coast, the Almoravid movement, which originated in [Mauritania]* among the Sanhaja Berbers, constitutes the beginning of Sunni Islam in West Africa. The first Muslim black African states develop in the Saharan region, in contact with the expanding Muslim world. The expanding mercantile relations between the Muslims and sub-Saharan Africa especially facilitated the gradual spread of Islam, which merged with pre-existing religions. Around 1000, the first conversions of African chiefs occur. The Khariji influence, which had crossed the Sahara during the 9th and 10th centuries, dims and eventually disappears.

The end of the period is marked by the rise of the empires of Mali and Kanem and their contact with Islam through caravan trade and raids, by the Arab push up the Nile valley, and by the emergence of the first large Muslim city on the eastern coast of Africa: Kilwa.

*In brackets are the *present* names of countries that had different names prior to 1960.

The First Conversions

Before 990/380
The Egyptian geographer al-Muhallabi notes that the king of Kawkaw [Gao, Mali] is Muslim.

1108-1009/399
Za Kosoi, the first king of Gao, converts to Islam, according to an Arab-African source from the 17th century.

1040-1041/432
Death of War Dyabi b. Rabis, first Muslim king of Takrur, town in central Senegal.

Circa 1075-1086/467-478: Reign of Hummay
First sovereign of Kanem [Chad], converts to Islam. Founder of the thousand-year dynasty of the Saifawa.

The Almoravid Movement

1038-1039/430
The Sanhaja Berber chief, Yahya b. Ibrahim, returns from a pilgrimage to Mecca to [Mauritania] accompanied by the Sunni missionary 'Abd Allah b. Yasin, native of southern Morocco. Ibn Yasin will become a theoretician of the Almoravid movement.

1042-1043/434
After Yahya's retreat to an unknown location (Atlantic coast or Senegal), because of criticism of his proselytizing among certain Berber tribes, he forms a coalition of tribes that are called the Almoravids (*al-murabitun*). They launch a *jihad* against rival tribes.

1054-1055/446
Capture by the Almoravids of Awdaghust, storage town for trans-Saharan trade (southwest of [Mauritania]).

1058-1059/450 or 1059-1060/451

Death of Ibn Yasin.

1061-1062/453 or 1064-1065/457

Abu Bakr b. 'Umar, leader of the Almoravid movement, hands power over to his cousin Yusuf b. Tashfin and goes to the desert of [Mauritania] to quell a tribal uprising. Yusuf prevents Abu Bakr from returning; Abu Bakr remains in the Sahara where he fights his enemies until he dies.

1076-1077/459 or, more likely, 1102-1103/496

The kingdom of Ghana, the center of the gold trade, is converted to Islam. The most recent historical research disputes the claim that the capital of Ghana had been conquered by the Almoravids.

1087/980

Death of Abu Bakr b. 'Umar (in combat with the Sudan, according to one source).

Beginning of 12th century/beginning of 6th century

Timbuktu founded, at first a simple camp.

1100-1264/494-663

Funerary steles from Gao-Sane [Mali] with epitaphs containing names and dates point to the Islamization of a ruling family in Gao or the surrounding area.

The Growth of New States

1st half of 13th century/7th century

Islamized Ghana conquered by the animist Soso, a southern people. Later, the founder of the empire of Mali, Sunjata Keïta, conquers the Soso and lays the foundations for the state's hegemony.

1210-1248/607-646

Muhammad b. Jil, known in the tradition under his African name, Dunama Dibale (from his mother's name, Dibale), spreads the word about Kanem [Chad] in the Arab world. Zenith of Kanem during the reign of this Islamicizing ruler.

Circa 1242/640

Muhammad b. Jil constructs an inn for the pilgrims of Kanem in Cairo.

1257/655

Kade, son of and successor to Dunama, sends a delegation to the Hafsid ruler of Tunis: among the gifts, a giraffe.

Eastern Coast of Africa

Circa 957/346

According to histories written much later, Kilwa was founded by Shirazi colonists from the Persian Gulf. The same origin is attributed to most of the Muslim trading posts on the eastern coast of Africa and the Comoro islands.

Ghana in the 11th Century

"The town of Ghana is made up of two towns, situated on a plain. One of the two is inhabited by Muslims: there are 12 mosques, one of which serves as a public gathering site (Fridays). They all have their *imam*, their *muezzin*, their readers (of the Qur'an). The town also has lawyers and learned men. . . . The king's town is six miles from this one. . . . The buildings are made of stone and acacia wood. The king has a palace and huts with rounded roofs. These structures are surrounded by a wall. In the king's town, there is one mosque for the Muslims in town on business, not far from the royal audience hall."

Al-Bakri, Andalusian author, 1068/460.

Circa 1120/514

Kilwa supplants Mogadishu and monopolizes the gold market in Sofala. It becomes, during three centuries, the capital of a Muslim merchant state: transit site for gold, ivory and slaves. The Swahili civilization develops in this environment.

End of the 12th century/end of the 6th century

First money minted by the sultan of Kilwa.

Disintegration in the West, Regrouping in the East

The history of Islam is, of course, not linear, but varies from one period to another, one region to another: the period of the 13th to the 15th centuries exemplifies these varying historical tides. In Spain, Muslim political power is progressively reduced by the Reconquista; however, the latter movement will declare victory only two centuries later with the capture of Grenada from the Nasrids in 1492. In North Africa, these centuries see three competing dynasties that, despite a period of cultural brilliance, never manage to control the forces which tear them apart, nor can they avoid the penetration into the coastal perimeter of the Portuguese and the Spaniards. Meanwhile, in the Near East, the Mamluk sultanate is established. It will dominate Egypt and Syria and become the vital political center of the Muslim world, despite the many changes in the leadership of the state. It also becomes the dominant force economically (the Mamluks control the maritime passage from the Indian Ocean to the Mediterranean), and religiously (the al-Azhar University of Cairo is the most significant school of Islamic theology).

To the north, small Turkoman emirates succeeded the Seljuqs of Rum. One among them, during the second half of the 14th century, begins to control the others: Osman, the founder of the Ottoman dynasty, establishes an empire that suddenly appears on the scene with the capture of Constantinople in the 15th century and puts an end to one thousand years of Byzantine hegemony. Moreover, the Ottomans invade the Balkans, intending to create an empire in eastern Europe and Asia Minor; at this point, they are already a threat to the Europeans and their neighbors in the Near East.

To the east after the domination by the Mongol Khans of Iran and central Asia, a short period of domination by Tamerlane (who controls an immense territory from Turkestan to the Aegean Sea) begins in 1370. After his death, his empire splinters into diverse Turkoman tribes (Black Sheep, White Sheep, Safavids), who will in turn succumb to the Ottomans. Afghanistan and central Asia witness the establishment of small local dynasties, while Muslim India has yet to find its unifying leader.

Pulling Out of Spain: The Kingdom of Grenada

With the decline of the Almohads, autonomous Andalusian Muslim power is reestablished, first under the leadership of the Banu Hud in Cordoba, then under the Banu Nasr (Nasrids) in Grenada.

Caught between their allegiance to Castile, to which they pay a tribute, and the military might of the Moroccans, on whom they call for assistance, the Nasrids perform a skillful balancing act that permits them to remain in power. Allied Grenadans and Moroccans lose the battle for the Straits of Gibraltar. Furthermore, the political instability in Castile and Morocco, in the second half of the 14th/8th century, allows Grenada to enjoy a period of calm and growth.

From 1391 to 1482, intradynastic struggles and the permanent pressure applied by the Reconquista lead to the progressive dissolution of Nasrid power. The unification of Castile and Aragon, the end of the Castilian civil wars and the Hispano-Portuguese reconciliation inaugurate the last period of the Reconquista, which will conclude with the surrender of Grenada.

The kingdom of Grenada, rich and prosperous, is heavily populated: Muslims from the regions conquered by the Christians come in large numbers to settle there. The Plain of Grenada offers a model for agricultural development using irrigation. Grenada produces and markets silk. In the active ports of Malaga and Almeria, Italian merchants have trading posts.

As regards intellectual and religious orientations, Grenada follows established trends: a practical and theoretical medical tradition, intellectual formation dominated by religion and literature, religious life framed by official Malikism, persistance of Sufi trends. The Alhambra, palace-city of the Nasrid government, remains one of the great examples of the monumental art of the Muslims of Spain.

The Almohad Decline and the Kings of the Ta'ifa

1224–1225/620–622

Internal struggles over secession among the Almohads. Al-Bayyasi, Almohad governor of Cordoba, proclaims his independence in the towns of Cordoba, Baeza, Jaen and Quesada.

1227/624

Abu al-'Ula, governor of Seville, Almohad pretender. Drought and food shortage in Andalusia. Seditions in Murcia and Valencia.

1228/625

Muhammad Ibn Hud (a descendant of the Hudids of Zaragoza) conquers Murcia.

1229/626

The Almohad caliph al-Ma'mun besieges Murcia. During his retreat to Morocco, where he faces internal strife, a general insurrection occurs in Andalusia. Zayyan Ibn Mardanish takes Valencia. Cordoba and Seville ally with Ibn Hud.

1230/627
Ferdinand III of Castile defeats Ibn Hud's supporters at Jerez de la Frontera.

1231/628
Alfonso IX of Leon defeats Ibn Hud at Merida. Algeciras and Gibraltar pledge their allegiance to Ibn Hud.

1232–1233/629–630
Muhammad b. Yusuf b. Nasr assumes the title Sultan in his capital Arjona, takes Jaen and Porcuna.

1234/631
Alliance pledged between the Nasrids and Ibn Hud.

1236/633
Cordoba taken by Ferdinand III of Castile with the support of the Nasrids.

1237/634
Grenada submits to the rule of Muhammad b. Yusuf b. Nasr, who makes it the capital of his small empire. Assassination of Ibn Hud in Almeria. Almeria submits to the rule of the Nasrids.

1238–1239/635–636
Alliance pledged between the Banu Ashqilula of Malaga and Muhammad b. Yusuf b. Nasr.

The Spanish Reconquista

1229–1245/626–643
Aragonian conquests: Baleares (1229–1239), Valencia (1238), Peñíscola, Alcira and Jativa (1245).

1236/633
Cordoba taken by Ferdinand III of Castile.

1244/641–642
Arjona taken by the Castilians. Castile-Aragonian treaty at Almizra for the division of conquered lands.

1246/643
Jaen taken by the Castilians.

1248/646
Seville taken by Ferdinand III of Castile.

The Nasrids and Their Spanish and Moroccan Neighbors

1237–1273/634–671:
Reign of Muhammad I
1238–1239/635–636
The Alhambra ("Red Castle") of Grenada, government city, founded.

1243/641
Ibn Hud's son, the ruler of Murcia, becomes a vassal of Ferdinand III.

1245–1246/643
Jaen besieged and taken by the Castilians. During the ensuing period of peace, Muhammad I consolidates his empire, and establishes good relations with the Marinids and Hafsids. Grenada pays tribute to Castile.

1262/660
Attempt to conquer Ceuta, in Morocco.

1264–1266/662–664

Dealings with the Marinids of Fez and the Hafsids of Tunis. In the regions of Jerez and Murcia, support given to Muslims revolting against Castilian domination (*mudjares*). Rebellion by the Banu Ashqilula, governors of Malaga and Guadix.

1273–1302/671–701: Reign of Muhammad II al-Faqih
1274–1275/673–674

Alliance with the Marinids of Fez. The Marinids take Tarifa and Algeciras. Militias and permanent Moroccan bases in Andalusian territory (the *ghuzat*).

1278/676

The Banu Ashqilula from Malaga submit to Marinid rule. Castilian troops blockade Algeciras. Merchants from Aragon begin to settle in the port cities.

1279/677

The Nasrids again take control of Malaga. Alliance between the Nasrids and Marinids against the Castilians in Algeciras.

1280–1281/679–680

Alliance between the Castilians, the Marinids and the Banu Ashqilula against Grenada.

1288/687

The Banu Ashqilula abandon Guadix to the Nasrids and settle in Morocco.

1292/691

Tarifa taken by Sancho IV of Castile.

1295/695

Nasrid offensive against Castile. Quesada taken.

1300/699

New offensive against Castile. Alcuadeta taken, incursions into Campina and as far as the outskirts of Jaen.

1302–1309/701–708: Reign of Muhammad III al-Makhlu' ("The Dethroned")
1303–1305/703–704

Truce between Grenada and Castile. In the peace of Agreda between Castile and Aragon, Grenada is included as a vassal of Castile.

1306/705

Ceuta taken by the Nasrids, from the Banu al-'Azafi.

1308/707

Treaty of offensive alliance between Castile and Aragon against Grenada.

1309/708

Palace revolution. Muhammad III deposed.

1309–1314/708–713: Reign of Abu al-Juyush Nasr
1309/708

Ceuta retaken by the Marinids. Gibraltar taken by the Castilians. Algeciras and Ronda are fortified Marinid strongholds. Siege of Algeciras by the Castilians and Aragonians.

1310/709

Siege on Algeciras lifted. Peace treaty.

1312/712

Alcuadeta retaken by Castile. Restoration of Algeciras and Ronda to Grenada.

1313/712

Abu al-Walid Isma'il, Nasr's cousin, pretender to power in Grenada with Marinid support. Grenada taken by Isma'il.

1314–1325/713–725: Reign of Isma'il I
1316/716

Castilian offensive against Guadix.

1319/719

Castilian offensive against Grenada. Failure.

1325/725

Isma'il I assassinated.

1325–1333/725–728: Reign of Muhammad IV
1327–1328/727–728

Nasrid-Marinid alliance; installation of a Marinid auxiliary corps in Grenada. Castilian conquests furthered under the direction of Alfonso XI. Castile-Aragon alliance and plan for a crusade.

1333/733

Siege and capture of Gibraltar by the the Nasrids and Marinids with the help of a Genoese fleet. Muhammad IV assassinated.

1333–1354/733–755: Reign of Yusuf I
1340/741

Nasrid-Marinid alliance. Siege on Tarifa. In the battle at the Rio Salado Muslims suffer a devastating defeat by Castilian and Portuguese troops (under Alfonso XI.)

1343–1344/743–744

Siege on Algeciras by Alfonso XI, with help from Aragon and other Christian rulers. Algeciras falls after two years of resistance. End of invasions from the North African coast.

1349/750

The *madrasa* of Grenada founded.

1354/755

Assassination of Yusuf I.

1354–1359/755–760: First Reign of Muhammad V

Truce with Castile. Political balancing act between Castile, Aragon and Morocco. Palace revolution. Muhammad V, dethroned by his step brother Isma'il II, takes refuge with the Marinid sultan of Morocco.

1359–1360/760–761: Reign of Isma'il II
1360/761

Isma'il II assassinated by Muhammad VI.

1360–1362/761–763: Reign of Muhammad VI

Muhammad V exiled in Morocco; his prime minister, Ibn al-Khatib, and his Christian guards follow him. With the aid of Pedro I the Cruel of Castile, Muhammad V retakes Grenada.

1362–1391/763–793: Second Reign of Muhammad V

Castile is subject to policy of destabilization, prudent intervention and defense of borders. Occupation of Gibraltar. Close ties with Tlemcen, Tunis and Cairo.

1363/763

Ibrahim Ibn al-Hajj al-Numayri, ambassador from Grenada to the Abdelwadid king of Tlemcen.

1364/765

Ibn Khaldun is ambassador from Grenada to the king of Castile, Pedro I the Cruel, in Seville.

1369/771

Reconquest of Algeciras.

1371/773

Ibn al-Khatib, a victim of intrigues, finds refuge in Morocco with the Marinid sultan.

1375/776

Accused of publishing Sufi works antithetical to orthodoxy, Ibn al-Khatib is judged, condemned and executed in Fez.

1382–1386/784–787

Rule of Grenada over Ceuta.

1391–1464/793–870

Slow disintegration of Nasrid power. String of short-lived reigns.

1410/812–813

Antequera taken by the Castilians.

1431/835

Castilian offensive; Muslim victory in the battle of the Higueruela (in the Vega of Grenada). Muhammad IX dethroned for the first time; four reigns, interrupted by palace revolutions, from 1419 to 1447/821 to 851.

1462/868

Loss of Gibraltar.

1464–1482/870–887: Abu al-Hasan 'Ali, King of Grenada (Muley Hacen in Spanish chronicles)

Rigid domestic policy. Reorganization of the army. Alternation between truce and conflict with the Christian kingdoms.

1469/873

Marriage of Ferdinand of Aragon and Isabella of Castile.

1479/884

Treaty of Alcacobas: end of the civil war in Castile, Hispano-Portuguese reconciliation.

1481/886

The castle of Zahara taken.

1482/887

March/Safar. Alhama conquered by the Castilians.

July/Jumada II. Castilians defeated in Loja.

1482–1484/887–889

Civil war in Grenada; power seized by Abu 'Abd Allah Muhammad ("Boabdil"). Abu al-Hasan 'Ali keeps power in Malaga.

1483/888

Spanish defeat at al-Sharqiyya (Malaga region). Offensive by Abu 'Abd Allah against the Christians in Lucena. Defeat and capture of Abu 'Abd Allah. Abu al-Hasan 'Ali takes control of Grenada.

August/Jumada II. Treaty of Cordoba between Castile and the captive Abu 'Abd Allah — he appoints himself vassal of Castile as well as king of Guadix.

Letter from Yusuf I, King of Grenada, to His People:

" . . . Arise from your deep sleep! Collect your scattered wishes! Be prepared to face the thunder and the dazzling lightning of evil. . . . For the Great One of Christianity [the Pope], the one who is their guide, the one they hope to please in being hostile toward us, the one before whose cross they prostrate themselves in exalting him saw that they are devoured, crunched and even nibbled by dissension, and in the end broken and absorbed, to such a degree that there remains of them neither nerve nor bone. He saw that these discords were dispersing that which had been brought together. He then tried to think of ways to reunite that which was separated, to rebuild that which had been torn down, to mend that which was lacerated and in pieces. He then released against Islam a nation whose flood pours forth like rain."

Letter cited by al-Maqqari, *Nafh al-Tib*, VI
translated by A. L. de Prémare

1483–1484/888–889
Offensives launched by the Castilians; internal strife in Grenada.

1486/891
Fall of Loja, Salar, Illora, Moclin, Colomera, Montefrio. Civil war in Grenada. Return of Abu 'Abd Allah.

1487/892
Fall of Malaga.

1489/894–895
Siege on and fall of Baza; surrender of Almeria and Guadix.

1490/895
Unfruitful negotiations between Abu 'Abd Allah and Spanish rulers.

1491–1492/896–897
Castilian campaign against Grenada.

1492/897
January 6/Rabi I. Surrender of Grenada.

Religion and Culture

1266/664
Establishment by Alfonso X the Wise of a college open to Christians, Muslims and Jews in Murcia. Muhammad Ibn Ahmad al-Raquti, from Murcia, teaches there.

1292/692
The traditionalist Ibn Rushayd, from Ceuta, *imam* and preacher at the Great Mosque of Grenada, makes mention, in the recounting of his travels to the East, of his meeting with leaders in cultural and religious thought of the period.

1308/708
In Grenada, death of Ibn al-Zubayr, traditionalist and historian, author of a collection of biographies on famous Andalusians from the 12th and 13th centuries/6th and 7th centuries.

1315/715

Death of Muhammad ibn al-Raqqam, mathematician, astronomer and doctor.

1336–1339/736–739

Voyage of the *qadi* Khalid al-Balawi to the East and the sacred Muslim sites. Accused of plagiarism in his travel narrative.

1340/741

During the battle of the Rio Salado, death of the lawyer Ibn Juzay al-Kalbi, author of a commentary on law.

1344/745

Cairo: death of Abu Hayyan, philologist from Grenada, master of the Turkish language and concerned with matters of comparative linguistics.

1348/749

Work by the doctor Muhammad al-Shaquri on the Black Plague.

1349/749

Ibn al-Jayyab, chief of the chancellory of the Nasrid state, dies of the plague. He is succeeded by his disciple Ibn al-Khatib.

1349–1350/750–751

Ibn Battuta visits the kingdom of Grenada where he meets members of the Banu al-Mahruq, representatives of Sufi circles in the capital.

1353/754

Ibn Marzuq, learned man and Maghribi statesman, teaches at the *madrasa* in Grenada.

After 1367/768

Death of Ibrahim Ibn al-Hajj al-Numayri, a well-read, highly placed civil servant of the Maghribi and Andalusian dynasties. Accounts of his travels in the East and the Maghrib.

1371–773

Ibn al-Hasan al-Nubahi, great *qadi* of Grenada, has the works of Ibn al-Khatib burned. Ibn al-Khatib was author of a collection of biographies of Andalusian judges and of a historiographic work on the Nasrid rulers.

1375–776

Execution of Ibn al-Khatib in Fez.

1396/798

Execution of Ibn Zamark, politician. Known as the "poet of the Alhambra," since his poems decorate the walls of the Nasrid governmental palace.

1411/814

Expedition by the knight Guillebert de Lannoy into the kingdom of Grenada, after the capture of Antequera by the Castilians; leaves an account of his voyage.

1426/829

Death of Ibn 'Asimo, great *qadi* of Grenada, author of a treatise of Maliki law in verse, the *Tuhfa*.

1445/849

Alfonso de Mella, Franciscan persecuted in Castile for heterodoxy, finds refuge in Grenada.

1481/886

Sa'dyah Ibn Danan, great rabbi of Grenada, faced with legal problems posed by the Marrans seeking refuge in Grenada and wishing to return to Judaism. Lawyer, chronicler, author of a Hebrew lexicon and of poems in Arabic.

North Africa: Hafsids, Marinids and 'Abdalwadids

From the 13th to the 16th centuries, the Hafsids maintain, not without difficulty, the Almohad heritage in the eastern Maghrib, an important place for Mediterranean trade. They are faced with internal schisms and turbulence caused by Bedouin Arabs, and have to confront outside intervention (from Tlemcen, Fez, Grenada, Aragon and Sicily). The domestic policy practiced by the rulers consists of a delicate mixture of official Malikism, saint worship, and recourse to the legitimacy of the *sharifs*. Besides demographic changes brought about by the settlement of Arab tribes, the urban cultural landscape is marked by the arrival of refugees from Andalusia, the anti-Jewish pogroms of 1391, and the expulsion of all Jews from Spain in 1492.

In Morocco, Marinid foreign policy is characterized both by their incursions into Spain and by their desire to break with the 'Abdalwadids of Tlemcen to be able to control the trade routes for which the central Maghrib is an important connection. But their incursions into Tunis are failures. After 1358/759, the dynasty sinks in the mire of its internal struggles. It is followed by the Wattasid dynasty, which is unable to stop the Portuguese from getting a foothold on the Moroccan coast.

The 'Abdalwadids, in the central Maghrib, establish and maintain a power that waxes and wanes, with the aid of Arab confederations. The Marinids blockade Tlemcen on several occasions. The town is, in fact, taken on two occasions. In the second half of the 14th century, under Abu Hammu Musa II, the dynasty regains a certain vitality and acquires political importance in the diplomatic game being played by Grenada, Fez, Tunis, Castile and Aragon. The final period of 'Abdalwadid history (first half of the 16th century) witnesses the successive domination of Tlemcen by Spaniards, Turks from Algiers, Sa'dians from Morocco and finally the Ottoman Empire.

1228-1249/625-647: Reign of the Hafsid Abu Zakariyya' Yahya in Tunis

Zenith of Hafis power. Abu Zakariyya' Yahya, governor of Gabes, assumes the title emir; break with the Almohad caliphate of Marrakesh (1229/627); the official prayer in Tunis is said in the name of the Hafsid king (1236/634); construction of the mosque in the Casbah of Tunis.

1230/627

Conquest of Constantine and Bijaya.

1231/628

Trade treaty with Venice.

1234/632

Trade treaty with Pisa.

1235/633

Hafsid conquest of Algiers.

1235–1283/633–681

The 'Abdalwadid Yaghmurasan (Yaghamrasan) Ibn Ziyyan, independent ruler of Tlemcen. The 'Abdalwadids recognize Hafsid suzerainty (1242/640). Construction of the minaret of the Great Mosque of Tlemcen.

1236/634

Hafsid trade treaty with Genoa.

1238/635

Nasrids (Grenada) and Marinids (Morocco) recognize Hafsid suzerainty.

1239/636

The Hafsids pay tribute to Sicily to guarantee the security of their trade. In Tunis, Spanish, French, Genoan and Pisan trading posts.

1248/646

The Marinid ruler Abu Yahya Abu Bakr (1244–1258) is master over eastern and northern Morocco after his conquest of Miknas (Meknes) in 1245 and Fez (1248).

1253/650

Hafsid king Muhammad assumes the title of caliph under the name of al-Mustansir. (1249–1277). He is recognized by the Sharif of Mecca (1259) and possibly by the Mamluks (1260).

1255 or 1257/653 or 655

In Tunis, death of Saint 'A'isha al-Mannubiyya, disciple of al-Shadili.

1258/656

Mecca: death of Abu al-Hasan al-Shadili, native of Ceuta or Tunis, founder of the Sufi order that carries his name.

1260/658

Tunis: execution of the historian and biographer Ibn al-Abbar, (born 1199) native of Valencia, one of the most significant intellectuals of his time.

1269/668

Conquest of Marrakesh by the Marinid governor of Fez, Abu Yusuf Ya'qub; he recognizes the suzerainty of the Hafsid caliph.

1270/668–669

Louis IX's crusade against Tunis. The king dies of the plague in Carthage. Retreat of the Crusaders.

1272/670

Marinid victory over the 'Abdalwadids in Isly. Siege on Tlemcen.

1274/673

The Marinids victorious over the 'Abdalwadids in Sijilmasa.

1275/674

Marinid incursions into Spain to help the Nasrids against the Reconquista; taken up again in 1277–1278/675–676.

1276/674

Fez al-Jadid, "The New Fez," also known as "The White City," home to the Marinid government and main headquarters of the army.

1279/677

Abu Ishaq, Hafsid pretender against al-Watiq, takes Bijaya (Bougie) with the support of the Dawawida Arabs, the Nasrids and the 'Abdalwadids.

1279/678

Abu Ishaq triumphs in Tunis with the aid of Peter III of Aragon, who has his sights set on Charles of Anjou's Sicily.

1280/671

The Marinid Abu Yusuf Ya'qub builds the Qur'anic school of the Saffarins in Fez.

1281/680

Incursion by the Marinid Abu Yusuf Ya'qub into Tlemcen.

1282/680–681

Pierre III of Aragon crowned king of Sicily after the "Sicilian Vespers." He attempts to take Bijaya (Bougie).

1284/683

The Aragonians in Jerba.

1285/686

The Hafsid king of Tunis pays tribute to the kingdoms of Aragon and Sicily. Bijaya (Bougie) and Constantine, autonomous Hafsid emirates. Marinid attack on Spain.

1286–1287/685–686

The king of Aragon and Sicily supports the pretender Ibn Abi-Dabbus against Abu Hafs, Hafsid king of Tunis.

1289/688

Voyage to the East by the Moroccan al-'Abdari; he leaves behind an account, *al-Rihla al-maghribiyya* ("Journey to the Maghrib").

1290/689

Attack on Tlemcen by the Marinid Abu Ya'qub Yusuf (1286–1307).

1294/693

Bijaya (Bougie) annexes the Zab. Allegiance of the governor of Gabes to the Hafsids in Bijaya.

1295/694

Beginning of a 12-year-long struggle of the Marinids against the 'Abdalwadids.

1298–1306/698–706

Blockade of and siege on Tlemcen by the Marinid Abu Ya'qub Yusuf. Construction, near Tlemcen, on the site of Agadir, of the siege town al-Mansura, complete with a palace, a mosque, baths and a market.

1305–1309/705–708

The Tunisian scholar al-Tijani travels to eastern Maghrib and Libya; account of the voyage.

1307/706

Assassination of Abu Ya'qub Yusuf.

1307/707

The Marinid Abu Thabit founds Tetouan as his base of operations for the recovery of Ceuta.

1309/708

The Marinids retake Ceuta from the Nasrids.

1312–1313/712

Ibn Idhari writes his *Chronicle of the Andalusian and Maghribi Kings*.

1313–1315/713–715

'Abdalwadid expeditions against Tunis, renewed between 1319 and 1330/719 and 730, from which springs a Hafsid-Marinid alliance against Tlemcen.

Circa 1315/715

Death of Ibn Abi Zare, Marinid chronicler, author of the *Rawd al-qirtas*. The purpose of his work is legitimizing Marinid rule.

1320–1323/720–723

The Marinid Abu Sa'id 'Utman II (1310–1331) founds three Qur'anic schools in Fez (in Fez el-Jadid, (1320) the Madrasa al-Sihrij (1321), and the Madrasa al-'Attarin).

1321/721

Marrakesh: death of Ibn al-Banna', Moroccan mathematician.

1331–1351/731–752: Reign of the Marinid Abu al-Hasan

Zenith of the dynasty. Numerous Qur'anic schools in Fez and other Moroccan cities; the ramparts of Shella, necropolis of the Marinid kings, built near Rabat.

1333/733

Algeciras taken by Abu al-Hasan.

1337/737

Tlemcen taken by Abu al-Hasan: the city remains under direct Marinid administration until 1359. Decline of the 'Abdalwadids.

1339/739

Construction of the mosque of the great mystic and patron of the city Sidi Bu-Madyan in Tlemcen.

1340/741

Marinids and Nasrids defeated by the Spaniards at the Rio Salado, near Tarifa.

1344/744

Definitive capture of Algeciras by the Spaniards after two years of siege. Ibn Tadrart, poet and important Marinid civil servant, evokes these events in his poems.

1346/747

Abu al-Hasan builds the Misbahiyya Qur'anic school in Fez, modeled on the one in Sala (Salé) (1341).

1347/748

Qur'anic school in the al-'Ubbad quarter of Tlemcen.

1347–1350/748–750

Abu al-Hasan conquers the eastern Maghrib including Tunis. Defeated by the Arab tribes revolting in Kairuan. Abu 'Inan, his son, revolts against him and takes power in Morocco. 'Abdalwadid restoration in Tlemcen.

1351/752

Death of Abu al-Hasan.

1351–1358/752–760: Reign of the Marinid Abu 'Inan

Construction of the Bu 'Inaniyya Qur'anic school in Fez; completion of the Qur'anic school in Miknas (Meknes) begun by his father.

1352/753

Abu 'Inan retakes Tlemcen.

1353/754

Tlemcen: construction of the Sidi al-Hawli mosque by Abu 'Inan.

1356/756

At Abu 'Inan's request, Ibn Juzay commits to writing the account of Ibn

Battuta's travels to the East, the Far East and Africa from 1325 to 1353/ 725 to 754.

1357/758

Abu 'Inan completes his triumph over the eastern Maghrib. Bijaya (Bougie) (1353), Constantine and Tunis (1357) taken. Arab tribes effectively resist. Ibn al-Hajj al-Numayri, from Grenada, important Marinid civil servant, gives an account of the expedition in his *Fayd al-'ubab*.

1358/760

Death of Abu 'Inan.

1359-1389/760-791: Reign of Abu Hammu Musa II in Tlemcen

'Abdalwadid restoration. The sovereign's memoirs in the form of a political testament, the *Wasitat al-suluk*, addressed to his son.

1370-1488/772-893: Hafsid Restoration in the eastern Maghrib

The reigns of Abu al-'Abbas (1370–1394/772–796), Abu al-Faris (1394–1434/796–837), al-Muntasir (1434–1435/837–839), and 'Uthman (1435–1488/839–893). Restoration and political unity; Hafsid power extended as far as Algiers (1410/813); rule over Tlemcen; Franco-Genoan expedition against al-Mahdiyya sabotaged (1390/792); victory over Alfonso V of Aragon in Jerba (1432/835); suzerainty over the Wattasids, successors of the Marinids in Fez (1472/877).

1375-1379/776-780

Retreat of Ibn Khaldun to the castle of Ibn Salama (Oran): writes the *Muqaddima*, an introductory essay to his historical work.

1379/780

Death of Ibn Marzuq, from Tlemcen; politician, author of a work on Abu al-Hasan's reign, the *Musnad*. Death of Yahya Ibn Khaldun, politician, important civil servant and chronicler of the 'Abdalwadids of Tlemcen on whom he writes in the *Bughyat al-ruwwad*. Brother of the historian 'Abd al-Rahman Ibn Khaldun.

1381/783

Death of Abu al-Qasim b. Ridwan, from Malaga. Important Marinid civil servant, poet, author of an essay of advice to the king.

1390/792

Death of Ibn 'Abbad of Ronda, disciple of Ibn 'Ashir, author of the *Letters (Rasa'il)* for spiritual instruction. Official preacher at the mosque of the Qarawiyin in Fez.

1391/793

Pogroms in Spain lead to Jewish immigration to North Africa.

1401/803

Death of Ibn 'Arafa, Maliki lawyer from Tunis, Ibn Khaldun's rival.

1406/808

Cairo: death of 'Abd al-Rahman Ibn Khaldun.

1407/810

Death of Ibn Qunfudh, from Constantine, lawyer, traditionalist, chronicler of the Hafsids and biographer of the Sufis. Death of Ibn al-Ahmar, from Grenada, chronicler of the Marinids.

1415/818

The Portuguese occupation of Ceuta opens the door for European trade in North Africa.

1458/862

The Portuguese in al-Qsar al-Saghir, on the Straits.

1463/868

Death, in Tunis, of Saint Ahmad b. 'Arus. (Sidi ben 'Arus), one of the two patrons of the city.

1465/870

The Wattasids, cousins of the Marinids, take power in Fez.

1469/874

The Portuguese in Anfa, on the Atlantic coast of Morocco.

1471/875

The Wattasid al-Shaykh concludes a 20-year truce with the Portuguese.

1488–1489/894

Death of al-Zarkashi, chronicler of the Almohads and Hafsids, author of *Tarikh al-dawlatayn.*

1492/897

Expulsion of all Jews from Spain; many settle in North Africa.

1504–1505/910

The Portuguese in Safi and Agadir.

The Maghrib in Turmoil

"Today, or rather, at the end of the 8th century [of the Hijra], the situation in Maghrib has undergone a profound transformation . . . and has been turned upside down: Berber tribes, living in these lands since very early on, have been replaced by Arab tribes who, having arrived in the 5th century, destroyed and subjugated them, took away the greater part of their territory and forced them to divide the joy of possessing the lands they still held. Let us add to this the arrival, in the middle of this 8th century, of a ravaging plague which descended upon the peoples of the East and the West; . . . the plague took away the greater part of this generation, stole and destroyed the best results of this civilization. It appeared at the moment when the empires were in an era of decadence and were reaching the end of their existence. . . . It seems to me that the voice of Nature, having ordered that the world be forgotten and erased, got complete cooperation in these matters from the world. As conditions of life are turned upside down, it is possible to say that creation is being changed in a fundamental way, and that the universe is witnessing radical changes. . . . "

Ibn Khaldun, *Muqaddima*
translated by J. E. Bencheikh, Hachette, 1965

1509/915
The Spaniards in Oran. Suzerainty over Tlemcen.

1510/916
The Spaniards in Bijaya (Bougie) and Tripoli.

1517/923
The Turks of Algiers rule in Tlemcen; 'Aruj, the brother of Khayr al-Din Barbarossa, the governor of Algiers, expels the Spaniards.

1534–1535/941–942
The pasha of Algiers, Khayr al-Din, Barbarossa chases the Hafsid al-Hasan from Tunis. Al-Hasan is re-established in Tunis by Emperor Charles V of Spain one year after the conquest of La Goulette.

1535–1536/942
Struggle between the Hafsids and the Turks who had settled in Kairuan.

1536–1541/942–948
Charles V launches an expedition against Algiers and Tunis.

1540/947
Struggle between the Hafsids and the Marabuti state of the Shabbiyya in Kairuan.

1549/956
Fez taken by the Sa'dids. Sa'did expedition against Tlemcen and Mostaganem.

1550/957
The Turks take control of Tlemcen.

1554/961
The last Wattasid sultan, Abu Hassun, regains a foothold in Fez; retaken by the Sa'dids nine months later.

1556–1557/964–965
The pirate Turghud (Dragut) successor of Khayr al-Din Barbarossa, named pasha of Tripoli by the Ottomans, takes Gafsa and Kairuan and completes Turkish conquest of the North African coast.

1557/964
Assassination of the Sa'did Muhammad al-Shaykh by the Turks.

1569/976
The pasha of Algiers takes Tunis in the name of the Ottomans.

1571/979
Sea battle of Lepanto: a Spanish Venetian fleet (led by Don Juan of Austria) of the Holy League destroys the Ottoman fleet.

1573/981
Don Juan of Austria puts a Hafsid back in power in Tunis.

1574/982
The Ottomans take Tunis; end of the Hafsid dynasty.

The Mamluks in Egypt and Syria

From the middle of the 13th century until the beginning of the 16th, Egypt and Syria are under the authority of military leaders, the Mamluk sultans, originally slaves recruited in Georgia, Armenia and Azerbaijan (Azarbayjan) to serve in the army who eventually took power from the Ayyubid rulers. Sultans such as Barsbay, Qalawun and Qaytbay left an indelible impression on their time. With a sense of security due to their military might, they impose a remarkable administration characterized by severe discipline.

Victorious over the Mongols, without rivals in the Near East until the end of the 15th century, rulers over all the land and sea routes from the Indian Ocean to the eastern part of the Mediterranean, they have access to large revenues from international trade. Their pre-eminence is manifested as well by the construction of mosques and palaces, which add an artistic dimension to their glory.

It is under the Mamluks that the writers Dhahabi, Ibn Taghribirdi, Ibn Iyas and Abu al-Fida lived.

The Mamluk Dynasty in Egypt and Syria

1250/618
A princess, Shajar al-Durr, governs Egypt after the assassination of the last Ayyubid sultan Turan Shah by his Turkish soldiers.

1260-1277/658-676: Reign of the Mamluk Sultan Barsbay in Cairo
1260/658
Aleppo sacked by the Mongols. Damascus conquered by General Kitbugha.

September 2/25 Ramadan. At 'Ayn Jalut (north of Jerusalem), victory of the Mamluks over the Mongols stops the Mongol invasion.

1261/659
The 'Abbasid caliphate established in Cairo; politically insignificant, it bestows legitimacy on Mamluk rule.

1262/660
Hülegü takes Mosul.

1265/663
Barsbay takes Caesarea and Arsuf.

1266/664
Barsbay takes Safad and attacks Cilicia.

1268/666
Barsbay reclaims Jaffa and Antioch from the Franks.

1271/669
Barsbay conquers the Crac des Chevaliers (Hisn al-Akrad), the citadel of the Knights of St. John. End of the tolerant cohabitation of Christian crusader states and Muslims.

1274-1275/673
The Mamluks ravage Cilicia.

1276/674
Voyage of sultan Barsbay to Petra. Barsbay invades Ilkhanid Anatolia.

1277/beginning of 676
Death of Barsbay.

1279-1290/678-689: Reign of the Mamluk Sultan Qalawun
1281/680
The Mamluks defeat the Mongols at Hims.

1282/681

Truce, to last 10 years and 10 days, agreed to by the Mamluks and the Crusaders.

1287/686

Qalawun takes Latakia (al-Ladhiqiyya).

1289/688

The Crusaders' capital Tripoli (Tarabulus) taken by Qalawun.

1291/690

Fall of Saint John d'Acre, during the sultanate of Qalawun's son al-Ashraf Khalil (1290–1293/689–692). Beirut and all other Crusader towns along the coast surrender. The Christians can only hold the tiny island of Arwad (at Tartus).

1293/693

March/Muharram. Assassination of al-Ashraf Khalil. Qalawun's son al-Nasir Muhammad b. Qalawun proclaimed sultan at nine years of age; supported by the emirs Zayn al-Din Kitbugha and 'Alam al-Din Shuja'i.

1294/694

November 2–December/Muharram. Al-Nasir deposed, judged to be too young. Kitbugha is proclaimed sultan.

1296/696

November 3/Muharram. Assassination of Kitbugha.

1299/698

January/Rabi II. Assassination of sultan al-Malik al-Mansur Lajin.

February/Jumada II. Reinstatement of al-Nasir Muhammad. Receives the title of caliph for the second time. Salar al-Mansuri and the *atabeg al-'asakir* Barsbay al-Jashnagir serve as his advisors.

September/Dhu'l-Hijja. The Mongols reach the Euphrates. Ghazan, son of Arghun, occupies Aleppo; defeat of the Mamluks near Hims. Damascus occupied by the Mongols, except for the citadel.

1300/699

March–April/Rajab. Retreat of the Mongols. The Mamluks reclaim Damascus, Aleppo and all of Syria.

1301/700

January/Rabi II. Ghazan sends a delegation to Cairo to negotiate. Failure.

1303/702

April 3/Shawwal. The Mongol Qutlushah crosses the Euphrates. Barsbay al-Jashnagir enters Damascus.

April 20/2 Ramadan. Battle of Shahqah: Mongols defeated.

August 8/23 Dhu'l-Hijja. Earthquake in Egypt.

1305/704

The Shi'is of northern Lebanon crushed by the Mamluks.

1309/708

March 8/25 Ramadan. al-Nasir Muhammad decides to abdicate.

April 5/23 Shawwal. Barsbay proclaimed sultan. Intrigue perpetrated by Salar against Barsbay and al-Nasir, who is in Damascus when the Syrian emirs come to his defense. Barsbay abdicates.

1310–1341: Sultanate of al-Nasir Muhammad
1313/712
January/Ramadan. The Mongols under Öljeytü, Ghazan's brother and successor, threaten Syria, besiege Rahba on the Euphrates, then retreat.

1315/715
Mamluk expedition against Malatya; other incursions into Asia Minor.

1316/716
Intervention of al-Nasir in Nubia.

1317/717
Al-Nasir's authority recognized in Mecca and Medina.

1323/723
Al-Nasir Muhammad signs a peace treaty with Ilkhan Abu Sa'id.

1325/725
Intervention of al-Nasir in Yemen with the support of the Meccans.

1335/735
November/Rabi II. Hasan Buzurg offers to recognize al-Nasir's suzerainty on condition that he receive military support from al-Nasir.

1340
Death of al-Nasir Muhammad.

1341–1342/741–743
Al-Mansur Abu Bakr, al-Ashraf, Kujuk and al-Nasir Ahmed follow in succession.

1342/743
Accession of al-Salih Isma'il. Trade treaty with Venice.

1344/745
May/Shawwal. Karak taken by Isma'il.

1345/746
Death of al-Salih Isma'il.
August 4/4 Rabi I. Accession of al-Kamil Sha'ban; assassinated September 21 1346/3 Jumada II 747.

1346/747
November/Rajab. Accession of Hajji. Favors Circassian factions. Death due to strangulation (December 16 1347/11 Ramadan 748). The Mamluks take Ayas (Lajazzo) in Cilicia (Armenia) from the Christians.

1347/748
December 18/14 Ramadan. Accession of al-Nasir Hasan, the most famous of the sons of Ibn Qalawun. He is 11 years old.

1348–1350/747–751
Plague in the Mediterranean area; Europe, North Africa, Egypt and the Near East ravaged.

1351/752
When he becomes an adult, Hasan abdicates. Accession of Hasan's brother, Salih.

1354/755
October 20/2 Shawwal. Salih deposed. He will later die in prison. Return of al-Nasir Hasan.

1358/759
The emir Manjak named governor of Damascus with the directive of reorganizing of the city's defenses on the Syrian-Lebanese coast, threatened at that time by the Franks in Cyprus.

June 4/14 Jumada II. Manjak, arrested on two occasions, taken to Cairo and then released, goes to Jerusalem where he settles.

1359/760

Sultan Hasan rejects the request of Peter of Lusignan, King of Cyprus, to travel to Tyre.

1362/763

March 9/13 Jumada I. Assassination of sultan Hasan by his general Yilbugha al-'Umari.

1365/767

October/Muharram. Alexandria attacked by a naval force led by the king of Cyprus, Peter I of Lusignan.

1367/769

Peter I of Lusignan attacks Tripoli, Latakia and Ayas.

1370/770

Peace negotiations with Cyprus, mediated by Venice and Genoa.

1375/776-777

Conquest of the Christian kingdom of Little Armenia in Cilicia by the emir of Aleppo, in the name of the sultan al-Ashraf Sha'ban. Adana, Tarsus, Mamistra and Sis taken. The last king, Leo VI, taken prisoner and incarcerated in the citadel of Cairo.

1377/778

Al-Ashraf Sha'ban, in the middle of a pilgrimage, has to turn back because of strife in his entourage. Back in Cairo, he finds his son has been sultan since May 17, 1377/8 Muharram 779.

1378/779

Barquq al-Jarkasi promoted to *atabeg al-'asakir.*

1382-1517/784-923:
The Reign of the Burji or Circassian Mamluks

They put an end to the dynastic principle of electing their sultans from the heart of a military aristocracy.

1382/784

May/Safar. 'Ali dies of plague at seven years old. Barquq grants the position of sultan to 'Ali's brother, Hajji. The council of the four great *qadis,* presided over by the caliph, depose him. Barquq takes the place of al-Salih Hajji, last Qalawunid descendant; first sultan of the Jarkas line (Circassians). Faced with the Mongol threat, special fiscal measures put in place to create an army.

1383/785

Incarceration in Cairo of the caliph al-Mutawakkil, replaced by al-Wathiq.

1386/788

Dismissal of al-Wathiq, return to power of al-Musta'sim, briefly caliph in 1377/778-779.

1389/791

March 10/11 Rabi I. Rebellion against Barquq by all the governors of Syria, led by Mintash, governor of Aleppo.

May/Jumada I. Numerous officers desert Barquq's second army; fighting in the streets of Cairo. Barquq in captivity in Karak; al-Salih Hajji returned to the throne. The emir Yilbugha al-'Umari becomes *atabeg al-'asakir.* Mintash revolts in Cairo. Wronged by Yilbugha, he removes him by incarcerating him in Alexandria; Mintash becomes *atabeg al-'asakir.*

December/Dhu'l-Hijja. Army of Cairo marches on Damascus where Barquq and an army await.

December 21/2 Muharram. After a reversal of fortunes in Shaqhab, Barquq comes away with the victory. The sultan Hajji abdicates, the caliph and the four great *qadis* pledge loyalty to Barquq.

1390/792

February 2/16 Safar. Barquq returns to Cairo.

1391/793

Attempt by Mintash to become ruler of Syria; betrayed in Aleppo, he is brought before the governor, who has him beheaded and sends the head to Cairo.

End of 1393/beginning of 796

New threat from Timur.

1394/796

Timur in Edessa (al-Ruha). A Mongol ambassador in Cairo demands the recognition of Mongol supremacy; Barquq has the messenger executed.

January/Rabi I. The Jalayrid sultan, Ahmad b. Uways, driven from Baghdad by the Mongols, finds refuge in Cairo.

March/Jumada I. Barquq in Aleppo receives a delegation from the Ottoman Bayezid I Yïldïrïm ("the Thunderbolt") proposing an alliance against Timur; the accord is signed.

1399/801

June 20/15 Shawwal. Death of Barquq. Timur in Georgia fighting against Toqtamïsh, leader of the eastern Qipchaqs. Faraj succeeds his father Barquq at 11 years old.

November/Rabi I. With the announcement of Faraj's adult status anticipated, revolt among the emirs.

1400/802–803

April 28/3 Ramadan. Death of Tanibak al-Hasani, rebel governor, executed after being defeated near Gaza.

May/Ramadan. Appointment of Sudun Sharaf al-Din, Barsbay al-Dawadar's brother, Barquq's nephew, to the position of governor of Damascus.

September/Muhurram. A vanguard of Timur's appears in 'Ayntab; panic in Syria.

October 29/10 Rabi I. Bloody defeat of Syrian troops and the Egyptian contingent by the Mongols. Aleppo sacked; Hama, Hims and Ba'albek surrender without resistance. Siege on Damascus by Timur.

1401/803

January 21/10 Jumada II. The sultan Faraj returns to Cairo where he recruits a new army.

February–March/Rajab. Damascus resists Timur. Negotiations. The 70-year-old historian Ibn Khaldun tries to persuade Timur to treat the defeated Syrians moderately.

Mid-March/Rajab. Unconditional surrender: Damascus sacked. Mass deportation of intellectuals, artists and artisans to Samarkand.

March 19/3 Shawwal. The backup army from Egypt repulsed; Timur, called to Anatolia, leaves Syria to fight the Ottomans.

1403/805

Timur makes a proposition for peace; Faraj signs on and Egypt enters an economic crisis due to destruction and war-related expenses. Famines, plague, poor harvests and Bedouin invasions exacerbate the situation.

1404/806
Return of Mongol troops to Transoxiana; the Mamluks immediately renew their intrigues. Neither the governor of Damascus, Taghribirdi al-Zahiri, nor the governor of Aleppo, Aqbugha, recognize the sultan.

1405/808
End of September/beginning of Rabi I. Faraj, deposed, flees to Syria. 'Abd al-'Aziz, one of his brothers, is recognized as sultan; 70 days in power.

1407/809–810
March/Ramadan. Two emirs vie for power with the sultan. Jakam, governor of Aleppo, proclaims himself sultan. Dies in combat during the same year.

July–August/Safar. Nawruz, governor of Damascus, arrested; when liberated, he will play an important role in Cairo.

1412/814–815
March–April/Dhu'l-Qa'da. Faraj defeated in Lajjun by Nawruz and the *atabeg al-'asakir* Shaykh al-Mahmudi.

May 7/25 Muharram. Faraj deposed in Damascus.

May 28/16 Safar. Execution of Faraj. The emirs name the caliph Musta'in bi-Allah sultan while awaiting their return to Cairo.

November 6/1st Shawwal. Shaykh al-Mahmudi has himself proclaimed sultan.

1413/815–816
March 16/13 Dhu'l-Hijja. The Sultan leaves Cairo to subdue Nawruz, who has barricaded himself in Damascus.

May–April/Muharram. Shaykh al-Mu'ayyad camps at Damascus, which surrenders; Nawruz is captured and beheaded.

1415/818
The sultan goes to Syria to quiet the emir Qanibay's rebellion. Plague in Egypt and Syria.

September/Rajab. Execution of Qanibay in Aleppo.

1417/820
New expedition in northern Syria against the emir Aqbay al-Dawadar, governor of Damascus; he is executed.

1420/823
November 20/24 Dhu'l-Qa'da Death of the sultan Shaykh al-Mu'ayyad.

1421/824
Succession of three sultans; between 1422 and 1430, there will be six.

1422/825
Barsbay chosen as sultan. Turmoil in the northeastern part of the Mamluk empire, due to the machinations of the Timurid shah Rukh against the leader of the Qara Qoyunlu Iskandar, son of Qara Yusuf, who requests Barsbay's help. Barsbay suppresses the governor of Aleppo's revolt, and changes governors in Damascus, replacing him with the emir Sudun al-Dawadar. He subjugates Hasan b. 'Ajlan, sharif of Mecca. Egypt's suzerainty over the sacred towns and Jidda is recognized.

1424/827

Barsbay initiates a reconnaissance mission to Cyprus. Janus, king of Cyprus, retaliates on the Mamluk coast.

1426/829

July/Shawwal. Cyprus taken by Barsbay; Janus of Lusignan, taken prisoner. Cyprus comes under Mamluk rule.

1429-1432/829-835

Mamluk expeditions carried out against the Aq-Qoyunlu Turkoman tribe, led by Shah Rukh.

1430/833

January/Rabi II. Plague in Egypt reaches Asia Minor via Syria.

1438/end of 841-842

New plague in Egypt and Syria.

June 7/13 Dhu'l-Hijja. Barsbay dies of the plague. Yusuf al-'Aziz succeeds his father. He reigns 94 days with the *atabeg al-'asakir* as his regent.

August 7/18 Safar. Attack on the citadel of Cairo by friends of Jaqmaq.

September 9/19 Rabi I. Jaqmaq proclaimed sultan. Yusuf, relieved of his position, finds himself in the citadel of Cairo.

December 29/12 Rajab. Qurqmas executed.

1439/842

February/Ramadan. Inal al-Jakami, governor of Damascus, refuses to recognize Jaqmaq, who subsequently sends troops against him; executed on May 4, 1439.

March 16/Ramadan. Yusuf al-'Aziz

escapes; recaptured, he remains under house arrest and surveillance in Alexandria.

April/Dhu'l-Qa'da. In Syria, the governors of Aleppo and Damascus support Yusuf; they are decapitated.

1440/843

August/Rabi I. Jaqmaq harassed by Corsairs who are supported by the Hospitallers of Saint John of Rhodes.

1444/847

July 28/30 Rabi I. Second Mamluk expedition departs from Damietta and Alexandretta.

August/Rabi II. Arrival of these forces and combat between Egyptians and the Hospitallers of Rhodes.

October 25/1 Rajab. Peace treaty signed by Jaqmaq and John of Lastic, great leader of the order of the Knights of St. John (Hospitallers).

1453/857

February 13/3 Safar. Jaqmaq dies at 80 years of age without having designated a successor. The caliph, the four great *qadis* and the emirs choose his son 'Uthman (19 years old).

March 12/1 Rabi I. Mamluks revolt. Siege on the citadel by the Mamluks who rally around the *atabeg al-'asakir* Inal al-Ajrud; 'Uthman imprisoned in Alexandria.

1453-1461/857-865: Reign of Inal al-Ajrud

Violence and disorder; the *julban*, the Mamluks of the sultan, are all-powerful.

1460/864

Terrible plague in Egypt.

1461/865

February 26/15 Jumada I. Death of Inal. Ahmad, his oldest son, *atabeg al-'asakir*, proclaimed sultan. Favors reform but is hostile to Mamluk uprisings.

June/Ramadan. Agreeing to depose al-Mu'ayyad Ahmad, the emirs attack the citadel. Ahmad surrenders. Khushqadam, *atabeg al-'asakir*, proclaimed sultan with the title of al-Malik al-Zahir. His rival in Damascus, Janim al-Jarkasi, finds refuge in Edessa (al-Ruha).

1463/867

August/Dhu'l-Qa'da. The emir Janibak al-Zahiri, former governor of Jidda, arrested and assassinated. Rivalry between the sultan of Egypt and the Ottoman sultan.

1466/870

Bedouin tribes terrorize Upper Egypt, Syria and northern Arabia. They attack the *hajj* pilgrims.

1466–1470/870–874

Conflicts, without results, between Mamluks and Ottomans.

1467/872

October 9/10 Rabi I. Khushqadam dies without naming a successor. The *atabeg al-'asakir* Yalbay becomes sultan; the emir Timurbugha becomes *atabeg*.

December 4/8 Jumada I. Plot: Yalbay deposed and imprisoned. Timurbugha succeeds him with the support of Khayrbak.

1468/872

January 31/6 Rajab. Timurbugha deposed. Khayrbak chosen as sultan but without the endorsement of the *atabeg* Qaytbay, who seizes the sultanate.

1468–1496/873–901: Reign of Qaytbay
1477–1478/882

September–January/Jumada I–Shawwal. Qaytbay travels to the Syrian provinces to conduct an inspection. Ottoman retaliation on the border provinces of Syria where Turkish is spoken.

1481/887

September/Shawwal. Qaytbay receives Jem, the son of Mehmed II and brother and rival of the Ottoman sultan Bayezid II, in Cairo.

1483/888

The Dhu'l-qadirid prince 'Ala' al-Dawla, supported by Mehmed II, enters into a conflict with Qaytbay.

1484/889

Two meetings with 'Ala' al-Dawla; defeat of the Mamluk troops.

1485/890

October/Shawwal. Aleppo: the reinforcement army of the *atabeg* Azbak arrives. Three months later, Ottomans are defeated.

1486/891

Cilicia: Mamluk positions occupied by Ottoman troops.

1487/892

Cairo: the Nasrid ambassador in Grenada, Abu 'Abd Allah (Boabdil). The sultan guarantees his support against Castile.

1488/893

Azbak returns to Cairo because of demand issued by Mamluks in his army.

1489/894

Qaytbay reprimands Catherine Cornaro, queen of Cyprus, for not having paid the tribute to Egypt since 1478.

1490/895

Azbak victorious over the Ottomans in the Qaysariyya region.

1491/896

Peace accord reached with Bayezid II after offer from Qaytbay; peace lasts until 1512. The Ottomans cede Adana and Tarsus to the Mamluks.

1492/897

Violent outbreak of plague in Egypt; nearly 200,000 dead, of whom more than one-third are Mamluks.

1494/899

Famine in Egypt.

1495/900

The sultan defuses a plot without bloodshed. Intrigues.

1496/901

June/Ramadan. Qaytbay foils, at 85 years old, a plot by the great *dawadar* against Qansawh Khamsmiya; abdication of Qaytbay who is replaced by his son Nasir Muhammad (14 years old).

July 27/17 Dhu'l-Qa'da. Death of Qaytbay.

1497/902

January/Jumada I. The emir Qansawh Khamsmiya pressures Nasir Muhammad to eliminate the supporters of his rival, the emir Aqbirdi, who has fled to Syria.

February 1/28 Jumada I. Aqbirdi's followers drowned in the Nile. Qansawh recognized as sultan the next day. He reigns three days, then flees to Palestine. Nasir Muhammad, declared old enough to reign, descends, along with the Mamluks, into a life of excess in Cairo. He recruits a troop of black archers, but the Mamluks revolt.

1498/903

March/Rajab. Strong outbreak of plague.

October 31/15 Rabi I. Assassination of Nasir Muhammad by the emir Tumanbay's men. Qansawh becomes sultan thanks to support of Tumanbay.

1499/904

May/Shawwal. Death of Aqbirdi in Aleppo.

End of 1499/beginning of 905

Plot led by emir Qansawh, governor of Damascus; along with Tumanbay, he revolts against the sultan.

1500/905

June/Dhu'l-Qa'da. Tumanbay, leading a punitive expedition into the Sa'id, revolts and returns to Cairo.

June 24/27 Dhu'l-Qa'da. The citadel of Cairo, where Qansawh had entrenched himself, captured. The sultan escapes. Tumanbay proclaims his dethronement; he proposes Janbulat, *atabeg*, for the position.

1501/906

January 9/18 Jumada II. Accord between Qansawh and Tumanbay to bring down Janbulat, who surrenders; he is strangled in the prison of Alexandria.

January/Jumada II. Tumanbay has himself proclaimed sultan. Qansawh becomes *atabeg*.

April 19/Ramadan. After 100 days of cruel reign, Tumanbay is exiled on the last day of Ramadan.

April 20/1 Shawwal. Qansawh al-Ghawri (60 years old) proclaimed sultan the day after the end of the fast (*'Id al-Fitr*). In order to deal with the deficit, he levies in one act 10 months-worth of taxes collected in a brutal fashion. Revolt.

1503/908–909

April and July/Shawwal and Muharram. Delegation sent by the Venetian Benedetto Sanuto to seek cooperation in the Indian Ocean against the Portuguese, settled in Calcutta since 1500.

1504/909–910

Message from Qansawh al-Ghawri to the Pope Julius II: threat to destroy the holy sites of Palestine if Manuel of Portugal continues to attack merchant Muslim ships in the Indian Ocean.

June/Muharram. Plague.

1505/911

September/Rabi II. Establishment of an "Indian force"; military occupation of Jidda, construction of ports on the Red Sea, and an important naval force in the Indian Ocean with which to face the Portuguese.

1506/911

May/Dhu'l-Hijja. Sawakin becomes a naval base.

Middle of 1506/912

Blockade of the straits of Bab al-Mandab by Albuquerque.

1507/912

Mamluk expedition into Yemen.

1508/913

First naval battle in the Indian Ocean between the Egyptians and the Portuguese, near the port of Shawl; Mamluk navy victorious.

1509/914–915

Revenge of the Portuguese off Diu. Rapid decline in Mamluk trade with India.

June 12/23 Safar. The Ottoman Korkud, oldest son of Bayezid II, seeks asylum in Cairo.

1510/916

November 16/14 Shawwal. Qansawh al-Ghawri, seeking allies, sends a message to the king of France; Louis XII sends a delegation.

1511/917

Easter/Muharram. Declaration by the sultan ensuring free trade and the right to make pilgrimages to holy sites; it is ceremoniously published in Lyon during the fair.

1512/918

April/Muharram. Accession of Selim I.

May 10/24 Safar. Venetian delegation in Cairo, led by Domenico Trevisani.

1515/921

The Ottomans destroy the Dhu al-Qadr, the vassals of the Mamluks, in Armenia.

1515–1516/921–922

Mamluk conquest of Yemen; attempt to take Aden fails.

1516/922

August 26/25 Rajab. Battle of Marj Dabiq, north of Aleppo. Ottoman victory; Ottomans greater in number and have more effective artillery. Qansawh al-Ghawri dies in combat.

September 26/28 Shawwal. Damascus capitulates. The *khutba* is performed in the name of the Ottoman sultan.

October 10/14 Ramadan. Solemn arrival of Selim I in Damascus.

October 17/Ramadan. The great *dawadar* Tumanbay chosen as sultan.

November–December/Shawwal–Dhu'l-Qa'da. Ottoman army moves towards Gaza. Refusal on the part of some Mamluks to participate in the campaign.

December 22/27 Dhu'l-Qa'da. Mamluk army defeated in Baysan.

1517/922–923

January 22/28 Dhu'l-Hijja. Mamluks led by Tumanbay, Qansawh's nephew and successor, defeated in Raydaniyya (close to Cairo).

January 26/3 Muharram. Solemn entry of Selim I into Cairo.

February/Muharram. Pillaging and fires in Cairo. Massacre of the Circassians.

April 10/19 Rajab. Battle of Wardan, to the north of Cairo; Mamluks defeated.

April 14/23 Rajab. Taken prisoner, Tumanbay is hanged at Bab Zuwayla, one of the gates of Cairo.

September 10/Ramadan. Selim I, undisputed leader of Egypt and the Syrian territories, takes the caliph Mutawakkil to Istanbul.

The Economy

1302/701

Trade treaty between Venice and Egypt.

1313–1316/712–715

Al-Nasir Muhammad increases the property holdings of his court from $\frac{1}{6}$ to $\frac{5}{12}$ of the Egyptian iqta' land.

1322/722

The Mamluks pillage Lajazzo, port in Little Armenia used by Genoan and Venetian merchants for spices and silks.

1347/748

Lajazzo surrounded by Muslims but supported by the West. The Mamluks take Lajazzo and make the town pay tribute to the sultan of Cairo in order to reroute trade from the East towards Egypt.

1348/749

Plague in Damascus.

1359/760

Decline of the port of Aydhab on the Red Sea benefits Sawakin, further to the south. The Mamluks take Adana and Tarsus, where the Venetians purchase goods from the East.

1399–1412/801–815

Under the sultan Faraj, several severe measures enacted against foreign merchants.

15th century

Collapse of agriculture due to more than a dozen plague epidemics. The revenue from agriculture declines from 9 to less than 2 million Dinar. The Mamluks develop urban crafts and long-distance trade as an alternative source of revenue. Merchants gain positions of power in the Mamluk court.

1415/818

Treaty with Venice. Number of civil servants decreased to reduce government spending.

The Mamluk "Order"

The regime in Egypt, during the Mamluk era, is organized around Islamic culture, disseminated thanks to charitable endowments (*waqf*), the mosques, the *madrasas*, the *dar al-hadith*, the *khanaqah* and the *zawiya*.

The state is based on a military oligarchy with its origin in slavery. The military class constitutes an instrument of war to be reckoned with. At the time of military campaigns, the regular army receives the help of militias, which contain in their ranks Bedouins who are a real danger for the government.

At the beginning of the 15th century/9th century, the emir, raised to the sultanate, marked his accession to this supreme function by awarding those who had helped him reach it. To ensure his safety, the sultan purchased new Mamluks to enlist in his army. He set them up in the citadel of Cairo, after having expelled the troops of his predecessor. But he remained at the mercy of jealous emirs close to power.

1421/824

Al-Zahir Tatar eliminates the concessions granted to foreigners and limits their stay to four months.

1422–1438/825–842

Barsbay confirms the concessions of the treaty of 1415. Futile protests by the consul of Venice, Dandolo. In autumn of each year, the great fair (the *mudda*) of Alexandria, where Europeans are forced to pay high entry taxes.

From 1426/829

Monopoly of the state over spices from the East and local sugar and the local trade of meat and grains leads to shortages and increases in prices, and the devaluation of the currency. Inflation depresses agriculture, industry and trade. Fiscal policy does not look forward; the state exists on emer-gency measures and profits gained in the transit trade. Jidda, important trading post for trade coming from the Indian Ocean via the Red Sea.

1426 and 1430/829 and 835

Barsbay fails in an attempt to coin local Egyptian currency (Ashrafi gold dinars) to replace the Venetian and Florentine gold coins that had replaced local Egyptian currency.

1438/841

Aydhab, supplanted by Sawakin, had been until now the port of embarkation for pilgrims from the Bilad al-Sudan.

1458/862

Monetary reform of Inal: gold and silver coins dating from his predecessor removed from circulation, and a more stable currency is minted. Punishment of counterfeiters.

1487/893

Discovery of the maritime route from the Cape of Good Hope to India. Ibn Majid hired as captain of a ship in Melindi by Vasco da Gama.

1491/898

Sultan Qaytbay decrees that the *waqfs* pay five months-worth of revenues, in order to fill his empty treasury.

1498/903

May 18/26 Ramadan. The Portuguese dock at the Muslim port of Kalikat; beginning of "colonial" trade. Decline of Mamluk long-distance trade.

Beginning of 1500/905

First Portuguese foreign trade office in Calcutta.

Circa 1505/910

The economies and financial situations of Egypt and Venice suffer from the rerouting of trade around the Cape.

Circa 1512/918

Transfer to Lisbon of the European spice trade, further weakening the position of Venice and Egypt.

Religion and Society

1258/656

Death of al-Shadhili (b. 1196/593), founder and luminary of the Shadhilyya, one of the most important Sufi orders of Egypt and North Africa.

1263/661

The sultan Barsbay names one great *qadi* for each of the four "schools" of Sunnism.

1276/675

Death of Ahmad al-Badawi of Tanta, founder of the Egyptian order of the Ahmadis.

1296/695

The Nasiriyya of Cairo. Adaptation of the cruciform mosque to the four schools of Sunnism (*madhahib*).

1317/717

Revolt of the Nusayris, Shi'i extremists from Syria.

1326/726

Death of 'Allamah al-Hilli (b. 1250/648); a.k.a. Ibn al-Mukhtar; theoretician of "twelver" Shi'ism, author of 75 treatises on Shi'ism. He is buried in Najaf.

1328/728

Ibn Tamiyya (b. 1263/661), Hanbali lawyer and theologian, major explicator of orthodox Islam, dies at the citadel of Damascus. He is one of the precursers of Wahhabism.

1448/852

The pious Jaqmaq adds to his titles that of *al-imam al-a'zam*, "the supreme imam," a privilege of the caliphs of Baghdad.

1453/857

With the imamate already hereditary, the sultanate follows suit.

1478/882

Pilgrimage by Qaytbay to Mecca. He concerns himself with the protection of sacred sites in the Hijaz, and has a *madrasa* built, future residence (*dar al-diyafa*) in the 16th/10th century of the emir in charge of the pilgrimage from Egypt to Mecca.

1501/906

End of April/Shawwal. Madrasa and mosque of Qansawh al-Ghawri built in Cairo.

1508/914

Aqaba serves as port for the pilgrims from Egypt, the Maghrib and central Africa. Qansawh al-Ghawri improves the stations along the route of the *hajj* in Sinai, between Aqaba and Cairo.

Art, Architecture

1266/664

Construction of the Zahiriyya, mosque with a cruciform layout, in Cairo.

1282–1283/681

Qalawun's monuments: Ribat al-Mansuri, in Jerusalem; Bimaristan (hospital) al-Mansuri, in Cairo, endowed by a charitable *waqf*.

1284/683

Mosque of Qalawun in Cairo.

1303/702

Completion of the mosque of Barsbay II Jashankir in Cairo.

1317/717

Mosque of Nasr on the Citadel of Cairo built, ornamented with Persian art.

1356/757

Madrasa of the sultan Hasan in Cairo, at the foot of the citadel, one of the most important monuments of Mamluk architecture.

1384/786

Mosque of Barquq.

1412/815

The sultan al-Mu'ayyad Shaykhi has a mosque constructed in Cairo that becomes a center of religious life until the 18th century.

1449/853

A mosque and, two years later, the Jami' Abu Sa'id *madrasa* founded by Jaqmaq.

1475/880

Funerary mosque of the sultan Qaytbay.

Civilization and Culture

1270/668–669

Death of Ibn Abi Usaybi'a, doctor, author of the *'Uyun al-anba'*, collection of 380 biographies of doctors. Death of Ibn Sab'in, a partisan of "existential monism," a contemporary of Thomas Aquinas.

1274/672

Death of Ibn Malik, grammarian.

1282/681

Death of Ibn Khallikan (b. 1211/608), author of the *Wafayat al-a'yan*, a biographical dictionary containing information on more 800 great men.

1288/687

Death of Ibn al-Nafis (b. 1213/610), Egyptian doctor who discovered pulmonary circulation.

1290/689

Ibn Manzur completes the *Lisan al-'Arab*, a dictionary.

1311/711

Death of Ibn Daniyal, Arab writer from Egypt and ophthalmologist. Author of the oldest "shadow" plays from medieval Egypt written in rhyme and free verse.

1331/732

October/Muharram. In Hama, death of the Ayyubid prince Abu al-Fida, historian and geographer, author of the *Taqwim al-Buldan* and the *Mukhtasar Ta'rikh al-Bashar*.

1332/732

June/Ramadan. In Cairo, death of al-Nuwairi, author of the *Nihayat al-arab, fi funun al-adab*, an encyclopedia.

1348/749

Death of Shihab al-Din Ahmad Ibn Fadl Allah al-'Umari, author of the encyclopedic work, *Masalik al-absar fi mamalik al-amsar*, and a handbook on administration, *Ta'rif bi al-mustalah al-sharif*.

1360/761

Death of Jamal al-Din Ibn Hisham, lawyer and grammarian, born in 1310/708; wrote treatise on syntax, *Mughni al-labib*.

1363/764

Death of Salah al-Din Safadi, born in 1296 or 1297/696 or 697, encyclopedist of Turkish descent; 33 works, among them *al-Wafi bi al-wafayat*, a biographical dictionary in 30 volumes.

1373/774

Death of Ibn Kathir (born circa 1300/700), historian and traditionalist, disciple of Ibn Taymiyya; wrote *al-Bidaya wa al-Nihaya*, a history of Islam (14 vol.) and *Kitab al-Jami*.

1418/821

July/Jumada II. Death of Shihab al-Din al-Qalaqashandi, Shafi'i lawyer born in 1355/756; wrote *Subh al-a'sha fi sina'at al-insha*, a writing manual for secretaries in the administration, a seven-volume encyclopedia, and *Nihayat al-'Arab*, a genealogical text.

1429/833

October/Muharram. An envoy sent by Shah Rukh asks for manuscript copies of the *Commentary on the Collection of hadith by al-Bukhari*, by Ibn Hajar al-'Asqalani, and the *History of the Mamluk Sultans* by Maqrizi.

Beyliks and Ottomans

The destruction of the sultanate of the Seljuqs of Rum (Asia Minor) by the Mongols allowed for the formation of small emirates (*beyliks*) created around tribes of Turkoman origin who had settled on the periphery of the sultanate in the second half of the 13th century. The most active of these *beyliks* conquer the last Byzantine territories in Asia Minor; among them, the *beylik* of Osman ('Uthman, which gives us *Ottoman*) by the end of the 14th century dominates all of Western Asia Minor and gets a foothold in the Balkans. Temporarily destabilized by Tamerlane's campaign in Asia Minor in 1402, it finds its vitality again in 1420 and reaches its zenith in 1453 with the conquest of Constantinople.

The goal of the Ottomans is nevertheless to build an empire capable of imposing its will on the Muslim dynasties of the Near East and on the European powers, Austria and Spain, which block the Ottomans' path of expansion toward the West.

If the Ottomans do not yet have a noteworthy literary tradition, they do develop a religious architecture that, in Bursa, Edirne (Adrianople) and Istanbul (Constantinople), reveals an original and powerful artistry, reinforced by a ceramic decor whose zenith is reached in the 16th century.

The Turkoman Beyliks of Anatolia

Qaraman (southwest of western Konya and Taurus)

Circa 1256/654
The Ermenak region under control of Qaraman.

Circa 1263–1277/662–676
Mehmed b. Qaraman intervenes in the Seljuq sultanate.

1300–1307/700–707
Extension of the *beylik* into Seljuq territory.

1356–1396/757–799: Reign of 'Alae al-Din b. Khalil Bey
The Ottomans take Konya and Qaraman.

1402–1423/805–826
After the reconstitution of the *beylik*, the region is shaken by multiple crises; the Ottomans intervene.

Eshref (Beyshehir region)

End of the 13th century–1326/7th century–726
In competition with Qaraman; Eshref wiped out by the Mongols. Territory divided between Qaraman and Hamid.

Hamid (western Pamphylia and Pisidia)

Before 1300/700
One *beylik* leader in the Egridir region, another in Antalya.

1373–1381/775–783
Antalya occupied by the Cyprians.

1391–1392/793–794
Annexation of the *beylik* by the Ottomans.

1402–1423/805–826
Reconstitution of the *beylik*, followed by permanent occupation by the Ottomans.

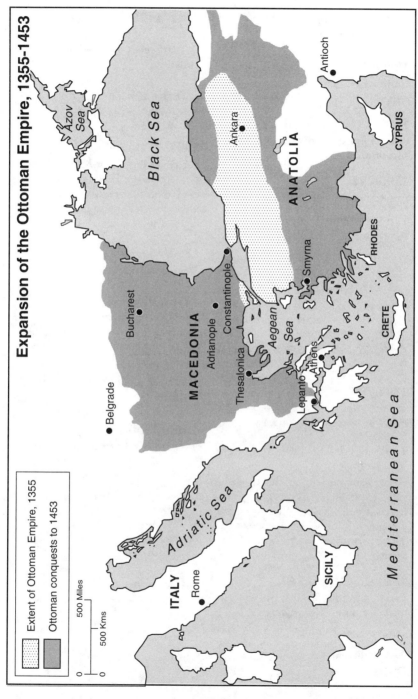

Expansion of the Ottoman Empire, 1355-1453

Extent of Ottoman Empire, 1355

Ottoman conquests to 1453

500 Miles

500 Kms

Azov Sea

Black Sea

Antioch

CYPRUS

Ankara

ANATOLIA

RHODES

Smyrna

Bucharest

Constantinople

MACEDONIA

Adrianople

Aegean Sea

Thesalonica

CRETE

Belgrade

Athens

Lepanto

Adriatic Sea

ITALY

Rome

SICILY

Mediterranean Sea

Menteshe (southwest of Asia Minor)

1280/679

Certified existence of a bey of Menteshe.

1300-1310/700-710

Occupation of Rhodes by the bey of Menteshe.

1390/792

Annexation by the Ottomans.

1402-1410/805-813

Momentarily independent, the *beylik* is permanently annexed.

Aydin (west central Asia Minor)

1307/707

Aydinoghlu Mehmed Bey creates the *beylik*.

1308/708

Conquest of Birgi (Pyrgion), hegemony in western Anatolia.

1334-1348/734-749: Reign of 'Umur Bey

He initiates attack on the Cyclades and Thessalonica, takes Chio and comes to the aid of the Byzantine pretender John VI Cantacuzenos in Thrace, helping him to become emperor.

1344-1348/745-749

Latin expedition against Smyrna (Izmir). Death of 'Umur Bey.

1390/792

Annexation of the *beylik* by the Ottoman Bayezid I.

1402-1425/805-828

Reconstitution of the *beylik*, followed by permanent annexation by the Ottomans.

Sarukhan (north of the beylik of Aydin)

1305-1346/704-747

Sarukhan Bey, from Manisa (Magnesia), fights the Persian king's Catalonian mercenaries. Imposes the payment of a tribute upon the Genoans of Phocia.

1390/792

Annexation by the Ottomans.

1402/805

Barely re-established, the *beylik* is permanently conquered by the Ottoman sultan.

Qaresi (northwest of Asia Minor)

Circa 1330/730

Two brothers (names unknown), sons of Karesi, beys in Balikesir and Bergama, attain hegemony in northern Anatolia.

Circa 1340/741

Annexation of the *beylik* by the Ottoman Orkhan.

Germiyan (west of the Anatolian plateau)

Circa 1300/700

Independence of the *beylik*; flourishes until the middle of the 14th century.

1363–1387/764–784: Reign of Sulayman Shah

Policy of strengthening ties with Murad I. His daughter marries the Ottoman heir Bayezid.

1390/792

Annexation of the *beylik* by Bayezid.

1402–1428/805–831

Good relations between Ya'qub II and the Ottomans, who annex the *beylik* following his death.

Sahib Ata (the Afyon Karahisar region)

After 1250/648

The region is ceded as *iqta'* to the Seljuq vizier Fakhr al-Din 'Ali (Sahib 'Ata).

Beginning of the 14th century/8th century

The *beylik* becomes independent.

1324/724

Comes under the suzerainty of the Germiyans.

After 1341/742

Annexation by the Germiyans.

Jandar or Isfandiyar (northern coast of Asia Minor)

End of the 13th century/7th century

A Mongolian vassal *beylik* founded near Kastamonu, by Shams al-Din Jandar.

1301–1340/700–741

Sulayman, son of Shams al-Din Jandar, gains his independence. He takes Sinope.

1392/794

The *beylik* comes under Ottoman domination.

1402–1440/805–843

The *beylik* is reconstituted. Good relations with the Ottomans.

1460/864

The bey Isma'il deposed by sultan Mehmed II.

Pervane (Sinopean region)

Before 1277/676

The Sinopean region is the domain of the Seljuq vizier Mu'in al-Din Pervane.

1300–1322/700–722

After the death of Gazi Tshelebi, the *beylik* is annexed by the Jandar.

Eretna (eastern Anatolia)

Circa 1250/648

Eastern Anatolia a Mongolian protectorate governed by Tshobanoghlu Timurtash.

1326–1352/726–753

Eretna is governor.

1380/782

Quarrels over succession; Burhan al-Din of Amasya controls the territory.

Burhan al-Din
(Amasya-Sivas)

1377-1381/779-793

The *qadi* Burhan al-Din Ahmed takes power in Amasya, then in Sivas, and proclaims himself sultan.

1384-1387/786-789

The *qadi* is victorious over the Ottomans; vanquished by the Mongols.

1398/801

After the death of Burhan al-Din Ahmed, the Ottomans occupy the territory.

The Ottomans (beginning of the 14th century-1512)

War and Foreign Relations

Circa 1280–circa 1324/679-724

'Uthman (Osman) I (1300–1324) leads a *beylik* in northwestern Anatolia.

1291-1300/690-700

Conquest of northern Phrygia and eastern Bithynia.

1308/708

The shores of the North Sea and the Marmara taken.

Circa 1324–1360/724–763: Reign of Orkhan, 'Uthman's son
1326/726

April/Jumada I. Bursa taken, becomes capital of the Ottomans.

1329

Defeat of the Byzantines in the battle of Maltepe (Pelekanon).

1331/731

March/Jumada II. Nicaea (Iznik) taken.

1332-1338/732-738

Izmit and Üsküdar (Skutari, near Constantinople) taken.

Circa 1340/741

Occupation of the *beylik* of Qaresi; access to the Dardanelles.

1346-1348/747-749

Military assistance to the Byzantine pretender John VI Cantacuzenos by Orkhan; he marries Cantacuzenos' daughter Theodora and sends Ottoman troops into Thrace.

1353/754

Suleyman Pasha, Orkhan's son, supports John Cantacuzenos at Adrianople (Edirne).

1354-1356/755-757

The Gallipoli peninsula taken by Suleyman Pasha, followed by the capture of several towns in eastern Thrace.

1360/761

Death of Orkhan.

1361-1389/762-791

Reign of Murad I, Orkhan's son. He for the first time takes the title of sultan.

1362/763

Andrianople (Edirne) and Philippopoli (Filibe) taken. Edirne becomes the new Ottoman capital. The Byzantines acknowledge Ottoman suzerainty and pay regular tribute, while the Ottomans pledge not to interfere in the food supply of the Byzantines, which comes from Ottoman-controlled territory.

1364/765

Defeat of the Hungarian-Bosnian-Serbian-Valachian-Papacy coalition by the Ottomans, near the Maritsa River. Bulgaria partly controlled by Murad I.

1366/767

August/Dhu'l-Qa'da. Gallipoli reclaimed by Amadeus of Savoy.

1371

Defeat of the Bulgars and Serbs (under Tzar Shishman) in the battle of Samako. Devastating defeat of the Serbs at Tshernomen on the Maritsa River; eastern Thrace taken and Macedonia taken.

1376-1382/778-784

Sofia taken. The Czar of Bulgaria a vassal of the sultan.

1385-1387/787-789

Gallipoli reoccupied by Murad. Ottoman raid on Albania.

1386/788

Salonika taken. Expeditions into the Balkans.

1388/790

Defeat of the Ottomans at Plocnik by a coalition of Serbs, Bulgars and Bosnians.

1389/791

June 20/24 Jumada II. Defeat of the Serbs in Kosovo. Assassination of Murad I.

1389-1402/791-804: Reign of Bayezid I Yildirim ("The Thunderbolt"), Murad's son

1389-1391/791-793

Ottoman suzerainty in Serbia, Bosnia and Valachia. Annexation of several *beyliks* in western Anatolia.

1390/792

Conquest of Philadelphia, the last Byzantine stronghold in Asia Minor.

1393-1395/795-797

Occupation of southern Albania. Conquest of Tivarno and the Danube territory from the Bulgars.

1394/796

Bayezid assumes the title "Sultan al-Rum."

1395-1397/797-799

Siege on Constantinople by Bayezid. Conquest of Thessalonika.

1396/798

September 25/20 Dhu'l-Hijja. Crushing Ottoman victory in Nicopolis over an army of Venetian, Hungarian and Byzantine Crusaders. Total occupation of Bulgaria.

1397/801

Argos and the Peloponnes taken.

Spring 1402/804

The Mongol Tamerlane (Timur) in Anatolia.

1402/804

July 27/28 Dhu'l-Hijja. Bayezid defeated and taken prisoner by Tamerlane near Ankara. He dies several months later.

1402–1413/804–816

Struggle for power among Bayezid's sons: Suleyman (1403–1411 in Edirne/Rumelia), Mehmed (in Amasya, later Bursa/Antatolia), 'Isa (in Bursa), and Musa.

1403/805

Autonomy of the *beyliks* restored, Byzantium relieved of Ottoman pressure.

1413–1421/816–824: Reign of Mehmed (Muhammad) I "Tshelebi"

Restoration of the Ottoman state to the area defined by the borders established prior to 1402, after Mehmed defeats his rival Musa. He attempts to unify the state politically and religiously.

1416/820

Venetian naval victory over the Ottomans at Gallipoli.

1421–1444: Reign of Murad II
1422/825

Unsuccessful attempt to take Constantinople.

1424/827

Byzantium, Serbia, Valachia and Hungary under Ottoman suzerainty.

1430/833

March/Shawwal. Thessalonika taken from Venica.

1438/842

Semendria in Hungary taken.

1439–1443/843–847

John Hunyady, important military officer from Transylvania, triumphs over the Ottomans and reclaims southern Serbia, leading a Crusader army of Hungarians, Poles, Serbs and Rumanians. Revolt led by George Castriota (Skander Beg) in Albania and Epira.

1444/848

November 10/28 Rajab. Ottoman victory over an army of Crusaders at Izaldi (Zlatica). Peace of Szegedin: the Danube becomes the border. Hungarians break the treaty; decisive Ottoman victory in the battle of Varna. Murad II abdicates in favor of his son Mehmed II.

1446/850

The despots of Morea, vassals of the sultan.

1446–1451/850–855

Murad II back in power.

1448/852

Second battle of Kosovo. Defeat of Serbs and Hungarians led by John Hunyady; conquest of Transylvania.

1451–1481: Reign of Mehmed II
1453/857

April 6/26 Rabi I. Beginning of the siege on Constantinople.

May 29/18 Jumada II. Constantinople taken; it becomes capital of the Ottoman Empire.

Summer 1458–summer 1460/ 862–864

Conquest of Morea.

1455/859

The Genoese island empire in the Aegean taken.

1456/860
Unsuccessful siege of Belgrade. Ottomans pushed back to Bulgaria: death of John Hunyady gives them relief.

1457–1458/861–862
Defeat of Serbia.

1459/863
January/ Rabi I. Athens taken.
Summer. Total occupation of Serbia, except Belgrade.

1461–1462/865–867
Annexation of Valachia.

Summer 1463/867
Conquest of Bosnia.

Spring 1468/872
Death of Skander Beg (Albania).

1473/878
August/Rabi I. Treaty between Mehmed II and the Aq-Qoyunlu Uzun Hasan after defeat of the latter. Occupation of the area from eastern Anatolia to the Euphrates.

1474/879
Conquest of Cilicia.

1475/880
June/Safar. Crimea under Ottoman suzerainty. Kefe (Kaffa, Theodosia) taken from the Genoese.

1476–1478/881–883
Total occupation of Albania, which becomes an Ottoman province.

1479–1481/884–886
August to July/Rajab–Jumada II. Incursion into southern Italy (Otrante).

1479/884
Peace with Venice as a result of a siege of Scutari (from 1474).

1481–1512/886–918: Reign of Bayezid II
1481/886
June 20/22 Rabi II. Defeat of Jem, who revolted against the sultan Bayezid II, his brother; he finds refuge with the Mamluks in Syria, is later found in Cairo, and threatens the empire until his death (1495).

1482/887
May–September/Rabi II–Shawwal. New attempt by Jem in Anatolia. Vanquished, he flees to Rhodes where the Knights of St. John send him to France, an action initiated by the great ruler Peter of Aubusson. He dies in Naples in February of 1495.

1483/888
Permanent conquest of Herzegovina.

1484/889
July/Jumada II. Control of the northwestern coast of the Black Sea (Kilia, Akkerman).

1485–1491/890–896
War with the Mamluks for Cilicia.

1488/893
Ottomans defeated at Qaysariyya (Agha Chayri).

1491/895
Peace treaty with the Mamluks; loss of Adana and Tarsus.

1492/897
Expeditions to Syria, Carinthia, Carnolia, defeated at Villach.

1496-1501/901-907
Occupation of Montenegro. Lepanto and Durazzo taken.

1497-1499/902-905
Invasion of Poland; this action is not pursued.

Spring 1511/917
Southeastern and central Anatolia partly occupied by the Safavid Isma'il, who retreats to Iran in August.

1512/918
May 26/10 Rabi I. Death of Bayezid II, dethroned on April 25/8 Safar by his son Selim, who was not designated as his successor.

Internal Affairs, Institutions

1326/726
Bursa becomes capital of the Ottoman state.

Circa 1339/730
Creation of a regular corps of infantrymen (*yaya*) and of cavalrymen (*müsellem*).

Circa 1340/741
Organization of the *beylik* into provinces (*sanjak*).

1346/747
Orkhan marries Theodora, daughter of John VI Cantacuzenos, in return for his support against emperor John V Palaidogos.

Circa 1360-1363/761-764
The *penjyek* (*penjik:* the fifth) instituted, according to which the Ot-

toman bey would keep only ⅕ of all booty. Organization of the Janissary corps, the elite troops of the sultan from the conquered Balkan regions (see box: *devshirme*) on page 127.

1362/763
The Ottomans gain control of the *akhi* fraternity of Ankara from the Germiyans.

After 1362/763
Creation of the *beylerbeyilik* (district) of Rumelia (European provinces).

After 1376/778
The conquered territories on the Balkans are divided into *timar*. Turkomans from Anatolia are resettled in different regions of the Balkans.

1385/787
Jandarli Qara Khalil, first Ottoman grand vizier (*sadr-i a'zam*). The position remains with his family, the Jandarli, during the next centuries.

1388/790
The title of sultan appears in the official title of Murad I.

1393/795
The *beylerbeyilik* of Anatolia is founded.

Around 1395/797
Devshirme ("levy of boys") of Christian children in the Balkan provinces instituted and a corps of *'ajemi oghlan* ("foreign children") created.

1402-1413/804-816
War between the sons of Bayezid I over succession. Reconstitution of the Turkoman *beyliks*.

1413/816

July/Rabi II. A victorious Mehmed I reunifies the Ottoman state. Creation of the *beylerbeyilik* of Rum (Amasya-Sivas).

1413-1421/816-824

Restoration of the *ghazi* tradition under the pressure of the old Turkish aristocracy; political importance of the Jandarli grand viziers; ties to the *akhi* fraternity.

1418-1420/821-823

Revolt of a religious and social nature by the shaykh Badr al-Din begins in Anatolia, then moves to Valachia and Dobroja. Appearance of the alleged son of Bayezid I, Düzme Mustafa, ("the false Mustafa") who, once vanquished, hides in Constantinople.

1428-1429/831-832

All of western Anatolia under Ottoman domination.

1444/848

August/Jumada I. Abdication of Murad II in favor of his son Mehmed. Retakes power in August of 1446 because of outside threats.

1452/856

The Rumeli Hisar fortress on the European coast of the Bosphorus built.

1453/857

May 29/18 Jumada I. Constantinople, henceforth known as Istanbul, taken.

June 1/21 Jumada I. Reorganization of the Ottoman government; beginning of importance of soldiers gathered through the *devshirme*. Appointment of Sulayman Bey as governor of Istanbul and of Gennadios Scholarios as orthodox patriarch.

1453-1456/857-860

First rules (*qanunname*) decreed by Mehmed II concerning living conditions and obligations of subjects of the empire.

1454-1460/858-864

Ordinances on the repopulating of Constantinople.

1458/862

Mehmed II settles in Istanbul, which becomes the capital.

1470/874

Decree made by Mehmed II on the "secularization" and confiscation of the *waqf* in order to raise revenues.

1476/881

The organization of the state is regulated, institutionalized and codified in a number of collections of laws (*qanunname*).

1481/886

May/Rabi II. Revolt led by Jem, Bayezid II's brother.

Circa 1490-1495/895-900

Development of the Ottoman navy, which is led in the western Mediterranean by Kemal Reis. Palace of Galata (Galata Saray) founded for the teaching of the *'ajemi oghlan*.

1501/906

Additions to Mehmed II's *qanunname*.

1510-1511/916-917

Revolt in southern and central Anatolia by the Turkomans (*alevi*) linked to the Safavi shah Isma'il. After initial hesitation, Bayezid defeats the rebels at Bursa.

1512/918

April 25/8 Safar. Selim, son of Bayezid, but not a designated successor, dethrones his father with the help of the Janissaries and becomes sultan.

Aq-Qoyunlu ("White Sheep")

Beginning of the 14th century/7th century

Creation of a federation of Turkoman clans in Diyar Bakr.

Circa 1390/792

Vassal federation of Qadi Burhan al-Din.

1396/798

Qara Yölüq 'Uthman, who established the power of the Aq-Qoyunlu, frees himself from the rule of Burhan al-Din. Obtains complete sovereignty over Diyar Bakr from Tamerlane.

1435/839

Death of Qara Yölüq 'Uthman. Conflicts between his sons until 1453/857.

1453–1478/857–883: Reign of Uzan Hasan

The most important Aq-Qoyunlu ruler.

1460–1461/864–865

Defeated by the Ottomans.

1467–1468/872–873

Victories over the Qara-Qoyunlu Jihan Shah and the Timurid Abu Sa'id. Domination over an area that reaches as far as Baghdad, Herat and the Persian Gulf.

1472/877

Venice seeks an alliance with the Aq-Qoyunlu against the Ottomans.

1490/896

After the death of Ya'qub b. Uzan Hasan, struggles among his sons and nephews. Beginning of the intervention of the Safavid Isma'il.

1502/908

Defeat of the Aq-Qoyunlu Alvand by Isma'il, who assumes control over the territory. An autonomous principality exists for several years in the Mardin-Urfa region.

1524/920

Death of the last Aq-Qoyunlu, Murad b. Ya'qub, in Urfa.

Qara-Qoyunlu ("Black Sheep")

1351/752

Appearance of the Qara-Qoyunlu led by Bayram Khoja, who controls the Mosul, Ahlat and Erzerum regions.

1372/774

Bayram Khoja extends his dominion to eastern Anatolia and Azerbaijan.

1377/779

Khoja forced to recognize the suzerainty of the Jalayrids. He dies in 1380/782.

1380–1389/782–791: Reign of Qara Mehmed

He frees himself from his Jalayrid tutelage and takes Tabriz.

1390-1420/792-823: Reign of Qara Yusuf

1402-1405/805-808

The Qara-Qoyunlu territory occupied by Tamerlane.

1405-1420/808-823

Qara Yusuf restores the Qara-Qoyunlu state, triumphs over the Aq-Qoyunlu, extends his domain from eastern Anatolia to western Iran and all of Iraq.

1408/811

Defeat of the Timurid Miranshah.

1412/814

Baghdad taken.

1420-1428/823-831: Reign of Iskandar

He reinforces the Qara-Qoyunlu domination of Azerbaijan and the territories conquered by his father.

1439-1467/843-872: Reign of Jihan Shah

Zenith of the Qara-Qoyunlu state.

1467-1469/872-874

Jihan Shah vanquished and killed by Uzan Hasan; his territories under the domination of the Aq-Qoyunlu.

The Economy

1327/727

First silver money (*akçe* = asper) minted by Orkhan.

1352/753

Political and economic accord with Genoa.

1388/790

Trade treaty with Venice.

Devshirme

This Ottoman term refers specifically to the removing of Christian children in the Balkan provinces of the Empire. This practice, which apparently started during the reign of Bayezid I around 1395, does not seem to have been annual. It consisted of a recruitment, by an officer of the Janissaries, of children and adolescents, between eight and 16 years old, in the Balkan villages chosen randomly; this recruitment was imposed on a few hundred individuals. These young people were sent to Anatolia to live with Turkish families, where they became Muslim as well as Turkish. Assembled next in Gallipoli (and, later, in Istanbul), they constituted the *'ajemi oghlan* ("foreign children") corps, then, based on their qualities and capabilities, were directed either toward the palace (becoming in that case the *iç oghlan* — "the children on the inside") where they served the sultan directly, or toward the Janissary corps. Starting in the middle of the 15th century, the most important functions of the Ottoman state, notably the grand vizierate, were carried out by individuals who were products of the *devshirme*.

1453/857

June 1/23 Jumada I. Renewal of the trade privileges accorded to the Genoans from Galata.

1454/858

Right to trade accorded to the Venetians in exchange for 200,000 ducats.

1455/859

Beginning of the construction of the Great Bazaar of Istanbul.

1463–1464/867

Construction of an arsenal in Istanbul (in the Kasim Pasha area, in the Golden Horn).

1478/883

First gold money minted in Istanbul.

1482/887

January/Muharram. Treaty with Venice; renewal of trade privileges, abandonment of the 200,000 ducat tribute.

1488/893

Declaration of rules concerning mining in Serbia.

1492/897

Jews expelled from the Iberian peninsula, received in Avlona, Salonika and Constantinople.

1496/901

Ottoman ports closed to Venetian ships.

1502/908

December 14/13 Jumada II. Peace with Venice. Trade with Venice resumes.

Literature

1271–1332/670–732

Ashik Pasha, author of the *Gharibname*.

Circa 1300/700

Gülshehri, lyric poet and mystic.

End of the 14th century/8th century

Qadi Burhan al-Din Ahmed, head of state, lawyer and poet.

1390/792

The *Iskendername* by Ahmedi.

Beginning of the 15th century/9th century

The *Mevlid* by Suleyman Çelebi. The chronicles of Yazijizade 'Ali: *Tarikh-i Al-i Seljuq; Mogholname; Oghuzname.*

1464/868

The *Düsturname* by Enveri.

1474/879

Death of the mathematician and astronomer 'Ali Kushju, student of the Timurid Ulugh Bey.

1400–1480/802–885

'Ashikpashazade, chronicler.

1497–1499/903–905

First Hebrew printing press in Istanbul.

1497–1499/903–905

Dursun Bey: *Tarikh-i Abu al-Fath.*

1501/907

Hesht Bihisht, by Idris Bitlisi.

Beylik Art, Ottoman Art

1302/702
Great Mosque of Ermenak built.

1336/736
Establishment of the Orkhan *madrasa* in Iznik.

1340–1347/741–748
Mosque of Orkhan in Bursa built.

1363/764
The Murad I *madrasa* in Bursa.

1366/767
Great Mosque of Manisa built.

1374/776
Mosque of Isa Bey built in Seljuq.

1378/780
The Green Mosque of Iznik built.

1390–1395/792–797
Mosque and *madrasa* of Bayezid I built in Bursa.

1394–1399/796–801
The Great Mosque of Bursa built.

1396/798
Anadolu Hisar (Anatolian fortress) built on the Asiatic coast of the Bosphorus.

15th century/9th century
Mosque of Haji Bayram built in Ankara.

1405/807
Bedesten (market) built in Bursa.

1415–1420/818–820
Green Mosque in Bursa embellished with faience.

1421/824
Green Türbe (tomb), built for Mehmed I in Bursa, embellished with faience.

1426/829
Creation of a Muradiye *madrasa* in Bursa.

1437–1447/841–851
Mosque of the three balconies (Üç Sherefeli) built in Edirne (Adrianople).

1452/856
Rumeli Hisar (European fortress) built on the European coast of the Bosphorus.

1454–1458/858–862
Eski Saray palace built in Istanbul.

1461/865
The Great Bazaar built in Istanbul.

1463–1471/867–871
Mosque of the Conqueror (Fatih) built in Istanbul.

1472/877
The Faience Pavillion (Çinili Köshk) built in Istanbul.

1472/877
Topkapi palace built in Istanbul.

1483–1484/888–889
Mosque, *madrasa* and hospital built under Bayezid II in Edirne.

After 1490/895
Iznik becomes the most important center for ceramics in the empire.

1501–1505/907–911
Mosque of Bayezid II built in Istanbul.

The Mongols in the Middle East and Central Asia

While certain Mongol Khans in the Middle East convert to Islam, others react violently to the presence of Muslims, such as Hülegü, who exterminates the Assassins then conquers and destroys Baghdad, forcing the 'Abbasid caliph to flee, or Arghun, who seeks, without success, to ally with the Europeans.

During the same era, Marco Polo crosses the Mongolian states, from Asia Minor to the heart of China. Tamerlane (Timur Lang) imposes, little by little, his authority over the many states that had appeared in central Asia in order to recreate the empire of Genghis Khan. Having made it first as far as Syria, then Asia Minor, where he triumphs over the Ottoman sultan Bayezid I, he dies soon after his return to Samarkand. His son Shah Rukh is unable to prevent the Turkoman tribe of the Qara-Qoyunlu (Black Sheep) from taking the western part of the territories (Iran, Azerbaijan); this tribe is succeeded by the Aq-Qoyunlu (White Sheep).

The end of the 15th century sees the emergence of another Turkoman group, the Safavids, who profess Shi'ism; they dominate eastern Anatolia and western Azerbaijan, but will soon be under the sway of the Ottomans.

Political Life

1252/650
Batu, the khan of the Golden Horde, converts to Islam.

1256–1265/654–663:
Reign of Berke, khan of Qipchak, and a brother of Hülegü, Islamic Convert
1256/654
Hülegü founds the Mongol dynasty of Persia. Hülegü takes Alamut, the fortress of the Assassins, whom he exterminates.

1258/656
February 12/6 Safar. Baghdad taken by Hülegü; end of the 'Abbasid caliphate. The *atabeg* of Mosul submits to the rule of the Mongols. The Ayyubids of Syria, except those in Damascus, seek help from Hülegü to reconquer Egypt.

1259/657
Ultimatum issued by the Mongols to the Ayyubid al-Malik al-Nasir of Damascus; they cross the Euphrates; al-Malik al-Nasir asks for support from Qutuz, the sultan of Egypt.

1260/658
Siege and destruction of Aleppo, conquest of Damascus (by general Kitbugha). Hülegü returns to Qaraqarum after the death of his brother Möngke, Great Khan of the Mongols. Qubilay becomes Great Khan. The Mamluks under Baybar stop the Mongol invasion by their victory of 'Ayn Jalut.

1260–1262/658–660
War between Hülegü and the khan of Qipchak.

1265/663
Death of Hülegü.

1265–1281/663–680: Reign of
Abaqa Khan, Hülegü's son
Establishment of the Ilkhan dynasty
in Iran.

1266/664
Qaydu Khan takes Kashgaria from
the Çaghatayds.

1267–1280/665–678
Möngke Temür becomes khan of the
Golden Horde; he is a follower of
tribal shamanism.

1277/678
Baybar defeats the Mongols in Elbistan (Asia Minor).

1281/680
Qalawun defeats the Mongols at
Hims (Syria).

1284/683
Anti-Muslim policy of the Ilkhan
Arghun, son of Abaqa, adept of Bud-
dhism; his vizier, Sa'd al-Dawla, remaining faithful to his Judaism, still
holds de facto power.

1288–1290/687–690
Arghun attempts to form an alliance
with European Christians against Islam.

1290/690
In Delhi, accession of the Khalji,
Afghan dynasty of Turkish origin.

1291/690
Exchange of letters between Arghun
and Philip the Fair concerning a Crusade.

1294/693
The Ilkhans try to introduce paper
money; collapse of the Iranian economy.

1295/694
Ghazan Khan, son of Arghun, sets up
his capital in Tabriz. Converted to
Sunni Islam, he organizes a government based on Islamic principles.
The Ilkhans become the national dynasty of Iran.

1296/695
'Ala al-Din Khalji Muhammad Shah
becomes sultan of Delhi; he reconquers Gujarat in 1297/696.

1299/698
Ghazan defeats the Mamluks of
Egypt at Hims; temporary occupa-
tion of Syria.

1304/1316–703/716:
Reign of Öljeytü Khudabanda,
son of Arghun and successor
to Ghazan
Attempts to make twelver Shi'ism official; friendly relations with the European powers.

1307/706
Öljeytü builds Sultaniyya as his new
capital.

1310/710
Öljeytü becomes a Shi'i Muslim.

1313/713
Öljeytü besieges Rahba on the Euphrates; siege unsuccessful. Inauguration of Sultaniyya, the new capital of
the Mongols from Persia.

1313–1341/713–742
Özbeg, khan of the Golden Horde, converts to Islam.

1317–1335/717–735:
Reign of Abu Saʿid
First Ilkhanite ruler to have Muslim name. Adheres to Sunni Islam.

1320/720
The Tughluqid Turks replace the Khalji in Delhi.

1323/723
Peace between the Ilkhans and the Mamluks.

1324/724
A Venetian resident in Tabriz.

1325/725
Accidental death of Ghiyath al-Din Tughluq, sultan of Delhi. Accession of his son Muhammad.

1333/734
Tarmarshirin, prince of the Çaghatay khanate, converts to Islam and takes the name ʿAla al-Din. In central Asia, revolt of the Mongol Buzan against his uncle Tarmarshirin. Death of Abu Saʿid. Disintegration of the Ilkhan state, rise of local dynasties.

1336/736
April/Shawwal. Birth of Timur Lang (Tamerlane) in Kadr, in Transoxiana.

1336–1412/736–815
The Mongol Jalayrids dominate Iraq and Azerbaijan.

1347–1358/748–759
ʿAla al-Din Hasan Bahman Shah founds the independent kingdom of the Bahmamids of Madura (India).

1359–1361/760–762
The Golden Horde disintegrates.

1365/766
Beginning of Timur's conquests.

1369/770
Timur, sole ruler of Khurasan and Transoxiana, from whose lands he expelled Tugha-Timur. Expedition against the Çaghatayads of Kashgaria.

1370/771
April/Ramadan. Timur, ruler of Balkh.

1376–1405/778–807
The Golden Horde is united for the last time under Toqtamish.

1378/780
Timur conquers Khwarizm.

1380/782
Timur invades Khurasan. Occupation of Herat, strategic site on the trade routes leading from the Mediterranean to India and China.

1382/784
Timur threatens the Aq-Qoyunlu (White Sheep) tribes settled in Diyar Bakr; threatens the Qara-Qoyunlu (Black Sheep) tribes from the Mosul region, and allies with the prince of Baghdad, Ahmad b. Uways al-Jalayri. Unification of the White and Golden Hordes by Toqtamish; Moscow is taken.

1383/785

Timur reaches the Caspian Sea.

1386/788

Timur takes Isfahan, Shiraz and Baghdad. The Jalayrid Ahmad b. Uways, forced to leave Baghdad, beckons Barquq, the sultan of Egypt, to his side.

1386–1387/788–789

Timur occupies Fars, Iraq, Luristan and Azerbaijan and forces the sultan Ahmad al-Jalayri to flee.

1387–1391/789–793

Timur defeats the khan of Qipchak.

1393/795

July/Ramadan. Beginning of the "Five Years War." Timur crushes the revolt led by Mansur Shah, eliminates the Muzaffarids and becomes the ruler of Fars.

1393/796

Birth of Ulugh Beg, in Sultaniyya.

1395/797

Timur destroys Siraf and Astrakhan.

1396/798

Timur repulses the attack by Toqtamish; the Qipchak tribes capitulate.

1398/801

September/Muharram. Timur crosses the Indus; in December/Rabi II, he battles the sultan Mahmud near Delhi, which he occupies and sacks. Mahmud Tughluq seeks refuge in Kanawj.

1399/801

Timur chases Ahmad al-Jalayri, sultan of Baghdad, out of Azerbaijan.

Turmoil in Syria. The sultan of Egypt, Faraj, refuses to free a parent of Timur Lang and kills the negotiators.

1400/802

Timur sacks Aleppo, Hama, Hims and Ba'albek. Defeat of the Mamluks of Faraj. Siege on Damascus, during which Timur receives the historian Ibn Khaldun.

1401/803

Damascus capitulates. Timur takes many artisans captive.

July/Dhu'l-Hijja. Timur takes Baghdad by surprise.

1402/805

Defeat of the Ottoman army in the battle of Ankara. Smyrna (Izmir) taken from the Hospitaller Knights of St. John.

1403/806

Autonomy of the Anatolian *beyliks* is restored.

1404/807

Timur returns to Samarkand, where he receives Ruy Gonzalez of Clavijo, who will write an account of his voyage.

1405/807

January/Shawwal. Death of Timur in Otrar, after a reign of 36 years. Shah Rukh succeeds his father. The Qara-Qoyunlu retake Azerbaijan from the Timurids.

1407–1409/809–811

Shah Rukh conquers Transoxiana.

1407/810

Ulugh Beg, governor of a part of Khurasan and Mazandaran.

1408/811

Shah Rukh takes Samarkand, Turkestan and Transoxiana from Khalil Sultan and turns them over to Ulugh Beg.

1410/813

The Qara-Qoyunlu occupy Baghdad. The khan of Qipchak expels the Venetians from Tana.

1426–1486/829–892

Hajji Giray, a descendant of Genghis Khan, founds an independent khanate in the Crimea.

1447/850

March/Dhu'l-Hijja. Ulugh Beg succeeds his father.

1448/852

Ulugh Beg occupies Herat. The Uzbeks invade Transoxiana; Samarkand sacked.

1449/853

October/Ramadan. Ulugh Beg held captive in Shahzukhiya by his son 'Abd al-Latif, who executes him. End of the Timurid Empire.

1451–1526/855–936

The Afghan Lodi dynasty rules in Delhi.

1451–1469/855–873

The Timurid Abu Sa'd rules over Transoxiana, western Turkestan and eastern Iran.

1466/871

Accession of Uzan Hasan Tawil, Dhu'l-Qadirid prince, leader of Aq-Qoyunlu. Zenith of the Turkoman dynasty of the White Sheep (Aq-Qoyunlu), who will reign over a section of Persia and Diyar Bakr, Azerbaijan and Iraq.

1467/872

The Qara-Qoyunlu Empire overthrown by Uzan Hasan. End of the alliance between Safavids and the Aq-Qoyunlu. The Aq-Qoyunlu expand into Persia and Iraq.

1468/872

Uzan Hasan, conqueror of the sultan of Samarkand.

1469/873

Death of Abu Sa'id after his campaign against the Aq-Qoyunlu in Azerbaijan fails.

1469–1506/873–912

Husayn Bayqara, the last important Timurid ruler in Herat (Khurasan).

1470/874

Treaty between Venice and the Aq-Qoyunlu.

1473/878

Uzan Hasan suffers a decisive defeat by the Ottoman Mehmed II.

1478/882

January 6/1 Shawwal. Death of Uzan Hasan. Succeeded by Ya'qub b. Hasan Tawil. Revolt by Shah Isma'il Safavi against the Aq-Qoyunlu.

1483/888

Campaign by Haydar, "twelver" leader of the Safavid Tariqa, against the Cherkesses.

1488/893

July/Shawwal. Defeat of the Safavids in Tabarsaran, southwest of Darband. The shaykh Haydar dies in combat.

1499/905

The Safavid dynasty founded by Shah Isma'il, spiritual and worldly leader of the Qizil bash ("Red caps"), the followers of Haydar organized as military troops.

1500/905

Autumn/Shawal. Isma'il routs Alwand Aq-Qoyunlu in Sharur. Muhammad Shaybani, the khan of a Siberian Mongol state, defeats the last Timurids and establishes the Uzbeg dynasty (Khwarazm and Transoxiana).

1501/907

Shah Isma'il returns to Tabriz, which he makes his capital. Enthroned as the first shah of the Safavid dynasty. Proclaims the Ja'farid rite of "twelver" Shi'ism as the state religion. Shi'ism accepted by the population.

1503/908

Success of Shah Isma'il, near Hamadan, over the sultan Murad.

1504/909

Conquest of Manzandaran and Gurgan.

1506/911

Death of Husayn Bayqara, the Timurid ruler in Khurasan.

1507/913

Diyar Bakr annexed by Shah Isma'il.

1508/914

Shah Isma'il takes Baghdad and occupies Fars.

1509/915

The body of Shaykh Haydar buried in the Safavid necropolis of Ardabil.

1510/916

In Merw, victory over the Uzbek Shaybani; Shah Isma'il annexes Khurasan. Persia under his control.

1512/918

Safavid rout in Gurgan. The Uzbeks in Mashhad. Shah Isma'il reaches a truce. The Safavid state trapped in a vise between two Sunni powers: Uzbeks to the east, Ottomans to the west. Crushed by the Ottomans in 1514/920 in Chaldiran (Azerbaijan).

Religion

1274/673

Death in Baghdad of Nasir al-Din al-Tusi, theoretician of "twelver" Shi'ism. Served the Assassins and, after 1256, the Mongols.

1389/791

Death of the Sufi Muhammad Baha' al-Din Naqshabandi, teacher of the Naqshabandi brotherhood (Turkestan).

Architecture, Art

1322–1412/722–815

Great Mosque (*Jum'a*) of Veramin built.

1371/772

Mausoleum built for Tushuk Bika in Samarkand.

1392/794

Necropolis for Shah Zinda built in Samarkand.

1399/801

In Samarkand, construction of the mosque-*madrasa* of Bibi Khanum, Timur's first wife.

1420/823

Completion of the mosque built by Ulugh Beg in Samarkand. Monastery (*khanaqah*) with the highest dome in the world.

1433/837

December/Jumada I. Death of Baysonghor, son of Shah Rukh and grandson of Timur; protector of the arts and master of the craft of illumination.

Middle of the 15th century/9th century

The Blue Mosque of Tabriz built.

1490/895

In Samarkand, mausoleum of Timur built: the Gur-i-mir ("tomb of the nobles"), masterpiece of Timurid art.

Civilization and Culture

1257/655

The Persian poet Sa'di, (1184–1292/580–692), from Shiraz, writes the *Bustan* ("The Fruit Garden"), followed by the *Gullistan* ("The Rose Garden") in 1258/656. He was a Sufi, who traveled to Gujarat, Delhi, Yemen and North Africa; died in Shiraz.

1271–1295/669–694

Second voyage to China by Marco Polo; crosses Persia.

1294/693

Return of Marco Polo; he then moves on to Persia (Iran).

1317/712

Wassaf becomes court historian of the Mongols in Sultaniyya.

1318/718

Death of Rashid al-Din Tabib, vizier of Ghazan, born around 1247/645, author of *Jami 'al-Tawarikh*, history of the Mongols, followed by a history of the Islamic world and a geographical appendix. His works cover the Islamic world, the Christian West, India, China and Judaism.

1338/739

Death of al-Qazwini Khatib Dimashq, Shafi'i grand *qadi* of Syria and Egypt, author of *Talkhis al-Miftah* and *Idah fi 'Ulum al-Balagha*, works on rhetoric.

1352 or 1361

Death of Khwaju, court poet of the Ilkhans, Jalayrids and Muzaffarids.

1389/791

Death of Sa'd al-Din al-Taftazani, Persian historian and philosopher at Timur's court.

1390/792

Death of Hafiz, born in Shiraz around 1320/720. Persian poet and panegyrist who spoke Arabic and knew the Islamic sciences; he was the author of the famous *Diwan*, a collection of Sufi poetry.

1413/816
Death of 'Ali al-Jurjani, philologist and historian at Timur's court.

1424/832
The Samarkand Observatory built by Ulugh Beg, inventor of powerful instruments for astronomical research. In his own work, he started with Ptolomy's theorem, which he hoped to correct.

1498/903
Death of Mir Akhund (Mirkhond), historian, native of Bukhara who lived in Herat. Author of *Rawdat al-Safa'* ("Garden of Purity"), a universal history in seven volumes.

1501/907
Death of 'Ali Shir Neva'i, poet of Çagatay Turkish at the Timurid court at Herat.

Sub-Saharan Africa

In those lands that have never come under the control of any central caliphate, the conquest of Baghdad by the Mongols passes practically unnoticed. South of the Sahara, Islam is ascendant. In the western part of the continent, vast hegemonic powers are declaring themselves Islamic: Mali, then Songhay; Kanem, then Borno. New territories, such as the Hausa states, are also influenced. In Nubia [Sudan]*, Islamization, coupled with a slow Arabization, progresses toward the south; the last Christian Nubian state disappears in 1504. In [Ethiopia], after several centuries of unequal confrontation between the divided Muslim emirates and the Christian Amhara kingdom, the *jihad*, unleashed on Harar in 1506, gives a sense of unity to the Muslim forces for the first time. On the eastern coast, the Portuguese conquest, in 1505, brings Kilwa's hegemony to an end, closing the first period of splendor for Swahili Islam.

In many regions, the first years of the sixteenth century signal a decisive turn in the evolution of African Islam. Several names from this period stand out: Mansa Musa, the ruler of Mali who leads a pilgrimage that is recorded; Ibn Battuta, the Moroccan globetrotter, the first Arab author to visit Kilwa, Mali and Timbuktu, the intellectual metropolis of West African Islam.

*The names in brackets refer to the *present* country names, which, prior to 1960, were different.

West Africa

After 1260/659
Pilgrimage to Mecca by Uli (Oule), son of and successor to Sunjata and to the leadership of the empire of Mali.

Circa 1300/700
Pilgrimage to Mecca by Sakura, officer who began as a serf, sixth sovereign (*mansa*) of the empire of Mali; he dies during his return.

1307–1331/707–732: Reign of Mansa Musa (or Kankan Musa), ruler of Mali
1324/724
Mansa Musa comes to Mecca by way of Cairo. The pilgrimage spreads

knowledge of Mali in the Middle East and North Africa.

1353/753-754

The Moroccan Ibn Battuta, first author to visit and describe Timbuktu, which marks the beginning of its increased power under the aegis of the empire of Mali.

Circa 1400/803

Mali's hegemony wiped out in the Saharan regions.

1464 or 1465-1492/869-898: Reign of Sonni 'Ali

The wise men of Timbuktu, who suffered during his reign, left in their writings an image of him as a debauched and impious tyrant.

1469/873

Sonni 'Ali takes Timbuktu and stifles its religious aristocracy, judged to be lenient with the Tuaregs.

1493/898

Sonni Baro, son of and successor to Sonni 'Ali, vanquished by Muhammad Turé, leader of the "Muslim party." The new Askiya dynasty takes control of the Songhay Empire for a century. In Timbuktu, zenith of the "University of Sankore."

1493-1528/898-934: Reign of the Askiya Muhammad Turé
Circa 1494-1500/898-906

Voyage of the Algerian reformer Muhammad b. 'Abd al-Karim al-Maghili in the northern regions of present day [Niger], [Nigeria] and [Mali]. Writes treatises on governing and provides advice to the princes of the countries he visited (among them the Hausa city-states of Kano and Katsina). His arrival in Gao comes soon after the coup d'etat by the Askiya Muhammad Turé, to whom he responds in writing when asked how his power can be legitimized.

1505/911

Death of the Egyptian historian, philologist and encyclopedist Jalal al-Din al-Suyuti in Cairo. He had received the Askiya Muhammad at the time of his pilgrimage to Mecca (between 1496/901 and 1498/904) and maintained a regular correspondance with the African rulers and wise men of [Mali], [Niger] and [Nigeria].

Around Lake Chad

End of the 14th century/ beginning of the 9th century

Beginning of the exodus toward the south by nomadic Arabs settled in Egypt and chased out by the Mamluks; they arrive in the Chad basin.

1382/784

The Saifawa, chased out of Kanem by the Arabs and the new local dynasty of the Bilala, emigrate from the other side of Lake Chad to Borno.

Circa 1385/787

The first Muslim missionaries, the Wangarawa, from Songhay or Mali, begin the Islamization of the Hausa. Yaji dan Tsamiya, *sarki* (sultan) of Kano, is one of the first converts.

1391-1392/794

Barquq, the Mamluk sultan of Egypt, receives a letter from 'Uthman Bir, ruler of Kanem (1389-1421/791-825) who presents himself as the "sword of Islam" in his country; he complains about the demands of the "devastating Arabs."

The Inhabitants of Mali, According to Ibn Battuta

"Account of what I considered admirable in the behavior of the Sudan (Blacks) and what I considered blameful.

Among their good actions:

Few injustices; they are of all men the furthest from them.

Their sultan does not tolerate the smallest breach of justice.

The total security in their country; neither someone who is traveling through nor someone who is staying need worry about robbers or aggressors . . .

Their diligence in prayer and their devotion to conducting it in groups, (even) including their children. Friday, if one does not arrive early at the mosque, it is impossible to find room because of the large number of people there. Typically, a man sends a young servant to lay out the prayer mat in his regular space prior to leaving for the mosque . . .

Their diligence in trying to learn the sublime Qur'an by heart; they put constraints on their children if they seem to be learning too slowly and do not remove these constraints until the Qur'an is known by heart . . .

Among their bad actions:

The fact that the servants, slaves and young women must be nude in public, their shameful parts visible . . .

The fact that women present themselves to the sultan nude, without a veil. Even his daughters are nude. I saw, on the 27th night of Ramadan, a hundred nude women slaves leave the palace with food; there were among them two of the sultan's daughters, both with round breasts and no veils . . . "

Circa 1450–1497/870–903

Reign of Muhammad Rumfa, *sarki* (sultan) of Kano; originator of the power of this city. He is the first to pursue a systematic policy of Islamization. Welcomes the reformer al-Maghili around 1493/899; accepts his advice.

1465–1497/870–903: Reign of the Mai (Sultan) 'Ali Gaji b. Dunama

He consolidates royal power in Borno; new capital, Ngazargamu, near Lake Chad. 'Ali Gaji b. Dunama

completes the pilgrimage in 1484/889; receives an appointment from the caliph al-Mutawakkil.

[Sudan] and [Ethiopia]

1276/674

[Sudan]: defeat of the Nubian Christian kingdom of Maqurra (capital: Dongola), which becomes a Mamluk protectorate.

1317/717

First Muslim king on the Dongola throne; royal residence transformed into a mosque.

1328/729

In [Ethiopia], the Muslim sultanate of Ifat subjugated by the Amharan Christian kingdom of Shoa (founded circa 1270/669). The other Muslim emirates in the region become vassals one by one.

1386-1387/788

The sultan of Ifat, Haqq al-Din II, reclaims his independence and attacks the Christian kingdom; vanquished and slain in combat.

Beginning of the 15th century/beginning of the 9th century

The Ifat dynasty, vanquished and exiled, gives birth to the new sultanate of Adal, settled in Harar, a fair distance from the Christian plateau.

2nd half of the 15th century/2nd half of the 9th century

A wave of militant Islam, led by newly converted Afar and Somali nomads, leads to a dynastic change in the Adal sultanate and more aggressive policy.

1473-1474/878

Defeat of the two Christian armies sent to Adal.

1504-1505/910

[Sudan]: destruction of the last Nubian Christian state, Alwa (or Alodia), whose capital, Suba, was near present day Khartoum. Emergence of the southern people of Funj; they establish the Sinnar sultanate, Islamicized during the following 20 years.

1506/912

The *imam* Ahmad b. Ibrahim al-Ghazi, nicknamed Gragn ("the left-handed one"), launches an important *jihad* against the Christians in [Ethiopia].

Eastern Coast of Africa

1331/731

Ibn Battuta visits Kilwa, Swahili Muslim province.

1505/911

Kilwa occupied by the Portuguese. Christian domination, destined to last nearly two centuries, begins on the eastern coast.

Ottoman Hegemony

The period from the 16th to the 18th century is, for Muslim states, first one of grandeur, then one of more or less marked decline depending upon the region. The Ottoman Empire experiences its golden age during the 16th century: the sultans Selim I and Suleyman I (Suleyman the Magnificent) are the prime movers in a considerable territorial expansion; their empire stretches over the greater part of the Mediterranean and controls the routes coming from Asia and Africa. The victories over Charles V and the judicious administration of the provinces are elements of a state at its zenith. The Ottoman Empire, whose brilliance is corroborated by a significant artistic movement, a sort of eastern Renaissance, is at this time the greatest power in the Old World. Most of the travel accounts from the 16th and the beginning of the 17th century celebrate its power, the splendor of its capital, the majesty of its sovereign, the rigor of its administration; if one does not consider religion, it stands as the model state for the West. If the Ottomans are viewed with such scrutiny, it is because, by virtue of their immediate proximity, they represent a major preoccupation for the Europeans.

The Ottoman hegemony over the Muslim world is, however, subject to limits that permit the other states to affirm their independence. Thus, Morocco, after having endured internal strife and the occupation of several cities by the Portuguese and Spanish, experiences under two successive dynasties — first the Sa'dians, then the 'Alawis — a period of stability, prosperity and territorial integrity. Further to the east, Iran becomes the domain of the Safavid dynasty. They establish Shi'ism, and remain in nearly permanent conflict with the Ottomans and Afghans. In India, Turks from central Asia establish the empire of the Great Moghul, which will unify the continent and lead to a period of political and artistic splendor. Indonesia becomes Islamic as well. This is a privileged moment in Islamic history.

The 17th century can be seen as a period of stabilization, during which most Muslim countries rely on their past achievements.

Meanwhile, the European states develop their plans for political, territorial and economic expansion: the 17th and 18th centuries witness developments in the West to which the Islamic countries will be unable to adapt, in spite of several attempts. As the 18th century draws to a close, Islam is on the defensive everywhere and will soon have to reckon with the influence, in all domains, of the West.

Morocco

The Sa'dian dynasty marks the beginning in Morocco of what is called the Sharifian kingdoms, since the Sa'dians, like their successors the 'Alawis (beginning in 1654), profess to be descendants of the Prophet (*sharif*). The founder of the Sa'dian dynasty, Muhammad al-Shaykh (al-Mahdi), was a distinguished head of state who imposed his authority on all of Morocco, including religious fraternities. His grandson's appeal to the Portuguese made possible the "Battle of Three Kings" (see box on page 149) and had as a consequence the rise to power of Ahmad al-Mansur; his reign, the most brilliant of the dynasty, witnessed a large number of administrative and military innovations. But the rivalries and dynastic quarrels that follow his reign lead to a decline in the ruler's authority.

In the second half of the 17th century, the 'Alawi sultans re-establish the prestige of their rule, especially during the reign of Mawlay Isma'il, a particularly brilliant ruler who was efficient and respected both in his country and abroad. Thirty years of rivalries and rebellions followed, and the 'Alawi dynasty was only able to reclaim power in the final third of the 18th century.

These two centuries allowed Morocco to affirm its independence not only from the Algerian Turks, but also from the Portuguese and Spanish, who both lost the powerful positions they had once occupied and the trade advantages they had held.

Internal Events

1502/907
The Portuguese build a small fort on the site of what will become Mazagan.

1504/909
The Portuguese build a small fort in Santa Cruz de Cap de Gue (Agadir).

1505–1524/910–931: Reign of the Wattasid Muhammad al Burtughali
1506/912
Mazagan founded.

1508/914
The Portuguese in Safi.

1511/917
The sharif of Tagmaddart (the valley of Dra) and leader of the Banu Sa'd, Muhammad b. 'Abd al-Rahman al-Qa'im, becomes, with support from the Marabouts, leader of the Muslims in their fight against the Portuguese. His sons, Ahmad al-A'ruj (1517–1544/923–951) and Muhammad al-Shaykh (1544–1557/923–985) control southern Morocco. Al-Qa'im establishes a central administration in the Sous, intensifies the production of sugar

cane, and revivifies the trans-Saharan gold trade, which until then the Portuguese had re-routed to La Mina on the West African coast.

1513/919

The Portuguese in Azemmour (Azammur).

1517/923

Death of Muhammad al-Qa'im. The inhabitants of the Sous recognize Ahmad al-A'ruj as their leader, and he settles in Taroudant. Support from the Marabout Sidi 'Abd Allah b. al-Mubarak.

1524/931

October. Marrakesh taken by Ahmad al-A'ruj.

1524–1549/931–955: Reign of the Wattasid Abu al-Abbas Ahmad
1536/942

Conquest of central Morocco by the Sa'dians. Victory over the Wattasids, with the help of English and French weapons.

1541/947

March 12/14 Dhu'l-Qa'da. Agadir taken from the Portuguese.

1542/948

Safi and Azemmour taken from the Portuguese.

1544/951

Muhammad al-Shaykh (Muhammad al-Mahdi) triumphs over his brother Ahmad al-A'ruj. He is recognized as ruler of Marrakesh.

1546/953

Muhammad al-Mahdi takes Meknes (Miknas) and Fez-Jedid from the Wattasids.

1549/956

Fez al-Bali taken. The Wattasid Ba Hassun seeks aid from Algerian Turks. Qasr al-Saghir and Arzila taken. End of the Portuguese domination of the Atlantic coast.

1550/957

Muhammad al-Shaykh takes Tlemcen from the Algerian corsairs, who recapture the city one year later.

1553/960

Fez temporarily retaken by Ba Hassun.
September 23/14 Shawwal. Death of Ba Hassun. End of the Wattasid dynasty.

1553–1654/960–1065

The Sa'dian dynasty.

1557/964

Assassination of Muhammad al-Mahdi by Ottoman agents.

1557–1574/964–982: Reign of the Sa'dian Sultan 'Abd Allah al-Ghalib

Al-Ghalib victorious over the Turks, near Fez.

1557–1578/964–986

Reign of King Sebastian of Portugal, who favors a war against the Muslims.

1574/981

January 20/27 Ramadan. Death of 'Abd Allah al-Ghalib. Accession of his son Muhammad al-Mutawakkil. Opposition from two of his uncles.

1575–1576/983

'Abd al-Malik, al-Mutawakkil's uncle, triumphs over his nephew with the aid of the Turks; al-Mutawakkil flees to Portugal.

1578/986

July 12/7 Jumada I. Arrival of King Sebastian and al-Mutawakkil's army in Arzila.

August 4/30 Jumada I. Battle of Wadi Makhazin (a.k.a. Battle of the Three Kings at Qasr al-Kabir [see box on page 149]). 'Abd al-Malik floods the battlefield by destroying a dam. Total defeat of the Portuguese; deaths of Sebastian, al-Mutawakkil and 'Abd al-Malik (the last by disease).

1578–1603/986–1012: Reign of Ahmad al-Mansur

Zenith of the dynasty.

1582/990

Al-Mansur pledges allegiance to the Ottomans in return for a cessation of corsair attacks.

1591/999

West African campaign with an army of 4,000 men led by the Spanish renegade Qudar.

March/Jumada I. Gao taken from the Askiya.

April 25/1 Rajab. Timbuktu taken. Capture of enormous wealth, which is sent to the north. Due to the long distances, the Sa'dians cannot maintain their control over these West African regions.

1595/1003

Spanish invasion in the north gains wide popular support.

1596/1004

Al-Mansur stops the Spanish invasion.

1603–1627/1012–1037: Reign of Mawlay (Mulay) Zaydan

Violent opposition by his two brothers. His authority limited to Marrakesh.

1610/1020

First Larache (al-'Ara'ish), then al-Ma'mura taken by the Spaniards. Movement of national and religious reaction led by Abu Mahalli, who occupies Tafilelt and takes Marrakesh. In Salé (Sala), organization of voyage by al-'Ayashi, who retakes al-Ma'mura not long thereafter.

1612/1021

The sultan loses interest in Timbuktu.

1613/1022

Abu Mahalli killed in Marrakesh.

1621–1627/1031–1037

Disintegration of the Sa'dian kingdom.

1627/1037

September 20/9 Muharram. Death of Zaydan.

1627–1631/1037–1041: Reign of 'Abd al-Malik b. Zaydan

1631–1636/1041–1045: Reign of Walid b. Zaydan

1636-1654/1045-1064: Reign of Muhammad al-Shaykh b. Zaydan (Muhammad al-Asghar)

Controls only Marrakesh.

1640/1050

The Marabouts of Dila' settle in Fez. Mawlay al-Sharif b. 'Ali, from the 'Alawi or Filalian family, first to hold the title of *sharif*, subjugates Tafilelt.

1640-1664/1050-1075

Mawlay Muhammad extends 'Alawi domination to eastern Morocco.

1655/1065

Ahmad al-'Abbas is killed in Marrakesh. End of the Sa'dian dynasty.

1664-1672/1075-1083: Reign of Mawlay al-Rashid

Founder of the 'Alawi dynasty.

1666/1076

June 6/13 Dhu'l-Hijja. Mawlay al-Rashid enters Fez and assumes the title of sultan. Triumph of the corsair Ghaylan in Qsar al-Kabir. Ghaylan annexes Rabat. Taza taken.

1668-1669/1078-1080

Occupation of Marrakesh by Ghaylan; the Marabouts from Sous (*zawiya* from Dila') no longer a force.

1672-1727/1083-1139: Reign of Mawlay Isma'il

Zenith of the dynasty.

1672/1083

June 4/7 Safar. Mawlay Isma'il first reclaims Marrakesh, then puts down sedition in Fez and triumphs over Ghaylan.

1673/1084

The Spaniards establish themselves on the Peñon of Alhucemas.

1677/1088

June/Rabi II. Marrakesh retaken. Meknes chosen as capital.

1679/1090

Mawlay Isma'il recognizes Tafna as the border between Morocco and Turkish Algeria.

1681/1092

Al-Ma'mura taken by Mawlay Isma'il.

1684/1095

Tangier taken.

1689/1100

Larache taken. Taroudant sacked.

1691/1102

Arzila taken. All of Morocco under the domination of Mawlay Isma'il, except Mazagan, which is controlled by the Portuguese, and four spots on the northern coast that are controlled by the Spanish.

1692/1103

Defeat at the hands of the Turks.

1694/1105

Oujda taken from the Turks.

1700/1112

Mawlay Isma'il positions his black militia in Salé.

1701/1113

Defeat at the hands of the Turks in the Chelif valley.

1727–1757/1139–1170

Thirty years of anarchy. Proclamation signed by 12 sultans.

1727/1139–1140

Insurrection in Rabat. 14-month siege.

1729–1757/1141–1170: Reign of Mawlay ʻAbd Allah

Proclaimed and overthrown six times.

1730/1142

Fez once again the capital.

1757–1790/1170–1204: Reign of Mawlay Muhammad

Relative stability. Campaigns against the Marabouts. Reorganization of the army, inclusion of Arabs and Berber tribes.

1765/1179

Mogador (al-Suwayra) founded; becomes the main port of southern Morocco, export of goods from the Sudan.

1769/1183

Portuguese expelled from Mazagan. Campaign against the Spanish in Melilla fails.

1790–1792/1204–1206: Reign of Mawlay Yazid

Revolt by the tribes.

1792–1824/1206–1238: Reign of Mawlay Sulayman

Prohibition of piracy.

Society: Internal Organization

Beginning of the 15th century/10th century

The Marabout Sidi ʻAbd Allah al-Mubarak supports the Saʻdian leaders.

1509–1517/915–923

Muhammad al-Qaʼim, a member of the Banu Saʻd, joins forces with the tribe of the Maʻqil in the Sous. He establishes a centralized administration and intensifies the production of sugar cane for export to Europe.

1544–1557/951–964

Muhammad al-Shaykh (Muhammad al-Mahdi) eliminates all opposition. The Marabouts are banished or executed. The *zawiya* is closed. The *kharaj* is imposed on mountain dwellers.

1557–1558/964–965

The Jewish population of Marrakesh brought together in a separate quarter, the *mellah*.

1557–1574/964–982

Campaign by Sultan ʻAbd Allah al-Ghalib against the Marabouts. Members of the Yusufiyya massacred.

1574–1578/982–986

Religious brotherhoods oppose al-Mutawakkil.

1578–1610/986–1020

Ahmad al-Mansur. Organization of the *makhzan* for maintaining order and collecting taxes. A regular army, composed of renegades, Moors, Andalusians, blacks and Turkish advisors. Lands given in exchange for military service to the tribes from eastern Algeria who had been chased out by the Turks.

After 1590/998

Poor harvests and epidemics after al-Mansur's expedition to West Africa.

1609/1018

A few thousand Andalusian Moriscos arrive in Salé (Sala) after their expulsion from Spain by Philip III. They seize power in the city until the 'Alawi Sultan Mawlay al-Rashid unifies the country in 1668/1078.

1610-1613/1020-1022

Religious and tribal uprising led by Abu Mahalli.

1668-1669/1079-1080

The Marabouts from the Sous greatly weakened.

1672-1727/1083-1139

Mawlay Isma'il. Elimination of any and all opposition. Organization of the *makhzan* tribes who are directly responsible to the central government. A solid army is established, with a troop composed of black slaves (the *'abid* or *haratin*), in order to prevent reliance on tribes, or on Turkish mercenaries. There is vocal opposition against Isma'il's state and his black soldiers. Shaykh Gassus of Fez (d. 1691/1102) accuses him of enslaving Muslims and using slaves for a holy war. After Isma'il's death, the black army shrinks and once again tribal factions dominate the army.

1727-1757/1139-1170

Central power diminished. Tribes play dominant role.

1757-1790/1170-1204

Mawlay Muhammad. Restoration of the sultan's power. Campaign against the Marabouts.

2nd half of the 18th century/12th century

Casablanca becomes peopled by Berbers.

Foreign Relations and Trade

1502-1513/908-919

The Portuguese on the Atlantic coast.

1511/917

Beginning of English trade with Morocco.

1533/940

Relations established between France and Morocco.

1549/956

End of Portuguese domination of the Atlantic coast.

Middle of 16th century/10th century

The Portuguese evacuate Ceuta, Tangier and Mazagan.

1577/985

Creation of a French consulate in Salé.

1578-1603/986-1012

Amicable relations with the Spanish, the French and the English.

1585/993

Creation of the Barbary Company with an office in Marrakesh by Queen Elizabeth I of England (1558-1603).

1589/997
Philip II of Spain returns Arzila.

End of the 16th century/10th century
Safi opens up to European commerce.

1600/1009
Queen Elizabeth I of England rejects al-Mansur's plan for a Moroccan-English alliance, due to the obvious Moroccan weakness during the Spanish invasion (1595). Instead, she proposes a joint colonization project in the Spanish provinces of the Americas, to which al-Mansur cannot adhere.

1627/1036
The republic of Bu Regreg founded (the corsairs of Salé).

1631/1040
Treaty between France and Morocco.

1635/1045
Confirmation of the treaty; ratified by the corsairs of Salé.

1662/1072
The English take the port of Tangier.

1665/1075
Creation of the French Company of Albouzine (Alhucemas). Little success.

1670/1081
Creation of the Levant Company. Does not survive.

1673/1084
The Spanish take Alhucemas.

1681–1691/1092–1102
The Moroccans reclaim Tangier, Larache, Arzila and al-Ma'mura.

1681/1092
Peace and trade treaty with France.

1699/1111
Ben Aysha sends a delegation to France.

Beginning of the 18th century/12th century
English and Dutch in Safi. The English first in Moroccan trade.

1712/1124
Creation of a French consulate in Tetouan.

1751/1164
The Danish monopolize trade in Safi and Agadir.

1769/1183
The Portuguese leave Mazagan.

1782 and 1789/1196 and 1203
Merchants from Cadiz and Madrid in Casablanca.

1785/1189
Peace with Spain.

Sa'dian and 'Alawite Monuments

1524/930
Casbah of Marrakesh built.

1540/947
Casbah of Agadir built.

The Battle of the Three Kings*

In spite of the advice to the contrary from his military officers and his uncle Philip II of Spain, the king of Portugal, Sebastian (1557–1578), who believed he was destined to convert Maghribi Muslims to Christianity, undertook a military expedition that had as its objective the conquest of Morocco. He was encouraged to pursue this plan by a former sultan of Morocco, Muhammad al-Murawakkil, deposed from the throne by his uncle 'Abd al-Malik. Near the wadi Makhazin, facing poorly organized Portuguese troops and attacking without a battle plan, 'Abd al-Malik presented a coherent and determined army supported by Andalusian archers. 'Abd al-Malik destroyed a dam and flooded the hastily chosen battlefield at al-Qsar al-Kabir. The battle ended in a complete rout of the Portuguese and in the death of three sovereigns: Sebastian, al-Mutawakkil and 'Abd al-Malik. The consequences were the subsequent Spanish domination of Portugal and, in Morocco, the accession to power of 'Abd al-Malik's brother, Ahmad, nicknamed al-Mansur ("the Victorious"), who benefitted from his prestige and collected the spoils of the battle. He governed wisely and competently; his reign represents the zenith of the Sa'dian dynasty.

*Also called the battle of the wadi Makhazin (or Qsar al-Kabir): 4 August 1578/30 Jumada I 986.

1557–1558/964–965
Bab Dukkala mosque built in Marrakesh.

1562–1572/969–980
Al-Mu'asin mosque built in Marrakesh.

1564–1565/971–972
The Ben Yusuf *madrasa* founded in Marrakesh.

After 1569/977
Restauration of the mosque at the casbah in Marrakesh.

1578–1603/986–1012
Construction of the al-Badi palace in Marrakesh.

1605/1014
Sidi Bel-Abbès mosque and *madrasa* built in Marrakesh.

1666/1076–1077
The ramparts of Fez built.

1670/1081
Casbah of the Shararda built. The al-Sharratin *madrasa* built in Fez.

1684/1095
Dar al-Makhzan built in Tangier.

1689/1100
Filada *madrasa* built in Meknes.

1697/1109
The Dar Kabira Palace built in Meknes.

End of the 17th century/12th century

Dar al-Makhzan built in Taza. Great Mosque of Tangier built. Khalifa palace built in Tetouan. Sa'dian tombs built in Marrakesh.

Beginning of 18th century/12th century

Mawlay Isma'il mausoleum built in Marrakesh.

2nd half of the 18th century/12th century

Madrasa bath and fort built in Casablanca. Numerous new building projects in Fez, among them the Bab Ghissa' Dar Ayad al-Kabira and Bab al-Qibla *madrasas*.

1760/1173

Mogador (al-Suwayra) founded.

1773/1187

Mosque and stores built in Muhammadiya.

End of the 18th century/12th century

Dar al-Bayda built in Meknes. Fonduq al-Sultan built in Qasr al-Kabir. *Madrasa* and fortifications built in Larache.

The Ottoman Empire

Expansion is the dominant feature in the history of the Ottomans during the 16th century. The sultan Selim I extends his domination to eastern Anatolia, Azerbaijan, Syria, Palestine and Egypt; he is even recognized as the "protector of the sacred sites of Islam." Suleyman I (Suleyman the Magnificent) continues his father's achievements in Muslim countries by conquering Iraq, Yemen and, through the intermediary of his corsairs, North Africa (with the exception of Morocco). In Europe, Hungary is annexed, Austria, Poland and the Ukraine threatened; the Ottoman Empire is at its peak, both in terms of power and wealth, which is corroborated by the construction of expansive monuments, the work of an architectural genius, Mimar Sinan.

The European states believe that they have stopped the Ottoman expansion with their naval victory at Lepanto (1571), but the Turks recapture Cyprus and Tunis. These victories, however, mark the end of their conquests except for one in Crete, which passes into their hands during the second half of the 17th century.

The empire then rests on its prestige, power and accumulated wealth, but eventually a need emerges for more energetic rulers, who are capable of understanding the evolution of the outside world. While the Western powers are launching their colonial enterprises and accelerating their economic development, and while Austria and Russia exert pressure on the Ottoman provinces of central Europe and the Balkans, the Ottoman Empire stagnates, conserves the rhythms of the past and, at the end of the 17th century, assumes a defensive posture. During the 18th century, the empire starts to lose territory. Much later, several open-minded leaders see the need for reforms and look to the West.

Wars and Foreign Relations

1512–1520/918–926: Reign of Selim I

1514/920

August 23/2 Rajab. Victory over the Shi'i Safavids in the battle of Chaldiran (Azerbaijan): the Ottomans under Selim I defeat Shah Isma'il who attempted to expand Shi'i-controlled territory. As a result, the Ottomans control eastern Anatolia and occupy Tabriz.

1515/921

June–September/Rabi II–Shawwal. Occupation of Cilicia and Kurdistan.

1516/922

Algiers taken by the Ottoman corsair 'Aruj.

August 24/25 Rajab. Ottoman victory over the Mamluks led by Qansawh al-Ghawri in Marj Dabiq, followed by the occupation of Aleppo and Damascus (September).

September/Shawwal. Defeat of the Spanish navy off Algiers.

1517/922–923

January 22/25 Dhu'l-Hijja. Mount Muqattam in Cairo conquered, which leads to the capture of the city by the Ottomans and the end of the Mamluk state.

April 13/21 Rabi I. Defeat, capture and execution of Tuman Bey, the last Mamluk sultan.

1520/926

The Turkish pirate Khayr al-Din Barbarossa puts his conquests in Algeria under Ottoman control.

1520–1566/926–976: Reign of Sultan Suleyman (a.k.a. Qanuni, "the Law Giver," or "the Magnificent"), Selim's son

1521/927

May/Jumada II. First campaign by Suleyman I against Hungary.

August 29/25 Ramadan. Belgrade taken.

1522/928–929

June/Rajab. Attack on the island of Rhodes, defended by the Knights of St. John of Jerusalem (the Hospitallers).

December 10/1 Safar. Surrender of the citadel of Rhodes. The Knights first settle in Tripoli (in Barbary), then Malta. Several thousand Christians accompany them.

1525/932

December 6/20 Safar. The sultan receives Jean Frangipani, the extraordinary envoy of the King of France, Francis I, who comes to discuss the foundations for an accord between France and the Ottoman Empire.

1526/932

August 29/21 Dhu'l-Qa'da. Victory over the Hungarians under King Louis in the battle of Mohacs.

September/Dhu'l-Hijja. Buda and Szeged taken. Devastation of the countryside. Hungary under Ottoman suzerainty.

1527–1528/933–934

Occupation of Bosnia, Croatia, Slavonia and Dalmatia.

1529/935–936

May 27/19 Ramadan. The Peñon of Algiers taken. A new port is built.

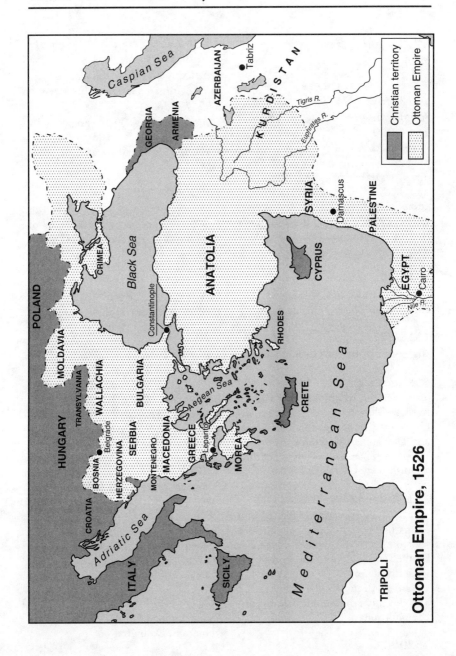

Ottoman Empire, 1526

September 27–October 15/23 Muharram–11 Safar. Vienna under siege by the Ottomans. Siege fails. Khayr al-Din Barbarossa pledges allegiance to the Ottomans, becomes responsible for the construction of a fleet.

1530/936
Aden taken.

1533–1534/939–940
June 22/29 Dhu'l-Qa'da. Peace treaty with the Habsburgs of Austria signed after conquest of Güns; confirmation of the status quo. "Campaign of the two Iraqs" — incursion into eastern Anatolia and Iraq.

1534/941
August 22/11 Safar. Tunis taken by Khayr al-Din Barbarossa. Lost in 1535.

November 28/21 Jumada I. Baghdad taken. Campaign against Shah Tahmasp of Persia.

1535/941
May/Dhu'l-Qa'da. Arrival in Istanbul of the first French ambassador, Jean de La Forêt.

1536
Commercial treaty with France, directed against Charles V.

1538/945
Jassy taken; annexation of Bessarabia. Ottoman fleet in the Indian Ocean. Occupation of Yemen and Aden. Defeat of the fleet of the Holy League (Venice, the Papal States, Charles V) in the battle of Preveza. The Ottoman fleet dominates the Mediterranean.

1540/947
October 20/18 Jumada II. Peace treaty with the Venetians signed. Venice keeps Cyprus, Crete and Corfu, but surrenders its possessions on the Aegean islands, the Peloponnese and Dalmatia.

1541/948
August 29/7 Jumada I. Occupation of Pest. Hungary becomes Ottoman province (Budin).

1543/950
July–August/Rabi II–Jumada I. Khayr al-Din Barbarossa's navy in Provence. Nice taken from the Spanish.

September 4/4 Jumada I. Szekesfehervar (Stuhlweissenburg) taken.

1547/954
Death of Khayr al-Din Barbarossa. Turghud Reis (Dragut) (1485–1565/890–972) succeeds him.

1548–1549/955–956
Ottoman-Persian war. Occupation of Azerbaijan. Van taken.

1551/958
August 15/12 Shawwal. Tripoli (in Barbary) taken.

1552/959
April/Rabi II. Incursion by the Admiral Piri Reis into Masqat and Hormuz. Condemned to death and executed for having failed.

1554/961
August/Ramadan. Defeat of the Admiral Seydi 'Ali Reis by the Portuguese in Hormuz.

1555/962
May 29/8 Rajab. Peace treaty with the Safavids of Iran signed.

1556/963

Defeat of the Ziyarids of Western Algeria. Naval war with the Portuguese in the Indian Ocean.

1557/964

July/Ramadan. Oran taken. Ottoman-Austrian treaty confirms vassal status of Hungary.

1560/967

March/Jumada II. Victory over the Spanish in Jerba.

1566/973-974

April 14/24 Ramadan. Island of Chios taken from the Genoans.
September 6–7/20–21 Safar. Death of Suleyman I. Citadel of Szigetvar taken.

1566-1574/973-982:
Reign of Selim II, "the Sot"
1568/975

February 17/18 Shawwal. Peace treaty with Maximilian of Austria signed.

1569/976

An Ottoman fleet in the Indian Ocean comes to the aid of the Sumatran Muslims against the Portuguese. Tunis occupied, lost again in 1572; attempt to take La Goulette fails.

1570/977-978

May–September/Dhu'l-Hijja–Rabi II. Incursion into Cyprus. Nearly the entire island is occupied. Peace with the Muscovites.

1571/979

August 1/9 Rabi I. Famagusta taken. Completion of the conquest of Cyprus.

October 7/17 Jumada I. Defeat of the Ottoman fleet in the battle of Lepanto. The Spanish-Venetian fleet of the Holy League, led by Don John of Austria, destroys the Ottoman fleet. Within only a few years, the Ottomans rebuild their fleet, regaining their naval dominance over the eastern Mediterranean.

1574/982

August–September/Jumada I. La Goulette and Tunis taken. Tunisia becomes an Ottoman province.

1574-1595/982-1003:
Reign of Murad III
1578/986

September/Rabi II–Rajab. Incursion into Iran. Akhiska and Tiflis taken. Fez taken from the Portuguese.

1579/987

May/Rabi II. Establishment of diplomatic relations with England; trade privileges granted.

1585/993

September 23/28 Ramadan. Annexation of Azerbaijan.

1590/998

March 21/14 Jumada I. Peace treaty with Iran signed. The Ottomans gain Luristan and Tabriz.

1593-1606/1001-1015

Ottoman-Austrian war.

1595-1603/1003-1012:
Reign of Mehmed III
1596/1004

Victory over Austria in the battle of Keresztes.

1603/1012

September–November/Rabi II–Jumada I. Iranian attacks on Azerbaijan and Armenia. Tabriz lost.

1603–1617/1012–1026: Reign of Ahmed I
1605/1014

Persia defeats the Ottomans at Lake Urmia.

1606/1015

November 11/10 Rajab. Peace of Szitvatorok with Austria. Austria loses territory in Hungary.

1612/1021

November 20/26 Ramadan. Peace with Iran. The Ottomans lose Georgia and Azerbaijan. Trade privileges granted to Dutch merchants.

1615/1024

War with Iran resumes. Siege of Yerevan falters. Peace treaty signed in 1618/1027.

1617–1618/1026–1027: Reign of Sultan Mustafa I, deposed in palace revolution because of imbecility

1618–1622/1027–1031: Reign of Sultan 'Osman II
1622/1031

English bombardment of Algiers in retaliation for piracy. End of campaign against Poland; Ottoman losses.

1624/1033

January/Rabi I. The Iranians take Baghdad and occupy Iraq.

1633/1042

Suppression of the rebellion in Lebanon led by the Druze Fakhr al-Din, supported by Spain, the Papal States and Tuscany. Fakhr al-Din executed in 1635/1044.

1635/1044–1045

March–September/Ramadan–Rabi I. Incursion into Yerevan. Temporary reoccupation of Tabriz.

1637/1047

July 5/11 Safar. Azov taken by the Don Cossacks.

1638/1048

December 14/17 Shawwal. Baghdad retaken from the Iranians.

1639/1049

May 17/14 Muharram. Peace of Qasr-e Shirin with Iran; Iraq and Tabriz given to the Ottomans, Yerevan and part of the Caucasus to the Iranians. Peace treaty allows the Ottomans to mass their troops on their western borders.

1622–1623/1031–1032: Second Reign of Mustapha I, deposed by the Shaykh al-Islam
1623–1639/1032–1049

War with Iran.

1623–1640/1032–1050: Reign of Murad IV

1640–1648/1050–1058: Reign of Ibrahim I
1645/1055

April/Rabi I. Beginning of the war for Crete against the Venetians.

August 19/26 Jumada II. Canea taken.

1648–1687/1058–1098: Reign of Sultan Mehmed IV
1648/1058

May–June/Jumada I–Jumada II. Dardanelles blockaded by the Venetians. Second blockade in 1650/1060.

1651/1061

Venetian victory in the sea battle of Paros.

1655/1066

British bombardment of Algiers.

1657/1067

The Danube principalities again under Ottoman rule.

1663–1664/1073–1075

War with Austria.

1664/1075

August 1/8 Muharram. Battle at Saint Gotthard; Ottoman defeat.
August 10/17 Muharram. Peace of Vasvár (Eisenburg) with Austria; 20-year truce.

1665/1076

French bombardment of Tunis and Algiers.

1669/1080

September 5/8 Rabi II. Crete occupied. Armistice with the Venetians in the Peace of Venice. Venice keeps three strongholds on Crete.

1672/1083

British bombardment of Algiers.

1672–1676/1083–1087

War against Poland.

1676/1087

October 17/19 Shawwal. Peace of Zurawno with Poland; Podolia annexed by the Ottomans; Ukraine becomes a vassal state.

1677–1681/1088–1092

War against Russia.

1681/1092

July/Rajab. Incident at Chio with the French Admiral Duquesne. Peace of Radzin with Russia. The Ottomans cede Kiev.

1683/1094

April/Rabi II. Beginning of the war with Austria.
July–September/Rajab–Ramadan. Failure of the siege on Vienna led by Qara Mustafa after the defeat at Kahlenburg.

1683–1699/1094–1110

War between the Holy Alliance (Austria, Venice, Poland, Russia, the Papal States, Tuscany and Malta) and the Ottoman Empire.

1684–1687/1095–1098

Preveza, Navarin, Budin and Athens lost.

1687–1691/1098–1102: Reign of Suleyman II
1688/1099

Loss of Belgrade to Austria.

1690/1101

Conquest of Nish and Belgrade.

1691/1102

August 19/24 Dhu'l-Qa'da. Battle of Szalankamen. Death of the grand vizier Fazil Mustafa Köprülü Pasha.

1691–1695/1102–1107: Reign of Ahmed II

1695-1703/1107-1115:
Reign of Mustafa II
1696/1108
August 6/7 Muharram. Azov taken by Peter the Great.

1697/1109
Ottoman defeat at Zenta on the Theiss by the imperial army led by Prince Eugene of Savoy.

1699/1110
January 26/24 Rajab. Peace of Karlowitz among Austria, Poland and Venice: Austria receives Hungary, Transylvania, Slovenia and Croatia; Venice receives the Peloponnes and most of Dalmatia; Poland receives the Ukraine, Podolia and Kameniecz.

1700/1112
July 17/27 Muharram. Peace treaty with Russia, which keeps Azov.

1703-1730/1115-1143:
Reign of Ahmed III
1711/1123
April–July/Safar–Jumada II. Defeat of Peter the Great at the Prut. Azov retaken. Charles XII, king of Sweden, flees to Turkey.

1713/1125
June 24/30 Jumada II. Peace of Adrianople with Russia.

1715/1127
August–September/Shawwal–Ramadan. Reconquest of Morea. Suda on Crete taken.

1716-1717/1128-1129
War with Austria. Temesvar and Belgrade taken.

1718/1130
July 21/22 Shawwal. Peace with Passarowitz. Austria gains the Banat region of Temesvar, western Valachia and northern Serbia, including Belgrade.

1723/1135
Tiflis taken.

1723-1727/1135-1140
Campaign against Safavid Iran. Azerbaijan and western Iran conquered in three campaigns between 1722-1725/1135-1137.

1727/1140
October 4/17 Safar. Peace of Hamadan. The Ottomans get western Iran and the southern Caucasus.

1730/1143
The Safavids reconquer Azerbaijan and Hamadan.

1730-1754/1143-1168:
Reign of Mahmud I
1731-1736/1144-1149
New war against Iran. The peace treaty of October 1736/Jumada II 1149 names the Araxa River as the border between the two states.

1736/1149
The Safavids reconquer Armenia, Georgia, Shirawan and lands in the Caucasus.

1736-1739/1149-1152
War against Austria and Russia.

1739/1152
September 18/14 Jumada II. Peace of Belgrade. Status quo with Russia, return of Azov. Austria loses its con-

quest of 1718. The Ottomans regain naval supremacy over the Black Sea.

1746/1159

Sept. 4/17 Shawwal. Renewed peace with Iran. Return to the borders of 1639.

1754–1757/1168–1170: Reign of 'Osman III

1757–1774/1170–1188: Reign of Mustafa III
1761

Treaty of friendship with Prussia.

1768/1182

October/Jumada I. Beginning of war with Russia.

1770/1184

July 6–7/12–13 Rabi I. Severe defeat of the Ottoman navy in Çeshme, near Smyrna.

1771/1185

June/Rabi I. Russians invade the Crimea.

1774/1188

July 21/12 Jumada I. Treaty of Küçük Kaynarji. Many advantages gained (including trade agreements) by the Russians in the Crimea and in the Black Sea. Russia becomes the protector of Orthodox Christians in the Empire.

Domestic Events

1515/921

February/Muharram Revolt by the Janissaries, which is severely put down.
September/Shawwal. Kurdistan comes under Ottoman suzerainty.

1519/925

April/Rabi II. Revolt in Anatolia by a nomad chief, Jelal, a relative of the Safavids. The movement, which has both religious and social characteristics, is quickly put down. First of the "Jelali" revolts.
May/Jumada I. Khayr al-Din Barbarossa offers the sultan suzerainty over the territories in North Africa conquered by the corsairs.

1520/926

Revolt led by the governor of Syria, Janbirdi Ghazali. Captured and executed in February 1521/Safar 927.

1523–1536/929–942

The grand vizierate of Frenk Ibrahim Pasha, of Greek or Italian descent. Executed in March 1536/Ramadan 942.

1524–1525/930–931

January–June/Rabi I-Shawwal. Revolt led by the Ottoman governor of Egypt, Arnavut Ahmed Pasha.

1526–1527/933

June/Muharram-Shawwal. Jelali revolt in Elbistan.

1544–1553/951–960

First grand vizierate of Rüstem Pasha, of Croatian descent.

1565–1579/972–987

The grand vizierate of Soqullu Mehmed Pasha, of Bosnian descent, who controls the administration.

1589 and 1592/997 and 1000

Revolts by the Janissaries.

1591–1635/996–1044

The Druze Emir Fakhr al-Din Ma'n in Lebanon extends his sphere of influence to include Gharb, Jurd and Matn.

1595/1003

January 15/4 Jumada I. Death of Murad III. Control of the government assumed by the sultan-mother Safiye.

1601/1010

Jelali revolt in Anatolia.

1606/1015

September/Jumada I. Revolt led by the Druze leader Janbulad in Kilis and Aleppo.

1608/1017

Fakhr al-Din concludes a treaty of assistance with the Medici.

1612/1021

The Ottomans force Fakhr al-Din to flee to Tuscany. The Iraqi local lord Afrasiyab and son 'Ali (1624/25–1652/1033–1062) and his grandson Huseyn (1652–1668/1062–1079) make Basra a semi-autonomous province.

1618/1027

February 26/Rabi I. Mustafa I deposed in a palace revolution; reason: imbecility. Return of Fakhr al-Din, who continues expansionist politics. His territory extends from the *sanjak* of Latakia to the *sanjaks* of Nablus and Ajlun.

1619/1028

Revolt in Baghdad led by the Janissary Subashi Bakr.

1622/1031

May 18/7 Rajab. Revolt by the Janissaries and Sipahis in Istanbul after peace with Poland.

May 19–20/8–9 Rajab. Palace revolt. Sultan 'Osman II deposed and executed; Mustafa I restored. The government controlled by the sultan-mother Kösem until 1632/1041 and again from 1640 to 1651.

1622–1628/1032–1038

Revolt led by the governor of Erzerum, Abaza Pasha (executed in 1634/1044).

1623/1032

September 10/15 Dhu'l-Qa'da. Mustafa I deposed again.

1631/1041

Insurrections in Egypt, Yemen and Lebanon.

1632/1041

June/Dhu'l-Qa'da. Sultan Murad IV assumes leadership of the state. Declaration of *qanunname* to take effect in the capital and provinces.

1635/1044

April 13/24 Shawwal. Execution in Istanbul of the Druze emir Fakhr al-Din Ma'n.

1648/1058

August 8/18 Rajab. Ibrahim I deposed and put to death on August 18.

1651/1061

August/Ramadan. Revolt of the guilds in Istanbul.

September 3/17 Ramadan. Execution of the sultana Kösem. Domination by the sultana-mother Turhan.

1656–1661/1067–1072

The grand vizierate of Mehmed Köprülü Pasha. Political rehabilitation by internal reforms; elimination of the influence of the Janissaries and the harem.

1658–1659/1069

Revolt by the governor of Aleppo, Abaza Qara Hasan Pasha, is put down severely.

After 1659–1660/1070

After Ottoman actions against the Janissaries, there are two Janissary corps in Damascus: the *qapi qullari* (regular troops) and the *yerliyya* (local recruits).

1661–1676/1072–1087

The grand vizierate of Köprülüzade Fazil Ahmed Pasha, Mehmed's son.

1671/1083: Regime of the Deys in Algiers (lasts until 1830)
1676–1683/1087–1094

The grand vizierate of Merzifonlu Qara Mustafa Pasha, brother-in-law of Ahmed Köprülü; he is executed after the failure of the siege of Vienna.

1687/1098–1099

September–November/Shawwal–Muharram. Revolt by the Janissaries, who depose Sultan Mehmed IV.

1689/1100

Mustafa Köprülü Grand Vizier. He reorganizes the financial system and the army.

1702/1114

Ibrahim al-Sharif takes power in Tunis; has the sultan recognize him as *bey* and *dey*. Taken prisoner by the Algerians in 1705.

1703/1115

July–August/Rabi I–Rabi II. Revolt by the Janissaries, the *'ulama'* and members of guilds in Istanbul. Sultan Mustafa II deposed.

1705/1117

Husayn b. 'Ali, *agha* of the Sipahis, becomes *bey* and *dey* of Tunis and receives the title of *beylerbey*. Founder of the Husaynid dynasty that lasts until 1957.

1710/1122

Ahmed Qaramanli, *dey* of Tripoli (in Barbary); *beylerbey* in 1713. Founds the Qaramanli dynasty (lasts until 1835). Domination of Zahir al-'Umar and the Zaydani family in Galilee.

1713/1125

The *dey* of Algiers, 'Ali Çavush, recognized as *beylerbey* of Algeria.

1725/1137

The 'Azm family dominates in Syria. Encourages import-export trade of luxury goods with Europe.

1726/1138

In Mosul, Isma'il Pasha b. 'Abd al-Jalil establishes the Mamluk dynasty of the Jalilis (lasts until 1834).

1730/1143

September–November/Rabi I–Jumada I. Revolt by the Janissaries, led by Patrona Khalil.

October 2/19 Rabi I. Ahmed III abdicates.

1730–1754/1143–1168

During the sultanate of Mahmud I, the French renegade Bonneval reorganizes the army and the government.

1757-1763/1170-1177

The grand vizierate of Koja Raghib Mehmed Pasha. New laws passed that limit the power of notables and high civil servants. He restricts the Timariots and re-establishes the financial health of the state.

1768-1773/1182-1187

Revolt in Egypt led by the Mamluk 'Ali Bey.

Society, Institutions and Religion

1515/921

Revised legal system established: new penal code, increased power for provincial judges.

1517/923

July/Rajab. The 'Abbasid caliph al-Mutawakkil led to Istanbul with Egyptian artisans and merchants in tow. Selim I recognized as "guardian of the Holy Places." He receives the keys of the Ka'ba in Mecca and takes the title of caliph.

1517-1519/923-925

Promulgation of the *qanunname* regarding the administration of the provinces.

1518/924

Construction of a new maritime arsenal in Istanbul (the Qasim Pasha area).

1522-1548/928-955

Promulgation of many *qanunname* for the provinces; thus, the surname of *qanuni* (legislator) given to Suleyman I. The *shaykh ül-islam*, Abu al-Su'ud

Efendi, plays an important role in the promulgation of *qanunname*. Creation of new taxes levied to pay for exceptional expenses (*tekalif-i divaniye*).

1536/942

February 18/25 Shawwal. Concessions granted to France.

1544/951

April/Muharram. Beginning of the construction of the Shahzade mosque in Istanbul, attributed to the architect Sinan. Completed in August of 1548/955.

1550/957

June 13/27 Jumada I. Cornerstone laid for the mosque of Suleyman I (Suleymaniye), built by Sinan; completed 1556/963.

1555/962

Beginning of coffee consumption in Istanbul.

1561/968

January/Jumada I. Mosque of Rüstem Pasha, decorated with faience from Nicaea.

1568/975

Beginning of the construction of Selim II's mosque (Selimiye) in Edirne, Sinan's magnum opus. Completed in 1574.

1571/979

Mosque of Soqullu Pasha in Istanbul built by Sinan.

1574/982

August 23/5 Jumada I. Death of the *shaykh ül-islam*, Abu al-Su'ud Efendi, the greatest lawyer of his time.

1578/986
Death of the architect Sinan; he built 318 buildings and became an example for future generations of Ottoman architects.

1579/987
March/Muharram. Diplomatic relations established with England. Concessions (known as capitulations) granted.

1581/989
July 6/4 Jumada II. Renewal of concessions granted to France.

1598/1004
April 9/10 Shawwal. Cornerstone laid for the Yeni Valide mosque in Istanbul; completed only in 1664.

1605/1014
Tobacco first imported into Turkey.

1609/1018
October 8/7 Rajab. Beginning of the construction of the mosque of sultan Ahmed (the "Blue Mosque") in Istanbul. Inaugurated June 9, 1617.

1633/1043
September 2/27 Safar. Furious fire in Istanbul; 20% of the town destroyed.
September 16/12 Rabi. Tobacco use prohibited. Coffee houses closed.

1650–1651/1060–1061
The grand vizierate of Melek Ahmed Pasha. Devaluation of the currency. Additional taxes.

1656/1067
Control of the government and administration reappropriated by the grand vizier Mehmed Köprülü.

1660/1071
July 24/16 Dhu'l-Qa'da. The largest fire in Istanbul's history: 4,000 casualties; 28,000 houses and 300 palaces destroyed.

1666/1076
The Sabbatai Zevi (Jewish pseudo-prophet) affair.

1669/1080
An envoy sent by Suleyman Agha to Paris. Failure.

1686–1687/1097–1098
Levy of a special tax, the *imdad-i seferiye,* to cover military expenses.

1718–1730/1130–1142
The grand vizierate of Nevshehirli Damad Ibrahim Pasha, who favors opening up to the West.

1719–1723/1131–1135
Ambassadors sent to Vienna, Paris, Moscow and Warsaw.

1720–1721/1132–1133
Successful delegation sent by Yirmisekiz Mehmed Çelebi to Paris.

1720–1730/1132–1142
The "Tulip Age" (*lale devri*) in Istanbul (named after the import of Dutch tulips by the nobility), during which a French artistic influence is felt. Period of considerable construction (palaces, mosques, fountains). Reforms end with Patrona Revolt (1730).

1731/1144
September/Ramadan. Reorganization of the artillery by the French renegade Count de Bonneval (Khumbarajibashi Ahmed Pasha Bonneval). Creation of a corps of bombardiers.

1732/1144

January/Shawwal. Law decreed by Mahmud I reorganizing the *timar* system.

1734/1147

September/Rabi I. First engineering school established for the training of artillery officers. Closed in 1750/1163.

1755/1169

December 5/9 Ramadan. The Nur-u 'Osmaniye mosque opened to the faithful in Istanbul.

1760/1174

April 10/15 Ramadan. Cornerstone of the Laleli mosque ("mosque of the tulips") laid in Istanbul.

Literature and Science

1468?-1534/873?-940

Ahmed Shems al-Din b. Kemal (Kemalpashazade), author of *Tarikh-i Al-i 'Osman* ("History of the Ottomans").

1480?-1553/885?-960

Piri Reis, sailor and geographer, author of the *Kitab-i bahriye* ("Book on Navigation," 1521, re-edited in 1525), and maps of the Old and New Worlds.

1480-1556/885-963

Mehmed b. Suleyman Fuzuli, one of the greatest Ottoman poets.

1488-1563/893-970

Lutfi Pasha, author of the *Asafname*, a treatise on political morality and administrative and social history.

1490-1574/895-982

Abu al-Su'ud (Ebussuud) Efendi, *shaykh ül-islam*, lawyer; contributed

to the writing of rules (*qanunname*) enacted by Suleyman I.

1521-1585/927-993

Takiyüddin Mehmed, astronomer, built an observatory in Istanbul/Tophane in 1579; destroyed the following year by order of the *'ulama'*.

1526-1600/932-1008

Mehmed 'Abd al-Baki, known as the "sultan among poets," greatest Ottoman poet.

1534?/940?

Death of Matrakçi Nasuh, author of *Beyan-i menazil-i sefer-i Irakeyn* ("Description of the faltering of the campaign into the two 'Iraqs' "), illustrated manuscript recounting Suleyman I's voyage from Istanbul to Baghdad in 1533-1534.

1536-1599/943-1007

Sa'd al-Din Efendi, *shaykh ül-islam* and chronicler (*Taj al-Tawarikh* [The Crown of Histories])

1541-1599/948-1007

Mustafa 'Ali, chronicler, author of the *Kunh al-Akhbar* (The Essence of Current Events).

1553/960

Death of Tashköprüzade Ahmed Husam al-Din Efendi, author of *Shakayik-i nu'maniye*, biographical dictionary listing Ottoman writers up to the 16th century.

1562/969

Death of Seyyidi 'Ali Reis, geographer, author of the *Muhit* (The Ocean, 1554), a treatise on nautical astronomy, and a description of the southern coasts of Asia.

Praise for the Town of Constantinople

" . . . Within the jurisdiction of the four districts, there are 660 tribunal offices of the Prophet's Law. In addition, there are 74 Ottoman sultanian mosques, 1,985 grand vizier mosques, 6,990 neighborhood shrines, 6,665 mosques and shrines for important people and notables, 19 imarets where food is served, 9 hospitals, 1,993 primary schools, 53 Qur'anic schools, 135 schools for the study of traditions, 557 monasteries of the dervishes, 6,000 dervish *zaviye*, 91 inns for travellers, 979 caravanserais, 556 *khans* for merchants, 686 *khans* for individuals, 9,990 Muslim districts, 304 Greek districts, 657 Jewish districts, 17 Frankish districts, 27 Armenian districts, 8,900 residences for viziers, important people and *'ulama'*, 14,536 private baths, 4,000 fountains in the residences of viziers and *'ulama'*, 9,995 private and public fountains, 200 *sebilhane* . . . 600,000 wells, 55 cisterns. . . . "

Evliya Çelebi, *The Book of Travels*, Vol. I (2nd half of 17th century)

1574-1650/982-1060
Ibrahim Peçevi, chronicler of Hungarian descent; used Western works in his *Ta'rikh* ("Chronicle").

1582-1635/990-1044
Nef'i, satirical poet, executed because of the virulence of his attacks.

1591/999
Treatise on arithmetic by Hamza al-Maghribi ('Ali b. Veli).

1599?/1007?
Death of Mustafa Selaniki, chronicler.

1600/1008
Death of Baqi, who eulogized Suleyman; an example for subsequent poets.

1600-1657/1008-1067
Haji Khalifa (Katib Çelebi), encyclopedist and author of chronicles. Used Western sources.

1611-1683/1020-1094
Evliya Çelebi, author of the *Seyahatname* (*The Book of Travels*). Detailed description of the sights seen in and around the Ottoman Empire.

1630/1040
First appearance of the *Risale* ("The Treatise") by Qoçi Bey, which inspired reforms enacted by Murad IV.

1642-1712/1052-1124
Yusuf Nabi, poet, represents Iranian influence.

1660-1735/1070-1148
Mehmed Rashid, chronicler of the period from 1660 to 1722.

1665-1716/1075-1128
Mustafa Na'ima, author of a chronicle (*Ta'rikh*) of the years from 1591 to 1659, which is considered the peak of Ottoman historiography.

1681–1730/1092–1143

Ahmed Nedim, principal poet of the "Tulip Age."

1691/1102

Death of Husayn Hezarfen, civil servant in the Treasury. Maintained relations with Westerners (Nointel, Galland, Marsigli). Author of the *Talhis ül-beyan fi kavanin-i Al-i'Osman* ("Exposé on the Ottomans' Laws"), one of the most important books on the organization of the Ottoman state.

1703–1730/1115–1143

The "Tulip Age," reign of Ahmed III. Westernization (French influence) of Ottoman art and architecture. The tulip serves to embellish gardens and

is also a decorative motif; import of Dutch tulips by the aristocracy.

1720/1132

The first map printed in Turkey (the Marmara Sea).

1724/1137

Map of the Black Sea printed.

1727/1140

Firman commissions Ibrahim Müteferriqa to create a printing press with Arabic characters: 20 volumes printed between 1728 and 1745, year that the press is closed by order of the *'ulama'*.

1731/1144

Death of 'Abd al-Ghani al-Nabulusi, a Syrian poet and commentator on mystical literature.

Iran

At the beginning of the 16th/10th century, the town of Ardabil, in Azerbaijan, serves as the center for a Sunni mystical order, founded by the shaykh Safi al-Din, whose message is very popular among the Turkoman tribes of eastern Anatolia; perhaps under the influence of these groups, the order orients itself toward Shi'ism, most notably as regards the belief in the incarnation of God in the spiritual leader (*murshid*) of the Safavi order. During the 16th century, under pressure of the shaykhs Junayd and Haydar, the order goes even further and claims that the Safavid leaders are descendants of the Husaynid imams, which leads to their becoming a politico-religious group supported by the Turkoman tribes known as the Qizil bash (Red caps) because of the color of the headgear they wear. Staking out this position leads the Safavids into a victorious struggle against the Turkoman dynasty of the Aq-Qoyunlu, who practice Sunnism.

As Shah Isma'il ascends to power, he is considered to be a *murshid*; imposes Shi'ism on Iran, with the help of "twelver" *'ulama'*, which constitute the foundation of a powerful clergy. Nevertheless, Iran's conversion to Shi'ism is not completed until the 18th/12th century.

The Safavid dynasty also made its mark on Iran's history on the military front, in its disputes with Afghanistan and its conflicts with the Ottomans, and especially on the artistic front; the Safavids transformed Isfahan into one of the most remarkable cities in the Muslim world.

Wars and Foreign Relations

1499/905
Isma'il, leader of the Turkoman Safavids from eastern Anatolia, Armenia and Ghilan, begins his ascent to power.

1501/907
Isma'il arrives in Tabriz and has himself crowned shah (*shahanshah*). The Ja'farid rite of "twelver" Shi'ism becomes the state religion.

1503/908
Victory over the Aq-Qoyunlu Murad. Isma'il ruler of central and southern Iran.

1508/914
Conquest of the Iraq-i 'Arab; Baghdad taken.

1510/916
Khurasan annexed after the victory over the Uzbeks led by Muhammad Shaybani Khan in Merw.

1514/920
August 23/2 Rajab. The Ottoman Selim I victorious over Isma'il, in the battle of Chaldiran (in Azerbaijan). Diyar Bakr and western Kurdistan lost.

1517/923
Conquest of eastern Georgia.

1524/930
May 23/19 Rajab. Death of Isma'il. Successor: his son Tahmasp I (10 years old); a period marked by struggles between Qizilbash tribes.

1533-1534/940
Tahmasp I takes power.

1533-1553/940-961
Ottoman attacks on Azerbaijan.

1534/941
Iraq conquered and Baghdad captured by the Ottomans. Tahmasp moves his capital from Tabriz to Qazvin.

1548-1555/955-962
Turkish-Persian war.

1555/962
Treaty between Amasya and the Ottomans: 30 years of peace. Division of Georgia, the Ottomans keep their conquests in Mesopotamia.

1576/984
Death of Tahmasp.

1577-1590/985-999
Turkish-Persian War.

1578-1588/985-996: Reign of Muhammad Shah
1578/985
Ottoman conquest of Tiflis.

1585/993
Ottoman occupation of Tabriz and Kars.

1588-1629/996-1038: Reign of Shah 'Abbas I
1589/998
Treaty with the Ottomans, unfavorable for the Safavids. The Ottomans acquire Georgia, Karabag, Shirwan, Tabriz and Luristan.

1598/1007
Victory over the Uzbeks. Herat recaptured. Transfer of the capital from Qazvin to Isfahan.

1602-1612/1010-1021
Turkish-Persian war.

1603/1012
Reconquest of Tabriz, Eriwan, Kars and Shirawan.

1605/1014
Defeat of the Ottomans at Lake Urmia; reconquest of Mosul, Baghdad and Diyar Bakr.

1607/1016
Ottomans chased out of Safavid territory. Arrival of Spanish, Portuguese and English ambassadors. Carmelite, Augustinian and Capuchin monasteries established.

1612/1021
Peace treaty with the Ottomans; Azerbaijan and Georgia again under Safavid rule.

1629-1642/1038-1052:
Reign of Safi I
Son of Safi Mirza, the oldest son of Tahmasp I. Safi Mirza was murdered by his father to prevent dangerous competition.

1638/1047
Loss of Iraq to the Ottomans. Treaty of Qasr-i Shirin: definite delineation of boundaries between the Safavids and the Ottomans.

1642-1666/1052-1077:
Reign of Shah 'Abbas II

1666-1694/1077-1105:
Reign of Shah Sulayman

1694-1722/1105-1135:
Reign of Shah Husayn
1709/1121
The Ghalzay Afghans take Kandahar (which had belonged to the Safavids since 1648/1058). Abdali Afghans ravage Khurasan.

1719/1131
The Ghalzay Mir Mahmud occupies Kirman.

1722/1134
October/Muharram. Isfahan in Afghan hands until 1729/1142. Shah Husayn deposed.

1723/1135
Shah Tahmasp II proclaims himself sovereign in Qazvin.

1726/1138
Ottoman-Iranian peace disintegrates. The Afghan ruler Ashraf forced to recognize Ottoman control of northern and western Iran.

1729/1142
The leader of the Turkoman Afshar tribe Nadir Khan expels the Afghans from Isfahan and re-establishes the Safavid monarchy with Tahmasp II. Nadir becomes governor of eastern Persia.

1730/1143
Nadir reconquers Azerbaijan (Tabriz) and Kirmanshah (Hamadan).

1732/1145
Tahmasp II deposed. Accession to power of 'Abbas II, with Nadir Khan serving as regent.

1733/1146
November 9/Jumada II. Victory over the Ottomans.

1736/1148

'Abbas II deposed. Nadir Khan ruler under the name of Nadir Shah. The Afshar dynasty founded. Georgia and eastern Armenia recaptured by the Ottomans.

1736–1747/1148–1160: *Reign of Nadir Shah*
1738/1150–1151

March–June/Safar. Kandahar and Ghazna taken. Arrival in Peshawar.

1739/1151

Capital moved from Isfahan to Mashhad.

March 20/9 Dhu'l-Hijja. Defeat of the Moghul army. Nadir Shah plunders Delhi, annexes the territories north and west of the Indus, then invades Turkistan and Khwarizm.

1741–1742/1154–1155

Disastrous campaign in Daghestan.

1747/1160

Azerbaijan and the Caucasus taken from the Ottomans.

June 10/1 Jumada II. Nadir Shah assassinated by his officers.

1750–1779/1163–1193: *Reign of Karim Khan Zand, of Persian origin*

Rules from the southern city of Shiraz.

1795/1209

Agha Muhammad Khan, leader of the Qajar tribe, takes power, establishes his capital in Teheran and founds the Qajar dynasty. Crowned shah in 1796/1210.

Domestic Policy

1501/907

Shah Isma'il attempts to create a nation-state.

1514/920

The defeat of Chaldiran diminishes the Qizilbashs' confidence in Shah Isma'il.

1524–1533/930–940

Period marked by struggles and rivalries between Qizilbash factions. State subsidies for *'ulama'* and *sayyids* (descendents of the Prophet Muhammad); import of Shi'i scholars from abroad.

1534–1535/941 and 1548/955

Rebellion led by Shah Tahmasp's brothers results in no changes. Progress in civic sectors to the detriment of religious institutions.

After 1568/975

Revolts led by Qizil bash, also involving dissatisfied peasants and artisans.

1576–1578/984–986

Struggles between Qizilbash, Georgians and Circassians (the *ghulaman*).

1589/998

Creation of a permanent army, composed primarily of Georgians, Circassians and Persian peasants. Many lands become the property of the crown and are managed in such a way as to bring in funds to the royal Treasury. Diminished economic prosperity, due to the employment of temporary tax collectors who are only interested in extracting as much revenue as possible in as short a time as possible.

1598/1007
Isfahan, capital; substantial public works program.

1607/1016
Strengthening of the *ghulamans'* role to the detriment of the Qizilbash. Increased role for the Armenians.

1668-1722/1077-1135
During the reigns of Sulayman and Husayn, importance of the *lala*, the dancers in the harem. Incompetence and corruption. Decline of the army. Growing influence of the Shi'i *'ulama'*, who amass enough wealth to publicly challenge the authority of the ruler.

1736-1747/1148-1160
Iranian prestige re-established, but internal administration is decadent, leading to the impoverishment of the country. Special taxes levied, primarily on Kirman, to finance military campaigns. Confiscation of *waqf* land to reduce the influence of the *'ulama'*

1747-1799/1160-1193
Period of anarchy and civil war. The Zand make their presence known in the south. Agha Muhammad from the tribe of the Qajars is held captive by Karim Khan Zand. After Zand's death, Agha Muhammad flees to his home province Masenderan, obtains the support of his clansmen.

1779-1795/1193-1209
Dynastic quarrels. The Qajar first dominate southern Iran then triumph over the Zand. Agha Muhammad conquers Kirman, the seat of Lutf

'Ali Khan, the last Zand. The entire population of 20,000 men is blinded, the women become slaves of the Qajar army.

Religion and Culture

End of the 15th century/9th century
A religious sect is founded by Shaykh Safi al-Din (d. 1335/735), the leader of a Sufi order in Ardabil (Azerbaijan). It gets its name Safawi/Safavid from this leader, and orients itself toward Shi'ism; large number of followers from Turkoman tribes of eastern Anatolia. Confrontations with the Aq-Qoyunlu, Sunnis.

1501/906
Shah Isma'il imposes "twelver" Shi-'ism and creates a powerful clergy to disseminate it; the Iranian population does not offer substantial resistance to this propaganda campaign.

1519/925
Death of the writer Umidi, a panegyrist for Shah Isma'il.

1533/940
Death of Shaykh 'Ali b. 'Abd al-'Amili (Muhaqqiq al-Thani or Muhaqqiq al-Karaki), the leading Shi'i scholar of the time; leads propaganda campaign for Shi'ism.

Middle of 16th century/10th century
Religious men see their role in government passing to the "secular" men, often of Georgian or Circassian descent. Renaissance of Iranian art (painting, illuminations, ceramics, textiles, rugs).

2nd half of the 16th century/10th century

Many Persian poets immigrate to India, a movement launched by 'Urfi of Shiraz.

1587–1588/996

Death of Muhtasham of Kashan, the greatest Safavid poet, author of works that celebrate 'Ali and the martyred saints of Shi'ism.

1591–1592/1000

Farigh of Ghilan celebrates the conquest of Ghilan by Shah 'Abbas I.

Beginning of the 17th century/11th century

Construction of religious and public structures in the new capital Isfahan: mosques, *madrasas*, caravanserais, public baths and palaces.

1603/1012

Beginning of the construction of the Shaykh Lutfallah Mosque in Isfahan.

1612/1021

Death of Mullah 'Abdullah Shushtari, who played an important role in making Isfahan the major religious center.

1612–1613/1021

Beginning of the construction of the Masjid-i Shah, a magnificent royal mosque.

1620/1029

Construction of the Grand Bazaar.

1622/1031

Death of Muhammad Baha' al-Din al-'Amili, author of works that intend to make the Shi'i religion more popular.

1631/1040

Death of Muhammad Baqir al-Astarabadi (Mir Damad), the founder of the Ishraqi (Illuminationist) school of philosophy ("School of Isfahan").

1640/1050

Death of Sadr al-Din Muhammad b. Ibrahim Shirazi (Mullah Sadra), the greatest figure in the School of Isfahan.

1658–1659/1069

Death of Jalal-i 'Asir, known as the "drunken" poet. Death of Muhammad Taqi al-Majlisi (born 1594), together with his son Muhammad Baqir

---

Isfahan, the Most Beautiful City of the East

Chardin (*Voyages* . . .), who spent time in Persia from 1664 to 1670 and from 1671 to 1677, refers to Isfahan as "the largest and most beautiful city in the East." There one finds inhabitants of every creed: Christians, Jews, Muslims, gentiles, fire worshipers, and merchants from all over the world. He mentions that Isfahan contained within its walls 162 mosques, 48 colleges, 1,802 caravanserais, 273 public baths and 12 cemeteries. 2,000 lambs were slaughtered in the city each day, 500 in the suburbs, 90 in the shah's kitchens. He surmises that the city is as populous as London, with 600,000 to 700,000 inhabitants.

al-Majlisi (d. 1699/1110) two of the most important Safavid theologians.

1677–1678/1088

Death of Sa'ib, one of the most talented Persian poets.

1680/1091

Death of Mullah Muhsin-i Fayd of Kashan, author of *al-Wafi*, the most important work on Shi'i *hadith*.

1706–1714/1118–1126

Construction of the Mader-i Shah *madrasa* and a nearby caravanserai.

Middle of the 18th century/12th century

New school of poetry in Isfahan and Shiraz, led by Mushtak (d. in 1757/1171) and Shu'la (d. in 1747/1160). Return to traditional literature.

1766/1180

Death of 'Ali Hazin, author of the *Tadhkirat al-Ahwal*, description of Iran in the first decades of the 18th century.

Afghanistan

Situated between the Safavid state of Iran and the Moghul Empire in India, Afghanistan was a constant point of contention between those two states from the 16th to the 18th century. Its people only begin to imagine the possibility of an independent existence after the demise of the Safavids and the decline of Moghul power, but in the end the quarrels and rivalries between the most important clans would not cease and, prior to the middle of the 18th century, there would be no peace.

Political History

End of the 15th century/9th century

Dhu al-Nun Beg Arghun establishes a Mongol state in Kandahar.

1507/913

His successor, Shah Beg, is threatened by the Timurid Zahir al-Din Muhammad Babur, who is established in Kabul.

1510/916

The Safavid Shah Isma'il takes Herat. Introduction of Shi'ism.

1520/926

Shah Beg invades the Sind; he establishes the Arghun dynasty there.

1522/928

Zahir al-Din Babur takes Kandahar and its province.

1526/932

Babur defeats the Lodi dynasty of Delhi in the battle of Panipat. He founds the Empire of Great Moghuls. Eastern Afghanistan, including Kabul, is incorporated into it. Herat and Sistan occupied by Persia. Possession of Kandahar disputed by the Safavids and the Moghuls; the country's northern part controlled by the Uzbeks.

1530–1556/936–963: Reign of Nasir al-Din Humayun
1531/937

Kamran, the brother of the Moghul Humayun, reunites Kabul and Kandahar with the Punjab.

1535/941

Attack on Kandahar by the Safavids.

1540–1555/947–962

Interregnum of Shir-Shah Sur and his successors. Nasir al-Din Humayun in exile.

1545/952

Humayun takes Kandahar from his brother.

1556–1605/963–1014: Reign of Akbar, founds a syncretistic universal religion

In North and Central India, the Moghul Empire reaches its zenith.

1558/965

The Safavid Tahmasp takes Kandahar. After having been under Persian control for 40 years, it is then disputed by the Persians and Moghuls.

1586/994

Moghul troops vanquished by the Yusufzay clan's troops. The Ghalzay clan extends its influence to the Kandahar region; the Abdali tribe from Herat becomes the ruling force in the region.

1605–1627/1014–1036: Reign of Jahangir
1613–1689/1022–1100

The poet Khushhal Khan Khattak encourages the Afghan tribes to defend their independence from the Moghuls.

1628–1658/1037–1068: Reign of Shah Jahan
1637/1047

Kandahar recaptured by the Moghul Shah Jahan.

1648/1058

Kandahar recaptured by the Safavid 'Abbas II.

1658–1707/1068–1119

Awrangzib defeats his brother Dara Shikoh in a struggle of succession. Assures the dominance of Islam in the Deccan and northwest India. After his death, the empire disintegrates.

1709/1121

Mir Ways, a Ghalzay leader, takes Kandahar and its province back from the Safavids; declares its independence.

1715/1127

Death of Mir Ways.

1716/1128

The Abdali forces conquer the Persians, take Herat and its province, and declare the region's independence.

1722/1134

The Ghalzay under Mir Ways' son Muhammad occupy Isfahan and depose Shah Husayn.

1729/1142

Tahmasp Quli Khan, later known as Nadir Khan, expels the Ghalzay from Persia; many perish in the deserts of Baluchistan.

The Tribes of Afghanistan

The most important of the Afghan tribes are the *Abdali*, or *Durrani*, a name derived from *duri-i duran* (pearl of all pearls) and adopted by Ahmad Shah Abdali. They establish themselves, at first, in the regions located to the west and southeast of Kandahar. Seven groups can be identified: Popalzay, Barakzay, Alizay, Nurzay, Ishakzay, Ashakzay and Alikozay. The Durrani, having attained power in the second half of the 18th century, led by Ahmad Shah, managed over time to gain control of the government and economy of Afghanistan.

The *Ghalzay* represent the second largest tribe, possibly of Turkish origin. Rulers of Afghanistan at the beginning of the 18th century, they were conquered by Nadir Shah of Iran and forced to submit to the rule of Ahmad Shah. They had been settled between Kandahar and Ghazni.

The *Khattak* are located in the eastern part of Afghanistan, along with the *Afridi*, who had controlled the Khyber Pass for a long time. This same region is home to the *Yusufzay* and, further to the north, the *Shinwari*. The *Tajik*, a sedentary tribe, had been established around Kabul, Kuhistan and the Panshir valleys as well as the Upper Oxus for some time. They speak Persian, like the inhabitants of the outskirts of Herat and several groups from the northeastern part of the country.

The *Harazas*, for a long time considered to be descendants of Mongol-Tartar troops, represented a mixed population of Iranians and Mongols. Dispersed throughout Afghanistan, they speak a Persian heavily laden with Turkish and Mongolian, and they practice Shi'ism.

Other groups are made up tribes of Turkish origin: Uzbek, Turkoman and Qizilbash.

1738/1150

Nadir Shah takes Kandahar, then Kabul; with the aid of the Abdali, he becomes the ruler of all Afghanistan.

1747/1160

Assassination of Nadir Shah by Asfar and Qajar leaders. The Abdali sever ties with the Persians, declare their independence and proclaim Ahmad Shah Durrani, from the Sadozay clan of the Abdali, the sovereign of Afghanistan. He chooses Kandahar as his capital and extends his sphere of influence to Ghazni, Kabul and Peshawar.

1747–1769/1160–1183

Ahmad Shah invades India nine times.

1751/1163

Ahmad Shah takes Herat, Mashhad and Nishapur.

1757/1170

Ahmad Shah occupies Lahore and plunders Delhi.

1761/1174

January 14/21 Jumada II. The Maratha of India crushed in Panipat; Ahmad Shah annexes the Punjab.

1773/1187

Death of Ahmad Shah; his state stretches from the Oxus to the Indus and from Tibet to Khurasan.

1773-1793/1187-1208

Timur Shah, his successor, continues Ahmad Shah's policies, but with little success.

Central Asia

1510/916

Defeat and death of Muhammad Shaybani, a descendent of Ghengis Khan, by the Safavid Shah Isma'il II.

1512/918

The Moghul Babur removed from Transoxiana, after an unsuccessful attack on the Uzbeks.

Uzbek (Transoxiana)

1551/958

Region unified under the Shaybanid 'Abd Allah II.

1557/964

'Abd Allah conquers Bukhara.

1573-1583/981-991

He takes Balkh, Samarkand, Tashkent and Ferghana.

1583/991

'Abd Allah assumes the title of khan. Introduces reforms, improves administration.

1585/993

Attempt to form alliance with the Ottoman Murad III and the Moghul Akbar.

1598/1006

Death of 'Abd Allah II. Made last attempt to unify Transoxiana. His son deposed soon after his accession. The Janids (Astrahanids), who are related to the Uzbeks, take power.

Moghulistan

16th century/10th century

The Çaghatay dynasty establishes itself in the eastern part of the territory. Mansur and Sa'id Khan, who hold power, open Tarim to the civilization of Bukhara and Samarkand. Progressive disappearance of Chinese influence.

1517/923

Mansur establishes his capital in the oasis of Qomul and launches attacks against China. Sa'id invades Ladakh.

1533/939

'Abd al-Rashid, son of Sa'id, succeeds his father in Kashgar.

1565?/972?

Death of 'Abd al-Rashid. Successor: his son 'Abd al-Karim, who reigns until 1593/1001.

End of the 17th century/11th century

The last Çagatay descendants disappear, except in Bukhara. Conquest of the oases Semiresh, Turfan and Qomul by the Buddhist-Lamaist Jungars.

1757/1170

The Turks liberate themselves from the Jungars' authority. Sun-Kiang recaptured by the Chinese. Kirghiz and Kazakh regain control over their own territories.

Bukhara

1599/1007

Baqi Muhammad, the Shaybanite ruler in Transoxiana. Loses territory to the Kazakhs.

1611–1643/1020–1053:
Reign of Khan Imam Quli

1645–1680/1055–1091:
Reign of 'Abd ul-'Aziz
1710/1121

Ferghana secedes and creates the Khokand state.

1711–1747/1123–1160:
Reign of Abu al-Fayz
Persia occupies Balkh.

1785/1198

The Mangit, led by Murad Ma'sum Shah, take power.

Khokand

Beginning of the 16th century/10th century

Uzbek government.

End of the 16th century/10th century

Kirghiz government.

17th century/11th century

Increased importance of the Qipchak.

1722/1135

Death of Shah Rukh, ruler of the Ferghana valley.

After 1759/1172

Khokand forced to recognize Chinese suzerainty.

Khiva

1613/1022 and 1632/1042

Attacks by the Kazakhs.

Circa 1615/1024

The capital moved from Urgenç to Khiva.

1644–1663/1054–1074: Reign
of Abu al-Ghazi Bahadur Khan
Kazakh attacks driven back.

1663–1687/1074–1099:
Reign of Anusha
End of the 17th–beginning of 18th century/12th century

Ascent of the Kungrat dynasty, which escapes the suzerainty of the Persian Nadir Shah.

India

India's history was profoundly marked by the dynasty of the Great Moghuls, who led the greater part of the country from the 16th century until British domination in the 19th century.

This period witnessed great rulers leading the dynasty: Babur, Humayun, Akbar, Jahanghir, Shahjahan and Awrangzib; some of them even became legendary figures. In any case, they all worked to enlarge their empire, as much in matters of political rule as in matters of culture, civilization and art. Adhering to Islam and being of Turkish descent, they had the ability to assimilate Indian traditions to create an original society and civilization; several of the architectural and artistic works left behind bear witness to this fact.

States Independent of the Moghul Empire

Gujarat
Center of maritime trade with Muslim countries of the Middle East. The Mamluks of Egypt (Qansawh al-Ghawri) and the Ottomans (Suleyman the Magnificent) had sent naval support against the Portuguese.

1458–1511/862–917
The dazzling reign of Mahmud I Begra; great prosperity. Propagation of Islam.

1508/913
Victory over the Portuguese navy.

1509/914
Mahmud's navy defeated off Diu. Decline of Muslim trade in this part of the Indian Ocean.

1526–1537/932–943: Reign of Bahadur Shah
Struggle with the Portuguese and Moghuls. Last great sovereign of Gujarat.

1531/937
Malwa (central India) conquered.

1534/941
Bassein taken by the Portuguese. Beginning of a long war with Humayun.

1537/943
Assassination of Bahadur by the Portuguese. Period of rivalries and anarchy.

1538/944
Ottoman attack on Diu.

1546–1547/953–954
Massacre by the Portuguese of Muslims from Diu and Bhoroç.

1572–1573/980–981
Conquest of Gujarat by Akbar.

1573–1574/981–982
Devastating famine.

1601/1009
Annexation of Gujarat by the Moghuls.

Khandesh

1509–1520/914–926: Reign of 'Adil Khan III, of the Faruqi dynasty
1564/972
Khandesh, province of the Moghul Empire.

Malwa

1500–1511/906–917: Reign of Nasir al-Din
1511/917
Mahmud II becomes sultan, in spite of opposition from his father Muhammad and Sikandar Lodi, the ruler of Delhi, and Muzaffar II of Gujarat, but with support from Hindu ministers, especially Medini Rai.

1517/923
Mahmud expelled by Medini Rai.

1518/924
Mahmud II restored. Northern Malwa annexed by the duchy of Mewar.

1531/937
Malwa annexed by Bahadur of Gujarat.

1535/941
The capital Mandu taken by Humayun.

1536/942
Mallu Khan, Khalji officer, becomes king but is deposed by the Afghan Shir Shah Sur.

1545/952
Shuja'at Khan, governor of Malwa.

1555/962
His son and successor, Baz Bahadur, refuses to recognize Moghul suzerainty.

1561/968
Malwa conquered by Akbar.

Delhi

1489–1517/894–923: Reign of Sikandar Lodi
Forces the Rajput states to submit to his rule. Iranization of the lower echelons of the administration. Attraction of scholars.

1504/910
The capital established in Agra.

1517–1526/923–932: Reign of Ibrahim Lodi
1526/932
Defeat against Babur in the battle of Panipat. End of the dynasty.

Bengal

1493–1519/899–925: Reign of 'Ala' al-Din Husayn Shah
1498/904
Annexation of a portion of Assam.

1519–1531/925–938: Reign of Nusrat Shah
Large numbers of Afghans arrive from Delhi.

1528/934
Skirmishes with the Portuguese.

1538/945
Shir Shah Sur becomes king of Bengal, but is immediately deposed by Humayun.

Northern Deccan

Berar: Dynasty of the 'Imad-Shahis (1485–1572/890–990)

Bijapur: Dynasty of the 'Adil-Shahis (1490–1686/896–1097)

Ahmednagar: Dynasty of the Nizam-Shahis (1491–1633/897–1042)

Golkonda: Dynasty of the Qutb-Shahis (1512–1687/918–1089)

Bidar: Dynasty of the Barid-Shahis (1526–1619/932–1028)

1565/1075

Union against the powerful Hindu kingdom of Vijayanagara, which is defeated.

1574/992

Ahmednagar annexes Berar.

1619/1028

Bijapur annexes Bidar. The religion of Ahmednagar, Bijapur and Golkonda was Shi'ism, and they maintained good relations with the Safavids.

The Moghuls

1494/899

Death of the Timurid 'Umar Shaykh Mirza, ruler of Ferghana, who bequeaths his territory to his son, Babur (11 years old).

1504/910

Babur occupies Kabul, after he fails to prevail at home against the Uzbek Muhammad Shaybani Khan.

1510/616

Death of Shaybani Khan.

1511/617

Babur captures the kingdom of Samarkand from the Safavid Shah Isma'il in an attempt to reestablish the empire in Central Asia.

1512/918

Babur loses Samarkand, retreats to Kabul. He leaves for India after he is invited to invade by Rana Sanga, the head of the Rajput confederation.

1524/930

Lahore captured.

1526/932

Battle of Panipat; Babur victorious over Ibrahim II Lodi; he occupies Delhi, sends his son to Agra. Babur's name read at the *khutba*. Beginning of the Moghul dynasty.

1527/933

The Rajput confederation defeated in the battle of Khanua.

1529/936

Mahmud Lodi vanquished. Jawnpur occupied. Treaty with Nusrat Shah of Bengal.

1530/937

December 29/9 Jumada I. Death of Babur. Had designated his son Humayun as his successor.

1531/938

Humayun subjugates the rajah of Kalinjar and triumphs over the Afghans.

1535/941

February–May/Shawwal–Dhu'l-Qa'da. Failure of an invasion into Moghul territory by Bahadur Shah of Gujarat.

1537/944

July/Safar. Humayun attacks the Afghan Shir Khan; four difficult years follow.

1539/946

Decisive defeat of Shir Khan.

1540/947

Defeat at Kanawj. Humayun goes into exile at the court of the Safavid Tahmasp.

1540–1555/947–962: Reign of Shir Khan (until 1545), Islam Shah (until 1554), and 'Adil Shah (until 1555)

1545/952

May/Rabi I. Humayun occupies Kandahar with Safavid support.

November–December/Ramadan. He takes Kabul from his brother Kamran.

1553/960

August/Ramadan. Kamran conquered and delivered to Humayun.

1555/962

February/Rabi II. Humayun enters Lahore.

July 23/4 Ramadan. Humayun enters Delhi.

1556/963

January 26–27/13–14 Rabi I. Death of Humayun as a result of falling down the stairs in his library. Successor: Akbar (13 years old). Bairam Khan, one of Humayun's viziers, leads the government for Akbar.

1556–1557/963–964

The Hindu leader Hemu, from Rewari, takes Delhi and Agra. Van-quished in the second battle of Panipat, Hemu is executed; the towns previously lost are recaptured.

1558–1560/965–967

Conquest of the Hindu principalities Gwalior and Ajmer, as well as the province of Jaipur.

1560/967

Rebellion led by Bayram Khan, Akbar's former tutor. Execution of Bayram.

1561/968

Malwa taken from Baz Bahadur.

1564/971

Annexation of the Hindu kingdom of Gondwana. Bengal recognizes Akbar's suzerainty.

1568/975

Defeat of the Rajputs.

1573/981

Ranthambor, Kalinjar and Gujarat taken.

1576/984

Da'ud of Bengal defeated; incorporation of Bengal into the empire.

1577/985

Khandesh occupied.

1581/989

Campaign against Akbar's brother Muhammad Hakim, who had started a rebellion in Kabul.

1583/991

Administrative reform.

1585/993

Incorporation of the province of Kabul after Muhammad Hakim's death.

1586/994

Kashmir subjugated, then annexed in 1590/999 in order to create a buffer against growing Uzbek power.

1593/1001

Sind, Urisa and Kathiawadh all subjugated.

1596/1004

Berar, a province of Deccan, falls to Akbar.

1599/1008

Salim, known by the name Nur ud-Din Jahanghir, leads a revolt against his father Akbar; he declares his independence in Allahabad.

1600/1009

Ahmednagar in the Deccan occupied, Khandesh annexed.

1601/1010

Jahanghir unable to capture Agra. Allows himself to be subjugated.

1605/1014

October 16/3 Jumada I. Death of Akbar. Jahanghir ascends to the Moghul throne.

1605–1627/1014–1037:
Reign of Jahanghir
1611/1020

He marries Nur Jahan, who has an important influence on how Jahanghir governs.

1612/1021

First English factory built in Surat.

1620/1029

Conquest of the principality of Kangra (at the foot of the Himalayas).

1623/1032

Revolt led by Jahanghir's son Khurram (Shahjahan); the rebellion spreads throughout India.

1626/1035

March/Jumada II. Khurram subdued.

1627/1037

October 28/17 Safar. Death of Jahanghir. Shahjahan becomes sultan. A war over secession ensues.

1628–1657/1038–1067:
Reign of Shahjahan
1633/1042

Dawlatabad taken.

1636/1045

Prince Awrangzib named viceroy of the Deccan.

1638/1047

Kandahar surrendered to the Moghuls by its governor. The town is recaptured, 11 years later, by the Persians.

1657/1067

Struggle over secession among the ailing Shahjahan's four sons. Awrangzib victorious against Shahjahan's chosen successor Dara Shukoh; has his father admitted to a hospital in Agra, then holds him captive in his palace.

1658–1707/1068–1118: Reign of Awrangzib
1662/1072
Revolt in the region of Assam.

1666/1076
Death of Shahjahan. Victory over the Marath leader Shivaji, in the western Deccan (battle of Purandar). Subjugation of Assam; the empire now borders on Burma.

1667/1078
Rebellion by the Afghan Yusufzay tribe.

1672/1083
The Afridi revolt.

1674/1085
Shivaji occupies the regions of Madras and Mysore; establishes a state that will be the rival of Awrangzib's state. Bombay becomes the headquarters of the British East India Company.

1678/1089
Marwar comes under direct Moghul control.

1682/1093
Death of Shivaji.

1686/1097
Bijapur taken.

1687/1098
Golkonda taken.

1689/1100
Capture and execution of the Marath leader Shambhuji.

Circa 1690/1101
The Moghul Empire at its largest, covering almost the entire subcontinent with the exception of its southern tip.

1707/1118
March 2/27 Dhu'l-Qa'da. Death of Awrangzib.

1707–1712/1119–1124: Reign of Bahadur Shah I
Uprising by Sikhs who favor Shi'ism in the Punjab. Turmoil in Delhi and Lahore.

1712/1124
Accession of Jahandar Shah, who is rapidly supplanted by Farrukhsiyar.

1719/1132
Farrukhsiyar, deposed by the Sayyid family. Provincial governors and nobles gain independence from Delhi.

1724/1136
The governor of the Deccan gains his independence and establishes his capital in Hyderabad.

1735/1148
Baji Rao recognized as governor of Malwa.

1739/1151
Nadir Shah, from Persia, occupies Kabul, pillages Delhi, drives Muhammad Shah back and annexes the provinces above the Indus.

1747/1160
Ahmad Shah Durrani, successor to Nadir Shah, vanquished in the Punjab by the Moghuls.

1749, 1751/1162, 1164
Repeated Afghani invasions of the Punjab.

1757/1170
Delhi devastated by the Afghans.

1761/1174
Third battle of Panipat. The Durrani become the true rulers of the Moghul Empire.

1765/1178
Shah 'Alam III seeks the protection of the British East India Company, which receives the revenues from land tax of the eastern provinces Bengal, Bihar and Orissa.

Islam in India

15th century/9th century
Shi'ism appears in a few states in the Deccan.

End of the 1st half of the 16th century/10th century
Increased influence of Shi'ism in northern India, after Humayun's return from exile in Safavid Iran.

2nd half of 16th century/10th century
Under Akbar, Shaykh Mubarak and his son Abu al-Fazl spread the ideas and syncretist views of the mystic Ibn al-'Arabi (1165–1240/560–638). Large emigration of Shi'is from Persia to India.

1562/969
Abolition of the *jizya* (head tax for non-Muslims).

1563–1603/971–1012
Khwaja Baki bi-Allah introduces the Sufi Naqshabandi brotherhood in India.

1579/987
The *'ulama'* issue an edict, proclaiming that if the theologians are divided, the final decision rests with the emperor (as long as he does not contradict Qur'an and *sunna*).

1580/988
Arrival of the first Jesuit mission to Agra.

1582/990
Akbar founds the Din-i ilahi sect, a heterodox, elitist and humanitarian grouping, which merges Jaini, Catholic, Zoroastrian and Muslim elements.

First half of the 17th century/11th century
Shah Jahan and Awrangzib devoted to Ahmad Sirhindi's doctrines, which condemn pantheism. The succession of Awrangzib marked by religious conflict. Defeat of his son Dara Shukoh, who favors Hinduism and eclecticism.

1650–1729/1060–1142
Shah Kalim Allah seeks a return to the original principles of Islam.

1669/1080
Wide-scale destruction of Hindu temples.

1679/1090
Reintroduction of the *jizya* for Hindus and non-Muslims.

1703–1763/1114–1176

Shah Wali Allah, last great thinker among those who attempt to reinterpret Islamic thought using reason; according to him, the *shari'a* must take into account social, religious and legal practices of each region concerned.

Architecture

1509/915

The Jam Nizan al-Din mausoleum in Thatta (Sind).

1515/921

Construction of the Rani Rupawati mosque.

1518/924

Octagonal tomb built for Sikandar in Khayrpur, near Delhi.

Moghul Architecture

1532/939

Humayun founds the Din Panah complex in Delhi.

1535/941

Hasan Khan mausoleum built in Bihar.

1536/943

Jamali mosque built; richly decorated tomb for Jamali.

After 1540/947

Construction activity in Delhi by Shir Shah.

1545/952

Mausoleum of Shir Shah built in Sasaram.

1565–1569/972–977

The Humayun mausoleum built; strong influence of Iranian architecture.

1570/978

Construction of the Jodh Bai palace.

1570–1574/978–982

Establishment of Fathpur Sikri by Akbar; attempt to merge different architectural styles.

After 1571/979

Tomb for Salim Çishti in Fathpur Sikri.

1572–1573/980

The Shaykh Sa'id al-Hafshi mosque built.

1577/985

Masjid-i jami' of Bijapur.

1605–1627/1014–1037

Summer palace of Jahanghir (Jahanghir-i Mahal) built.

1613/1022

Mausoleum of Akbar built in Sikandra, near Agra; contains elements of Buddhist architecture.

1626/1035

Mausoleum of Jahanghir built near Lahore.

1634/1043

Taj Mahal, mausoleum for Nur Jahan, built in Agra.

1636/1045

Shahjahan begins construction of New Delhi.

1638/1047

The fort of Delhi built of red sandstone.

1644-1658/1054-1068
The Jamiʻ mosque in Delhi built, the biggest mosque in India.

1662/1072
Moti mosque in the fort of Delhi.

1678/1089
Bibi-ka-Maqbara in Awrangabad.

1739-1753/1151-1166
Mausoleum of Safdar Jung, last great Moghul monument.

Painting

16th century/10th century
Humayun invites the Persian painter Mir Sayyid ʻAli, author of the *Amir Hamza-name* ("Life of the Prophet's Uncle"), starting point of the Moghul miniature school; it has no relation to the Indian tradition of painting. Artistic activity pursued by ʻAbd al-Samad.

17th century/11th century
Continuation of the Moghul miniature school under Jahanghir and Shahjahan: during the latter's reign, the zenith of Indian painting is attained, with works by Manohar and Govardhan. Growing influence of Indian painting; the stylized landscape is replaced by naturalism and realistic pictures of animals.

Literature

Beginning of 16th century/10th century
Babur grants the Turkish language a dominant position in his court (inherited from Timurid culture of Samarkand). Principal work, the *Baburname*, written in eastern Turkish.

Middle of the 16th century/10th century
Persian becomes a literary language, especially after Humayun's return from Iran. But poetry is characterized by a very intellectual "Indian style" (*sabk-i hindi*), e.g. byʻUrfi (1555-1591/962-999) and Bidil (1644-1721/1054-1133).

Late 16th-17th century/10th-11th century
Emigration of outstanding writers from Iran to India as a result of the decline of the Safavids.

18th century/12th century
The Indian Muslim elite tends toward the elimination of outside influences; they use Urdu, not Persian, as their poetic language.

Indonesia

The Spread of Islam and the Dutch Incursion

Beginning of the 15th century/9th century
The ruler of Malacca converts to Islam. Pasai (northeast of Sumatra)

and Malacca are centers of Islamic thought and contribute to the spread of Islam throughout the archipelago.

Middle of the 15th century/9th century

Islam introduced into the court of Majapahit (Java) thanks to the missionary Raden Rahmat, who settles in Ampel (Surabaya) and is venerated under the name of Sunan Ampel.

1467/872

Death of Sunan Ampel. Ampel becomes the great center of Islamic culture.

1475/880

Sayyid Abu Bakr of Malacca founds the Islamic Sultanate of Sulu; mass conversions to Islam, construction of mosques, initiation of caliphal authority.

1488/894

A mosque in Demak (north of Java); along with Raden Patah, an important Islamic center. Use of the *wayang* (shadow theatre) for the dissemination of Islam.

End of the 15th century/9th century

Beginning of the Islamization of the southern parts of Sumatra and Borneo as well as the Moluccas.

1486–1550/891–905: Reign of Zayn al-'Abidin

First Muslim ruler of the Moluccas.

1495/900

The ruler of Ternate travels to Gresik (northern Java) to convert to Islam.

1505/911

Islamization of Macassar (south of Celebes).

Beginning of the 16th century/10th century

Large number of conversions in western Java.

1511/917

Malacca taken by the Portuguese; Muslim refugees in various Indonesian port towns.

1521–1524/927–930

Pasai occupied by the Portuguese.

1521/927

Report of an Islamic ruler in the northwestern part of the island of Halmahera.

1524/930

'Ali Mughayat Shah, sultan of Atjeh (north of Sumatra), conquers Pasai.

First quarter of the 16th century/10th century

Islamization of the coast of Brunei.

1526/932

Bantam (west of Java) and Jakarta adopt Islam.

1530/937

Death of 'Ali Mughayat Shah.

1537/944

Conquest of central Sumatra (Batak) by the sultan of Atjeh.

Circa 1539/946

Ottoman military assistance for Atjeh in its struggle against the Portuguese.

1546/953

Demak becomes a de facto Muslim state under Sunan-Kudus. His influence extends as far as central Java.

1548–1571/955–979: Reign of 'Ala' al-Din, sultan of Atjeh

Conflict with the Portuguese over Malacca; receives material aid from the Ottomans.

Circa 1550/957

Foundation of an Islamic dynasty in Sukadana (on the western coast of Borneo).

1575/983 and 1582/990

'Ulama' from Mecca, Yemen and Gujarat arrive in Atjeh.

1591/1000

The coast of Borneo entirely Islamized. Islam introduced into Luzon and certain parts of Manila.

1595/1004

Dutch merchants arrive in Java.

Second half of the 16th century/10th century

Islamization of the Lampung and Bangkahulu (Sumatra) regions; Java and Madura entirely Islamized. Ternate, under Moluccan control, is a center for the spread of Islam.

1602/1010–1011

Creation of the Dutch East India Company.

1605/1014

In Celebes, the prince of Tallo embraces Islam; the princes of Macassar convert to Islam.

1607–1636/1016–1046: Reign of Iskandar Muda, sultan of Atjeh

Atjeh reaches its economic and military zenith, becomes an important naval power, and develops a sophisticated philosophy of religion.

1613–1646/1022–1056: Reign of Agung, sultan of Mataram (south of Java)

The major part of island is conquered, except for Batavia.

1619/1028

Batavia founded by the Dutch.

1629/1038

Failure in the attempted siege on Malacca by Iskandar Muda. He establishes a monopoly on pepper.

1637–1641/1047–1051: Reign of Iskandar II in Atjeh

Continuation of Iskandar Muda's policies.

1641/1051

Malacca taken by the Dutch. Agung, the ruler of Mataram, replaces his Javanese title of susuhunan with the title of sultan. His successor Mangku-Rat I reverts to pre-Islamic practices, has 6,000 Muslim theologians killed, and once again takes the title susuhunan.

1641–1699/1051–1111

The Atjeh throne occupied by four successive queens. Decline of the sultanate.

Circa 1661/1072

Followers of Ahmad Qushashi of Medina spread this Dervish order in Sumatra and Celebes, later in Java and Malaya.

1663/1074
Treaty of Painan; the Dutch obtain ports in Sumatra.

1668/1079
The Dutch occupy Macassar. Atjeh sends Islamic missionaries to Siam.

1675–1682/1086–1093
Rebellions in Mataram. The rulers seek support from the Dutch, who will intervene on several occasions.

End of the 17th century/11th century
The Dutch East India Company acquires a monopoly on trade with Java.

1714/1126
The English settle in Bangkahulu. Rivalries and conflicts with the Dutch.

1755/1168
The kingdom of Mataram divided into two: Surakarta and Jogjakarta.

Literature

Muslim religious literature written in Malaysian is typically anonymous, as are the *suluk*, mystical chants in Malaysian.

End of the 16th century/10th century
Mystical poems, in Malaysian, by Hamza Fansuri (d. ca. 1608/1017), which are inspired by the neo-Platonist gnostic Ibn al-'Arabi (1165–1240/560–637).

1603/1012
Taj al-Salatin ("The Mirror of the Princes"), by Bukhari Johori, written for the sultans of Atjeh.

1630/1040
Death of Shams al-Din al-Samatra'i, author of religious texts in Arabic and Malaysian; saw an essential equality between man and god (*wujudiyya*).

1637–1644/1047–1054
Sojourn in Atjeh by the Arab Nur al-Din al-Raniri (died in India in 1658/1068), author of polemical orthodox works against Hamza Fansuri's mystical school; demanded the burning of the followers and writings of this school.

1638/1047
Bustan al-Salatin ("The Garden of the Princes"), encyclopedia of all Islamic knowledge.

Second half of the 17th century/11th century
The Qur'an translated into Malaysian.

End of the 17th century/beginning of the 12th century
Death of 'Abd al-Ra'uf of Singkel, author of mystical works and disseminator in Atjeh of the *tariqa shattariya*, a very popular text in Indonesia.

18th century/12th century
Publication of a large number of historical novels (Islamic heroes, Indonesian historical figures, etc.) in prose and in verse.

Sub-Saharan Africa

In West Africa, a passage from one type of Muslim presence to another occurs. Courtly Islam, associated with the upsurge in Islamized empires during the Middle Ages, is progressively replaced by a militant Islam inspired by men of letters who were the keepers of Arabic-Muslim written culture. This new tendency first appeared in the Senegambia, a region more exposed than others to social mutations brought about by the extension of European commerce. The fall of the Songhay Empire at the hands of the Moroccan conquerors in 1591/999 and the first West African *jihad*, a half century later, in [Mauritania]* and in northern [Senegal], point to an instability that is the result of the interface of two geographical zones and two types of Islam. At the same time, the Muslim commercial and intellectual network establishes itself as it diversifies, creating the foundations for mass Islamization.

Near Lake Chad, Kanem reaches its zenith just as Songhay is crumbling. Out of these two empires, a new civilization develops that is marked by a common language and is organized around a certain number of city-states: the Hausa world.

[Sudan] and [Ethiopia] provide the backdrop for similar events that are oriented in the opposite direction. While in the [Sudan] a Funj state puts the finishing touches on a total victory for Islam over the last vestiges of Christianity and introduces the first Sudanese Muslim ruling class, in [Ethiopia] the Christians succeed, not without difficulty, in maintaining their independence in the face of the *jihad* directed at them by the Muslims.

In East Africa, a long period of Portuguese and Christian domination progressively vanishes as it is replaced by a new Muslim hegemony that comes from the sultanate of Oman (Southern Arabia).

---

*In brackets throughout this section are the *present* names of countries that, prior to 1960, had different names.

West Africa

1549–1582: Reign of the Askiya Dawud
Golden Age of the Songhay Empire.

1590/999
October/Muharram. In retaliation against the Songhay's refusal to give up the Taghaza salt mine (in the middle of the Sahara), al-Mansur of Morocco sends an armed expedition of 3,000 to 4,000 men, led by the pasha Judar, a Spaniard converted to Islam.

1591/999
March 12/16 Jumada I. The Moroccan army crushes the Songhay army, led by the *Askiya* Ishaq II, on the road leading to Gao, in Tondibi.

Starting in 1591/999
The Moroccan pashas govern the principal towns in the Niger loop. Due to its distance from Morocco, this

regime slowly dissolves until it disappears in 1833/1249.

Circa 1645/1055

In [Mauritania], a member of the Berber tribe of the Awlad Dayman, known as the Nasir al-Din, assumes the title of *imam* and launches an Islamic reform movement.

Circa 1655/1065

Completion of two African chronicles written in Arabic that commemorate the history of the fallen Songhay Empire: *Tarikh al-Sudan*, by al-Sa'di and *Tarikh al-Fattash*, by Mahmud Ka'ti and his grandson Ibn al-Mukhtar.

1673–1677/1083–1087

Nasir al-Din launches a *jihad* against the pagan or only slightly Islamic rulers of the Senegal Valley. An Islamic revolution known as the War of the Marabouts or Toubenans (from the Arabic word *tawba*, "conversion, repentance") leads to the toppling of four Senegalese kings accused of colluding with European slave traders; they are replaced by militant clerics. Movement completely crushed in 1677; the overthrown kings are restored.

1674/1085

August/Shawwal. Nasir al-Din dies in combat; after his death, the *imams* do not attempt to rectify the situation. In [Mauritania], the "Toubenan" war develops into a confrontation between newly arrived Arab groups and Berber groups. After this war, known as the *Shurbubba*, Mauritanian society is restructured: the Hassani Arabs, warriors, generally in a dominant position, and the Zwaya Berbers, students

of Islam, mostly in an inferior position. This war also provides the model for the West African Islamic revolutions of the 18th and 19th centuries.

End of the 17th century/beginning of the 12th century

A Tukulor man of letters, Malik Sy, establishes the small state of Bundu in upper Senegal that, for some time, realizes the ideals of Islam and serves as an example for future experiences. Other Tukulor Islamic militants emigrate to Futa Jallon [Guinea].

Circa 1725–1726/1138

Nine Peuhl *'ulama'* from Futa Jallon assemble and declare a *jihad*. They appoint Ibrahim Sambeghu, better known as Karamoko Alfa, as their leader. Movement with ethnic (Peuhl immigrants against Jalonke natives) and religious dimensions.

1729/1141

Birth of Sidi al-Mukhtar al-Kabir, who established Kunta dominance.

1751/1165

Death of Karamoko Alfa, replaced by his cousin Ibrahim Sori, also known as Sori Mawdo ("The Great"), a well-known warrior.

1754/1168

Sidi al-Mukhtar al-Kabir becomes the shaykh of the sub-Saharan Qadiriyya movement.

1760/1174

New Islamic reform movement in Futa Toro (Tukulor state, middle Senegal). The participants, known as the *torodbe*, have as their leader Sulayman Bal, a man of letters.

Islam in Waalo*

Islam, which had until that time been a courtly type of Islam, a monopoly of the notables, begins to be rejected more and more by an aristocracy which will in fact become more or less hostile to Islam until the colonial conquest of 1855. On the other hand, the people, constantly pillaged, become more and more receptive to Islam, peaceably preached, this time around, by the Marabouts.

Boubacar Barry, *Le Royaume de Waalo. Le Sénégal avant la conquetre.*

*(Senegal)

Around Lake Chad

Circa 1548–1568/955–975: Reign of Malo Mbang

King of Bagirmi [Chad]. According to tradition he performed the Islamization of the country.

1564–1596/971–1004: Reign of Idris Aloma

Mai (sultan) of Borno. Borno's historical peak. The first 12 years — primarily the *jihads* carried out against neighboring peoples — are well-known as a result of two chronicles in Arabic written in 1576/984 by the *imam* of the court, Ibn Furtua.

1577/985

Bornoan delegation to Tripoli and correspondence between Idris Aloma and the Ottoman sultan Murad III over a border problem in the Fezzan. Borno hopes to obtain firearms from the Turks.

1582/990

Delegation sent by Idris Aloma to see the sultan al-Mansur; seeks guns and canon to combat the infidels. Three other delegations; no outcome.

Circa 1635–1655/1045–1065: Reign of 'Abd al-Karim

Founder of the Wadai state (eastern [Chad]) and propagator of Islam.

[Sudan] and [Ethiopia]

1506–1543/912–950

The *jihad* led by Ahmad b. Ibrahim al-Ghazi (Gragn) reconstitutes Muslim power; three-quarters of [Ethiopia] under his control. Ethiopian Christianity threatened with extinction.

1518/924

Nubia (northern part of [Sudan]) conquered by the Turks.

Before 1523/930

Sinnar [Sudan]: the first Funj king, Amara Dunkas, attains power in 1504–1505/910, and converts to Islam.

Beginning of the 17th century/beginning of the 11th century

Sinnar [Sudan]: large number of Muslim missionaries come from Arab countries. The first autochthonous Islamic missions appear in texts.

1529/936
Gragn defeats a Christian army in Shembura Kure.

1535/942
Rapid advance of Gragn; the Christian kingdom of [Ethiopia] calls on the Portuguese.

1543/950
Gragn killed by the Portuguese.

1545/952
The Galla nomads, from southern [Somalia], reach the Ethiopian high plateaus; they threaten Christians and Muslims.

1559/967
The Christian emperor (*negus*) Galawdemos (Claudius) killed in combat by Muslim forces.

1567-1568/975
The Galla nomads destroy the Muslim state of Harar. The Christian state returns to prominence.

1577/984
Muhammad IV, sultan of Harar, defeated by the Christian army and executed. End of a two-and-a-half-century competition between Christians and Muslims for control of the upper plateaus. The entire southeastern part of [Ethiopia] remains Islamized.

1660-1680/1071-1091: Reign of Sulayman Solongduno
According to tradition, it is he who makes Islam the religion of the

Darfur state (western part of [Sudan]), building mosques and encouraging Islamic practices in a country that has been entirely animistic.

Before 1730/1143
Darfur [Sudan]: Ahmad Bukr (d. ca. 1730/1143), Suleyman Solongduno's grandson, develops Islamic institutions and favors the progressive introduction of missionaries from neighboring countries.

1744/1157
April 7/23 Safar. Sinnar [Sudan] drives back an Ethiopian invasion, with the help of Darfur's allies.

Beginning in 1750/1164
In [Ethiopia], the Galla nomads convert to Islam, which modifies the balance of power between Christians and Muslims.

Eastern Coast of Africa

1505-1652/910-1062
The Portuguese control the coast.

1527/933
The sultan of Adal, Ahmad b. Ibrahim a Ghazi (called Gragn), declares a *jihad* against the Portuguese.

Circa 1651/1061
A delegation from Mombasa, one of the principal coastal regions, sent to Masqat (Muscat), capital of the sultanate of Oman, to seek the aid of the sultan against the Portuguese. Beginning of the Omani dominance of the region.

1652/1062

Omani raid on the Portuguese in Pate and Zanzibar. The rulers of the coastal towns begin to pay tribute to the sultan of Oman. War between the Omanis and the Portuguese until the end of the century.

1698/1109

Mombasa in Omani Arab hands, except for a brief Portuguese reoccupation in 1727–1729. The Portuguese driven back to Mozambique.

1699/1110

The Omani Arabs take Zanzibar. The Omanis are of the Ibadid persuasion, but do not spread their doctrine on the coast.

1772/1185

First document from the Comoro Islands written in Swahili: letter from one of the sultan's brothers from the coastal town of Pate.

The Disintegration of the Ottoman Empire and European Colonization

From Morocco to Indonesia, the Muslim states come under increasing pressure from the Western powers: Russia, France, Great Britain and the Netherlands. If some, such as Iran or Afghanistan, are able to maintain a semblance of independence, it is not without having made concessions, sometimes substantial, on both economic and strategic fronts; the confrontation between Russia and Great Britain has direct consequences for them. India, Indonesia, the states of central Asia and North Africa are henceforth under a direct colonial-style administration that allows for self-rule while the extraction of resources is in the hands of the dominant colonial power.

In all the Muslim countries, awareness of a backwardness in technological matters as well as in the domains of religious thought, politics and philosophy takes hold. Movements with modernist and reformist tendencies appear, which open onto nationalism, at the beginning of the 20th century, but do not yet have the means to realize these new ideals. Given what is taking place in Egypt, Syria and in the Ottoman Empire, spirits are moved; at that time doctrines are put forth that will find their true place in the 20th century.

The Eastern Question

The 150-year period referred to by Western historians as the Eastern Question corresponds to the slow decline of the Ottoman Empire under increasing pressure from the great European powers. In spite of the introduction of often far-reaching reforms (*tanzimat*) throughout the 19th century, the upsurge in local nationalisms supported by the intention of the West to have this power disappear, after it had been a threat for so long, leads to the progressive disintegration of the Empire and its disappearance at the beginning of the First World War. If the states created in the Balkans and eastern Europe manage to first acquire, then maintain, relative independence, the same cannot be said for the remaining provinces of the Ottoman Empire. They come under the domination of the colonial powers and are forced to accept a political tutelage that leaves them with no room for their own initiative; this period represents Europe's domination of the Muslim world.

Relations Between the Ottoman Empire and the Great Powers

1778–1779
Invasion, followed by annexation, of the Crimea by the Russians, recognized by the sultan in 1784 (the Aynali Kavak Accord); the sultan can no longer claim to rule over all Muslims.

1788
February 9. Austria declares war, following Russia.
March–May. Bosnia and northern Moldavia occupied by the Austrians.

1789
April 7. Death of 'Abdul-Hamid I.

1789–1807: Reign of Selim III
October–November. Belgrade taken by the Austrians, Bucharest and Valachia by the Russians.

1791
August 4. Peace of Sistowa with Austria, which is forced to return its conquests.

1792
January 9. Peace of Jassy with the Russians. The Dniester becomes the border between the two empires. The Ottomans lose the northern Black Sea coast and the Crimea.

1798
July 2. Alexandria taken by Napoleon Bonaparte. France's aims were to control the trade routes to India, to ensure Egyptian wheat exports and to open the Egyptian market for French merchandise.
July 21. Cairo taken.
August 1. Defeat of the French in Abukir. The Ottomans build an alliance with Britain and Russia, France's enemies.

1799
March 18–May 21. Failure of the attempted siege on St. John d'Acre (Akka) by Bonaparte.
August 22. Bonaparte secretly leaves Egypt, leaving his army behind.

1800
June 14. Assassination of General Kléber.

1801
August 31. French troops leave Egypt under the pressure of an Ottoman expedition corps led by Muhammad 'Ali and under the pressure of the British.

1802
June 25. Peace between the Ottoman Empire and France in the treaty of Amiens. British invasion of Egypt, naval attack on Istanbul; restoration of the country to Egypt.

1806
December. Ottomans declare war on Russia, which first occupies Moldavia, then Valachia and Bessarabia.

1807

June 7. Peace of Tilsit between the Russians (Tsar Alexander I) and French. The Russians give up their conquests. The French occupy the Ionian islands.

August 25. Russian-Ottoman armistice. Repulsion of British naval intervention before Istanbul. Defeat of British forces at Alexandria. Assassination of Selim III.

1807–1808: Reign of Mustafa IV

Deposed by supporters of Selim.

1808–1839: Reign of Mahmud II

1812

May. Treaty of Bucharest with Russia: Serbia autonomous; Bessarabia to the Russians.

1823

July. Accord of Erzerum between the Ottomans and the Iranians.

1826

March. Russian ultimatum concerning Greece.

1827

June. Alliance between Russia, France and Great Britain against the Ottomans.

October 20. Destruction of the Ottoman navy at Navarino.

1828–1829

Russian troops in eastern Anatolia, Moldavia, Dobruja, Bulgaria and Thrace. Edirne (Adrianople) falls.

1829

London Protocol: the European powers insist on the independence of Greece.

September 14. Treaty of Adrianople: Russia gives up its conquests in the European part of the Ottoman Empire. The Ottomans recognize the London Protocol.

1830

February. Conference of London: Greece independent; Serbia, Moldavia and Valachia autonomous. Bessarabia becomes Russian on a permanent basis.

June 14. The French land near Algiers.

July 5. Algiers taken.

1832

The Ottomans accept Russian aid against Muhammad 'Ali's incursions.

1833

July 8. Treaty of Hünkar Iskelesi between Russians and Ottomans. Its secret clauses give Russia full freedom of navigation in the Straits, while closing them to any power at war with Russia.

1837

Constantine (Algeria) falls.

1838

August. Treaty of Balta Liman between the British and the Ottomans. Removal of protective customs duties on British produce.

1839

Anglo-Austrian naval blockade of the Syrian coast to force Muhammad 'Ali's withdrawal.

April. Surrender of the Turkish fleet at Alexandria. The British take Aden to prevent the further expansion of Muhammad 'Ali.

June 30. Death of Mahmud II.

1839–1861: Reign of Sultan 'Abd ül-Mejid

1841

July. Treaty of London. Austria, Britain, Prussia, Russia, and France force Muhammad 'Ali to return to Egypt; he is made hereditary pasha of Egypt. Convention of the Straits: end of Russia's privileged position in the Straits.

1853

May 31. Russian ultimatum to the Ottomans: demands to protect all Orthodox Christians in the Empire (circa 12 million), and a treaty of alliance with the Ottomans. Russia invades two Romanian principalities to support the ultimatum.

December 23. British ultimatum to the Russians is rejected.

1854

March 28. Declaration of war against Russia by Britain, France and Sardinia: the Crimean War.

1855

September 9. Death of Tsar Nicholas I, fall of Sebastopol. Alexander II becomes Tsar.

1856

February 25–March 29. Congress of Paris. Integrity and independence of the Ottoman Empire. International commission of the Danube: freedom of navigation for all nations. Demili-

tarization of the Black Sea. End of Russian protectorate over the Rumanian principalities, which remain under Ottoman rule. Russia cedes southern Bessarabia to the Ottomans.

1861–11876: Reign of Sultan 'Abd ül-Aziz

1862

Moldavia and Valachia unite and form Rumania, led by Prince Alexander Couza. The Ottomans recognize the union.

1866

Rumania becomes independent.

1867

'Abd ül-Aziz is the first Ottoman sultan to visit Europe.

1876

Murad V, deposed because of mental illness.

1876–1909: Reign of 'Abd ül-Hamid

1876

July. Beginning of the Balkan crisis, as a reaction to Ottoman reprisals against the Bulgarian independence movement.

December 23. Opening of the international conference in Istanbul.

1877

January 20. Failure and end of the conference.

April 24. Declaration of war against Russia. Battles around Plevna and the Shipka Pass.

May–November. Invasion of Bulgaria and eastern Anatolia by the Russians.

1878

March 3. Treaty of San Stefano: Russia annexes some territory. Creation of a big Bulgarian buffer state, dependent on Russian support.

June 4. Cyprus given over to Great Britain in return for secret offer of aid to the Ottomans against Russia.

June 13–July 13. Congress of Berlin deprives Russia of most territorial gains. The Ottoman Empire loses almost all of its European territory; keeps only eastern Rumelia, Macedonia and eastern Thrace. Creation of a small Bulgarian state under Ottoman suzerainty. Austria occupies Bosnia and Herzegovina. Independence of Serbia, Montenegro, Rumania. Russia gains Kars, Ardahan, Batum and southern Bessarabia.

1881

Tunisia occupied by France; becomes a French protectorate through the Treaty of Bardo (1881) and the convention of La Marsa (1883).

1882

Egypt occupied by Great Britain after an anti-foreign revolt led by ʿUrabi Pasha. British bombardment of Alexandria and victory in the battle of Tell al-Kabir.

1885

Defeat of the British army and death of General Charles George Gordan in the Mahdi rebellion in Sudan.

1889

The German emperor William II visits Istanbul.

1897

April. Greco-Turkish war for Crete. The great powers intervene after Turkish success.

December. Crete granted its autonomy under a Greek governor.

1898

Second visit of William II to the Ottoman Empire. Defeat of the Mahdi movement by British-Egyptian troops under General Kitchener at Omdurman.

1899

Establishment of a British-Egyptian condominium over the Sudan.

1908

October 5. Annexation of Bosnia by Austria.

October 6. Annexation of Crete by Greece.

1909–1917: Reign of Mehmed V Reshad

1911

September. War between Italy and the Ottoman Empire. Italians land in Tripoli and Benghazi.

1912

April–May. Dodecanese Islands occupied by the Italians.

October 15. Treaty of Lausanne: Tripolitania to the Italians.

October 18. First Balkan War: the Ottomans lose Adrianople and Tripolitania.

November 12. Albania declares independence.

1913

May 30. Treaty of London. In Europe, the Turks control only one part of eastern Thrace and Constantinople.

June 30. Second Balkan War; the Ottomans regain Adrianople.

August 10. Treaty of Bucharest. The Turks retake Adrianople.

1914

August 2. Ottoman-German treaty of alliance and military convention.

September 7. Abolition of the capitulations.

October 29. Two Ottoman battleships, the *Sultan Selim* and the *Medilli*, bought from Germany, and manned with German crews, attack the Russian fleet in the Black Sea.

November 2 and 5. Russia, Great Britain and France declare war on the Ottoman Empire.

November 11. Declaration of Holy War (*jihad*) by the Sultan, addressed to all Muslims in the world. The declaration is signed by the highest religious dignitaries, including the *shaykh ül-islam*.

1914–1915

Violent combat in eastern Anatolia (Armenia).

1915

January. Jamal Pasha's attack on the Suez Canal ends in total failure.

February. Franco-British attacks in the Dardanelles.

March 18. Constantine Agreement: secret agreement among Russia, Britain and France concerning the future dismemberment of the Ottoman Empire.

April 25. An Allied force lands on Gallipoli; attempt fails, in January 1916 they retreat after losing ca. 25,000 men.

April 26. Treaty of London: secret treaty making territorial concessions to Italy.

April 27. Armenian population ordered to leave the Van, Bitlis and Erzerum regions; they are transferred to Iraq; Armenians from Cilicia and the northern Syria regions are transferred to central Syria.

May–July. Massacre of Muslims and Armenians.

1916

January 30. Accord between Sir Henry McMahon and Sharif Husayn promising a large independent Arab state in return for Arab military support of the British.

January. Franco-British forces retreat from the Dardanelles.

February–July. Russian occupation of northeastern Anatolia.

March 16. Sykes-Picot agreement between Britain and France concerning the division of the Ottoman Empire.

April 25. The British under General Townshend defeated in Iraq after a five-month siege of Kut al-Amara; circa 13,000 British soldiers die.

June. Beginning of the Arab Revolt in the Arab peninsula, led by Sharif Hussayn of Mecca, and supported by Britain (under T.E. Lawrence).

1917

March 11. Baghdad falls to General Maude's forces.

April 17. St. Jean de Maurienne Agreement. Territorial concessions to Italy in southwest Anatolia.

May. The German general von Falkenhayn and a mission of 65 German officers assume the command over the Turkish army in Palestine.

July–November. Arabs advance into Palestine.

November 2. Balfour Declaration concerning a Jewish national homeland in Palestine.

December 7. Russian-Turkish armistice (peace treaty signed on the 18th).

December 9. General Allenby enters Jerusalem.

1918

March. Eastern Anatolia reoccupied by the Turks.

September–October. Occupation of Syria, Palestine and Lebanon by Arab troops led by T.E. Lawrence, and of Iraq by British troops.

October 30. Armistice of Mudros, signed by the Turks. Large-scale occupation of the territory by the Allies. Independence of Yemen.

December. Clemenceau-Lloyd agreement between Britain and France. The Mosul area goes to Britain, France obtains northern Mesopotamian oil fields.

1919

January. Conference of Paris.

May 15. Greek troops land in Smyrna.

May 19. Mustafa Kemal (Atatürk) arrives in Samsun, leads Turkish war of independence against the Allies.

May–July. American King-Crane Commission to Syria and Palestine; recommends an American mandate for Syria; favors constitutional Arab monarchies; opposes the establishment of a Jewish state in Palestine.

1920

May 15. Greek troops land in Ismir. Subsequent occupation of Edirne, Thrace and Bursa.

June 20. Beginning of the Turkish War of Independence.

The Provinces: Toward Independence
In Europe

1788

Occupation of Bosnia and Moldavia by the Austrians.

1797

November. Beginning of the revolt led by Pazvanoghlu in Bulgaria.

1798

June 24. Execution of Constantin Rhigas, initiator of the idea of Greek independence.

1802

April. Ali Pasha Tepedelenli, first governor of Rumelia, then of Janina and Tirhala in 1803. Supported by the French.

1803

Extortions carried out by the Janissaries in Serbia, provoking the first Serbian rebellion led by Karageorgios (Karadorde) (1760–1817) and supported by Austria and Russia.

1805

Revolt led by Tirsiniklioghlu Isma'il Agha in eastern Bulgaria. The Serbs defeat an Ottoman military expedition.

1806

Belgrade falls. Mustafa Bayraqdar, new leader of the revolt in Bulgaria.

1812

May. Treaty of Bucharest between Russia and the Ottomans.

1815–1817

Second Serbian rebellion led by Miloš Obrenović; autonomy (1817).

1814

Reconstitution of the Hetairia Philike, in Odessa, a Greek emigre community, which consisted mostly of merchants and sailors.

1820

The local lord Ali Pasha of Janina (Albania and northwest Greece), removed from office, enters into open rebellion.

1821

February. The Greek prince Alexander Ypsilantis, since 1820 head of the Hetairia Philike, attempts but fails to incite a Romanian rebellion.

March 25. The patriarch Germanos declares the Greek war of liberation.

October. Massacre of the Turks in the Morea. The Greek patriarch of Istanbul hanged by the Ottomans.

December. Declaration of independence by the Greeks at Epidaura.

1822

January. Alexander Mavrocordato president of Greece. Defeat, escape and execution of Ali Pasha of Janina.

1823

Massacre of Greeks on the island of Chios.

1824

January. Lord Byron arrives at Missolonghi to join the Greek War of Liberation. Dies of fever three months later.

1825

February. Egyptian troops under Muhammad 'Ali and Ibrahim Pasha, having already occupied Crete and crushed Greek opposition there, land in the Morea.

1826

April. Missolonghi taken.

1827

April. John Capodistrias, a Greek who had been a Russian foreign minister, accepts the presidency of the Greek government.

June. Russian, French and British alliance against the Ottomans.

October 20. Defeat and destruction of the Ottoman-Egyptian navy in Navarino by the Anglo-French-Russian fleet.

1828

February. The Ottomans close the Straits to foreign shipping; this is a *casus belli* for Russia. Evacuation of the Egyptians from the Morea and Crete. Russian troops in eastern Anatolia, Moldavia, Dobruja, Bulgaria and Thrace.

1830

February. London protocol following the Conference of London. Greece granted independence. Serbia, Moldavia and Valachia autonomous.

August. Miloš Obrenovitć, hereditary prince of Serbia.

1831

Assassination of Capodistrias by rival Greek factions; the European powers agree on installing the Bavarian prince Otto as king of Greece.

1842

September 14. Alexander Karageorgios, elected to lead Serbia.

1857

Montenegro proclaims independence. Ottoman intervention.

1860–1861

Massacre of Muslims in Herzegovina by the Montenegrans. Ottoman intervention. Montenegro gains independence. Reforms in Bosnia.

1866

May. Revolt in Crete put down by the Ottomans.

1867

Ottoman forces leave Serbian fortresses.

1868

February. Reorganization of the administrative regime in Crete.

1875

Revolts in Crete until 1878.

July. Revolts in Bosnia and Herzegovina.

1876

May. Insurrection in Bulgaria. Serbia and Montenegro declare war on the Ottoman Empire.

July. Beginning of the crisis in the Balkans. Ottoman occupation of Serbia. Armistice under Russian pressure.

1877

July. Russians enter Bulgaria. Revolt in Bosnia-Herzegovina.

1878

January 24. Serbia declares independence.

March 3. Treaty of San Stefano. Rumania, Serbia and Montenegro recognized as independent; Bulgaria autonomous.

June–July. Congress of Berlin replaces Treaty of San Stefano. Occupation of Bosnia-Herzegovina by Austria. Special status for Macedonia.

October. Accord of Aleppo: new administrative status for Crete. Creation of Albanian League.

1884

Beginning of insurrections in Macedonia.

1889

The Règlement Organique suspended in Crete.

1893

Creation of the Macedonian Revolutionary Organization.

1896

The Règlement Organique reinstated in Crete. Incidents between Christians and Muslims.

1897

April. War between Greece and Turkey for Crete. Intervention of the great powers after Ottoman success.

December. New status of autonomy for Crete under Greek governor. Muslim exodus.

1900

Creation of the "Three Provinces" (Salonica, Kosovo, Monastir) in Macedonia.

1908

May–July. Incidents in Macedonia. Order restored in 1909.

September. Crete unifies with Greece.

October 5. Annexation of Bosnia and Herzegovina by Austria.

October 5–6. Bulgaria declares its independence from the Ottoman Empire.

October 6. Annexation of Crete by Grecce, officially recognized in 1912.

1909

Start of a struggle for independence in Albania; independence proclaimed on November 12, 1912.

1912

First Balkan War. Serbia, Bulgaria, Greece and Montenegro declare war on the Ottomans. Turkish defeats at Kirk, Kilisse, Lüle Burgas, Adrianople and Kumanowo.

1913

May. Peace of London: the Ottomans cede all territory west of the Enos-Media line, as well as the Aegean Islands.

June. Second Balkan War. The Ottomans intervene along with Rumania, Greece and Montenegro in Serbia.

Eastern Anatolia and Armenia

1844

Creation of the Council of the Armenian Community.

1860–1863

Reorganization of the Council of the Armenian Community.

1877

Russian troops in eastern Anatolia (Ardahan, Doghu Bayezid, Kars).

1878

Congress of Berlin: Kars, Batum and Ardahan granted to the Russians. The Armenian proposition for the creation of an Armenian state rejected.

1886

Creation of the Hunchak movement by students in France and Switzerland.

1890

Creation of the Dashnak Party (Armenian Revolutionary Federation).

1890–1893

Beginning of violence. Incidents in Samsun. Armenians seek European support.

1894

Suppression of Armenian revolts with the assistance of Kurdish irregular troops. Massacres of about 10,000–20,000 Armenians incite public opinion in Europe and America.

1895

September. Incidents in Istanbul.

1896

August 26. Attack on the Ottoman Bank of Istanbul. Following foreign intervention, first amnesty, then appointment of Christian civil servants in the Eastern Provinces. General appeasement.

1905

Armenian assassination attempt on 'Abdül-Hamid, when he leaves a mosque after the Friday prayer.

1914-1915

Violent clashes on the border between Russia and Turkey. The Russians advance.

August. The head of the Armenian church in Echmiadzin, Russia, declares that the tsar is the protector of all Armenians. Many Armenians leave the Ottoman army to fight for Russia.

1915

April 27. Armenian population ordered to leave because of alleged disloyalty to the Empire. Numerous massacres during the relocation. About two million people are affected, 600,000 of whom die.

May. Proclamation in Van of an Armenian state. Creation of the Armenian Legion.

July. The Turks counterattack, forcing the Russians to pull out. Many Armenians die.

1916

February-July. New Russian offensive in northeastern Anatolia. Massacre of the Turks.

1917

December 7. Russian-Turkish armistice. Armenia, Georgia and Azerbaijan form a Transcaucasian Federation, which declares independence.

December 18. Russia and the Ottoman Empire at peace. Armenian insurrection.

1918

March 3. German-Soviet Treaty of Brest-Litovsk. Russia cedes the districts of Kars, Ardahan and Batum to the Ottomans.

April 1 and 12. Ottoman occupation of Batum and Kars.

May 26. Creation of the Republic of Armenia, on both sides of the Russian-Turkish border. Capital: Yerevan. Dissolution of the Transcaucasian Federation. Georgia declares its independence, placing itself under German protection. Azerbaijan declares its independence one day later.

June 4. Treaty of Batum between Turkey, Georgia, Azerbaijan and Armenia. Armenia cedes territory, evacuates troops from Baku.

1919

Cilicia occupied by the French. Many Armenian refugees return from Syria. War between Turkey and France.

October. President Wilson appoints a commission to study the Armenian situation, led by Major-General James G. Harbord. Suggestion that the U.S. become a mandatory power over the Straits, Anatolia and Armenia. Wilson rejects.

1920

May. Armistice in Cilicia.

June. Accord between Turks and Russians.

July-August. Breakdown in negotiations between Turks and Armenians.

August 10. Treaty of Sèvres between the Allies and the Ottomans. Armenia recognized as an independent state, U.S. arbitration about boundaries.

September. Offensive led by General Kazim Qarabekir.

October 30. Kars taken.

November. The Bolsheviks conquer Yerevan and install a Communist government there.

December 2. The Armenians capitulate.

December 30. Treaty of Alexandropol. The Communist government of Yerevan cedes large portions of western Armenia to Turkey.

1921

March 16. Treaty of Moscow between the Russians and the Turks. The pre-1877 borders reestablished. End of the independent Republic of Armenia; becomes a Soviet Socialist Republic.

October 20. Accord between France and Turkey (the Franklin-Bouillon agreement). Evacuation of French troops. Exodus of Armenians from Cilicia to Syria.

The Arab States
Lebanon-Syria-Palestine

1775–1804

Ahmad al-Jazzar, a former Mamluk of Bosnian origin, governor of the *pashalik* Sayda, and pasha of Damascus.

1788–1840

The Reign of Bashir II Shihab, a distant relative of al-Jazzar, in Lebanon. Removes Druze feudal lords and favors the Maronites.

1815–1820

Revolts in northern Syria against the *a'yan* (notables).

1820–1831

Bashir II Shihab extends his dominion to Lebanon and part of Syria. Collaborates with Muhammad 'Ali.

1831–1840

Egyptian occupation of the region. Damascus becomes capital. The Egyptians strengthen central authority, modernize the administration and impose equality before the law for Muslims and non-Muslims alike. Mandatory military service, imposition of state monopolies on silk, oil and soap.

After 1834

Revolts against the Egyptians, supported by the Ottoman sultan Mahmud, and British agents.

1840

October Bashir II subjugated then deposed. Successor: Bashir III. The Druze attempt to regain their property, which had been appropriated by the Maronites. Ottoman support for the Druze in order to prevent an accumulation of power in the hands of the Maronites.

1841

Bashir III deposed. Britain and Prussia found the Protestant diocesis of Jerusalem.

1843

Division of Lebanon into two *sanjaks* (Maronite in the north, Druze in the south); Ottoman governor sent to Beirut after revolts spread from Dayr al-Qamar (1841–1842). Both districts have a mixed population and a weak government.

1845

Administrative separation of the Druze and Maronite communities. Start of "administrative confessionalism."

1850

The Protestants are recognized as a separate *millet*.

1857

Taniyus Shahin, the leader of a peasant revolt in Kairuan, installed as president of a peasant republic.

Late 1850s-early 1860s

Military campaigns against the powerful local lords of lower Galilee and the central Palestinian highlands. Final subjugation.

1860

May 27. Maronite raid on a Druze village; massacres of Christians (about 15,000 dead and 100,000 refugees).

July. Massacre of Christians in Damascus.

September 5. French fleet sent to the region.

1861

June 9. Règlement Organique for Lebanon under European pressure. A non-Lebanese Christian governor and an administrative council consisting of four Maronites, three Druzes, two Greek-Orthodox, one Greek Catholic, one Sunni, and one Shi'i.

1866

Protestant missionaries establish the American University of Beirut.

1866-1871

Rashid Pasha governor of Damascus.

1878-1880

Midhat Pasha governor of Damascus. Politics of centralization, expansion of the educational system, rise of a new class of wealthy property owners who dominate politics.

1882

Beginning of Jewish colonization of Palestine (first *aliya*) after pogroms in Russia.

1897

First Zionist Congress in Basel; aim: creation of a homeland in Palestine.

1905

Damascus becomes a center of activity for the Young Turks.

1915-1916

Jamal Pasha, governor of Syria, seeks to introduce reforms. Opposition by Syrian notables, who are executed.

July 14-March 10. The Husayn-McMahon correspondence on the future of the Middle Eastern Arab world; stipulates the creation of an independent Arab state, with the exception of Lebanon, and the status of Palestine undecided.

1916

March 16. Sykes-Picot agreement concerning spheres of influence of the Great Powers in the Middle East: internationalization of southern Palestine and Jerusalem, with Haifa as a British enclave.

1917

November 2. Balfour Declaration on the creation of a Jewish homeland in Palestine, approved by France (Feb. 18, 1918), Italy (Feb. 23, 1918) and the U.S. (Oct. 29, 1918).

1918

September. Haifa and Akka (Acre) taken by Arab troops.

October. Damascus, Homs and

Aleppo taken. Beirut occupied by the French.

1919

May–July. The American King-Crane Commission tours Syria and Palestine. Reports the population's desire for independence, their opposition to Zionism. Endorse Faysal for the kingship of Syria, under the Mandate system.

1920

March. The General Syrian Congress proclaims the creation of an independent greater Syria, which includes Lebanon and Palestine. Faysal, the son of Sharif Husayn, proclaimed king of Syria; his brother 'Abd Allah is emir of Iraq.

March 17. French reaction: Lebanon independent.

April. Anti-Jewish disturbances in Jerusalem and Jaffa.

April 25. San Remo Accord: mandate of France over Lebanon and Syria, of Great Britain over Palestine, Transjordan and Iraq.

July 25. Damascus occupied by the French; Faysal, isolated, becomes king of Iraq on August 23, 1921.

Iraq

1726–1834: Reign of the Mamluk dynasty of the Jalilis in Mosul

1749–1831: Reign of a Mamluk dynasty of Georgian origin in Baghdad

1780–1802: Reign of Sulayman the Great (Büyük Sulayman) in Baghdad

1801

The Wahhabis conquer and destroy the Shi'i pilgrimage sites Najaf and Karbala.

1810

Mehmed Sa'id Halet Efendi extinguishes power of the Mamluk Sulayman Agha in Baghdad.

1813–1828

Da'ud Pasha restores the Mamluks to pre-eminence.

1828

Open rebellion against the Ottoman sultan.

1831

Ottoman military expedition against Baghdad. Massacre of the city's inhabitants, who had survived a plague and a flood of the Tigris in the same year (53,000 out of 80,000 died).

1834

The Jalilis of Mosul are deposed by the Ottomans.

1861

The British Euphrates and Tigris Steam Navigation Company founded.

1869–1872

Governorship of Midhat Pasha, who introduces numerous reforms: introduction of a new land law (1858), which facilitates individual ownership of land; establishment of an administrative council; power of local lords curbed.

1870

The first British steamship docks at Basra directly from England.

1914

November 6. The British land in Fao. The arrival of a large expeditionary force from India follows.

November 20. Basra taken by the British.

1915

September 28. Kut al-'Amara taken; the Ottomans begin the siege of the British in late November.

1916

April 29. The British under General Townshend surrender with 13,000 soldiers. Death of the leader of the Ottoman army, General von der Goltz Pasha; the less competent Halil Pasha replaces him.

1917

February 25. Kut al-'Amara recaptured.

March 11. Baghdad taken by the British led by General Maude.

1918

Kirkuk taken.

November. Mosul taken when the Ottoman army withdraws after the armistice.

1919

May–July. The King-Crane Commission visits Iraq. Recommends the establishment of a large mandate, including Diyar Bakr, Dayr al-Zur, Mosul and Mohammera.

1920

April–December. Anti-British revolt; the British have to send reinforcements; almost 2,500 British casualties; revolt is quelled.

June 4. In the Treaty of Trianon, the British gain a mandate over all of Iraq, except for the Mosul region.

Egypt

1786

An Ottoman army led by Jaza'irli Ghazi Hasan Pasha sent to reduce the power of the Mamluk beys, Ibrahim Bey al-Qazdughli and Murad Bey al-Qazdughli. In spite of this, they reclaim power in 1787, but pledge to pay their tribute.

1789–1801

French expedition under Napoleon, occupation of Cairo and lower Egypt. French withdrawal after the landing of a British naval force.

1803

British troops retreat two years after the French.

1801–1805

Power struggle between the Mamluks, the Ottoman governor and the Albanian brigade of Muhammad 'Ali.

1805

Muhammad 'Ali, governor.

1807–1881

Reorganization of the Egyptian army with French officers and non-commissioned officers (*nizamiye*).

1809–1812

High revenues through the export of wheat to Europe during the Napoleonic war.

1813

Mecca and Medina recaptured from the Wahhabis.

1816
Confiscation of pious foundations (*waqfs*) and large estates.

1818-1820
The Wahhabis expelled from the Hijaz. Reorganization of finance administration, modernization of the infrastructure, foreign technicians called in, agriculture improved.

1820-1823
Conquest of the Sudan in order to gain slaves for the army and to explore the African market.

After 1821
Establishment of state-owned factories.

1824
Egyptian troops in Crete, then in the Morea (1825).

1826
Students sent to France (Rifa'at al-Tahtawi), in order to create a technical-administrative elite. Reforms initiated by al-Azhar. Control of Muslim institutions.

1828
October. Egyptian troops pull out of Morea after the defeat of the Ottoman-Egyptian fleet by Britain and France in the battle of Navarino (1827).

1831-1833
First Ottoman-Egyptian war. Conquest of Palestine and Syria by Ibrahim Pasha, son of Muhammad 'Ali, supported by a fleet.

1831
December. Ibrahim grants the minorities equality before the law; provokes the rage of Muslim notables.

1832-1833
Egyptian invasion of Anatolia; victory over the grand vizier Rashid Pasha in the battle of Konya (1832).

1833
May 14. The Kütahya accord: following the Ottoman-Russian treaty of Hünkar Iskelesi: Syria, Cilicia and Jidda go to Ibrahim Pasha; Muhammad 'Ali becomes governor of Egypt and Crete.

1834-1840
Revolts against Egyptian occupation in the wake of the disarmament and conscription of peasants: in Palestine (1834), south Lebanon and the Hawran (1838), in the entire Lebanon (1840).

1839
April. Ottoman offensive on Syria.
June 24. Ottoman defeat in Nisbin, defection of the commander in chief of the Ottoman navy to the Egyptians.

1840
July. Ultimatum by the Ottomans and the European powers to Muhammad 'Ali; rejected.
October. Ibrahim Pasha retreats to Egypt after the British navy begins to bombard Beirut and Ottoman troops land at Juniya.

1841
Muhammad 'Ali proclaimed hereditary governor and viceroy of Egypt, recognizes Ottoman suzerainty.

Schools in Egypt in 1875

—Seven higher or special schools, all located in Cairo: 69 professors, 356 students;

—Two *taghizi* schools (preparatory schools for higher schools): one in Cairo, with 34 professors and 192 students, the other in Alexandria, whose students are mixed with the primary school students;

—Two primary schools: one in Cairo, with 34 teachers and 539 students (school of the *mubtadiyan*), the other, in Alexandria, includes, with the *taghiziyya* school, 21 teachers and 298 students.

All the schools are supported and run by the government; the students are housed, fed and given a stipend.

—Seven schools in provincial towns, partially supported by the budget of the *waqf* and the *diwan al-madaris*. Total: 56 teachers and 1,133 students.

—Twenty-two similar schools in Cairo: 181 teachers, 2,480 students (among these schools, the Dar al-ʿUlum University, with 8 professors and 35 students). The students in this group are fed, housed and dressed, but are not given a stipend, except for the teaching assistants from the Dar al-ʿUlum.

Total: 395 teachers and 5,000 students.

—Foreign schools and non-Muslim religious schools include 438 teachers and 9,000 students, 500 of whom are Muslim.

—The educational system also includes:

- 4,685 primary schools, with 4,881 teachers and 112,000 students,

- the al-Azhar mosque: 325 professors, 11,100 students,

- the al-Ahmadi mosque in Tantah: 36 professors, 3,830 students,

- the Ibrahim Pasha mosque in Alexandria: 65 professors, 413 students,

- mosques in other provincial towns: precise totals unknown.

G. Delanoue: "La politique scolaire des vicerois-réformateurs" in *l'Égypte au XIXe siècle*."

1848: Reign of Ibrahim Pasha

Both Muhammad ʿAli and Ibrahim die in the same year.

1849–1854: Reign of ʿAbbas I Hilmi

Attempts to counteract his predecessors' modernization and Westernization projects.

1850–1860
Egyptian peasants gain hereditary right to their land.

1854–1863: Reign of Muhammad Sa'id
Muhammad 'Ali's economic policy pursued.

1854
The Frenchman Ferdinand de Lesseps given authorization to build the Suez Canal.

1859–1869
Construction of the Suez Canal by the Compagnie Universelle du Canal Maritime de Suez.

1863–1879: Reign of Isma'il

1864
First foreign loan.

1867
Isma'il takes the title *Khedive*.

1869
November 17. Inauguration of the Suez Canal. The construction of the canal costs Egypt £21.5 million, but Egypt receives no revenues from it until 1938.

1873
June 8. An Ottoman *firman* grants Egypt greater autonomy. It can now conclude international treaties, take loans, and command its army at will.

1873
Death of Rifa'at al-Tahtawi (born 1801), who advocates the modernization of Egypt.

1875
Egypt cedes its shares in the Suez Canal to Great Britain for £4 million.

1876
May. Creation of the Caisse de la Dette Publique, which fixes Egypt's foreign debt at £91 million. This amount is to be repaid within 65 years at an annual rate of 7 percent.
November. A French and a British controller supervise the Egyptian financial administration ("Dual Control").
July 26. Europeans force Isma'il to resign; exile in the Sudan.

1880
The Egyptian foreign debt fixed at £98.4 million (the so-called Liquidation Law).
September. Revolt led by Colonel Ahmad 'Urabi; crushed by the British in 1882. Reason for the revolt: repayment of debts resulted in the dismissal of officers and increasing indebtedness of the peasants.

1882
September 17. Bombardment of Alexandria; Cairo under British occupation (battle of Tell al-Kabir). British control over Egypt, which remains part of the Ottoman Empire.
October 24. Ottoman-British accord (not pursued); Ottoman suzerainty maintained; appointment of a British High Commissioner (Lord Cromer, from 1883).

1892–1914: Reign of 'Abbas Hilmi II
Supports the anti-British nationalist movement.

1892

The literary journal *al-Hilal* founded by Jurji Zaydan and other Lebanese Christian emigrés in Cairo.

1897

Death of Jamal al-Din al-Afghani (born 1839); advocates compatibility of Islam and modernity.

1898

The Salafi-reformist newspaper *al-Manar* founded by Muhammad Rashid Rida in Cairo.

1899

British-Egyptian condominium over the Sudan.

1905

Death of Muhammad 'Abduh (born 1849); calls for the reinterpretation of the *shari'a* along modernist lines.

1906–1907

The Dinshaway affair: provocations by British officers lead to nationalist resistance. Muhammad Kamil founds the Nation Party, and Lutfi al-Sayyid the *Umma* party.

1907–1911

Sir Eldon Gorst British proconsul in Egypt.

1911–1914

Lord Kitchener British proconsul in Egypt.

1914

December 18. Britain declares Egypt a protectorate.

1915–1917

Husayn khedive of Egypt.

1915

February. Ottoman attack, led by Jemal Pasha, on the Suez Canal fails. British-Egyptian expeditionary force under General Sir Archibald Murray, later under General Sir Edmund Allenby, advances toward Palestine and Syria.

1917

Fuad I khedive of Egypt.

1918–1920

Sa'd Zaghlul, leader of the Wafd Party, demands full autonomy and eventually total independence for Egypt.

1919

March. The British deport Sa'd Zaghlul to Malta; uprisings in Cairo; Zaghlul released, goes to the Paris Peace Conference, then to London to advocate his cause.

1919–1920

December–March. The Milner Commission recommends: replacement of protectorate by treaty of alliance, British control over Suez Canal, guidance of Egypt's foreign relations, defense of Egypt.

Arabia

1792

Death of the Hanbali scholar Muhammad b. 'Abd al-Wahhab, who instituted Wahhabism with the help of Muhammad b. Sa'ud (died 1765), and his son 'Abd al-'Aziz (died 1803).

1797 and 1798

Two punitive expeditions of the governor of Baghdad, Büyük Sulayman, fail.

1802
The Wahhabis take the Shi'i pilgrimage sites Najaf and Karbala; raids on Iraq.

1803–1805
Mecca and Medina taken. Pilgrimage route severed.

1813
Mecca retaken by Muhammad 'Ali. The Hijaz under Egyptian domination; local power of the *sharif* re-established.

1818
The Egyptians conquer Dar'iyya, the headquarters of the Sa'ud family. Capture of 'Abd Allah b. Sa'ud, execution in Istanbul.

1820
British treaty with the Gulf shaykhdoms.

1824
Reconstitution of the Sa'udi kingdom.

1839
The British take Aden to prevent Egyptian expansion in the area.

1840
The Hijaz under the sovereignty of the Ottoman sultan.

1843
The Sa'udi leader Faysal establishes control over the Sa'udi kingdom.

1847
The Ottomans in San'a.

1849
The Wahhabis, led by Faysal, expel the last Egyptian governor from the peninsula.

1872
The Ottomans conquer Yemen.

1891
Muscat and Oman under British protection.

1899
Kuwait under British protection.

1902
'Abd al-'Aziz (age 21) begins the reconquest of the Sa'udi kingdom.

1908
The Hijaz rail line (Damascus/Mecca/Medina) a pan-Islamic project, opens. Sharif Husayn b. 'Ali appointed emir of Mecca by the Young Turks.

1911
Treaty of Da'an between the Ottomans and the imam Yahya of Yemen.

1912
'Abd al-'Aziz conquers the coastal province of al-Hasa.

1913
January. The first *ikhwan* settlement founded at al-Artawiyyah.

1914
May. Sa'udi-Ottoman treaty: 'Abd al-'Aziz recognizes Ottoman suzerainty over the Najd, becomes *wali* of this province.

1915
October 24. Sir Henry McMahon and Sharif Husayn exchange letters concerning the Arab Near East.

Wahhabism

The doctrine of Muhammad b. 'Abd al-Wahhab (1703–1787), which claims to be Sunni, condemns dangerous innovations, disapproves of the worship of saints, visits to tombs, prayer rituals in the mausoleums, veneration of sacred trees, the mention of a prophet, angel or saint's name in a prayer, etc. It prescribes, on the other hand, literal readings of the Qur'an and Hadith and the strict application of the *shari'a*, even in legal matters; the consumption of tobacco is prohibited, attendance at ritual public prayer is mandatory as is payment of the ritual tithe on profits from trade.

In 1972, the Sa'udi authorities specify that "Islam, whose dogma is in absolute accordance with science, reason and contemplative thought, must be able to adapt to constantly changing conditions brought on by the passage of time, and must provide adequate answers to all questions of a constitutional, civil or penal nature and questions of a more personal nature, taking the public good into account each time these questions are not directly answered in the sacred texts. . . . It is indispensible to establish a distinction between general principles, which are not subject to alteration or change, and particular situations . . . , which demand changes that conform to alterations in interests and the evolution of social mores. . . . "

Taken from *Péninsule arabique d'aujourd'hui*, Vol. I (P. Rondot).

December 26. British-Sa'udi treaty of protection; Ibn Sa'ud refrains from attacking King Husayn of the Hijaz.

1916

May. The Sykes-Picot agreement: the interior of the Fertile Crescent seen as a state or a confederation of states under the protection of Great Britain and France.

June. Declaration of the Arab rebellion against the Ottomans. Husayn, king of the Hijaz.

October 29. King Husayn proclaims himself "King of all Arab Countries."

1917

May. Sir Mark Sykes and Georges Picot visit Husayn in Jidda.

November. End of the Ottoman resistance in the Hijaz.

1919

May. Battle at Turaba between the Wahhabis and Hijazi forces. Yemen independent, under the authority of the imam Yahya.

1920

The Wahhabis conquer Asir, a border principality between Yemen and the Hijaz.

Internal Affairs of the Ottoman Empire: Reforms

1774–1789: Reign of 'Abd ül-Hamid I

1774

Renovation of the artillery by the Baron de Tott; modernization of the fleet. Schools for military engineers open. The new troops have little impact, since they meet with the resistance of the old troops who vastly outnumber them.

1787

Conservative reaction; foreign technicians forced to leave.

1789

Death of 'Abd ül-Hamid I; accession of Selim III.

1789–1807: Reign of Selim III

1793

February 24. Army reorganized: formation of the *nizam-i jedid* (new system), new troops who are trained along European lines and exist parallel to the old troops.

1793–1796

Ambassadors sent to London, Berlin, Paris and Vienna.

1807–1808: Reign of Selim III

1807

May 25. Unsuccessful revolt led by Jannissaries opposed to the *nizam-i jedid.*

May 29. Selim III deposed. Accession of Mustafa IV.

August. Suppression of the *nizam-i jedid* and of the taxes levied by Selim III; officers massacred.

1808–1839: Reign of Mahmud II

1808

July 18. Mustafa Bayraqdar, a notable from the Danube region, enters Istanbul with his army and the supporters of Selim. Elimination of the Jannissaries' leaders and the *shaykh ül-islam*, 'Ata Allah; provisional restoration of Selim III.

July 28. Assassination of Selim III; Mustafa IV deposed; accession of Mahmud II.

July 28–November 15. Great vizierate of Bayraqdar; elimination of Selim III's adversaries.

October 7. Declaration of the *Sened-i ittifak,* an accord between the grand vizier and the notables based on the need for reforms.

November. Insurrection by the Jannissaries, death of Bayraqdar.

1809–1821

Mahmud II appoints those who support his reforms to important governmental posts.

1815

Restoration of Selim's army under the name *Sebkan-i jedid,* after defeats of the regular army against Russia, Greece and Serbia.

1826

June 15. Following another revolt, the Janissaries are massacred by Mahmud II without major opposition. This act is called *vaqa'a-i khayriyye* ("benevolent event").

July. Elimination of the Janissaries' allies.

1827

Reorganization of the army. Establishment of the School for Military Medicine.

1831

First official Ottoman newspaper, *Taqvim-i Veqayi* (government gazette), appears.

1833

Establishment of a translation office for the administration.

1834

Establishment of a military academy modeled after St. Cyr, with French as the language of instruction.

1836–1839

Creation of ministries: Foreign Affairs (1836), Justice (1837), Finance (1838), Trade (1839) and Administration of Pious Foundations (1837).

1838

Creation of the Council of the Sublime Porte; reorganization of the army.

1839–1861: Reign of 'Abdul Mejid

The principal reforming grand viziers are: Mustafa Reshid Pasha (d. 1858), Mehmed Emin 'Ali Pasha (d. 1871), Fu'ad Pasha (d. 1869).

1839

November 3. Public reading of the *Hatt-i Sherif* (imperial decree) of Gülhane (drafted by Reshid Pasha); it announces reforms (*tanzimat*), and is primarily intended to show the European powers that the Ottoman Empire is a serious ally. It announces equality before the law, and deals with the protection of property, taxation, conscription and the duration of military service.

1840

February. Tax system reformed. Reorganization of provincial administration after the French model; the provincial governors are assisted by an administrative council (*mejlis*). Reorganization of the army.

1843

Law concerning army recruitment; the number of recruits per family is limited to one, and 10 percent per village; the duration of the military service is limited to five years; establishment of a military reserve (*redif*).

1845

Establishment of a municipal police in Istanbul.

1846

Ministry of Agriculture. Council on Public Instruction.

1849

Creation of imperial money.

1856

February. Hatt-i hümayun: reaffirmation of the reforms, especially freedom of belief, legal and tax reforms, and the rights of non-Muslims.

1858

The land law; stipulates the gradual introduction of private property; in reality it gives rise to a class of large landholders.

1861–1876: Reign of 'Abd ül-'Aziz

1863

Creation of the Imperial Ottoman Bank.

1865

Civil code. Reorganization of the provincial administration. The Young Turks founded as an opposition movement.

1866

Ministry of Public Instruction.

1867

The State Council (shura-ye devlet) founded, a representative legislative body.

1868

Public instruction established. The Galata Saray High School opens. A municipal council in Istanbul.

1869

Establishment of the Crédit Général Ottoman.

1875

Financial collapse of the empire, after 16 foreign loans had been taken between 1854–1877. The government has to spend £15 million of its £18 million budget for repaying debt.
October 6. The government announces that it will issue new bonds to pay debt.

1876–1909: Reign of 'Abd ül-Hamid II

1876

May. Revolt in Istanbul by students from the religious schools.

May 30. The sultan 'Abd ül-'Aziz deposed by Midhat Pasha. Accession of Murad V.
August 31. Murad V deposed because of mental illness. Accession of 'Abd ül-Hamid II.
October 28. Declaration of the constitutional project and the electoral law.
December 19. Midhat Pasha, grand vizier.
December 23. Declaration of the Constitution: equal rights for all subjects, establishment of a parliamentary government; based largely on the Belgian constitution.

1877

February 5. Midhat Pasha forced to step down. Assassinated in exile in 1883.
March 19. Official opening of the Parliament. Municipal code applied to all cities.

1878

February 14. Dissolution of Parliament, suspension of the Constitution after crisis in the Balkans.

1881

November 23. "Decree of Muharram": the creditors of the Ottoman state guarantee borrowed capital by collecting from various revenue sources.
December 20. Creation of the Ottoman Public Debt Administration by Britain, France and Germany.

1883

Tobacco monopoly given to Franco-German Bureau of Tobacco (La Société de la Régie Coïntéressé des Tabacs de l'Empire Ottoman).

1885

Many schools open, among them professional schools. Increase in the number of foreign schools (religious).

1887

The Association for Union and Progress founded (Ittihad ve Teraqqi) in Istanbul by an oppositional student group of the department for medicine of the Military Academy.

1888

Creation of the Bank of Agriculture. Inauguration of the Orient Express.

1889

The Young Turks movement founded by students of the Military Academy.

1892

Attempted assassination of Sultan 'Abd ül-Hamid leads to the persecution of the opposition, many of whom flee to Geneva (led by Ahmad Riza), Paris (led by Mirzanji Murad Bey), London and Cairo.

1902

February. Congress of oppositional groups in Paris fails to unify the movement due to differences in opinion.

1905

Creation of the Society for Liberty and Country (Vatan ve Hürriyet).

1907

In Salonika, the Ottoman Society for Freedom (Osmanli Hürriyet Jem'iyyeti) unites with other exiled groups of Young Turks to form the Committee for Union and Progress (Ittihad ve Teraqqi Jem'iyyati).

1908

July 23–24. Revolution led by the Young Turks supported by rebel government troops. Constitution restored. Enthusiasm in the empire. Government by the Committee for Union and Progress (CUP) led by Enver Pasha.

November–December. Elections; the Young Turks win the majority.

December 17. Parliament reopens.

1909

January. Creation of the Turkish Society (Türk Dernegi).

April 12–13. 'Abd ül-Hamid II attempts to reclaim power. The CUP calls for a revolt.

April 27. After the army's triumphal march from Salonika to Istanbul (led by Mahmud Shevket Pasha), 'Abd ül-Hamid is deposed and sent into exile, and Mehmed V Reshad ascends to power. Government supported by the CUP. Beginning of the Turkification of the empire.

1909–1918

Mehmed V constitutional sultan.

1912

February. Dissolution of Parliament due to pressure by the liberal opposition.

March. Creation of the Association for a Turkish Homeland (Türk Ojaghi).

May. The new Parliament opens after rigged elections. Led by a CUP cabinet.

July. Fall of the cabinet. Uprising by the Free Officers' Group (Halaskaran Zabitan), the CUP adversaries.

August. Dissolution of Parliament.

1913

January 23. Coup d'état by the CUP.

June 11. Assassination of the grand vizier Mahmud Shevket. Government by the CUP, triumvirate: Tal'at, Enver and Jemal. An orientation towards pan-Turkism.

June 18–23. Meeting of the Arab Congress, an organization founded by Muslim and Christian students, in Paris; demands for a substantial decentralization of power and an Arabization of the administration of Arab provinces. Establishment of the Ottoman Decentralization Party by exiled Syrians in Cairo.

1914

September–October. The Ottoman state aligns itself with Germany.

September 5. The Ottoman Empire officially repudiates the capitulations.

October 10. The Ottoman Empire enters the war on the side of the Central Powers.

November 2 and 5. Russia, France and Great Britain declare war.

1918

July 3. Death of Mehmed V. Accession of Mehmed VI Vahid ül-Din.

October 13. The Young Turk government under Tal'at Pasha resigns. Ahmed Izzet Pasha new grand vizier.

October 30. Mudros armistice: opening of the Straits, demobilization of the Ottomans, occupation of Istanbul and parts of Anatolia by the Allies.

December 21. Dissolution of Parliament. The Young Turk cabinet is replaced by a government that favors the Allies (first Tevfik Pasha, then Damad Ferid Pasha). Creation of liberal parties.

1919

March–April. Resistance movements begin to fight foreign occupation in Anatolia.

May 19. Mustafa Kemal, the defender of Gallipoli, arrives in Samsun, organizes national resistance.

July 23. Congress of Erzerum.

September 4. Congress of Sivas (association for the Defense of the Rights of Anatolia and Romelia) confirms Kemal's leadership.

September 11. National Pact declares right of self-determination of Turks.

1920

April 23. Meeting of the first National Assembly in Ankara. Mustafa Kemal elected president of the Assembly.

June 20. Beginning of the Turkish War of Independence.

November 2. Leaders of the Committee for Union and Progress flee.

Society and Culture

1793

Ambassadors appointed to serve in the major European capitals; observing the major powers will give birth to ideas on modernization in the empire, which will take hold during the reign of Mahmud II.

1796

Publication of the *Gazette française de Constantinople*, first newspaper published in the Ottoman Empire.

1814

Construction of the Dolmabahçe palace, where Mahmud II will live.

1824

Publication of the newspapers *Le Smyrnéen* and *Le Spectateur Oriental*.

1829

Publication of the Egyptian newspaper *Vakayi-i Misriyye*. European dress as well as the fez adopted.

1831

Publication of the official Ottoman newspaper *Takvim-i Vekayi* and its counterpart *Le Moniteur Ottoman*.

1833

Creation of a "Translation Service" (Terjüme Odasi) in the Ministry of Foreign Affairs. Ottoman youths sent to Western Europe, mainly to France, for their studies.

1836

Construction of the Thiraghan palace, where the sultan 'Abd ül-Mejid will live.

1839

Publication of the first Ottoman private newspaper *Jeride-i Havadis*.

1844

First ocean liner offering service between Istanbul, the Aegean Sea and the Black Sea (*Feva'id-i Osmaniyye*).

1855

Telegraph first used.

1860–1866

Several new newspapers (*Jeride-i Havadis, Tasvir-i Efkar, Muhbir*).

1860

New status for the Greek community.

1863

New status for the Armenian community.

1866

First rail line, from Smyrna to Aydin.

1867

First Ottoman theater.

1870

February. University of Istanbul opens. Closes in 1871 following conferences by Jamal al-Din al-Afghani that are deemed provocative. Arrival of Turkish refugees from central Asia, conquered by Russia. Origins of a Turkish feeling of national identity, accompanied by anti-Christian and anti-Western reactions.

1873

Publication of *Vatan yahut Silistre*, work by Namiq Kemal, expressing sentiments of Turkish nationalism.

1876

First edition of the *Lehçe-i Osmani*, first Ottoman dictionary.

After 1878

New newspapers appear, but are very quickly forced to stop publication because of political censorship.

1880

Death of the poet Ziya Kemal (born 1825), a leader of the Young Ottomans.

1888

Death of the journalist Namiq Kemal (born 1840), a leader of the Young Ottomans.

1891

Servet-i fünun, journal put out by a literary movement with the same name, influenced by the French Parnassians.

POPULATION OF THE OTTOMAN EMPIRE					
	1872–1874	1881–1882	1896	1906	1914
Muslims	15,267,231	12,587,137	14,156,023	15,508,753	15,044,846
Non-Muslims	13,765,880	4,801,467	4,986,373	5,375,877	3,475,170
Total	29,033,111	17,388,604	19,142,396	20,884,630	18,520,016

1895

The newspaper *Meshveret* ("The Consultation"). Created by the Young Turks movement.

1908

More than 5,800 kilometers (3,600 miles) of train tracks constructed since 1866.

1909

The Qahtaniyyah society (*al-jam'iyyah al-qahtaniyyah*) founded by Syrian officers in Istanbul; support Arab nationalism.

1911

Türk Yurdu Jemiyeti association (Association for a Turkish Fatherland) founded. Creation of the Turkish Petroleum Co.

1912

March. The Türk Ojaghi ("The Turkish Homeland") movement founded; oriented towards pan-Turkism, under the influence of Ziya Gökalp (1876–1924).

The Maghrib

The history of the Maghrib from the end of the 18th century to the beginning of the 20th appears to be fragmented, but its destiny is anything but discontinuous: one after the other, the states of the Maghrib come under French or Italian domination. Piracy, which had brought them a large part of their resources until the 18th century, comes to a halt and the pressure applied by the Western powers increases, because the Maghrib is one of the primary routes to Black Africa.

Morocco, which had avoided coming under Ottoman control, is the object of colonial expansion plans by Spain, France and Germany; it will resist until the dawn of the 20th century and will maintain, as a French protectorate, the illusion of a royal government.

Algeria, conquered between 1830 and 1848, becomes a French colony, while Tunisia, occupied in 1881 by the French, keeps as its head of state a bey who has no real power.

Libya is conquered by the Italians between 1912 and 1920. Busy with defending its other territories, the Ottoman Empire can do nothing to protect these distant provinces. Foreign occupation contributes to the disintegration of the Ottoman Empire, and the emergence of European colonialism in the Mediterranean.

Morocco

1757–1790: Reign of Muhammad b. 'Abd Allah

1792–1822: Reign of Mawlay Sulayman
1818–1820
Insurrection in Fez. Uprising by the Darqawa and the Wazzani.

1818
Abolition of piracy under European pressure.

1822–1859: Reign of Mawlay 'Abd al-Rahman
1829
Austria destroys the Moroccan fleet after the resumption of piracy.

1830–1832
Attempts to occupy Tlemcen and western Algeria.

1844
Moroccans defeated by the French in Isly, when 'Abd al-Rahman tries to extend his influence to western Algeria by supporting 'Abd al-Qadir.

1856
Trade treaty with Great Britain.

1859–1873: Reign of Muhammad b. 'Abd al-Rahman
1859–1860
War with Spain, Moroccan defeat; payment of reparations; ceding of territory to Spain.

1861–1862
First foreign loans taken.

1863
Béclard Convention; trade treaty signed with France. Internal division of the *makhzan*.

1873–1894: Reign of Mawlay al-Hasan
1880
The Madrid Conference: beginning of the internationalization of the Moroccan question.

1881
Reforms, most notably in the financial sector, opposed by the religious fraternities.

1882 and 1886
Campaigns against British and Spanish penetration. Policy of modernization for the army.

1884
French quest to establish a protectorate is rejected.

1892
British quest to establish a protectorate is rejected.

1894–1908: Reign of Mawlay 'Abd al-'Aziz
Real power is in the hands of Si Ahmad b. Musa until his death in 1900.

1894–1897
Suppression of tribal revolts.

1900–1901
Occupation of Touat by the French.

1901

Fiscal reform (the *tartib*). Opposition led by Bu Hmara.

1904

Entente Cordiale between Britain and France, and subsequent secret negotiations with Spain: agreement about the future division of Morocco; Germany is left out.

1905

William II of Germany visits Tangier. French plans for reform. German opposition.

1906

January 16–April 7. Conference of Algeciras: confirmation of the status quo.

1909

Mawlay 'Abd al-'Aziz recognized as sultan by the great powers. Capture and execution of Bu Hmara.

1911

After internal unrest, French intervention in the Fez region, occupation of Fez, Spanish intervention in the north.
July. Crisis provoked by Germany.
November 4. Franco-German accord concerning Morocco and the Congo. Germany gives up all claims to Morocco.

1912

March 30. Treaty of Fez establishes French protectorate. Marshal Louis Lyautey becomes governor (1912–1925).
August. Mawlay Yusuf the next sultan.

1920

Start in the Rif of the revolt led by Muhammad b. 'Abd al-Karim ('Abd el-Krim).

Algeria

1766–1791

Baba Muhammad b. 'Uthman, dey of Algiers.

1771–1792

Salih Bey, bey of Constantine.

1775

Failure of a Spanish incursion into Algiers. Decline of piracy.

End of the 18th century

The Tijaniyya brotherhood founded by Ahmad al-Tijani (1737–1815). The Rahmaniyya brotherhood founded by Abd al-Rahman al-Gushtuli (died in 1793).

1793–1798

Algerian wheat exports to southern France. France owes the dey and his intermediaries—Jacob Bacri and Nephtali Busnach—seven million francs.

1800

France pays three million francs, but refuses further payment; growing tensions.

1816

Incursion by Lord Exmouth into Algeria, destruction of the Algerian fleet in revenge for piracy.

1818–1830

Husayn Dey.

1827

April 27. The "Fly Whisk Incident": the dey touches (or beats, according to the French) the French consul with a fly whisk; French blockade of the port of Algiers.

1830

January 31. French government decides to attack Algiers, for reasons merely of internal politics. The French navy comprises 700 ships and 37,000 soldiers; the dey has about 44,000 soldiers.

June 14. French troops land west of Algiers.

July 5. Occupation of Algiers. The French remove approximately 150 million francs.

1832

Ahmad, the bey of Constantine, and Muhyi al-Din, the deputy of the Moroccan sultan in West Algeria, resume the Algerian resistance.

1834

Creation of a general government of Algeria. Accord with the emir 'Abd al-Qadir, the son of Muhyi al-Din.

1836

'Abd al-Qadir defeats the French siege of Constantine.

1837

Second accord with 'Abd al-Qadir (treaty of Tafna): delineation of French borders; 'Abd al-Qadir gets eastern Algeria, where he establishes a state.

October. Constantine taken.

1840

December. General Bugeaud governor of Algeria; his aim is to conquer all of Algeria.

1844

'Abd al-Qadir and the Moroccans defeated at Isly. Creation of the Bureaux Arabes.

1847

'Abd al-Qadir surrenders. First exiled in Turkey (Bursa), then in Damascus, where he dies in 1883.

1848

Surrender of Ahmad Bey. Bugeaud leaves Algeria.

1852–1864 and 1864–1870

The struggle in the Kabylia and the Sahara continues.

1860

Project for an "Arab kingdom" led by 'Abd al-Qadir.

1863

Sénatus-Consulte: administrative division of the tribes, division of their territories, transformation of their land into private property.

1865

June 20. Letter from Napoleon III concerning French policy in Algeria.

July 14. The Sénatus-Consulte: all Algerians are declared Frenchmen. Muslims are allowed to vote if they abandon their legal status in favor of the Code Napoléon.

1870

October 24. Décret Crémieux granting French citizenship to Algerian Jews.

1871
Revolt led by Muhammad al-Hajj al-Muqrani and Shaykh al-Haddad, the head of the Rahmaniyya brotherhood.

1872
January. End of the revolt after al-Muqrani's sudden death. Eighty thousand French soldiers are involved. Beginning of large-scale European colonization.

1879–1880
Revolt in the Aurès. Expansion of colonial enterprise.

1881–1883
Revolt of the Saint Sidi 'Amama.

1896–1902
Administrative and financial organization established (assemblies, financial delegations).

After 1906
Algerian immigration into the industrial regions of France.

Tunisia

1782–1814
Hammuda Bey.

1784–1785
Plague.

1794–1795
Intervention in Tripoli.

1807
Failure of an incursion into Constantine.

1811
Revolt of the Janissaries.

1814–1824
Husayn Bey.

1816
Treaties with the European states. Revolt of the Janissaries.

1818–1820
Plague.

1819
Piracy prohibited. Creation of a tithe on olives.

1824–1835
Mustafa Bey.

1824
Reduction of the silver content of the Tunisian currency by one third.

1836–1854
Four cholera epidemics.

1837–1855
Ahmad Bey. Mustafa Khaznadar, prime minister (until 1873).

1840
The Military School of Bardo created; closed in 1869.

1841
Slavery abolished.

1854–1855
Tunisian participation in the Crimean war.

1855–1859
Muhammad Bey. The *majba* (money tax) replaces multiple taxes: every adult pays three piasters a month (except the inhabitants of Tunis, Kairuan, Susa and Sfax, and veterans and students of the Zietouna University).

1857

September 10. Declaration of the Fundamental Pact (*'ahd al-aman*): guarantees the equality and safety of all Tunisians; modeled on the Ottoman Hatt-i Sherif of Gülhane. Activity by reformers (Khayr al-Din, Ibn Abi al-Diyaf).

1858

Establishment of a municipal council in Tunis.

1859–1882

Muhammad al-Sadiq.

1860

The first Tunisian newspaper: *al-Ra'id al-Tunisi.*

1861

Constitution (*dustur*); introduces the separation of power, and a legislative council (*al-majlis al-akbar*), which includes notables of Tunis and religious scholars.

1863

First foreign loan (30 million francs) negotiated with the Parisian banker Erlanger.

1864

January. The *majba* doubled.

Spring Popular uprising, especially in the Sahel and in the northwest, in response to the doubling of the *majba* in order to pay the first installment of the loan. Dissolution of the Constitution and the Majlis.

1865–1868

Wave of epidemics, famines and droughts.

1869

July 5. Establishment of a Commission on International Finance by France, Britain and Italy, which supervises the repayment of Tunisia's foreign debt (about 160 million francs).

1870

The president of the Commission, Khayr al-Din (1822/23–1883) raises the *majba* from 36 to 40 piasters annually.

October 23. Firman from the sultan reaffirming Ottoman sovereignty has no effect.

1873

October. Khayr al-Din, prime minister: policy of reform announced in his manifesto *Aqwam al-masalik fi ma-'rifah al mamalik* ("The best way to know the situation of the countries").

1875

Reformation of the curricula of the Zaytuna University. Creation of the Sadiqiyya College for modern sciences. Its purpose is to train qualified personnel for administration and the army; adopts French curriculum.

1877

Khayr al-Din steps down.

1878

The fate of Tunisia determined at the Congress of Berlin.

1881

April. French troops in Tunisia.

May 12. Treaty of Bardo: establishment of a French protectorate.

1883

June. The convention of La Marsa.

Reaffirmation of the French protectorate.

From 1898

The French sell land of pious foundations (*hubus*) to acquire more territory.

1907

Creation of the Young Tunisian Party. Emergence of nationalism.

1920

Publication of 'Abd al-'Aziz Ta'albi's and Ahmad Sakka's book: *La Tunisie martyre. Ses revendications.* ("The Martyrdom of Tunisia: Its Rightful Claims").

June. Creation of the Liberal Constitutional Party (*al-hizb al-hurr al-dusturi al-tunisi*).

Tripolitania and Cyrenaica

1784

Devastating famine; about a quarter of Tripoli's 14,000 inhabitants perish.

1790

Power struggles among the Qaramanli.

1793

'Ali Barghul, a former janissary stationed in Algiers, occupies Tripoli.

1795

Return of the Qaramanli.

1796–1832

Government of Yusuf Qaramanli.

1801–1805

The U.S. navy destroys the navy of the Qaramanli in retaliation for piracy.

1830

Abolition of piracy.

1832

Revolt in Tripoli.

1835

May. Ottoman troops land. Reestablishment of direct Ottoman rule over Tripolitania; the Qaramanli are deposed.

1843

First *zawiyya* of the Sanusiyya brotherhood founded in the Cyrenaica by the Algerian Sayyid Muhammad 'Ali al-Sanusi (1791–1859); based on a mixture of Wahhabism and Sufism. After his death, his son Sayyid Muhammad al-Mahdi (died 1902) established hundreds of *zawiyyas*.

1856

The *zawiyya* of Jaghbub founded, which is the center of the Sanusiyya.

1858

Death of the tribal leader Jum'ah b. Khalifa; collapse of the resistance movement against the Ottomans. The Sanusiyya recognize the Ottoman sultan's authority.

1860

Administrative reorganization. Autonomy for the Cyrenaica.

1895

Kufra becomes the new center of the Sanusiyya.

1899

Quru (Guro) becomes the new center of the Sanusiyya.

Muslim Reformism

For the Muslim reformers of the late 19th century, the caliphate, a fundamental religious element, must serve as the foundation for a liberal and open Muslim society, but not one without religion. In addition to the revivers of Arab literature, who are often Syrian and Lebanese, Christians or Muslims, there appear the theoreticians of reform, of the modernization of Islam, and the propagandists of the renewal of the Arab world. Jamal al-Din al-Afghani (1839–1897), considered the "father of eastern nationalism" and founder of the pan-Islamic movement, sees reform as a means to fight the West while celebrating the traditions of the Arab states, which are under Turkish domination; he hopes for the creation of autonomous kingdoms gathered together in a confederation in which the caliph would be their spiritual leader, the symbol of unity in the Muslim world. Rashid Rida (1865–1935) resumes the propagation of these ideas by stressing the importance of anti-Turkish sentiment. Abd al-Rahman al-Kawakibi (1849–1902) questions the legitimacy of the Ottoman caliphate and proposes the establishment of a Qurayshi caliphate in Mecca with Arab nationalist tendancies. Muhammad Abduh (1849–1905) emphasizes the struggle against the corrupting influence of the West and Christianity.

The journal *al-Manar* was the principal medium for the spreading of reformist ideas, at first anchored in religious reform, later in political reform. The League de la Patrie Arabe (Arab Fatherland League), created in Paris in 1905, took up these ideas and declared itself in favor of independence for Arab states.

1906 and 1910
Accords with France concerning border with Tunisia.

1911
October 5. Soon after the establishment of a French protectorate over Morocco, Italian troops land in Tripoli. Ottoman-Italian war; Italy conquers Libya.

1912
October 17. Treaty of Lausanne-Ouchy. Tripolitania becomes an Italian colony.

1912–1923
Period of anti-Italian resistance.

1914
Tribes loyal to the Sanusiyya push the Italians back to the coast.

1918
The Tripolitanian Republic of Misurata established under Italian protection.

1919
Political and administrative organization of Libya, local parliaments.

From Iran to Central Asia

To the east of the Ottoman Empire, the Muslim states of the Middle East are subject to pressure from Russia and Great Britain: the former seeks to open a route to the Indian Ocean, the latter to protect its routes to India. Iran and Afghanistan experience internal strife, but they manage to begin modernization, a slow process that is nonetheless symbolic of an opening toward the modern world at the same time that it is an attempt to safeguard their independence. The Central Asian states, engrossed in fratricidal wars, come one by one, beginning in 1840, under Russian domination. The revolution of the Young Turks in 1908 awakens for a moment a nationalist awareness, especially during the First World War, but, after 1918, Russia finally takes possession of Turkestan.

Iran

Events

1779

The Zand dynasty weakened. The Qajars, of Turkoman descent, take over northern Persia.

1795

Agha Muhammad Khan Qajar overthrows the Zand ruler Lutf 'Ali Khan and executes him. Establishes his capital in Tehran. Strong, centralized administration. Invasion of Georgia. Tiflis sacked, thousands of Georgians deported as slaves. Conquest of Azerbaijan and Armenia.

1796

Agha Muhammad is crowned *shahanshah*.

1797

Agha Muhammad Khan assassinated by a servant he had condemned to death. Successor: his nephew Fath 'Ali Shah. Beginning of pressures by the great powers.

1797–1834: Reign of Fath 'Ali Shah

1800

The Russians annex Georgia.

1801

The Englishman Sir John Malcolm of the British East India Company concludes a treaty that calls for a Iranian-British military alliance, and the right of unlimited trade in Iran without paying taxes.

1807

Treaty with France: Iran cancels all relations with Britain.

1811

War against Russia.

1813

October 12. Treaty of Gulistan with Russia. Iran loses the Caucasian provinces; Russia is allowed to acquire property in Iran.

1826

Second war against Russia.

1828

February 22. Treaty of Turkoman-çay after Iranian defeat. Iran gives up Armenia; border established on the Araxes River. Trade privileges (capitulations) granted to the Russians in Iran; Iran pays reparations to Russia.

1833

Crown Prince 'Abbas Mirza, governor of the province of Azerbaijan, tries to take Herat.

1834

Death of 'Abbas Mirza, death of 'Ali Shah.

1834–1848: Reign of Muhammad Shah

1836–1841

A series of treaties with Britain, which gains the same rights as Russia.

1837

Iran threatens Herat. British counteroffensive.

1840

Revolt led by Hasan 'Ali Shah (Agha Khan), the *imam* of the Isma'ilis, in south-central Iran; defeat, flight to India.

1844

Babi protest. Political-religious revolt, led by Sayyid 'Ali Muhammad of Shriaz, denounces secularism and Western influence; demands social justice, improvement of the status of women, reduction of taxes, etc.

1848

Death of Muhammad Shah. The Babis establish their own authority in southern cities during the interregnum.

1848–1896: Reign of Nasir al-Din

1850

July 9. Execution of the *bab* in Tabriz. After continuing protests, mass tortures and executions. All remaining Babis are forced to emigrate, go underground or renounce their belief.

1852

Execution of Mirza Taqi Khan, who implemented numerous reforms.

1852–1856

New Iranian incursions into Afghanistan. Herat taken.

1856

Britain repulses an Iranian attack, lands at the port of Bushir in the Persian Gulf. Treaty of Paris. Afghanistan reclaims Herat as its independence is recognized.

1860

Britain gains concession to build a telegraph network.

1863

Baha'ullah declares himself the prophet of the Babis, founds the sect of the Baha'is, which is active in the Iranian underground.

1872

Exclusive rights given to the British citizen Baron Julius de Reuter for the extraction of all mineral resources in Iran, creation of a bank, installation of a telegraph network and rail lines — high Iranian officials are bribed. Strong Russian reaction; concessions nullified.

1874
Reorganization of the postal system with the help of Austrian advisors.

1879
Fishing concession in the Caspian Sea to a Russian company. Creation of the Cossack Brigade to serve as the royal guard; commanded by Russian officers; strengthens Russian influence in Iran.

1889
The British authorized to establish the Imperial Bank of Persia. Russians establish a bank for loans.

1890
Tobacco monopoly granted to a British company.

1891
December. Tobacco monopoly nullified under pressure from public opinion: a coalition of *'ulama'*, modernists, and urban population. Iran has to pay £500,000 compensation.

End of the 19th century
Formation of secret societies for the study of Western liberalism and the problems of social reform. Development of constitutional and nationalist movement.

1896
Assassination of Nasir al-Din Shah by a follower of Jamal al-Din al-Afghani.

1896–1907: Reign of Muzaffar al-Din Shah
1899
Revocation of the Reuter concession, transferred to William Knox d'Arcy in 1901.

1902
Customs treaty with Russia, preferential customs for Russian goods.

1905–1906
Revolutionary movements led by *mullahs*, mass protests, led by Agha Sayyid Jamal and Shaykh Muhammad.

1906
October 7. First National Assembly (Majlis) elected.
December 30. Constitutional law, modeled on the Belgian constitution.

1907
January. Death of Muzaffar al-Din Shah.

1907–1909: Reign of Muhammad 'Ali Shah
Muhammad Shah, supported by the Cossack Brigade, opposes the Constitution and the enactment of laws created by the Majlis; the result is a popular uprising.

August 31. Anglo-Russian entente overseeing the division of Iran into two politically separate zones separated by a neutral zone. The Russian zone includes north and central Iran with Teheran and Isfahan; the British zone comprises the southeast, with a neutral zone between them.

1908
Discovery of oil in the neutral zone.
March 26. Russian troops occupy Tabriz.
June 23. Martial law in Teheran. The Majlis suspended, execution of numerous populist leaders. Popular uprising in Tabriz, led by Sattar Khan and Baqir Khan.

Two Pressure Groups in Iran

Besides tribal chiefs, landowners, high military officers and civil servants, two groups play an important role in 19th-century Iranian society: clerics and merchants.

The Shi'i clergy is invested with the power to direct the Iranian people, and their dignitaries, the *mujtahids*, often stake out positions that differ from the decisions made by the rulers, especially after the reign of Fath 'Ali Shah (1797–1834), who had been favorable to their cause. The *mujtahids* fight against the increasing influence of the West and support the people in their protests against foreign monopolies (e.g., granting of rights to sale and export of tobacco to an English group, 1891–1892). They struggle as well, at the beginning of the 20th century, against the authoritarian government of the Qajar shahs, who tend to limit their privileges.

Until banks are established in Iran, merchants played a prominent role in the supplying and circulating of money, especially for the upper classes. It is among these merchants that provincial governors find the financial guarantees that are indispensible to the government. Little by little, the large merchants, through marriage, by the acquisition of land and wealth, and by their economic and political power, rise to the ranks of the upper classes; the bazaar merchants (the *bazaris*) find allies among religious dignitaries and, on many occasions, merchants and Shi'i dignitaries rise up together against the decisions of the Qajar government.

1909

Creation of the Anglo-Persian Oil Company. Counteroffensive led by nationalists, supported by the tribe of the Bakhtiyars (under 'Ali Quli Khan), who take Isfahan.

July. Shah deposed; flees into exile in Russia. Successor is his son Ahmad.

1909–1925: Reign of Ahmad Shah

Controlled by the constitutionalists.

1911

The Majlis invites the American William Morgan Shuster to reform the state finances; Russia protests.

July. Muhammad Shah's attempt to reclaim power fails. The Russians invade northern Iran.

November. Russian ultimatum to dismiss Shuster.

December 24. The Majlis dissolved; Russian ultimatum accepted; Shuster dismissed.

1914

The British government acquires the majority in the Anglo-Persian Oil Company.

November 1. Iran declares its neutrality in World War I. The army is split: the dominant Cossack Brigade favors Russia, while the *gendarmerie* is dominated by pro-German Swedish officers. Russia occupies positions in the north, Britain takes the south and the neutral zone. Election of a new Majlis to stabilize the state finances.

1915

Ottoman occupation of Azerbaijan, but Ottomans are expelled by the Russians. The German consul W. Waßmus incites a tribal rebellion against Britain in the south; tribes take Teheran, from a provisional government in Qum. Allied advance in the south.

1916

Renewed Russian invasion in the north. British conquest of the south; formation of the South Persian Rifles, a local army, under Sir Percy Sykes.

1917

Ottoman retreat after their defeat by Britain at Baghdad. Russian retreat after the Bolshevik Revolution.

1917-1918

The armed revolutionary movement of the Jangalis led by Kuchik Khan takes power in the province of Gilan.

1918-1919

Devastating famine.

1919

British propose to place independent Iran under British protection. Not ratified.

1920

May. Bolshevik occupation of Resht and Gilan. British withdrawal to Qazvin. The Bolsheviks destroy the Cossack Brigade, but Britain reorganizes it.

1921

February 21. Reza Khan, commander of the Cossack Brigade, takes power. Constitution suspended. Religious circles oppose the creation of a republic.

February 26. Soviet-Iranian treaty: the Bolsheviks renounce the imperialist policies of the tsars, agree to withdraw from Iran, abolish the capitulations and renounce all concessions.

1925

Ahmad Shah deposed, exile in Europe.

December. Reza Khan proclaimed Shah: first sovereign of the Pahlevi dynasty.

1926

April 25. Crowning of the Shah.

Religion

Second half of the 18th century

Sufi renaissance under Ma'sum 'Ali Shah, from India.

1797-1798

Persecution of the Sufis; execution of Ma'sum 'Ali Shah.

Beginning of the 19th century

Increased role for the Shi'i clergy. Fath 'Ali Shah depends on support from the clergy. Schism among Shi'is: traditionalist *usulis* against Shaykhis; controversy about the hidden imam.

1844

Sayyid 'Ali Muhammad (1819–1850), from Shiraz, puts himself forward as the *bab* (the "door" to knowledge and divine wisdom) and claims to begin a new prophetic cycle.

1848

The *bab* breaks away from the *shari'a*.

1848–1850

Persecution of the Babi. The movement becomes clandestine. Mirza Husayn 'Ali Nuri (Baha'ullah) succeeds the *bab*, reforms the Babi religion and creates the Baha'i religion.

1863

Baha'ullah founds the Baha'i sect.

1906

The Constitution, followed by the Complementary Law of 1907, confirms the privileged position of "twelver" Shi'ism as the state religion.

Literature

1797–1834

Fath 'Ali Shah attempts to revive royal patronage in Tehran. Creation of small literary societies (*anjuman*). Neo-classical poetry.

1800–1871

Reza Quli Khan, author of texts on political, literary and religious history; known as Hidayat in poetry: revives, along with Furughi, the tradition of the mystical *ghazal*.

1808–1854

The poet Ka'ani; return to classicism.

1816–1817

First printing press in Tabriz.

1822

Death of Saba, neoclassical poet; author of a *Shahanshahname*, which describes the wars against Russia.

1834

First newspaper, *Ruzname-i akhbar-i waqayi'*.

1852

The Polytechnic School (Dar al-Funun) founded, with some European teachers. Translation of European works. Literary activity by the Babists.

1857/1858

Death of Furughi.

1859

Kizabça-i ghaybi, political tract written by Malkam Khan, an Armenian from Isfahan (1833–1909).

1862

Malkam Khan sent into exile in Istanbul after he founds a Freemason-like lodge in Teheran.

End of the 19th century

Modern, politically committed literature written by Muhammad Baqir Bawanati and Agha Khan Kirmani (died 1890), disciple of Jamal al-Din al-Afghani. Appearance of a nationalist ideology, glorifying pre-Islamic past. Attempt to simplify the language.

1887

Al-Afghani is forced to leave Iran; readmitted in 1889; deported to Iraq in January 1891.

1890

The newspaper *Qanun* appears in London; banned in Iran due to its radical reformist ideas.

1910

Death of Zayn al-'Abidin Maragha'i, author of a fictional description of Iran at the end of the Qajar dynasty; devastating critique of Iranian society.

Afghanistan

Political Events

1773–1793: Reign of Timur Shah

Capital is moved from Kandahar to Kabul. The system of hereditary duties is reinstituted, and new ones are added that depend directly on Timur Shah. He regularly holds meetings with clerics (*majlis-i 'ulama'*). Forms an elite military corps composed of Persians and Tajiks.

1793–1800: Reign of Zaman Shah

Policy of centralization. Gradually abolishes the hereditary duties.

1795

Incursion into India fails.

1796

Invasion of the Punjab.

1800

Mahmud, brother of Zaman Shah, first takes Kandahar, then Kabul.

1803–1809

Period of disorder. Mahmud expelled.

1809

Fath Khan, leader of the Barakzay clan, re-establishes Mahmud as ruler, but holds power behind the scenes.

1818

Execution of Fath Khan. His brother Dost Muhammad, the ruler of Kabul, expels Mahmud from Kabul.

1819–1834

Tribal struggles. Loss of the eastern provinces (Multan, Kashmir, western Punjab). Russia's influence increases.

1834

Dost Muhammad takes the title *emir*.

1839

First British-Afghan war to check Russian influence. Kandahar falls, followed by Kabul. Dost Muhammad flees. Shah Shuja' al-Mulk, new ruler.

1842

January 4. Defeat of the British army.

December. Kabul recaptured from the British. Assassination of Shuja al-Mulk; Dost Muhammad returns to power.

1844

British-Russian accord concerning Afghanistan.

1863

The Persians expelled from Herat. Death of Dost Muhammad.

1863–1868

Struggle among Dost Muhammad's sons.

1873

Part of the western territories relinquished to the Persians.

1878–1880

Second war against the British.

1879

Death of the pro-Russian emir Shir 'Ali. Successor: his son Muhammad Ya'qub. Treaty of Gandamak with the English.

1880–1901: Reign of 'Abd al-Rahman Khan
1880

Ya'qub Khan deposed. His successor, 'Abd al-Rahman Khan, restores unity to the country, agrees to let Britain control Afghan foreign policy in return for an annual subsidy of £60,000 and assistance against foreign aggression.

1888

Border between Afghanistan and Russian central Asia drawn.

1893

New treaty with the English (Durand Agreement) determines the borders with India; millions of Afghans are excluded from Afghan jurisdiction, leading to the development of Afghan irredentism.

1901

Death of 'Abd al-Rahman, who had preserved Afghanistan's independence. Successor: his son Habib Allah Khan, an enlightened sovereign.

1901–1919: Reign of Habib Allah Khan
1905

Accord with the English: confirmation of British control of Afghan foreign politics. Increase of subsidy to £160,000 annually.

1907

Anglo-Russian convention guarantees neutrality for Afghan territory.

1915

A German-Ottoman mission led by Oskar Niedermayer and Herr von Hentig arrives in Kabul. Their attempt to persuade Habib Allah to join the German war effort fails.

1919

February 20. Habib Allah assassinated. Successor: his third son, Aman Allah.

August 8. After a brief war against the British, Afghanistan's independence recognized in the Treaty of Rawalpindi. An Afghan mission goes to Moscow, and a Soviet mission is received in Kabul.

1921

February 28. Afghan-Russian treaty of friendship.

November 22. New treaties with the U.S.S.R. and Great Britain. Afghanistan recognized as totally independent.

Central Asia

Political Events

1774-1797
Sirim Batir of the Kazakh tribe struggles against the Russians.

1785-1800: Reign of Murad Ma'sum Shah
Establishes the Mangit dynasty in Bukhara.

1799-1809
'Alim Khan, ruler of Khokand, unifies the Ferghana Valley.

1800-1826
Haydar, khan of Bukhara, fights against 'Alim Khan.

1808
'Alim Khan conquers Tashkent.

1811
Muhammad Rahim (1806-1825), khan of Khiva, takes Aral.

1809-1822: Reign of 'Umar in Khokand
1814
'Umar takes Samarkand.

1822
Muhammad Rahim takes Merv.

1826-1860: Reign of Nasr Allah, Ruler of Bukhara
Struggle against Khiva. Occupies Balkh (1826-1849).

1831
Occupation of the Tajik state by Muhammad 'Ali, 'Umar of Khokand's son.

1834
Beginning of Russian penetration into central Asia (Khiva).

1839
Nasr Allah, khan of Bukhara, imposes his suzerainty on the Tajik state.

1840
The Kazakh state under Russian control.

1842
Khokand taken by Nasr Allah; lost soon thereafter.

1843
Khokand and Tashkent taken by Nasr Allah.

1858
Russian attack on Khiva fails.

1860-1885: Reign of Muzaffar al-Din in Bukhara
1864
Decision made by Russian government to conquer central Asia.

1865
June. Tashkent taken by the Russians.

1866
May. Muzaffar al-Din, khan of

Bukhara, severely defeated by the Russians.

1868

May 1. Samarkand taken.
July. Muzaffar al-Din recognizes the Russian conquests.

1873

Bukhara and Khiva become Russian protectorates.

1875–1876

Total occupation of the khanate of Khokand.

1885

Merv taken. Afghan forces expelled.

1911

Students sent to Istanbul.

1913

The nationalist newspapers *Kazak* and *Alash Orda* published. Turkistan follows to the Turkish Committee for Union and Progress.

1915

Suppression of the khanates of Khiva and Bukhara.

1916

The Kirghiz, Kazakh and Uzbek revolt. Nationalist movement inspired by a similar movement led by Gaspirali in the Crimea.

1917

Violent Russian repression.

1918

The Bolsheviks control Tashkent.

India and Indonesia

British domination of India intensifies at an even pace, especially from the 19th century: by 1858, the Indian Empire is completely in British hands, and all Muslim power disappears after 1877. Nevertheless, a religious and intellectual movement appears in the second half of the 19th century; it too will eventually become political.

In Indonesia, the Dutch impose their political and economic authority by often applying excessive measures; here too an intellectual and religious Muslim Indonesian movement is born which will eventually fight for independence.

India

1771

Power reclaimed by Marartha.

1782–1799: Reign of Tipu Sultan in Mysore
Vanquished by the British; southern India comes under British control.

1788

Attack on Delhi and capture of the Moghul ruler Shah 'Alam II by Ghulam Khan.

1793

The East India Company's constitution is renewed. Lord Cornwallis and Sir John Shore introduce a new tax

237

law in Bengal (The Permanent Settlement) that makes Hindus tax collectors at the expense of Muslims; result is rise of a new Hindu middle class.

1798

Hyderabad becomes a British protectorate.

1803

The Maratha defeated by the English. Shah 'Alam II reclaims the throne, but the Moghul dynasty no longer has any power.

Beginning of the 19th century

Influence of Wahhabism.

1813

The East India Company loses its monopoly on trade. Beginning of a capitalist colonial economy.

1824

Death of the theologian 'Abd al 'aziz (born 1746), who declares British-controlled India to be enemy territory (*daral-harb*).

1830

Death of Hajji Shari'atullah, the leader of the anti-Hindu Fara'izi movement in Bengal.

1831

Death of Sayyid Ahmad Brevli, the leader of the *mujahidin* movement, which aims at the renewal of Islam and the elimination of Hindu influence. Defeat and death of the Muslim peasant rebel leader Titu Miyan in Bengal.

1835

English replaces Persian as the language of instruction and administration.

1843

The British control Sind, which becomes a British province.

1846

The British control Kashmir.

Muslim Intellectual Movements

In the second half of the 19th century, several Muslim intellectual movements come to life.

Working at the heart of the School of Aligarh are Sayyid Ahmad Khan (1817–1898), who fights medieval obscurantism, Abu al-Kulam Azad (1875–1938), influenced by Jamal al-Din al-Afghani and Muhammad Abduh, and Muhammad Iqbal (1876–1938), who seeks to rebuild Islamic religious thought in light of the problems posed by the modern world.

The Deoband Movement questions the pace and scope of modernization and extols the renaissance of religious knowledge.

The Nadwat al-'ulama' seek a compromise between these two schools, especially under Mawlana Shibli (1857–1914).

1849
The British control the Punjab.

1856
British annexation of Oudh, end of the local Shi'i rulers.

1857
Revolt (the Mutiny) by the army, crushed by Lord Canning. Muslim power in India suppressed; the Muslim community given a lower status than the Hindus.

1858
India under British administrative control through the intermediary of a viceroy.

1860
Death of Dudhu Miyan (born 1819), the son of Hajji Shari'atullah; he established Muslim courts and developed a parallel government in the Bengal countryside.

1875
Aligarh College founded by Sayyid Ahmad Khan, teaches modern subjects and classical Muslim theology.

1877
Queen Victoria proclaimed Empress of India.

1885
The Indian National Congress founded; leading party of Indian nationalism.

1891
Amir 'Ali declares that original Islam is the source of European progress.

1898
Death of Sayyid Ahmad Khan (born 1817); he attempted to improve the status of the Muslim community, while remaining loyal to the British.

1905–1911
Partition of Bengal, a British attempt to separate Muslims and Hindus.

1906
The Muslim League is founded.

1914
Death of Shibli Nu'mani, who reinterpreted *kalam*, influenced by the Egyptian Salafiyyah movement. Death of Hali, poet, revived Urdu literature.

1916
The partition of Bengal is cancelled.

Indonesia

1755
The kingdom of Java divided in two (Surakarta and Jogjakarta).

End of the 18th century
Ineffectual anti-Dutch movements.

1800
January 1. Dissolution of the Dutch East India Company. Direct exploitation by the Dutch state.

1802
A new colonial charter prepared.

1803–1839
Religious war (*Padri* war) of the Wahhabi movement against the Miankabau of southern Sumatra and the Batak of central Sumatra, launched from Atjeh; against saint worship,

alcohol and other un-Islamic practices.

1808–1811
Administrative reforms in Java.

1811
Java conquered by the British.

1812–1821
Revolts in Palembang.

Circa 1815
The travel report *Serat Tjentini* is written; a rhymed, syncretist work, it derides ritual duties of Muslims, but treats mystical topics seriously.

1816
Administration of Thomas Stamford Raffles: reform of the colonial system, abolition of forced labor, creation of a tenant farming system. The Dutch reclaim their possessions. Reforms sustained.

1817
Revolt on the Moluccas.

1819
January. Singapore founded by Raffles.

1821
The Dutch intervene in the *Padri* war; cannot prevent Islamization.

1824
New Dutch Trading Company.

1825–1830
The Java War waged by Prince Dipo Negoro.

1830–1834
Governor Van den Bosch establishes the "forced agriculture system": large tracts of land devoted to the harvest of coffee beans, sugar cane and indigo plants, all for export. The Dutch Trading Company prospers, but there are many abuses.

1844
The Christian dynasty of Bolaäng-Mongondon is converted by Muslim merchant missionaries.

1852
Abolition of the pilgrim tax; as a result, many Indonesians stay in Mecca to study.

1863
Attempt to correct abuse by the Dutch Trading Company.

1870 and later
Extensive colonial activity in the islands around Java.

1873–1904
Atjeh War. Unflinching defense of the Muslim community.

End of the 19th century
Political plan drawn up by the Dutch orientalist Snouck Hurgronje (1857–1936); it seeks to maintain Muslim religious practices and customs, while encouraging Muslims to assimilate into Dutch culture. Put into action in 1904.

1908
In Batavia, students create the Budi Otomo (Noble Effort) movement with the goal of modernizing Javanese culture.

1912

Creation of the Muslim reformist movement, Muhammadijah, by Kiaji Haji Ahmad Dahlan (1869–1923), a friend of Muhammad 'Abduh's. Creation of the Islamic Union (Sarekat Islam), initially a merchant's union, then a traditional religious movement and populist political party.

1915

Revolt in the southern and eastern Celebes, supported by the Ottomans; their aim is the restoration of the Muslim Empire of Makasar.

1920

Development of Communist movements leads to the decline of the Islamic Union. Secularizing tendancy.

Sub-Saharan Africa

This is the era of the great *jihads* in West Africa and [Sudan]*: the first ones, linked to local factors, are manifestations of a new balance of power between Muslims and non-Muslims in the sub-Saharan region: Usman dan Fodio in [Nigeria], al-Haj 'Umar in [Senegal] and [Mali], etc. The later *jihads* seem to stem from a reaction to European conquests: the Mahdi in [Sudan], "Mad Mullah" in [Somalia], and Samori in [Guinea] and [the Ivory Coast]. At the dawn of the 20th century, only the Sahara (and its outlying areas) can still be considered a theater for armed Islamic movements [Mauritania, Chad and Niger], while everywhere else, compromise seems to rule in the relations between colonial authorities and Islamic authorities.

In East Africa, the period is not defined by the *jihad*, but rather by the energetic acts of the dynamic and expansionist sultan of Oman, who extends the Swahili network deep into the heart of the African continent, until this Muslim hegemony, based on the island of Zanzibar, is suppressed by European colonization.

In all regions, but at a different pace, Sufi fraternities (especially the Qadiriyya and Tijaniyya) are established; Black Africa is for them a fertile area for expansion.

*In brackets are the *present* names of countries that, prior to 1960, appeared under different names.

West Africa

The First Generation of Jihads

1750s–1881

Sidi Makhtar al-Kunti, the West African head of the Qadiriyyah Sufi order, spreads his teachings along the African trade routes.

1776

Victory by Muslim troops in Futa Jallon [Guinea]. Ibrahim Sori proclaimed *almamy:* beginning of the Islamic State of Futa Jallon, which exists until the French conquest. 'Abd al-Qadir, successor to Sulayman Bal, killed in combat, is proclaimed *almamy* of Futa Toro [Senegal].

Circa 1780

'Abd al-Qadir overthrows the Denyanke dynasty in Futa Toro, establishes an Islamic state, then moves against the Moors on the northern bank of the Senegal River. This regime lasts until the French conquest.

Circa 1790

Defeat of the Muslims in Cayor [Senegal] who had revolted against the *damel* (king), Amari Ngone Cuba. Some are sold as slaves, others seek refuge on the Cape Verde peninsula.

1796

Invasion of the Wolof kingdoms of [Senegal] (Jollof, Walo, Cayor) by 'Abd al-Qadir, *almamy* of Futa Toro; failure. The Wolof monarchs, supported by a professional warrior class (*tyeddo* or *ceddo*), position themselves against Islam until the 19th century.

1807

Death of 'Abd al-Qadir at the age of 80.

First half of the 19th century

Cerno Mamadu Samba Mombeya (circa 1765–1852), Islamic man of letters from Futa Jallon, devises a system of graphic representation for the Peuhl language (Fulfulde) using Arabic characters, which allows the teaching of Islam in common languages and facilitates the spread of texts written in African languages.

West Africa and the Hausa States
The Second Generation of Jihads

1804

Islamic reform movement in one part of the Hausa states [northern Nigeria], by a group of Peuhl men of letters led by Usman dan Fodio and his brother Abdullahi.

February. Direct confrontation between troops from the Hausa state of Gobir and Usman's disciples. Usman recognized as imam of the new community at 50 years of age. When the king of Gobir plans a preemptive military strike, he orders a retreat (*hijra*) following the example set by the prophet Muhammad.

1804–1808

Usman dan Fodio wages a *jihad* against the Hausa armies.

1808

October 3. Alkalawa, capital of Gobir [Nigeria], captured by Usman dan Fodio's followers.

1808–1812

Caliphate created by Usman dan Fodio. The Hausa states as well as several territories in the south, as far down as the Benue River and the Adamawa Plateau, are integrated into this new state.

1815

Usman settles in Sokoto, headquarters set up by his son Muhammad Bello.

1817

April 20. Death of Usman dan Fodio. Muhammad Bello, his successor (1817–1837), is the true creator of the empire. The Sokoto caliphate lasts until the British conquest.

1818

Ahmadu Lobbo, Peuhl man of letters from Masina (the Niger Loop, [Mali]), launches a victorious *jihad* against the Peuhl and the pagan Bambara tribes of the region.

1818–1844

Ahmadu Lobbo, henceforth known as Seku (Shaykh) Ahmadu, creates an Islamic state (Dina) of which he becomes the *amir al-mu'minin* (Commander of the Faithful).

1821

Hamdallahi (Arabic for "Praise to God"), capital of Ahmadu Lobbo's state.

1826

Ahmadu Lobbo's successor captures Timbuktu. Apart from that conquest, the caliphate is generally not expansive.

1840–1841

After a lengthy stay in the Near East (three years) and Sokoto (seven years), al-Haj 'Umar Tal settles in Jegunko, on the edge of Futa Jallon ([Guinea]) and begins attracting disciples.

1852–1853

Al-Haj 'Umar's *jihad* victorious over the pagan king of Tamba near Dingirai ([Guinea]).

1855

April 11. Al-Haj 'Umar takes Nioro, capital of the Bambara state of Karta (western [Mali]), and transforms it into his power base.

Apology for the Peuhl Language

"I will cite the Authentics (the *hadith*) in the Peuhl language to make it easier for you to understand.

When you hear them, accept them.

Indeed, one can only truly understand the Authentics in one's own tongue.

Many Peuhls do not grasp what they are taught in Arabic and remain in a state of uncertainty.

The state of uncertainty, in the works of Duty, is sufficient neither for words nor deeds.

He who seeks knowledge free of incertitude must read these lines in Peuhl. . . ."

Cerno Mamadu Samba Mombeya, *Le Filon du bonheur éternel*, Peuhl text from the early 19th century, French translation by Alfa Ibrahim Sow.

1857

April–July. Siege on Médine, French fort in Upper Senegal. Defeat of 'Umar's followers.

1857–1859

Al-Haj 'Umar in Upper and Middle Senegal calls on his followers to immigrate to the west, in order to move away from the French and to fight the pagan Bambaras. More than 500,000 people leave for Nioro (in Peuhl: *fergo* = emigration).

1859

October. 'Umar's followers vanquished in Gemu by French troops. They nevertheless turn westward.

1860

September 5–9. Battle of Woitala. Al-Haj 'Umar victorious over the troops from the Bambara Empire of Segu; he controls the towns of Middle Niger.

1861

March 9. Al-Haj 'Umar enters Segu, the "city of paganism"; transforms it into the capital of his empire.

1862

May 15. Al-Haj 'Umar victorious over Masina in Cayawal.
May 17. Triumphant entrance of al-Haj 'Umar into Hamdallahi.

1864

February 12. Death of al-Haj 'Umar on the Degembere cliffs ([Mali]).

1864–1893

Ahmadu Seku, son and designated heir of al-Haj 'Umar, succeeds his father. Takes the title *Lamido Julbe*

(commander of the faithful). Opposition by some of his brothers.

1893

Arrival of the French: emigration to the west by Ahmadu Seku, who dies in 1897.

West Africa
The Third Generation of Jihads

1861–1887

'Umar's movement spawns imitators in Senegambia. The French intervene against new Islamic movements: Maba Diakho, 1861–1867, in [Gambia]; Amadu Ba, also known as Amadu Shaiku, in Jollof [Senegal], 1869–1875; Muhammad al-Amin Drame [Mamadu Lamine] in Upper Senegal, 1886–1887.

1884–1886

Samori Ture, Jula conqueror, native of the Kankan [Guinea] area, begins a movement in 1861 with no Islamic tendencies, and later assumes the title of *almamy* and forces his subjects to convert.

1891–1894

Pushed back to the east by the French, with whom he has been clashing since 1882, Samori conquers northern [Ivory Coast] and [Ghana].

1897

Samori destroys the great Muslim center in Kong (northern [Ivory Coast]) after its members refuse to come to his aide.

1898

September. The French stop Samori in Gelemu (the hinterland of [Liberia]), on his way to Guinea. He dies in exile in [the Congo] in 1900.

Beginning in 1902

Coppolani, with support from Shaykh Sidiyya and Shaykh Saad Bu, begins to extend French influence into southern Mauritania.

1905

Coppolani killed in Tagant, in a conspiracy arranged by Shaykh Ma' al-Ainin, organizer of resistance in the desert.

1908

Adrar conquered by Gouraud, who defeats Ma'al-Ainin's troops.

1910

Ma'al-Ainin vanquished by French troops in Morocco. Dies in Tiznit.

West Africa
From Military Jihad to Peaceful Jihad

1895

Faced with an increasing number of Ahmadu Bamba's disciples, the French arrest him and deport him to [Gabon].

1902–1907

Ahmadu Bamba back from Senegal; confined to a house and kept under surveillance in [Mauritania].

1902

Al-Haj Malik Si, a wise man of Tukulor descent, creates the *zawiya* of Tivuan [Senegal], a new Tijani center.

1903

March 15. The British in Sokoto. The last independent caliph, Attahiru, immigrates to the east; the vizier Muhammad al-Bukhari chooses to compromise. The caliphate of Sokoto made a British protectorate; keeps its "feudal" structure until the independence of [Nigeria].

1907–1912

Ahmadu Bamba under surveillance in Cheyen, a village in Jollof [Senegal]. In 1910, he advises his disciples in a letter to submit completely to the French authorities.

1912

Ahmadu Bamba authorized to return to Diourbel [Senegal].

1914–1918

Support of Ahmadu Bamba's disciples in the recruitment of soldiers for the French army.

1918

Ahmadu Bamba awarded the Legion of Honor. Avoids having to wear it by arguing that it is associated to Christianity.

Around the Shores of Lake Chad (except the Hausa region)

1808 and 1811

A Peuhl army, in favor of Usman dan Fodio's *jihad*, takes the capital of Borno. With the aid of Muhammad

The Muridiyya

The word *murid*, Arabic for the candidate in a Sufi initiation, took on a particular meaning in Senegal to describe the adepts of a movement founded by Ahmadu Bamba, a Senegalese mystic and man of letters (circa 1850–1927), which was repressed for a long time by French authorities. Basing its economic strength on the cultivation of peanuts, Muridism offers an original example of a religious fraternity engaged in agricultural production.

After the death of its founder, the Muridiyya becomes the mediator for all powers currently in place. Buoyed by the extreme fervor of its adherents, the movement seeks, even though it does not represent a majority in the country, to become the national fraternity *par excellence*.

al-Amin, more commonly known as Shaykh Laminu al-Kanemi, the sovereign of Borno reoccupies his capital.

1835–1850
'Umar succeeds al-Kanemi, his father. Overthrow of the Saifawa dynasty in 1846; takes power with the religious title of *shehu* (shaykh).

1850
Muhammad al-Sharif, sultan of Wadai [Chad], ally of the new Sanusiyya brotherhood, established in the Cyrenaica [Libya], moves his capital from Ouara to Abeshe. Rapid growth of the new trans-Saharan route Benghazi–Kufra–Abeshe.

1886
Rabih Fadlallah (Rabih Zubayr), adventurer from [Sudan], former lieutenant for the slave trader Zubayr Pasha, arrives in Shari.

1892
Rabih crushes Bagirmi [Chad]. Enters victoriously into Kukawa, the capital of Borno, which becomes the focal point of his empire. Loosely affiliated to the Sudanese Mahdi, he runs an autonomous government.

1899
Muhammad al-Mahdi, supreme shaykh of the Sanusiyya, settles in Guro (northern [Chad]). Creation of a Sanusi *zawiya* in Bir Alali, near Lake Chad.

1900
April 22. Rabih defeated then killed by the combined action of three French campaigns in Kusseri (northern [Cameroon]).

1901
November 9. Attack on the Sanusi *zawiya* in Bir Alali by a French light brigade, which is routed.

1902
January 20. The Sanusi *zawiya* of Bir Alali taken by another French division: beginning of the 11-year-long French-Sanusi War in northern [Chad].

1913

November 27. Colonel Largeau takes the fortified town of Ain-Galakka, the last Sanusi *zawiya* actively resisting in northern [Chad].

1916–1917

December 13–March 3. Agades taken by a Tuareg colonel, led by the Sanusi chief Kaossen; siege on the French fort lasts nearly three months.

1917

March 4. The Marabouts from Agades, hiding in the Great Mosque, are killed by the French forces involved in the reconquest. Wrongly accused by Kaossen of complicity in the occupation of the town.

[Sudan]

1820–1821

Conquest of [Sudan] by Turkish and Egyptian troops. The Funj state of Sinnar crumbles. Darfur resists and manages to maintain its independence.

1821–1881

Egyptian administration of [Sudan]. Slave merchants, such as Zubayr Pasha, control the captured regions in the south.

1871

Muhammad Ahmad, born in Dongola in 1843, member of the Sammaniyya brotherhood, retires to Aba island on the Blue Nile and begins gathering disciples.

1881

Muhammad Ahmad openly proclaims himself *mahdi*.

1883

November 5. Khedive Tawfiq's army crushed in the battle of Shaykan (near al-'Obeid) by the Mahdists. Result is the collapse of Turkish-Egyptian administration, Mahdist rule in Kardofan, Darfur and Bahr al-Ghazal.

1885

January 26. The Mahdi takes Khartoum. Gordon Pasha, British governor general, killed after a long siege of the city.

June 22. Death of Muhammad Ahmad; successor (*khalifa*) designated: 'Abd Allah al-Ta'aishi, Baqqara Arab leader, continues the *jihad*.

Rabih

"He then undertook the creation of an entirely original state in this part of Africa. Without historical origin, without tradition, without any popular mandate, it rested on a disciplined army, trained in the Turkish tradition, relying on the example set by the Mamluks. It was an incomparable instrument in the hands of an honorable leader."

J. Chapelle, *Le Peuple tchadien*, Paris, 1986.

1889

Mahdist forces led by 'Abd al-Rahman al-Nujumi invade Egypt; defeat at the battle of Tushki.

1891

Loss of Tokar.

1894

Loss of Kassala.

1896

Egyptian-British forces commanded by General Kitchener sent to Sudan with reconquest as their goal.

1898

April 8. Battle of Atbara: 3,000 Sudanese killed, more than 4,000 wounded.

September 2. Omdurman (near Khartoum) taken by the British in the battle of Karari. 11,000 Sudanese die, about 16,000 are wounded. The *khalifa* 'Abd Allah killed in the battle of Umm Diwaykrat on November 24, 1899.

Beginning in 1899

Joint British-Egyptian control of Sudan (until 1956).

1900–1914

A series of Mahdist uprisings in northern Sudan, most notably the uprising of 'Abd al-Qadir Muhammad Imam (Wad Habuba); defeat of a government force, but subsequent defeat of the Mahdi. He is publicly hanged on May 17.

1916

Revolt of Faki 'Ali in southern Sudan suppressed after two years.

The Horn of Africa: Ethiopia and Somalia

1875

An Egyptian campaign puts an end to the independence of the Muslim state of Harar. The Egyptian presence speeds the spread of Islam.

1876

March 5–7. Yohannes IV of Ethiopia crushed by the Egyptians near Gura. Mobilization against the Egyptian campaigns in the Horn of Africa in the form of a crusade against Muslims.

Beginning in 1878

Conversion campaign launched by Yohannes IV, aimed at the Muslims and pagans of the high plateaus.

1889

March 10. Death of Yohannes IV, killed in a battle against Sudanese Mahdists. Menelik, king of Shoa and Wallo, his successor, reincorporates the Islamized regions of the periphery and high plateaus into the empire.

1895

After several pilgrimages to Mecca, where he joined the Salihiyya brotherhood, Sayyid Muhammad 'Abdille Hassan (born between 1860 and 1870) settles in Berbera [Somalia]. He uses a religious reform movement to unify all Somalians against the Western presence and Christian colonization.

1899

Muhammad 'Abdille Hassan proclaims himself *mahdi*: raids against the British and Italians.

August. Occupation of Burao, the center of British Somaliland.

1900–1904

Four British campaigns against the Mad Mullah, Muhammad 'Abdille Hassan, whose forces are crushed after a number of British defeats (e.g., April 1903, the battle at Gamburu); Muhammad retreats to the Italian Midjurteyn Protectorate.

1909

Shaykh Muhammad Salih, ruler of the Salihiyya, disowns Muhammad 'Abdille Hassan, his disciple in [Somalia], for violence and infractions of the brotherhood's rules.

November. Muhammad forces the British to withdraw from the interior, after having mobilized his forces.

1913

Death of Menelik. Lij Iyasu, heir apparent, leads, with his father's support, a policy that is increasingly openly favorable to Islam.

1916

Lij Iyasu deposed. Menelik's cousin, Ras Tafari (the future Haile Selassie) proclaimed regent and heir apparent.

1920

November. Death of the Mad Mullah.

The Eastern Coast of Africa

1806

Sa'id b. Sultan becomes sultan of Oman.

Beginning in 1811

Sa'id b. Sultan undertakes the recreation of the old Omani hegemony on the coast of Africa.

Circa 1839

Caravans sent by Sa'id to the interior of the continent. Swahili merchants reach the region of the Great Lakes.

1840

Sa'id, who has already spent some time on the coast of Africa, moves his court to Zanzibar. Indian businessmen, mostly "twelver" Shi'i, called on to finance large ventures (clove plantations on the coast, slave trade in the interior).

1847

British treaty with Zanzibar prohibits slave trade.

1856

October 19. Death of Sa'id b. Sultan, who had returned to Oman in 1854. One of his sons, Majid, inherits the African domain.

1861

With British support, Majid, sultan of Zanzibar, declares his independence from Oman.

1870

Death of Majid; succeeded by his brother Barghash. Under pressure from the British, a series of measures against the slave trade (1873–1876).

Beginning in 1880

Arrival of Sufi shaykhs belonging to the Qadiriyya (from the north) or the Shadhiliyya (from the Comoros) tribes; spread of Islam among Africans of the interior.

Beginning in 1884

The British and Germans begin to partition eastern Africa; Zanzibar's authority limited to the coastal strip.

1887

February. Tippu Tib, merchant, adventurer and the sultan of Zanzibar's representative, is chosen by H.M. Stanley to be the governor of Maniema, the eastern province of the independent state of Congo [Zaire].

1890

Zanzibar officially becomes a British protectorate.

1891

Arab-Swahili (from Maniema) uprising, led by Rumaliza; revolt put down severely by the Belgians.

1905–1907

Maji-Maji uprising led by Kinjikitile Ngwale in the southern section of the German colony of Tanganyika as a reaction against the introduction of a communal cotton scheme. The Ngindo, the driving force behind the revolt, are not Muslims, but practitioners of Islamic magic; they eventually convert to Islam.

French and British Hegemony

The period between the two World Wars is witness, first, to the total supremacy of the colonial powers France, Great Britain, Italy and the Netherlands over the Muslim countries. The period is also marked by the birth, in most Arab countries, of political movements that demand independence. Meanwhile, Turkey and Iran, under their leaders Mustafa Kemal and Reza Khan, defend their independence, but also institute, mostly in Turkey, a regime where Western ideas and techniques are implemented. Turkey is the only country in the Middle East to embrace secularism.

World War II, which leads to a weakening of all the colonial powers, has as one consequence the achievement of true independence by several Muslim countries, while, in 1945, the first great political organization in the Islamic world, the League of Arab States, is being created.

The Maghrib

Morocco

1920

Beginning of the revolt led by 'Abd el-Krim ('Abd al-Karim) in the Rif mountains of the northern Spanish zone.

1922

February 1. Proclamation of the Islamic Rif Republic, expulsion of the Spaniards.

1924–1925

Offensives by 'Abd el-Krim on territories controlled by the French.

1925

August–September. Marshal Henri Pétain, successor to Marshal Louis Lyautey as governor.

1926

May 27. 'Abd el-Krim surrenders after a defeat at Fez; sent into exile on the French island of Réunion. Independentist youth groups formed: in Fez, by Allal al-Fassi, a leader of Arabic and Islamic studies; in Rabat, by Ahmad Balafrej, a student of literature in France. They combine in 1927 into the Moroccan League.

1927

November 18. Death of Mawlay Yusef. Successor: his son, Sidi Muhammad b. Yusef, with the help of the French.

1930

May 16. Declaration of the Berber *dahir:* creation of courts for Berber customary law, which later become subject to French jurisdiction. Goal is separation of Berbers from Muslims.

June–July. Protest movements against the *dahir* and French policy.

1933

August–December. Appearance of nationalist newspapers, among them, *L'Action du Peuple.*

1934

May. Nationalist newspapers suppressed by the French (*Maghreb, L'Action du Peuple*). The Comité d'Action Marocaine (CAM) founded; draft of a reform proposal (December), which would give greater freedom to the Moroccan people.

1936

June. The Party of National Reform founded in Tétouan by 'Abd al-Khaliq Torrès, united with General Franco in 1937.

August. General Noguès, resident general.

November. Nationalist agitation. Temporary arrests of the nationalists leaders al-Fassi and al-Wazzani.

1937

January. Nationalist newspapers allowed to reappear. Rupture between Allal al-Fassi and Hasan al-Wazzani. The Party of Moroccan Unity founded in Tétouan by Muhammad Makki Naciri.

July. The National Party for the Achievement of Reforms (PNRR) founded by Allal al-Fassi. The Popular Movement founded by al-Wazzani.

September–October. Confrontations with the French army in Fez, Meknès, Kenitra, Rabat and Marrakesh after conflicts with settlers. Arrest of the nationalist leaders after they protest the incidents. Al-Fassi is sent to Gabon into exile for nine years, al-Wazzani enters forced residence in the desert south.

1939

Twenty thousand Moroccan soldiers delegated to serve in the French army.

1940

The Vichy regime has the full loyalty of Noguès. Sultan Muhammad refuses to implement anti-Jewish laws.

1942

November 8. American troops land in Casablanca. Sultan Muhammad orders his subjects to cooperate with the Americans.

1943

January 22. Sidi Muhammad meets with Roosevelt in Anfa, a suburb of Casablanca. Roosevelt speaks favorably of a future independent Morocco.

June. Puaux replaces Noguès. Political pressure applied by the Americans.

December. The Independence (Istiqlal) Party founded by Ahmad Balafrej.

1944

January 11. Manifesto of the Istiqlal

Manifesto of the Istiqlal Party
(selected passages)

"The Istiqlal Party (The Independence Party) . . . , considering that Morocco has always been a free and sovereign state and that it has maintained its independence over the course of thirteen centuries until, under particular circumstances, the status of protectorate was imposed upon it, . . . considering that the Protectorate's authorities replaced the old regime with a regime characterized by direct and arbitrary administration to benefit the French colony . . . ;

considering that the regime thus installed tried to break, by diverse means, the unity of the Moroccan people, made it impossible for Moroccans to effectively participate in the government of their country and deprived them of all their civil and individual liberties;

considering that the present circumstances in world politics are different from what they were when the Protectorate was established . . . ,

considering that the allies have manifested, on several occasions, their sympathy toward peoples with an historical lineage less rich than ours and a degree of civilization inferior to Morocco's . . . has decided:

a. As regards general policy:

1. to demand the independence of Morocco in its territorial entirety under the aegis of His Majesty Sidi Muhammad Ben Youssef—may God bless him;

2. to ask His Majesty to undertake with other interested nations negotiations with the goal of obtaining a recognition and guarantee of this independence as well as the determination, within the framework of national sovereignty, of the legitimate interests of foreigners living in Morocco;

3. to demand the inclusion of Morocco in the Atlantic Charter and its participation in the Peace Conference.

b. As regards domestic policy:

to ask His Majesty to take the reform movement, which is developing, under his eminent control to insure that the country is effectively run and to allow His Majesty to establish with care a democratic type of government comparable to those already adopted by Muslim countries in the East, guaranteeing the rights of all segments and classes of Moroccan society while defining the rights of each."

Proclaimed in Rabat, 14 Muharram 1363 (January 11, 1944).

Party: declaration of independence. The French reject it.

January 29. Nationalist leaders arrested on a charge of collaborating with Germany. Balafrej exiled to Corsica. Riots in Rabat and Fez. More than 30 dead, thousands of prisoners. Qarawiyin closed.

1945

July. Nationalist leaders liberated.

Algeria

1925–1927

Maurice Violette governor general.

1926

Creation in Paris of a group known as Étoile Nord-Africaine (the North African Star), which demands independence and recruits its members in the industrial outskirts of Paris. Messali Haj, the son of a worker from Tlemcen, becomes its leader in 1927.

1930

Solemn celebration of the centenary of the French conquest.

1931

Creation of the Association of Algerian 'Ulama', reformists from Algeria, by Shaykh 'Abd al-Hamid Ben Badis. Their slogan: "Islam is our religion, Algeria our country, Arabic our language."

1932

Creation of the Sunni 'Ulama' Association. Appearance of *Histoire de l'Algérie jusqu'à nos jours* (History of Algeria to the Present) by Tawfiq al-Madani.

1934

June. Violent incidents in Constantine. Creation of the Federation of Elected Muslims in the Constantine region by Dr. Ben Jelloul and Ferhat Abbas. Abbas considers Algeria French territory, and regards his fellow Algerians as Frenchmen with Muslim personal status.

1935

The Communist Party of Algeria founded.

1936

June and August. Algerian Muslim Congress.

December. Blum-Violette project for the granting of political rights to certain distinguished Muslim Algerians. Not discussed by the French Parliament, because of settler resistance.

1937

January. The North African Star dissolves.

March. Creation in France of the Algerian People's Party (P.P.A.) by Messali Haj.

August. Messali Haj arrested, sent into exile to the Congo.

1938

April. Creation of the Algerian Popular Union (by Ferhat Abbas).

July. Algerian Franco-Muslim gathering (called by Ben Jelloul).

1939

September. Dissolution of the P.P.A.

1940–1943

Vichy regime in France: anti-Jewish legislation, revocation of the Crémieux law.

1940

April 16. Death of Shaykh Ben Badis.

1942

November 8. Anglo-American troops land (Operation Torch).

Reaction of Shaykh Ben Badis
to the Blum-Violette Project

" . . . If we have supported it on occasion, it is because we have ended up admitting that those who saw in it only a first step towards future improvements were right. We, the Algerian nation, have our own institutions and characteristics which determine our ethnic nationality in a precise fashion. The trials of the times have proven that, more than any other people, we have jealously preserved this ethnic nationality and that, over the course of centuries, we have never stopped hanging on to the fringes of its veils. It is therefore impossible to weaken our passion for it and, more importantly, to assimilate us or to annihilate us.

The Algerian nation, even though it is overjoyed, wishes to state that the Blum-Violette project does not give it total satisfaction. Also, it sees the project as only one step towards total equality, an indispensable condition for a good and sincere relationship.

The last word on the project will belong to the French Parliament on whom all eyes are turned. But let us not forget the word of God: 'Before and after, all things depend on God'."

Al-Shihab, February 1937

December 20. "Message from the Muslim representatives of Algeria," from Ferhat Abbas.

1943

April–May. "Manifesto of the Algerian people" by a dozen Muslim leaders, including Ferhat Abbas, as well as a reform project.

June. French Committee on National Liberation in Algiers. General Georges Catroux, governor general, rejects the manifesto, places Ferhat Abbas under house arrest.

December 12. de Gaulle in Constantine; promises certain reforms.

1944

March 7. Ordinance on the principle of equality allows citizenship for

16 categories of Muslims. Rejected by the Muslims. The Association of the Friends of the Manifesto and Liberty (A.M.L.) founded by Ferhat Abbas.

September. Yves Chataigneau governor general.

1945

May. Violent incidents between settlers and Algerian nationalists, especially in the Constantine region (Sétif) and Greater Kabylia. Many casualties (estimates vary between 1,500 in the official French version to 45,000 in the nationalist version); first military, then judicial repression. Rupture between the French and Algerian communities. Imprisonment of Ferhat Abbas.

Tunisia

1920

The Destour (Constitution) Party founded by 'Abd al-Aziz Ta'albi, as a reaction to the *habous* decrees, which threatens the property of the notables.

1922

April 3. An ultimatum given to the resident general by the bey requesting that the demands of the Destour be met. No result.

1923

Death of Muhammad al-Nacer. French citizenship offered to certain qualified Tunisians; few accept. Ta'albi sent into exile.

1924

Formation of the General Confederation of Tunisian Workers.

1930

Eucharistic Congress in Carthage, considered a provocation by Muslims.

October 1. Appearance of *La Voix du Tunisien* ("The Tunisian's Voice").

1932

November 1. Appearance of the Destour daily *L'Action Tunisienne* ("The Tunisian Action") by Habib Bourguiba; aim: open communication between France and Tunisia.

1934

March 2. Creation of the Néo-Destour (P.N.D.) at the Ksar-Hellal Congress, by the more nationalist younger guard of the Destour. The *al-'Amal* ("Action") newspaper appears.

September 8. Leaders of the Néo-Destour placed under house arrest by orders of resident general Peyrouton. New leaders, such as Mongi Slim, Hedi Nouira and 'Ali Belhouane, make sure that the party continues its work.

1937

March. After the Néo-Destour is outlawed, bloody incidents in Metlaoui — about 200 Tunisians are killed. Arrest of about 3,000 party members, including Bourguiba.

August. Rupture between Destour (Ta'albi) and Néo-Destour (Bourguiba).

1938

April 9. Violent incidents in Tunis.

April 10–12. Destour leaders arrested and deported to France by general resident Alphonse Juin; both Destours dissolved.

1940

May. France offers Italy a condominium over Tunisia; Italy declines.

1942

June 19. Muhammad al-Moncef, Bey of Tunis.

October 12. Violent speech by Moncef Bey against the French administration.

November 8. Anglo-American invasion.

December 9. The Germans in Tunis and Bizerte.

April. Habib Bourguiba transferred

1943

January. Formation by the bey of a totally Tunisian government; creation of groups and movements for young Destour members.

from France to Italy, from whence he returns to Tunis.

May 7. Tunis occupied by the Allies.

May 14. Moncef forced to step down, charged with collaboration with the Nazis, replaced by Lamina Bey.

1944

October 1. Death of Shaykh Ta'albi.

October 30. Manifesto of the Tunisian Front in favor of domestic autonomy.

1945

March 26. Bourguiba clandestinely leaves Tunisia for Egypt, where he seeks support.

Libya

1921

Beginning of the Italian conquest of territories of the interior.

November. Creation of a Central Reform Committee by the Libyans.

1922

Idris al-Sanusi goes into exile in Egypt. 'Umar al-Mukhtar takes over the leadership of the Sanusiyya, which resists the Italian forces.

1923

The Sanusiyya loses Tripolitania, which is completely occupied by the Italians in 1925.

1928

Decrees on colonization.

1931

The South occupied by the Italians.

September 11. 'Umar al-Mukhtar defeated and executed soon thereafter. End of the Sanusi rebellion.

1932

Complete occupation of the Cyrenaica; immigration of Italian settlers.

1936

The coastal provinces (from Tripoli to Derna) integrated into Italian territory.

1937

Creation of Italian Africa Ministry. Special status granted to the Libyans. Separation of the two communities.

1940

Formation, in Egypt, of a Sanusi army to fight the Italians.

1943

Libya liberated. British military administration of Tripolitania and the Cyrenaica, French administration of the Fezzan and Ghadamès. Idris al-Sanusi returns from Egypt to the Cyrenaica for a visit.

The Near East

Egypt

1918

Movement demanding independence. A delegation (*wafd*) sent to Europe demanding the full independence of Egypt. The Wafd Party is created in early 1919 by Sa'd Zaghlul.

1919

March. Sa'd Zaghlul deported to Malta; this act provokes a spontaneous uprising; release of Zaghlul, who proceeds to Paris to speak before the peace conference.

1920
The Misr Bank founded by the Egyptians.

1921
December. The leaders of the Wafd arrested and deported to Aden, Gibraltar and the Seychelles.

1922
The Liberal Constitutional Party founded, appeals mainly to intellectual and aristocratic circles.
February 21. British protectorate status abandoned.
February 28. Egypt recognized as a sovereign and independent state, but Britain maintains the right to preserve its interests, including the defense of Egypt against all foreign interference, direct or indirect. The nationalists reject this offer.
March 15. Fu'ad assumes the title of king; accepting the British offer.

1923
April 19. Fu'ad promulgates a Constitution: Parliament with two assemblies holding legislative power; executive power resides in the king, assisted by his ministers.

1924
January. First elections. Complete success for the Wafd. Zaghlul prime minister.
November 19. Murder of Sir Lee Stack, commander-in-chief of the Egyptian army and governor general of the Sudan, by a Wafdist fanatic.

November 24. Zaghlul resigns after increased British demands for Nile water to be channeled to British plantations in Sudan.

1926
May. New elections. Same outcome: Zaghlul elected president.

1927
April 23. Death of Sa'd Zaghlul. He is succeeded by Mustafa Nahas Pasha.

1928
Parliament dissolved, partial suspension of the Constitution. Hasan al-Banna founds the Muslim Brothers.

1929
Quasi-fascistic movement, Misr al-Fatat ("Young Egypt"), led by Ahmad Husayn.

1930
Isma'il Sidqi Pasha appointed prime minister; introduction of a new electoral law to curb the power of the Wafd.

1931
Elections, boycotted by the Wafd. Victory of Isma'il Sidqi's al-Sha'b governmental party (People's Party).

1933–1936
Direct rule by the king; focus on economic issues.

1936
The Constitution is re-established.
April 28. Death of Fu'ad. Successor: Faruq.
May. Elections: Wafd victory.

August 26. Treaty with the English, who, among other privileges, keep troops (10,000 soldiers) in the Suez Canal zone.

1937
May 26. Egypt admitted to the League of Nations.

1939
September. Proclamation of martial law, censorship, break of diplomatic relations with Britain, expulsion or internment of German nationals.

1940
Faruq refuses to declare war on Italy. The Wafd declares itself anti-Nazi. Contact between Hasan al-Banna and the Germans.
August. Italian troops enter Egypt, but the government does not declare war, because the action is directed only against Britain.

1941
April. Rommel's Afrika Korps enter Egypt.

1942
February. Wafdist government imposed by the English; Nahas prime minister.
November. Allied victory at al-Alamayn (Alamein).

1944
October. Expulsion of the Wafdist cabinet.

1945
January. Declaration of war on the Germans and Japanese. 'Ali Maher assassinated while reading the declaration of war in parliament (February 24).

Cultural Life

1919
Taha Husayn (1889–1973), named professor of ancient history at Cairo University.

1921
Creation of the Arab "Garden Theatre."

1922
"The Diwan" literary group.

1927
'Abd al-Hamid Sa'id founds the Young Men's Muslim Association (YMMA).

1930–1936
Creation of schools for theology, Arabic and Islamic law in al-Azhar.

1932
The "Apollo" literary group centered around 'Ali Shadi.

1933
The People of the Cave, novel based on an Islamic legend by Tawfiq al-Hakim (born 1902).

1934
Adib, by Taha Husayn (1889–1973).

1935
Death of the Muslim reformist Muhammad Rashid Rida.

The Muslim Brothers
(al-Ikhwan al-muslimun)

"The Muslim Brothers movement was founded in 1928 in Ismailia by a young teacher, Hasan al-Banna. He set up chapters in a large number of locales, especially after 1933, the date of his conversion in Cairo. The movement started with the goal of 'Islamization'; its aim was to resist the Westernization of institutions and ethics, which seemed to Hasan al-Banna and his followers — generally members of the middle class — to be an abandonment of Islam. But, in principle, it emphasized education, not politics. The Brothers established schools, night classes, hospitals, community clinics, etc. In fact, Hasan al-Banna vehemently criticized the parliamentary regime dominated by the Wafd with its pro-Western outlook as regards society.

During the years 1928–1940, the Muslim Brothers presented themselves as an association of devout and active Muslims. Their hostility toward the Wafd, parliamentarianism and Socialist and Communist doctrines were reassuring to wealthy landowners, and their dream of restoring the caliphate pleased King Faruq; the English did not fear these idealists.

. . . The doctrine of the Muslim Brothers contains the following points: Islam is a comprehensive system which must regulate all human actions, at the level of the individual as well as society. If a community is content to be Muslim simply in worship and imitates non-Muslims in everything else, its Islam is incomplete. Islam must be brought back to its original simplicity, moving beyond the deviations and forgery to which it has been subjected during the centuries of its decline; this simple and pure religion is capable of responding to the needs of all times. . . . The Muslim Brothers attempted to resuscitate the pan-Islamic ideal: 'Every parcel of land on which the flag of Islam has at one time flown is for all Muslims a fatherland that must be preserved, for which they must work and fight in holy war.' (Hasan al-Banna)."

G. Delanoue, "Le nationalisme égyptien," in *L'Égypte d'aujourd'hui*

1938

Maze of Justice: Diary of a Country Prosecutor, by Tawfiq al-Hakim. *The Future of Culture in Egypt*, by Taha Husayn; a call for a mixture of Arab and Western culture.

1939

The Call of the Unknown, by Mahmud Taymur (born 1894).

1943

Umm Hashim's Lamp, by Yahya Haqqi.

1944

The Tree of Misery, by Taha Husayn.

Syria

1920

March 7. The National Congress proclaims Syria's independence "within its natural limits" (i.e., including Palestine and Transjordan).

April 25. Mandate on Syria and Lebanon given to France.

July 25. French troops under General Gouraud in Damascus.

July 28. Faysal leaves Syria.

August 7. King Faysal deposed by the French.

September 1. Proclamation of Greater Lebanon by General Gouraud. Damascus, Aleppo and Latakia become separate units.

1922

Creation of the Syrian Federation. Jabal Druze is accorded the status of a separate state.

July. Brief Druze revolt led by Sultan al-Atrash.

1924

The autonomous *sanjak* of Alexandretta is created.

1925–1926

Revolt in Jabal Druze, which spreads to all of Syria; crushed by France.

1925

January 1. Unification of the states of Aleppo and Damascus as the state of Syria.

1928

April. Elections held; nationalists win in the cities, moderates in the countryside.

August. Constitutional project rejected by the high commissioner.

1930

May. The Assembly is dissolved. Declaration of a Constitution issued by high commissioner M. Persot.

1931

December. Elections won by the moderates. Organic laws for Jabal Druze and the 'Alawi territory (Latakia).

1934

Suspension of the Chamber.

1936

January. General strike in all of Syria.

September. Franco-Syrian treaty outlining Syrian independence and French privileges in Syria, not ratified by the French Parliament.

November. Elections go to the National Bloc (Kutla), which demands the full independence of Syria; ratification of the Franco-Syrian treaty.

1937

May. The *sanjak* of Alexandretta autonomous. Upheaval in Jabal Druze.

1938

Manifesto of the Free National Front.

July. Turkish troops in the *sanjak* of Alexandretta.

1939

Revolt in the Jabal Druze.

June. The *sanjak* becomes Turkish territory (Hatay).

July 10. Suspension of the Constitution, dissolution of the Chamber by high commissioner Gabriel Pueaux.

1940

July. Shukri al-Quwwatli, leader of the national movement. Zaki al-Arsuzi establishes the Ba'ath Party.

1941

April. Government led by Khalid al-'Azm. Meeting of the Assembly for consultation.

May. German aircraft permitted to refuel on Syrian airfields.

June 8. Free French troops and British troops enter Syria.

July 14. Armistice signed in Acre.

September 28. Declaration of independence, valid until the end of the war.

1942

The Constitution is restored. George Wadsworth appointed American consul general and diplomatic agent to Syria and Lebanon.

1943

July. Elections: majority to the National Bloc. Shukri al-Quwwatli elected president of the Republic. The Arab Ba'ath movement founded by Michel Aflaq and Salah al-Din Bitar.

1944–1945

Power transferred to the Syrians; France maintains air and naval bases, and the right to organize and command Syrian and Lebanese armies. Jabal Druze is incorporated into Syria.

1945

March 1. Declaration of war on Germany and Japan.

The Territorial Political Units

September 1920

   Creation of the state of Aleppo (with a separate regime for the *sanjak* of Alexandretta); the state of Damascus; an 'Alawi territory (Latakia).

March 1921

   Creation of the Jabal Druze territory.

1922

   The 'Alawi territory becomes a state; creation of the Syrian Federation, which groups the states of Damascus and Aleppo with the 'Alawis.

1924

   The 'Alawi state separated from the Syrian state.

June 1939

   The *sanjak* of Alexandretta becomes a Turkish province known as Hatay.

September 1944

   Jabal Druze is incorporated into the Syrian state.

May–June. Violence between French and Syrians in Damascus and several other places in Syria.

July 7. Transfer of the *Troupes Spéciales* to national control.

1946

April 7. End of the evacuation of Syria by the French.

Lebanon

1920

September. Creation of Greater Lebanon by the French.

1926

May 23. Declaration of the Constitution, establishing a balance between the communities, parliamentary institutions, a president, a cabinet, a two-chamber (later one-chamber) parliament.

1932

May 9. Suspension of the Constitution by high commissioner Persot, after a severe economic crisis, accompanied by general unrest.

1934

January 2. Promulgation of a new Constitution by high commissioner Count de Martel; limits authority of parliament, prevents irresponsible spending.

1936

Independence treaty with France, signed by Count de Martel and Emile Eddé; not ratified by France.

1937

Restoration of the 1926 Constitution.

1941

France proclaims Lebanon's independence.

1943

Elections: nationalist majority, which demands full independence. Turmoil in Beirut.

LEBANON:
The Distribution of Parliamentary Seats
by Community

30.5%	The Maronite community (Catholics)
6.5%	The Greek Catholic community
10.5%	The Greek Orthodox community
6.5%	The Druze community
18.5%	The Shi'i community
20.5%	The Sunni community
93.0%	

The remaining 7% can be attributed to other communities (e.g., the Armenian community) that are not recognized as institutions.

(The 1926 Constitution and the National Pact of 1943)

November 9 and December 7. "National Pact" concerning the cooperation of the different communities in Lebanon.

November 11. The president of the Republic, Bishara al-Khuri, is arrested (released on the 22nd). The Constitution is suspended. Emile Eddé appointed head of state.

1944–1945

Power transferred to the Lebanese.

1945

Lebanon joins the League of Nations

1946

December 31. French troops completely evacuated by December.

Transjordan

1921

January. 'Abd Allah, Faysal's brother, is given the right to govern the Karak region, which is later extended to include Amman and Salt.

March. 'Abd Allah, emir of Transjordan. Establishment of the Arab Legion by Captain F.G. Peake.

1922

September. British mandate established.

1923

May 25. Transjordan becomes independent, but the mandate continues. Britain has special prerogatives as regards legislation, fiscal matters, and the protection of foreigners and minorities.

1928

April 16. The Organic Law promulgated by Britain with 'Abd Allah's consent. A non-parliamentary regime in power; the emir is assisted by an executive and a legislative council.

1939

Major John Bagot Glubb becomes commander of the Arab Legion.

1941

'Abd Allah introduces a project for Arab unity in the form of "Greater Syria" (Syria, Lebanon, Palestine and Transjordan).

1946

March 22. End of the mandate.

April 25. 'Abd Allah assumes the title of king.

May 25. Declaration of independence.

December 7. A Constitution is granted.

Palestine

1917

November 9. British troops in Jerusalem.

1919

Zionist plan to parcel up Palestine. Rejected.

1921

Anti-Jewish disturbances after increased Jewish immigration into Palestine.

1922

July 22. British mandate, granted by the League of Nations; the mandate incorporates the Balfour Declaration.

1923

Beginning of the enforcement of the mandate; development of the Jewish community; guarantees given to the Arabs.

1929

Increase in land purchases by Jews. Violent disturbances in the wake of the Wailing Wall incidents.

1931

December. Islamic Congress in Jerusalem.

1936

After increased Jewish immigration, violence in Jerusalem, Haifa and Jaffa. Protests aimed against the grand mufti of Jerusalem, Haj Amin al-Husayni.

1937

July. British plan for parceling up Palestine into an Arab state, a Jewish state and a British-controlled neutral enclave around Jerusalem and Bethlehem. As a result, armed Arab revolt.

1939

May 17. British White Paper limiting Jewish immigration to 75,000 for the next 5 years, after which it would cease completely. Project to create an independent Palestinian state, linked with Britain; rejected by the Arabs and the Jews.

1942

November 10. The General Council of the Zionist Organization adopts the Biltmore Program presented by David Ben Gurion; it calls for a Jewish state in all of Palestine, and unlimited immigration.

1946

The Arab League proposes a single state with proportional representation. Rejected by the Jews.

1945

August 31. President Truman advocates the admission of 100,000 Jews to Palestine.

1947

February. State of siege. The English declare their mandate void as of May 13, 1948.

Iraq

1920

April. The ex-Ottoman provinces of Baghdad and Basra under British mandate.

1922–1924

Kurdish rebellion led by Shaykh Mahmud of Sulaymaniyya.

1921

March. Iraq becomes a kingdom; given to the emir Faysal (king as of August 23).

1922

October 10. British-Iraqi treaty confirming the British mandate. Treaties of January 13, 1926, and December 14, 1927 relax British control.

1925

March 21. Constitution: parliamentary monarchy.

1926

June 5. The Mosul district becomes part of Iraq.

1927

October 25. Large oil reserve discovered in Kirkuk.

1929

June 8. The Turkish Petroleum Company dissolved, replaced by the Iraqi Petroleum Company.

1930–1931

Kurdish rebellion led by Shaykh Mahmud of Sulaymaniyya.

1930

June 30. New Anglo-Iraqi treaty: use of military facilities granted to British troops. The anti-British Ikha' al-Watani (Brotherhood) party founded.

1931

The Ahali (People's) group founded by young intellectuals.

1932

Kurdish rebellion. The British air force helps the Iraqi army subdue the revolt.

October. Iraq independent. End of the mandate. Admission to the League of Nations.

1933

September 8. Death of Faysal. Successor: his son Ghazi (21 years old).

1934

July 14. Completion of the Kirkuk-Tripoli pipeline.

1935

Large tribal rebellion against the government subdued by the military.

1936

October 19. Coup d'état by Hikmet Sulayman. No fundamental changes in government policy.

1937

July 8. The Sa'dabad Pact with Turkey, Iran and Afghanistan signed; it stipulates mutual cooperation.

1938

December 24. Coup d'état; the pro-British Nuri al-Sa'id assumes the premiership.

1939

April 4. Death of Ghazi in a car accident. Regency of the prince 'Abd al-Ilah.

1941

April 1. Rashid 'Ali al-Gaylani takes power, calls on the Germans for aid. Vanquished by the British in May after Mosul had been under German control for a short while.

1943

January 16. Declaration of War on Germany, Italy and Japan. The "Fertile Crescent" project presented by Nuri al-Sa'id.

1945

Kurdish revolt, led by the Barzani tribe. The short-lived Kurdish republic at Mahabad collapses.

Arabia

1920

'Abd al-'Aziz Ibn Sa'ud (1902–1953) takes Asir and becomes sultan of Najd.

1924

March 11. Sharif Husayn, king of the Hijaz, proclaimed caliph in Amman. Ibn Sa'ud attacks the Hijaz.

October 5. Husayn abdicates the throne of the Hijaz so that his son 'Ali can take over.

1925

Mecca taken, followed by Jidda. Husayn's oldest son, 'Ali, abdicates. Husayn goes into exile in Cyprus.

1926

January 3. Ibn Sa'ud proclaimed king of the Hijaz and sultan of Najd and dependencies.

1927

January 29. Constitution for the kingdom of the Hijaz, Najd and its dependencies.

May 20. British-Sa'udi-Arabian treaty; reaffirms Ibn Sa'ud's independence.

June 7. Ibn Sa'ud convokes an Islamic Congress in Mecca.

1932

The kingdom assumes the name of the Kingdom of Saudi Arabia.

1933

First petroleum extraction by American firms (Aramco).

1934

War against Yemen. Borders drawn.

1936

Treaty of non-aggression and Arab brotherhood with Iraq.

1938

Prodigious increase in oil drilling.

1942

Arrival of an American agricultural mission, headed by K.S. Twitchell.

1943

Beginning of the construction of the U.S. Dhahran air base (finished 1946).

1945

February. Ibn Sa'ud meets President Roosevelt on board the U.S.S. *Quincy* in the Great Bitter Lake in Egypt.

March 1. Declaration of war on Germany.

Yemen

1918

Yemen liberated from Turkish occupation.

1921

Invasion of Dhala in the British Aden protectorate.

1925

March. Capture of Hodayda and Luhaya from the Idrisis.

1926

September 2. Italian-Yemeni treaty recognizing Yemen's full independence.

1929

Treaty with the Soviet Union, permitting a Soviet commercial mission to San'a.

1934

War against Saudi Arabia; ends in defeat. The San'a Treaty between Britain and Yemen. Yemen's inde-

pendence recognized. Treaty with Ibn Sa'ud. Imam Yahya I establishes a feudalistic and autocratic regime (he is assassinated in 1948).

1945

Yemen joins the Arab League, but does not declare war on Japan and Germany.

Turkey

1920

March 18. The Ottoman Chamber votes in favor of its own dissolution.

April 23. First meeting of the Grand National Assembly of Turkey in Ankara. Mustafa Kemal elected president of the G.N.A. and the Council of Ministers.

May 30. Franco-Turkish armistice.

June–July. The Greek army moves into western Asia Minor.

August 10. The Treaty of Sèvres, unfavorable to Turkey, signed by Turkey and European powers.

October 31. Kars taken by the Turks.

December 2. Turkish-Armenian peace treaty.

1921

January. Greek offensive; first Turkish victory near Inönü.

March 16. Turkish-Soviet friendship treaty.

March 23–30. New Greek offensive; second Turkish victory near Inönü.

June–October. Franco-Turkish negotiations. Accord signed on October 20.

July 10. Third Greek offensive.

August 23–September 13. Battle on

the Sakarya River: Mustafa Kemal victorious.

December 20. French troops pull out of Cilicia.

1922

August 30. Battle of the "Generalissimo." Decisive Turkish victory at Dumlupinar.

September 9. The Turks enter Ismir.

October 3–11. Armistice negotiations in Mudanya.

November 1. The G.N.A. votes to abolish the sultanate. Mehmed IV leaves Istanbul.

November 20. Beginning of the Peace Conference in Lausanne.

November 24. The new caliph, 'Abd ül Mejid, is appointed.

1923

April 8. Creation of the People's Party.

July 24. Peace treaty signed in Lausanne: Turkish sovereignty over the area of present-day Turkey; abolition of the capitulations.

October 13. Ankara, capital of Turkey.

October 29. Declaration of the Republic. Mustafa Kemal elected president, Ismet Pasha president of the Council.

1924

March 3. Abolition of the caliphate.
April 8. Suppression of religious tribunals.
April 20. Adoption of the Constitution.

1925

February–June. Kurdish insurrection led by Shaykh Sa'id of Palu, chief of the Naqshabandi dervishes. Severe repression.
September. Polygamy outlawed. Civil marriage required by law.
December. Neutrality and non-aggression treaty with the U.S.S.R. European calendar replaces the Islamic calendar.

1926

February 17. Ratification of the Swiss Civil Code.
March 5. Treaty with Great Britain and Iraq: Mosul turned over to Iraq.
May 30. Treaty with France.
June 5. British-Turkish treaty settling the Mosul problem; relinquishes claim to Mosul in return for 10 percent of its oil production.

1927

November 1. Mustafa Kemal reelected president of the republic.

1928

April 10. The Constitution is revised; Islam no longer the state religion.
November 1. The Latin alphabet adopted.

1930

Elimination of foreign-sounding geographical names: Constantinople be-comes Istanbul, Adrianople becomes Edirne, Smyrna becomes Izmir etc.
April 3. Women given the right to vote in municipal elections.
June 11. The Central Bank of Turkey founded.
October 30. Treaty of Ankara with Greece. Resolution of all unresolved issues.
December 23. Menemen: religious riot.

1931

April 12. Creation of the Turkish Historical Society (Türk Tarih Kurumu).

1932

January 22. First oration of the Qur'an in Turkish.
February 19. Abolishment of the "Turkish Hearths" (Türk Ocaği), clubs for national education, organizing lectures, courses etc. (founded 1912). "The People's Houses" (Halkevi) opened, expansion of activities.
June. Turkey joins the League of Nations.

1933

February 7. The *ezan* (a call to prayer) in Turkish.
June 3. Sümer Bank founded (industrial development).
September 14. Greek-Turkish friendship treaty.

1934

January 9. First Turkish five-year plan.
February 9. Balkans Pact (Turkey, Greece, Yugoslavia and Rumania).
June 21. Laws concerning the use of "last names"; every Turk has to adopt a surname.

The Treaty of Lausanne
(July 24, 1923)

A. *Clauses regarding Greek-Turkish relations:*
1. Exchange of civilian and military prisoners.
2. Establishment of the Turkish border on the left bank of the Maritza; Turkey recovers the islands of Imbros (Imroz) and Tenedos (Bozja Ada); the Greek isles closest to the Anatolian coast are to be demilitarized (Mytilene, Chio, Samos, Nikarya).
3. Exchange of the Greek population in Turkey and the Turkish population in Greece, except for Turks in western Thrace and Greeks in Istanbul.
4. As compensation for damages incurred during the Greek destruction of western Anatolia and eastern Thrace, the Greeks surrender Karaaghaç and Edirne station (Adrianopole).

B. *Clauses regarding the relations between Turkey and the Allied Powers:*
1. Delimitation of the Syrian border.
2. Recognition of Italy's sovereignty over Dodecanese Islands.
3. Recognition of Turkey's right to fortify the Straits in case of participation in a war. The Straits Commission will have jurisdiction only over foreign ships and no control over the demilitarized land zones.
4. The capitulations are abolished, but judicial guarantees for foreigners granted for five years.
5. Nationalization of coastal navigation.
6. Allied troops evacuated from Istanbul.

Unresolved Issues:
1. Payment of the Ottoman debt.
2. Establishment of the border with Iraq (the Mosul problem).

November 24. Mustafa Kemal given the name Atatürk (father-Turk), drops the Arabic Mustafa.

December 5. Women given the right to vote in national elections.

1935

June. Eti Bank founded (extraction of natural resources).

1936

July. The Montreux Convention: Turkey reassumes control of the Straits.

1937

January 27. The League of Nations puts forth the idea of autonomy for the *sanjak* of Alexandretta.

July 8. The Sa'dabad Pact (Turkey, Iraq, Iran and Afghanistan).

November 29. Independence granted to the *sanjak* of Alexandretta.

December. Turkey renounces the 1926 Treaty of Friendship with Syria.

1938

July 4. Turkish troops enter Hatay

after France agrees on establishing a Franco-Turkish condominium.

September. Referendum results in Turkish victory in the *sanjak.*

November 10. Death of Mustafa Kemal. Successor: Ismet Inönü.

1939

October 19. Mutual assistance pact between France, Great Britain and Turkey.

1941

March. Non-aggression pact with the U.S.S.R.

June 18. Friendship treaty with Germany.

October 9. Trade pact with Germany: chrome ore in exchange for war equipment.

1943

December Ismet Inönü meets Roosevelt and Churchill in Cairo.

1944

April 20. Shipment of chrome to Germany stopped.

August 2. Relations with Germany broken off.

1945

February 23. Declaration of war on Germany.

March 21. The U.S.S.R. denounces the nonaggression treaty of 1925 and demands control of Kars and Ardahan, the revision of the Montreux Convention, and military bases in the Bosphorus and the Dardanelles.

December. The Democratic Party founded.

Iran

1920

January–April. The British military withdraws.

1921

February 26. Russian-Iranian treaty of friendship.

1922–1927

The American Arthur Chester Millspaugh reorganizes Iran's public finances.

1923

October 28. Reza Khan, officer of the Cossack brigade, holds the post of prime minister.

1924

Reza Khan attempts to proclaim a republic and fails.

1925

February. Dictatorial power given to Reza Khan by the Majlis.

October 31. The shah is deposed while he is on a trip to Europe.

December 12. Reza becomes the shah. Founds the Pahlavi dynasty.

1926–1928

Ratification of a new penal code, followed by a new civil code.

1927

October 1. Neutrality treaty with guarantees from the U.S.S.R.

1927–1938

Rail lines built from the Persian Gulf to the Caspian Sea.

1928

Abolition of all trade advantages and capitulations granted to foreign countries. Prohibition of oriental dress.

1931

Foreigners are prohibited by law from owning agricultural land.

1932

Foreign primary schools are abolished.

1933

Accord with the Anglo-Persian Oil Co., which becomes the Anglo-Iranian Oil Co.

1934

The name Iran used in place of Persia.

1935

Teheran University founded; modern curricula. Prohibition of the veil for women.

1935–1939

Attempt to modernize the country (teaching, agriculture); army has important role; help of German technicians is sought; struggle against religious elements.

1937

Participation in the Sa'dabad Pact together with Turkey, Iraq, and Afghanistan.

1940

First government broadcasting station; mostly educational programs.

1941

June. Russians and Britons meet in Iran following the German invasion of Russia.

August 25. British troops invade southern and western Iran, the Soviets invade the north.

September 16. Reza Shah abdicates under Soviet and British pressure. Successor: his 22-year-old son Muhammad Reza. A pro-Allies regime set up.

1942

January. Creation of the Tudeh (the "Masses") Party; pro-communist.

January 29. Alliance treaty with Great Britain and the U.S.S.R gives the Allies transit and communication facilities, stipulates withdrawal within six months after the end of the war.

1943

Creation of the nationalist National Will Party (Irade-yi milli); counteracts Tudeh and Soviet propaganda.

November. Roosevelt, Churchill and Stalin meet in Teheran.

1943–1945

Millspaugh invited a second time to administer Iran's finances; resigns after a recriminatory press campaign.

1944

Muhammad Mossadegh, leader of the nationalists. Has a law passed that prohibits the granting of oil rights.

July 16. Death of Reza Shah in South Africa.

Fall. The Soviets are denied an oil concession in the northern provinces.

1945

Establishment of autonomous republics in Azerbaijan and Kurdistan (Mahabad) with the help of the Soviets and former Tudeh members.

1946

March. The British pull their troops out of Iran.
May. The Soviets withdraw their troops.
December 15. The Iranians reoccupy Azerbaijan.

Afghanistan

1919–1928: Reign of Amanullah
1919

August 8. The Treaty of Rawalpindi with the British: armistice and recognition of Afghanistan's complete independence.

1921

February 28. Treaty of friendship with Russia.
November 22. The Kabul Treaty with Britain. Independence confirmed. A Constitution declared.

1923

April 9. Promulgation of a Fundamental Law, with the aim of modernizing the country.

1924

March. Rebellion in Khost against modernization efforts. Legislation that favors women, especially in terms of education.

1926

Reforms. A new Constitution. Pact of neutrality and nonaggression with Russia.

1928

Tribal uprising. The king abdicates, goes into exile in Europe. Government by Baça-i Sakao ("water-carrier's son"), a Tajik brigand also known as Habib Allah Ghazi.

1929

Power appropriated by Muhammad Nadir Shah, former general and ambassador to France, who becomes king (October 16).

1931

Nonaggression pact with the Soviets.
October 31. A new constitution. Majority of power granted to king and prime minister; establishment of a two-chamber assembly.

1932

Creation of the National Bank.

1933

November 8. Assassination of Nadir Shah. Muhammad Zahir (19 years old) proclaimed king; regency until 1946 by his brother Sardar Muhammad Hashim Khan.

1936

Trade pact with the U.S.S.R. signed.

1937

Participation in the Sa'dabad Pact, signed on July 8. Pashto declared the official language, but its application proves very difficult.

1938
The Shami Pir rebellion; invasion of Afghanistan in an attempt to restore Amanullah; defeat.

1939
September. Declaration of Afghanistan's neutrality.

1941
Acceptance of the Allied demand to surrender all Axis nationals on Afghan territory.

1943
Establishment of diplomatic relations with the U.S.

1946
Official inauguration of Kabul University. Already in existence: Department of Law and Political Science, School of Sciences, School of Letters.

The Indian Ocean States

India

1919
Gandhi returns to India. Creation of the "Khilafat Conference," anti-British, pro-Ottoman and pan-Islamic; Hindu-Muslim cooperation.

1919-1935
Constitutional reforms increase the participation of Indians in the running of public affairs.

1920-1922
Two civil disobedience campaigns led by Gandhi.

1922
Violent confrontations between Hindus and Muslims in the Punjab.

1924-1937
Muslims lean heavily toward separatism. Jinnah recommends the formation of a federal Indian state.

1930
Muhammad Iqbal (1876–1938) seeks the creation of a Muslim India in the interior of India that would include the Punjab, Kashmir, the Sind and Baluchistan.

1933
End of the "Khilafat Conference."

1935
The "Government of India Act" rejected by the Congress Party and the Muslims. Increased Muslim power in India. The British recognize the "native states" governed by autonomous Muslim rulers; the most important among these is the Hydrabad state.

1936
Muhammad 'Ali Jinnah assumes leadership of the Muslim League.

1937
Reactivation of the Muslim League. Hostility from the Congress Party, which begins to dominate.

1938

Death of Muhammad Iqbal, the first theoretician and Urdu poet of Pakistan; combines Sufism and Western philosophy.

1940

The "Pakistan Resolution" by the Muslim League; repeats the proposals put forth by Muhammad Iqbal in 1930.

1941

Abu al-'Ala' Mawdudi creates the Jama'at-i Islami, a political-religious movement hostile to communism and Sufism.

1942

The Congress Party accepts the idea of partition.

1945

The Muslim League takes all the Muslim seats during the elections for the Central Assembly.

1946

The British government plans the transfer of power to the Indians.

Indonesia

1918

Creation of an advisory council (Volksraad).

1920

May. Creation of the Communist Party, outlawed in 1927.

1926

Creation of the Nahdatul 'Ulama' by traditionalist theologians.

1927

Creation of the Indonesian National Party led by Sukarno; dissolved in 1930.

1930

Sukarno arrested and deported. Opposition goes underground.

1934

Death of Tjokroaminoto (born 1883), leading figure of Sekaret Islam.

1935

The Greater Isles Party (Parindra).

1937

The Indonesian People's Movement (Gerindo). Creation of an Islamic council.

1939

Indonesian political coalition (Gapi).

1942

February 21. Japanese troops land in Java.

March 9. The Dutch Governor General capitulates.

Sumatra linked to Singapore. Economy totally controlled by Japan. Forced labor. Sukarno liberated.

1945

August 17. Sukarno proclaims independence.

August 18. Declaration of a Constitution. Sukarno president. Batavia becomes Jakarta.

September 29. English and Indian troops land. Dutch authorities return. Resistance throughout the land, especially in Surabaya. Economic situation declines.

Sub-Saharan Africa

The years from 1920 to 1945 are a period of transition in the history of sub-Saharan Islam. The colonial powers are from this point forth solidly entrenched and, for the most part, the Islamic authorities cooperate with the established powers, whether by conviction or necessity. At the beginning of the period, France loses two excellent intermediaries in al-Haj Malik Si (d. 1922) and Shaykh Sidiyya Baba (d. 1924), who had greatly contributed to garnering support for their Islamic policies in [Senegal]* and [Mauritania].

From 1930 to 1940, one of Haj 'Umar's grandsons, Seydu Nuru Tall, is in power. This voluntary or forced sharing of power bears fruit: in all of West Africa, Islam consolidates its position and, in fact, gains ground. However, resistance from Islamic communities is at a low point. The colonial authorities are nevertheless concerned by an increase in hostile sentiments: the French focus their attention on Shaykh Hamallah and his disciples, and the British on the Mahdists of [Nigeria]. In both cases, the local administrations exaggerate the danger, and repression follows.

*In brackets are the *present* names of countries which, prior to 1960, appeared under different names.

West Africa

1922

Death of al-Haj Malik Si, shaykh of the Tijani *zawiya* of Tivuan [Senegal]. Death of al-Haj Abdulay Niasse, founder of a new branch of the Tijaniyya (the Kaolack, Senegal branch). After a pilgrimage to Mecca in 1890, he maintains close ties with the Tijani *zawiya* of Fez (Morocco). Considered suspicious by the French, he goes into exile in [Gambia] from 1901 to 1910.

1923

March. Mallam Sa'idu, son of Hayatu, great-grandson of Usman dan Fodio, adept of Sudanese Mahdism, arrested in Borno [Nigeria] after being accused of subversive activities by the British. Deported without any other proof of wrongdoing; in exile

for 36 years (in Buea, Cameroon, then later in Kano). Liberated in 1959, he dies in 1978.

1924

Death of Shaykh Sidiyya Baba, an important man of letters, grandson of Shaykh Sidiyya al-Kabir (1775–1868), who spreads the teachings of the Qadiriyya. One of the primary mediators with the French authorities in [Mauritania]. Riot in Nioro [Mali] between partisans and adversaries of Shaykh Hamallah, who since 1902 has presented himself as the restorer of Tijani orthodoxy.

1924–1927

Construction of the mosque of Tuba [Senegal], capital of Muridism.

1925

French administration, encouraged by representatives of al-Haj 'Umar's family, condemn Shaykh Hamallah to 10 years imprisonment in [Mauritania].

1927

Death of Ahmadu Bamba in Diourbel [Senegal].

1928

First *magal* (annual pilgrimage of the Muridiyya) in Tuba.

1929–1930

Uprising in Kaedi [Mauritania] between supporters and opponents of Shaykh Hamallah; the French deport him to the [Ivory Coast] (1930–1936).

1937

First pilgrimage to Mecca undertaken by al-Haj Ibrahim Niasse, Abdulay Niasse's son and spiritual leader of the Kaolack branch of the Tijanis. Meets the emir of Kano, Abdullahi Bayero, whose alliance with the Tijaniyya is reaffirmed: beginning of a massive implantation of the Tijaniyya of Niasse in northern Nigeria.

September. Official reconciliation in Nioro between Seydu Nuru Tall, al-Haj 'Umar's grandson, and Shaykh Hamallah under the aegis of the French administration; not pursued in the future.

1938

Tierno Bokar Salif Tall (1884–1940), also a descendant of al-Haj 'Umar, comes from Bandiagara to Nioro to become a devotee of Hamalli Tijaniyya: ostracized by his people.

1938–1940

Bloody confrontations between followers and adversaries of Shaykh Ha

mallah over the border between [Mauritania] and [Mali].

1941

June 19. Shaykh Hamallah arrested and deported to Algeria.

June 30. Thirty-three death sentences handed down in Nioro against Shaykh Hamallah's partisans implicated in the conflict, including two of his sons.

1942

March 15. The Vichy government in France decides to transfer Shaykh Hamallah to France. Incarcerated in Vals-les-Bains and Evaux-les-Bains. He dies in a hospital in Montluçon (January 16, 1943).

Sudan

Beginning in 1920

Sayyid 'Abd al-Rahman (1885–1959), posthumous son of the Mahdi, *imam* of the Ansar (Mahdists), commits his movement to the colonial agricultural projects near Gezira, in cooperation with the British. He becomes a wealthy capitalist.

1921

September 26. Nyala revolt led by 'Abd Allah al-Sihayni in Darfur.

October 4. Al-Sihayni hanged in public.

1922

May. Suppression of the revolt.

1924

November. Attempted uprising by Sudanese soldiers to show sympathy with the Egyptian troops, whom the

British had ordered to withdraw from Sudan: the Ansar (Mahdists) hold their ground against the British. The total suppression of the revolt forces the educated class to concentrate on literacy and social activates, thus integrating the Mahdist movement into the colonial system.

Chapter 10   1945–1963

Political Independence

The spread of independence is dramatic in Algeria and Indonesia, in their struggle against the two colonial powers, France and the Netherlands. In Palestine and the Indian subcontinent, for internal ethnic and religious reasons, independence brings division and the creation of two new states, Israel and Pakistan. The exodus of many people is the consequence of such events: Muslims and Hindus, Palestinians and European Jews as well as Jews from Arab states in increasingly larger numbers. Many refugees are taken care of by the recently formed U.N.

Islam, which contributes to and upholds certain shifts in population, opposes others, especially in the face of Judaism, Hinduism and European Christianity. Islam also plays a role on the political scene. Nevertheless, with the exception of the Sudan, where ideological Arabism, competition between Muslim brotherhoods and the resurgence of Mahdism define the political scene, Islam does not enter directly into the debate. The determining inspirations of newly acquired independence are national. The countries that have gained their independence jealously guard their borders, which had often been drawn long before by European powers without consideration for ethnic and local allegiances — the most tragic examples of this occurring in Black Africa. The leaders of these young states attempt to prolong the domination that characterized the administration of the former colonial governors. They "forget" about, or even fight against, what they perceive to be retrograde local ethnic and/or denominational allegiances such as Islam. Strong leaders, such as Nasser in Egypt, Sukarno in Indonesia, and Muhammad Reza Shah in Iran, also adopt an accelerated statist economic development that gives rise to immense bureaucracies. The Arab world is suffused with a feeling of pan-Arabism, the fourth allegiance after the allegiances to Islam, the state and local ethnicity/denomination. The League of Arab States is created in 1945, meticulously designed by both Arab nationalists and Great Britain. Initially focused on the Zionist challenge, which becomes the Israeli challenge in 1948, the league represents divergent interests of states and gradually imposes Nasser's rule over this grouping of Arab states.

279

"Positive neutrality," formulated by the "non-aligned" camp, defines the relationships between Egypt, India and Indonesia, which establish rigorously defined alliances with the Soviet bloc, against a pro-American bloc that includes Turkey, Iran, Pakistan and Saudi Arabia, as well as Iraq for a short while. The extraction and sale of oil, as well as the economic exploitation of the international route that the Suez Canal represents, lead to struggles of nationalization. Mossadegh seizes the initiative in Iran, Nasser nationalizes the Suez Canal and OPEC is created.

With the exception of the countries that become socialist, on a societal level, the development of law and lifestyles is characterized by a synthesis of the colonial heritage and Muslim tradition. Religious men lose their teaching and tribunal positions at an increasing rate, but jealously guard their control over matters of personal status, except in Turkey and Tunisia. Unchecked population growth leads to a decline in standards of living. Education, while on the rise, is still far from responding to the needs of the people. Underdevelopment continues.

1945

May 10. Creation of the League of Arab States in Cairo as a loose regional confederation.

1947

December. The Arab League rejects U.N. Resolution 181, which calls for the division of Palestine into a Jewish state and an associated Palestinian state.

1948

The Arab League rejects the self-proclamation of the Israeli state.

1953

A worldwide Islamic Congress created in Cairo by Egypt, Saudi Arabia and Pakistan.

1957

Islamic conference in Lahore (Pakistan) on "Islamic Culture and Society."

OPEC MEMBERS

Iran (1960)	Libya (1962)
Iraq (1960)	United Arab Emirates (UAE) (1967)
Kuwait (1960)	Algeria (1969)
Saudi Arabia (1960)	Nigeria (1971)
Venezuela (1960)	Ecuador (1973)
Qatar (1961)	Gabon (1973)
Indonesia (1962)	

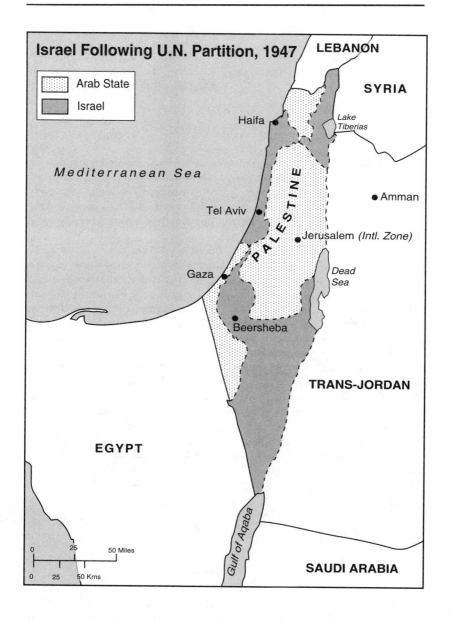

Israel Following U.N. Partition, 1947

Arab State

Israel

LEBANON

SYRIA

Haifa

Lake Tiberias

Mediterranean Sea

Tel Aviv

• Amman

PALESTINE

Jerusalem *(Intl. Zone)*

Gaza

Dead Sea

Beersheba

TRANS-JORDAN

EGYPT

0   25   50 Miles

0   25   50 Kms

Gulf of Aqaba

SAUDI ARABIA

1959

Islamic conference in Karachi (Pakistan), with the focus on "Islam and the Modern World."

1960

September 15. Creation of the Organization of Petroleum Exporting Countries (OPEC) in Baghdad.

The Maghrib

The Maghrib, or the Muslim West, gains national independence over the course of several years following a particularly long and brutal struggle in Algeria, which, after having been a French overseas *département*, becomes a sovereign nation-state. Maghrib unity, clearly envisaged from the first struggles for independence in 1946, becomes a secondary concern once independence is achieved.

In the struggles for independence, Islamic inspiration played an important role, together with local patriotism — particularly in Morocco, a state that had not been under Ottoman rule. But these independent regimes are primarily concerned with the modernization of their countries, the Provisional Government of the Algerian Republic (GPRA) having adopted a statist socialist plan based on Marxist ideology. Good relations with France are sought, but an exodus of the large community of French citizens living in Algeria (*pieds-noirs*) as well as other Europeans in Morocco and Tunisia is unavoidable.

The Maghrib becomes entirely Muslim and Arab once again, marginalizing the large Berber population. An accelerated "re-Arabization" is undertaken, Tunisia officially adopts bilingualism, but the call to pan-Arabism elicits only a feeble response. These societies, shaken and heavily mobilized during the struggles and wars for independence, and marked in a profound way by the French colonial experience, modernize in various ways: Tunisia adopts authoritarian reforms that, unlike in other places, affect family rights as well as the status of women and ensure literacy rates close to 100% for children; Morocco stagnates; Algeria reaps profits from oil and natural gas and benefits from the (French) Constantine Plan.

Political and Institutional Life

1946

Morocco: the new resident general, Eric Labonne, tries to improve relations with Morocco; release of political prisoners (including al-Fassi).

Libya: return of emir Idris al-Sanusi from exile in Cairo.

1947

Algeria: Messali Haj creates the Movement for the Triumph of Democratic Liberties (MTLD), which demands independence and creates a paramilitary Organisation Spéciale (OS), led by Aït Ahmed. New status for Algeria in the French Republic, the so-called Algerian Statute: an Algerian Assembly with two electoral colleges (one Muslim, one French);

plus Algerian-Muslim elite); French citizenship extended to all Algerians; representatives from both colleges to the French National Assembly; statute not implemented.

Morocco: speech in Tangier by Sultan Muhammad V (Muhammad V Ibn Yusuf) demanding independence (April).

Tunisia: Jean Mons, the French resident general, grants Tunisia six ministries; rejected by the Néo-Destour and by the settlers.

1948

Algeria: Edmond Naegelen new governor general.

1949

Algeria: Ben Bella replaces Aït Ahmed as leader of the OS.

Libya: Idris proclaims himself emir of the independent Cyrenaica (June 1).

1951

December 24. Libya gains its independence, after proclaiming a Constitution: Idris al-Sanusi, first king.

1952

Tunisia and Morocco encounter grave problems after demanding a genuine representative government; Bourguiba incarcerated, first at Tabarka, then on the island of Galite. Algeria enforces permanent exile on Messali Hadj, who is imprisoned in France.

1953

Turmoil in Morocco: the sultan abdicates under French pressure; exiled in December, first to Corsica, then to Madagascar. His elderly uncle Munlay b. Arafa becomes sultan; complies with French demands. Widespread resistance.

1954

Morocco: boycott of French goods; violent popular uprisings in Casablanca; revolt in the Rif.

November. Algeria: beginning of an armed insurrection led by the National Liberation Front (FLN), which has its origins in the Revolutionary Committee for Union and Action (CRUA), an exile group of nine former OS activists.

Tunisia: March. French reform program dismissed by the Néo-Destour.

1955

July. Tunisia: internal autonomy.

August. Algeria: large and violent riots; repression. Guerrillas kill 71 settlers and 62 Algerians in an attack at Philippeville.

November 17. Muhammad V returns to Morocco.

1956

August Algeria: program initiated by the FLN in the Soummam Valley Congress (Kabylia) exacerbates the guerrilla war; streamlining of the leadership structure; inclusion of women in the War of Liberation.

March 2. Morocco gains independence; an advisory Assembly named in November.

June 1. Independence for Tunisia; Salah b. Youssef's (secretary general of the Néo-Destour) partisans (Youssefistes) defeated by Bourguiba; Ibn Youssef had already fled to Cairo in January.

1957

Algeria: civil war, especially in Kabylia and in the "battle of Algiers"; exile of the leadership of the FLN; tensions between the domestic and foreign branches of the FLN.

1958

April 20–28. Algeria: conference at Accra (Ghana) attended by Morocco, Tunisia, Libya, Sudan, Liberia, Ghana, Ethiopia and the UAR; recognition of the FLN as Algeria's spokesman; pledge of support.

May 13. Protest by the "Algerian French" in Algiers, and a plea to Charles de Gaulle; Provisional Government of the Algerian Republic (GPRA) in exile.

1959

Morocco: schism in the Istiqlal Party, and creation of National Union of Popular Forces (UNFP), led by Mehdi Ben Barka.

June 1. Tunisia: constitution that establishes a presidential regime with an Assembly elected from a single party.

1960

Morocco: Muhammad V dissolves the Assembly after factional infighting and widespread violence; takes full power and appoints his son Moulay Hassan, as leader of the government; the situation is stabilized.

Algeria: widespread protests in Algiers in support of the FLN.

1961

January. Algeria: referendum in France finds 75% in favor of self-determination; in Algeria 69% in favor. Negotiations in Evian between the French government and the GPRA.

April 21–25. Failed putsch by French military in Algiers against Charles de Gaulle and self-determination.

February. Morocco: death of Muhamad V; succeeded by his son Hassan II.

Tunisia: assassination of Ibn Youssef.

1962

March 18. The Evian Accord; agreement on a referendum on independence.

April 8. Referendum in France with 91% in favor of Algerian independence.

July 1. Algeria independent, after referendum in Algeria finds 99.72% in favor.

September 20. Algeria: Constituent Assembly elected from a one-party FLN ballot.

Morocco: Constitution. Members of the bicameral parliament and the prime minister are named by the king.

Tunisia: institutionalization of a Néo-Destour (which eventually becomes the Destourian Socialist Party) one-party system. Assassination attempt on Bourguiba, possibly by Youssefistes.

1963

Morocco: the Front for the Defense of Constitutional Institutions (FDIC) becomes the government party; opposition by the Istiglal and the UNFP.

Foreign Policy

1946

Tunisia: Bourguiba pleads Tunisia's case before the U.N. in New York.

1947

The Committee for the Liberation of North Africa founded in Cairo by 'Abd el-Krim.

1951

An office of the Tunisian trade union (UGTT) opens in Washington under the supervision of Mehdi b. Aboud.

1954

Military and economic treaties between Libya, Great Britain and the United States.

1958

Morocco claims Mauritania and begins to question its border with (French) Algeria. The GPRA (Algeria) recognized first by China, then by the U.S.S.R. French bombing of the border town of Sakiet Sidi Yusuf (Tunisia), a "sanctuary" of the Algerian FLN.

1960

December 19. U.N. General Assembly declares the "right of the Algerian people to self-determination."

Morocco: Mauritania becomes independent from Morocco with Tunisian and French support.

1961

Military crisis between Tunisia and France, at the (French) navy base in Bizerte (Banzart).

Economy, Society and Religion

1946

Public borrowing for (French) Algeria to build roads, rail lines and ports.

1948

Morocco: first influx of European private capital for public works programs.

1952

Tunisia: assassination of the union leader Ferhat Hashed, of the General Union of Tunisian Workers (UGTT).

1954

Algeria: 984,000 Europeans and 9 million "Muslims" (3 million more than in 1931) on its soil.

1955

Morocco: stagnant economy, flight of capital.

Libya: creation of the Libyan University, with campuses in Tripoli, Benghazi and Beida.

1956

Algeria: opening of the Hassi R'mel-Arzew, Ejele-Skirra (in Tunisia), Hassi Messaoud-Bejaia gas pipelines. The secret General Union of Algerian Workers (UGTA) founded.

August 13. Tunisia: publication of the Personal Status Code, which forbids polygamy and non-judiciary repudiation while encouraging women to work; beginning of redistribution of tribal *habous* land to private owners.

1957

February Algeria: general strike ordered by the FLN.

Morocco: start of a cooperative farming project using modern equipment; does not flourish because of peasant resistance.

1958

March 6. Algeria: first delivery of Saharan oil.

Tunisia: reform and state control of the Islamic Zietouna University.

1959

Algeria: the "Constantine Plan" launched—accelerates development of the (French) overseas *départements* of Algeria; industrialization, development of the infrastructure; the plan is sabotaged by the FLN.

Libya: discovery of large oil reserves.

Tunisia: introduction of a large public works program, aimed at rehabilitating the unemployed by providing work on various projects.

1961

Tunisia: adoption of the Ben Salah option of "Decennial Perspectives" (an economic plan), creating most notably a system of agricultural cooperatives.

Morocco: project to alleviate rural poverty and illiteracy.

1962

Algeria: assessment of the "independence war": 1 million (1.5 million according to the FLN) "Muslims" dead, and an exodus of an additional 900,000 French settlers, primarily back to France; rapid and massive flight of capital. The war had devoured approximately 10–15 percent of France's annual budget.

Morocco: Cadastral survey, designed to rationalize cultivation.

Civilization and Culture

1954

Algeria: Malek Bennabi, *The Vocation of Islam.*

1955

Tunisia: Mes'adi, *The Barrage,* a symbolist drama.

1960

Algeria: Mouloud Ferraoun, *The Journal.*

1961

Morocco: Muhammad Aziz Lahbabi, *From Closed to Open: 20 Observations on National Cultures and Human Civilizations.*

The Arab Near East

The Arab Near East, independent except for the perimeter of the Arabian peninsula, is preoccupied first and foremost with the Israeli challenge. Nonetheless, Hashemite (Iraqi and Jordanian), Syrian, Palestinian, Saudi Arabian and Egyptian interests are hardly compatible, and the military mobilization against Israel, both economic and political, proves to be weak. Some 900,000 Palestinian refugees are received in neighboring countries, but (except in Jordan) they are not assimilated and are willfully kept in refugee camps as a passive argument against Israel. The Israeli threat also facilitates the emergence of "revolutionary" military dictatorships in Syria, Egypt and

COMPOSITION OF THE LEAGUE OF ARAB STATES
(ARAB LEAGUE)

Algeria (Algiers) 1963	PLO* (Jerusalem) 1976
Bahrain (Manama) 1971	Qatar (Doha) 1971
Comoro Islands (Moroni)	Saudi Arabia (Riyadh) 1945
1994Djibouti (Djibouti) 1977	Somalia (Mogadishu) 1974
Egypt (Cairo) 1945	South Yemen (Peoples Democratic
Iraq (Baghdad) 1945	Republic) unified with the Yemen
Jordan (Amman) 1945	Arab Republic in 1990 (Aden) 1967
Kuwait (Kuwait City) 1961	Sudan (Khartoum) 1956
Lebanon (Beirut) 1945	Syria (Damascus) 1945
Libya (Tripoli) 1951	Tunisia (Tunis) 1957
Mauritania (Nouakchott) 1973	United Arab Emirates 1971
Morocco (Rabat) 1957	Yemen Arab Republic (Sanaa) 1945
Oman (Muscat) 1971	

*(the Palestine Liberation Organization)

Iraq. Nasser bursts onto the Arab and international scene with the Aswan Dam, his celebrated rapprochement with the Soviet bloc, the nationalization of the Suez Canal Company and his "victory" against the tripartite aggression (Israeli-British-French) in 1956. Pan-Arabism, already elaborated in Ba'athi philosophy and by the Ba'ath Party, finds its champion in Nasser, up against the pro-British and pro-American "Baghdad Pact" and Israel, which he equates with a "base for imperialism."

Political and Institutional Life

1946

Syria: putsch first by Husni Za'im, then by Sami Hinnawi. The Transjordan emirate: end of the British mandate.

Jordan: May 25. Independence of the kingdom of Jordan.

December 7. Constitution of Jordan.

1947

Lebanon: constitutional amendment; the president's term increased to six years and amplified by the possibility of "emergency decrees."

1948

February 17. Yemen: coup d'état; civil war; emir Sayf al-Islam Ahmad new Imam.

Israel: May 14. Proclamation of the Israeli state.

Palestine: May 15. Unilateral end (at Great Britain's behest) to the mandate over Palestine. Arab Palestinian vote to be integrated into Jordan at the congress of notables in Jericho and Nablus.

Lebanon: Progressive Socialist Party (PSP) founded by the Druze notable Kamal Jumblat.

December 8. Egypt: the Muslim Brothers outlawed after the assassination of the Cairo chief of police, Salim Zaki Pasha.

1949

February 12. Egypt: Hassan al-Banna, leader of the Muslim Brothers, assassinated.

Syria: March 30. Bloodless coup by Husni Za'im.

August 14. Coup by Sami Hinnawi; execution of Za'im. Adib Shishakli exercises absolute power.

Lebanon: attempted coup d'état by the leader of the Syrian National Social Party (PPS), Antoun Saadeh, who is condemned to death, then executed (July 8).

Transjordan: change of the country's name to the Hashemite Kingdom of Jordan (April 26).

1950

Egypt: the Wafd Party returns to the government.

Syria: a new constitution adopted.

Iraq: Jews are permitted to renounce their nationality and emigrate. By June 1951, approximately 160,000 Jews have emigrated to Israel.

1951

Syria: November 28–29. New coup. Shishakli exercises total control over the country with the aid of the army.

Jordan: assassination of King Abdallah by a Palestinian member of Haj Amin al-Hussain's military group Jihad Muqaddas (Sanctified Struggle); his son Talal succeeds him.

1952

Creation of a Council of Arab Emirates; independence for the emirate of al-Fujayrah.

Lebanon: a popular movement led by the PSP. Jumblat forces President Bechara al-Khoury to step down (Sept. 18); Camille Chamoun is his successor (Sept. 23).

Syria: all parties dissolved for the greater good of the Arab Liberation Movement.

December 30. Dismissal of many army officers. Many Socialist leaders flee abroad (Akram Hourani, Michel Aflaq, Salah al-Bitar).

January. Egypt: suspension of the Constitution by the king after anti-British riots in Isma'iliyya and Cairo.

July 22. Military putsch by the "free officers": King Faruq abdicates; the Revolutionary Command Council (RCC) composed of 11 officers.

1953

Egypt: provisional constitution; all parties dissolved; the Liberation Movement, to serve as a single party for the people; declaration of the republic, emergency powers granted by the RCC to General Neguib; Egypt proclaimed a republic (June 18).

Syria: a new constitution gives great power to the president; elections won by the ALM (the Arab Liberation Movement), Shishakli's party; popular protests organized by the oppositional Popular Front (July).

December. Student demonstrations and lawyer strikes.

November 9. Saudi Arabia: Death of King Ibn Sa'ud; his oldest son Sa'ud b. 'Abd al-'Aziz becomes king.

Iraq: Faisal II, the cousin of King

Hussain of Jordan, declared king on May 2.

May 2. Jordan: Hussain, Talal's son, proclaimed king, after the deposition of Talal by the parliament.

1954

February 25. Syria: coup d'état led by Mustafa Hamdun; Shishakli leaves the country; re-establishment of the Constitution of Sept. 1950; reinstatement of dismissed army officers.

Egypt: all political parties dissolved; Nasser purges the RCC and the army eliminates General Naguib.

October 26. Alleged assassination attempt on Nasser in Alexandria; members of the Muslim Brothers arrested; six executions; the movement is outlawed.

1955

March 31. Yemen: Sayf al-Islam 'Abd Allah new *imam* after coup d'état; deposed by *imam* Ahmad's supporters; Ahmad reinstated (Apr. 4).

August 18. Syria: Shukri al-Quwatli in power; favors the Ba'ath Party, the army and Nasserism.

December 19. Sudan: Proclamation of independence.

1956

Jordan: Dismissal of the commander of the Arab Legion, John Bagot Glubb; replaced by a Jordanian officer.

January 16. Egypt: Nasser, the sole candidate, elected president; new constitution approved; the National Union, Egypt's only party, nominates the members of the National Assembly.

December 22. Syria: 47 Syrian politicians tried before a special military court for alleged involvement in an "Iraqi plot."

1957

May–June. Lebanon: Parliamentary elections; majority for Chamoun; non-Christian, pan-Arab leaders not elected.

Syria: electoral victory by the left-wing contingent (Ba'ath, Communist Party) of the National Front.

December 11. Trial of ten politicians for alleged involvement in an "American plot."

1958

United Arab Republic (UAR): February 10. The National Union, the only party for all of the UAR (Egypt and Syria).

May 8. Lebanon: assassination of Nassib Metni, editor of the pan-Arab newspaper *Al-Telegraf.*

May–July. Lebanon: civil war; General Fouad Chehab elected president on July 31.

July 14. Iraq: military coup by General Qasim. A provisional constitution for the Arab Republic of Iraq.

1959

March. Iraq: Communist insurrection led by Colonel Abdul Wahhab al-Shawaf in Mosul; bloody reprisals.

July. Bloody uprisings in Kirkuk.

UAR-Northern Province (Syria): July 8. Elections; thorough defeat of the former Ba'ath Party.

1960

Iraq: campaign by Qasim (Kassem) against the Communist Party (his ally since 1958), which he outlaws.

April 26. Lebanon: electoral law; multidenominational slates (at a national rate of 6:5 in favor of Maronites) elected by *all* voters in all districts.

1961

November 15. Syria: after secession from the UAR, provisional constitution; an Assembly elected on December 1, Nazim al-Qudsi president; pro-Iraqi Dawalibi government close to Syrian Muslim Brothers.

Kuwait: independent; election of a constituent Assembly.

Iraq: beginning of a nationwide Kurdish revolt led by Barzani.

December 31. Lebanon: another attempted coup d'état by the Syrian National Social Party, (ex-PPS) is immediately repressed.

1962

March 27. Syria: Army coup d'état; abolition of parliament; domination of the Ba'ath Party.

Egypt (UAR): charter for national action ratified by the congress of the Arab Socialist Union (ASU), a large single party that replaces the National Union; emphasis on Arab Socialism, nationalism and anti-imperialism.

Kuwait: constitution allows for a National Assembly to be elected through a system of political parties.

September 26. Yemen (San'a): coup d'état led by 'Abd Allah al-Sallal, a Nasserist officer, against the Zaidi imam Yahya; the Arab Republic of Yemen is declared; leads to civil war.

Foreign Policy

1946

June 15. Civilian air pact between Egypt and the U.S. British and French troops leave Lebanon and Syria. Anglo-American Commission of Inquiry on the political wishes of Arabs and Palestinians.

1947

November 29. U.N. Resolution 181 prescribing the mandatory division of Palestine into Jewish state linked to a Palestinian state.

December. Jewish-Arab civil war.

1948

First visit of the U.S. navy to Saudi Arabia (Dammam).

Palestine: the Jewish-Arab civil war intensifies.

Beginning May 15. Offensives by Jordan, Syria, Iraq, Lebanon and Egypt against the new Israeli state.

June 11–July 9 and July 19–October 29. Cease-fire under U.N. auspices.

November 9. Saudi Arabia refuses to sign the Universal Declaration of Human Rights at the U.N.

1949

February–April. Armistices between Israel and Egypt, Lebanon, Jordan and Syria (but not Iraq).

1951

Egypt: rejection of Anglo-American plan for a common defense system linked to NATO; unilateral abrogation of the Anglo-Egyptian treaty of 1936 by Premier Mustafa Nahas Pasha: guerrilla war (led primarily by the Muslim Brothers) against British military installations along the Suez Canal.

June 1. Syria: Prime Minister Khalid al-'Azm rejects American technical aid under the Point Four program.

June 18. Saudi Arabia: U.S.-Saudi Defense agreement.

1953

Egypt: accord with Britain concerning Sudan's gradual emancipation; end of the guerrilla war on the canal.

October 14. Israel: attack at Kibya (Jordan); 53 villagers killed.

1954

March. Israeli attack at Nahhalin (Jordan); 9 villagers killed.

June. U.S.-Jordan economic pact ($8 million aid).

October 19. Accord concerning the Suez Canal between Egypt and Great Britain, leading to the retreat of the British military in 1956.

1955

Saudi Arabia declines a Soviet arms offer; refuses to extend diplomatic recognition to Russia.

February 24. The Baghdad Pact between Iraq, Turkey, Pakistan, Iran and Great Britain, hostile to Egypt.

February 28. Israeli attack on the Gaza garrison headquarters of the Egyptian army; 38 Egyptians killed.

March 2. Egypt signs an accord in Damascus with Syria and Saudi Arabia.

April 18. Bandung Conference (Indonesia) launched by Nasser, Sukarno, Nehru and Tito in opposition to the Baghdad Pact.

August 26. Secretary Dulles proposes to resettle 900,000 Palestinian refugees.

September. Egypt: arms purchase from Czechoslovakia. Israeli raids on Egyptian troops in Gaza.

December 11. Israeli attack on Syrian outposts at Lake Tiberias: 65 Syrians killed.

1956

March. First conference of the Federation of Arab Labor Unions in Damascus.

June. Secret accord, in Sèvres (France), between Israel, France and Great Britain, allied against Egypt.

July 19. The U.S. withdraws its offer of a loan to Egypt to build the Aswan Dam.

July 26. Immediate nationalization of the Suez Canal Company.

August 20. Cultural agreement between Syria and Russia; students go to Communist bloc to study.

October 29. Israeli attack on Gaza and Sinai as far as the canal.

November 5. Franco-British bombing of the Suez Canal; French and British troops capture Port Said.

November 6. Soviet threat of armed intervention; a cease-fire, coupled with an Israeli retreat, brings an accord between the U.S. and the U.S.S.R. at the U.N. The U.N. Emergency Force (UNEF; the Blue Helmets) in position along the border with Egypt (Sinai).

1957

Lebanon, Jordan and Iraq adopt the anti-Communist "Eisenhower Doctrine." Accord between Syria and the U.S.S.R.; Syria threatened on land by Turkey and on the seas by the Americans (the 6th Fleet); Syria vehemently denounces the Eisenhower Doctrine.

March 9. Evacuation of Israeli troops from Gaza.

October 13. Egyptians land in Latakia to demonstrate Arab solidarity.

December. African-Asian conference in Cairo.

1958

January. Financial accord reached between Egypt and the U.S.S.R. for the construction of the Aswan High Dam.

February 10. Creation of the United Arab Republic (UAR) of Egypt and Syria.

February 14. Creation of the Arab Union of Iraq and Jordan, opposing the UAR

March 8. Creation of the United Arab States (UAR and People's Democratic Republic of Yemen).

Lebanon: U.N. observers arrive headed by the Swedish general Odd Bull.

July 15. American Marines in Lebanon at the request of President Chamoun.

October 24. The Marines withdraw from Lebanon, after the internal situation stabilizes.

December. The U.S. extends a $10 million grant to Lebanon.

1959

February 11. Britain establishes the Federation of Arab Emirates of the South, later called the Federation of South Arabia (1963). Iraq-U.S.S.R. accords.

1961

Kuwait: Iraq threatens annexation; Britain and the Arab League send forces.

Iraq: crisis concerning the Iraq Petroleum Company (IPC); annulment of the Anglo-Iraqi accord of 1928; the Iraq National Oil Company founded.

September 28. Syria breaks away from the UAR (Egypt).

1962

Syrian-Iraqi economic accord. Egyptian military support in Yemen for the Republic of General 'Abd Allah al-Sallal beginning in October. Saudi support for the resistance movement led by the imam Yahya. Iraqi boycott of the Arab League (October)

The Economy, Society and Religion

1946

Egypt: numerous strikes.

Lebanon: passage of laws affecting work.

1948

Some 900,000 Palestinians displaced to (or seek refuge in) Jordan (450,000), Lebanon and Syria, and Gaza (under Egyptian control); immigration to Saudi Arabia, Kuwait, etc.

1949

Kuwait and Qatar begin production of oil.

1950

UNRWA (U.N. Relief and Works Agency) installations of permanent refugee camps with health clinics and schools in Jordan, Gaza, Lebanon and Syria.

December 30. Saudi Arabian-Aramco agreement includes 50-50 profit-sharing formula.

1951

Jordan: the Muslim Personal Status Code concerning polygamy, repudiation and traditional inheritance.

1952

August 12. Egypt: strike in Kafr al-Dawar: two workers are hanged following trial.

September 8. Egypt: agrarian reform (limitation of individual holdings to 200 *feddan* [about 208 acres]) concerning primarily the crown's wealth.

Jordan: Ministry of Planning; creation of agricultural, trade and artisanal cooperatives.

Iraq: insurrection in Baghdad.

1953

Syria: the Personal Status Code keeps repudiation valid, regulates polygamy and reforms inheritance.

April 1. Egypt: decree encouraging the investment of foreign capital in business enterprises.

1955

Iraq: more riots in Baghdad; repression.

Egypt: project to build a high dam in Aswan to create a large reservoir.

November 9. Syria: economic pact with Saudi Arabia; Syria receives $10 million loan.

1957

August 6. Soviet-Syrian economic agreement.

1958

Lebanon: "Reform Decrees" as a result of managed economic development ("Chehabism").

Iraq: agrarian law; creation of unions.

Syria: land reform law.

1959

Iraq: unified Personal Status Codes for both Sunnis and Shi'is. Inherit-

ance reformed, polygamy regulated, legal divorce, but repudiation still valid.

Lebanon: creation of an Office for Social Development.

1960

Jordan: oil refinery in Zarqa.

Abu Dhabi: oil discovered.

1961

Egypt: reform at the al-Azhar Islamic University, enlarged to include all disciplines and opened to women. New agrarian reform law; system of state cooperatives.

UAR: nationalization laws.

December 11. Iraq: nationalization of the petroleum industry; the oil companies turn toward other countries, Iraq loses revenues.

1962

Saudi Arabia: law abolishing slavery; founding of Petromin State company with refineries and other petrochemical industries.

Civilization and Culture

1947

Egypt: Naguib Mahfouz (Najib Mahfuz), *Midaq Alley*, a realist novel.

1948

Iraq: Dhu al-Nun Ayyub, *The Hand, the Earth and Water*, a popular novel.

1949

Egypt: Taha Husayn, publication of the novels *The Tormented of the Earth, The Mirror of Modern Conscience*, and

Animals' Paradise; all critiques of social injustice. Theater: Tawfiq al-Hakim, *King Oedipus*.

1950

Egypt: publication of Shaykh Khalid's *From Here We Start*, a devastating condemnation of the traditionalism of the religious establishment.

1951

Egypt: Naguib Mahfouz, beginning of the *Trilogy*, a novel of social commentary.

1952

Cairo: 'Abd al-Razzaq Ahmad Sanhuri, *Treatise on New Civil Rights*, 1st volume (the 4th and final one appears in 1970); Yusuf al-Siba'i, *The Water-Carrier Is Dead*.

1954

Egypt: 'Abd al-Rahman Sharqawi, *Egyptian Earth*, a novel portraying the problems of peasant life. Sanhuri: *The Sources of Law in the Fiqh*.

Iraq: 'Abd al-Wahhab Al-Bayati, *Chipped Jugs*, peasant poems.

1962

February 28. Soviet-Iraqi cultural agreement; students sent to Soviet universities.

The Turkish and Iranian Middle East*

After the end of the Second World War, the Turkish-Iranian world is first confronted with the Soviet threat in Communist states with Turkish and Tatar populations, in Turkey itself and in northern Iran. An orientation toward the United States and Western Europe becomes evident when these countries agree on the common defense of the Middle East (the Baghdad Pact).

In Kemalist Turkey Islam makes a modest comeback. The aggressive secularism of the country is relaxed.

Iran, on its side, with the new shah, weakens Westernizing reforms and affronts the West when Mossadegh nationalizes foreign oil companies. This is the beginning of a wide-scale nationalization of oil in the Gulf. The shah establishes an unpopular police state when he starts to build a very modern army, redistributes lands, and starts industrialization and social reform, which the Parliament and the clergy often oppose — several from the latter group exile themselves to Iraq and Lebanon.

Afghanistan democratizes its political system using the traditional bases of the Great Assembly composed of notables, which endeavors to create a planned economy.

---

*This territory also includes the Muslim states of Southeast Europe, the heirs to the Ottoman Empire.

Political and Institutional Life

1946

Turkey: Displeasure with Inönü's authoritarian policies. Creation of new parties authorized: the National Party, the Party of National Recovery, on the right; the Democratic Party (DP), center-left and non-Kemalist.

1947

October 22. The Iranian Majlis refuses to ratify the oil agreement with the Soviet Union.

1948

End of martial law in Turkey.

1949

Iran: strong Parliamentary opposition to government, led by Mossadegh, leader of the National Front.

1950

May. Turkey: overwhelming victory for the Democratic Party, which takes 387 out of 487 seats; Adnan Menderes, Prime Minister.

July. Lifting of the ban on religious radio in Turkey.

September. Iran: Kurdish rebellion.

1951

Iran: Prime Minister Razmara assassinated by the Fedayan-e Islam ("Crusaders of Islam"); Mossadegh, now Prime Minister, plays the Parliament and public opinion against the shah.

1953

August 12. Iran: dissolution of Parliament; the shah flees the country; major riots.

Iran: coup d'état (led by General Zahedi) leads to Mossadegh's fall; the shah returns; imprisonments, execution of former Minister Fatemi.

September. Afghanistan: Prince Muhammad Daoud Khan, Prime Minister.

1954

May 2. Turkey: electoral victory of the Democratic Party (503 seats out of 541).

1955

March 30. Anti-Pakistan riots in Kabul, Jalalabad and Kandahar, after Pakistan announces the creation of a single province in western Pakistan (Pakhtunistan).

1957

Iran: martial law suppressed; two Conservative parties appear—the People's and National parties; rigged elections.

1960

May 27. Turkey: military coup led by General Cemal Gürsel; Menderes overthrown, then executed; arrests followed by quick sentencing.

November. Constitutive Assembly led by a the People's Republican Party (PRP). Kemalist majority.

1961

July 9. Turkey: new constitution, approved in a referendum, replaces 1924 constitution; government powers limited.

October. Elections less favorable to the People's Republican Party. Justice Party formed.

Iran: elections canceled because of corruption; Minister 'Ali Amini granted full power.

1963

Afghanistan: Dismissal of Daoud Pasha by King Zahir.

Foreign Policy

1945

Iranian Azerbaijan: Soviet military occupation; Soviet autonomy.

Turkey: U.S.S.R. demands the surrender of the Kars and Ardahan provinces and the establishment of a Soviet base in the Dardanelles; as a result the Turks come closer to the Americans.

1946

April. By U.N. decree, control of Azerbaijan returned to Iran.

1947

March 12. President Truman delivers a message to Congress, proposing assistance to Turkey and Greece to counter Communist threat.

Afghanistan: futile struggle with Great Britain over the border known as the "Durand Line" (1893), including Pakhtunistan, in what will become Pakistan.

July 12. Turkey: adheres to the Truman Doctrine of March 12: treaty for American military aid.

Iran: American aid, principally military.

1948

Spring. The U.S. delivers ships, submarines, attack bombers to Turkey.

1949

November 16. Shah Mohammad Reza on a trip to the U.S.

1951

April 30. Iran: Mossadegh nationalizes oil industries. British and American reaction; issue sent to the International Court of Justice; international blockade of Iranian oil.

1950

July 25. Turkey: Offer the U.N. to send 4,500 soldiers to Korea.

Afghanistan: U.N. mission investigating the country's economic needs.

1952

Turkey joins NATO; military accord with the United States.

October. Iran breaks off diplomatic relations with Great Britain.

1953

Turkey and Iran adopt the anti-Communist Eisenhower Doctrine.

May. U.S.S.R. gives up its territorial claims in Turkey.

Iran: plan to nationalize oil companies abandoned; relations with Great Britain resume; large amounts of American aid.

1954

Turkish and Pakistani defense pact with NATO.

April. Formation of an international consortium of eight oil companies that control Iranian oil production; 50-50 profit-sharing formula. Accord between U.S.S.R. and Iran concerning borders and war reparations; agreement pertaining to locally drilled oil between the new National Iranian Oil Company (NIOC) and foreign companies (the International Consortium).

1955

February. Baghdad Pact (Middle East Defense Organization, dubbed CENTO [Central Treaty Organization] in 1958) between Turkey, Pakistan, Iran and Iraq. Severe tensions between Turkey and Greece over Cyprus.

Afghanistan: improved relations with the Soviets.

1960

February 19. Cyprus independent, with two antagonistic national communities — the Turks and the Greeks.

March 4. U.S.-Iranian agreement.

March 5. U.S.-Turkish treaty of mutual defense.

August 16. A Turkish army unit lands on Cyprus (in accordance with the independence agreement).

1961

Crisis between Afghanistan and Pakistan over Pakhtunistan.

1962

September. Iran assures the Soviet Union that it will not allow foreign missiles to be positioned on its territory.

1963

December 2. The president of Cyprus, Archbishop Makarios, announces his intention to restrict the rights of the Turkish minority.

The Economy, Society and Religion

1946

Afghanistan: inauguration of the country's first university in Kabul.

Iran: the reformer Ahmad Kasrani assassinated by the Fedayan-e Islam.

1949

Turkey: teaching of Qur'an resumes in primary schools; creation of a separate school for the science of religion (Islam) at the University of Ankara.

1950

Close to 150,000 Turks expulsed from Bulgaria.

Iran: the shah distributes the crown's land in small parcels; laws limiting land ownership.

Turkey: religious and peasant movements; measures to insure religious tolerance.

Yugoslavia: wearing of veil by women prohibited.

Afghanistan: tribunal that consists of both of Shari'a and secular law (customary and "European").

1951

Mossadegh creates the National Iranian Oil Company (NIOC) to replace the AIOC; the result is a blockade of Iran, with attendant social malaise; Mossadegh challenged.

1953

Iran: new law concerning the distribution the state's wealth.

Turkey: serious financial difficulties and inflation.

September. Violent protests in Istanbul: Greeks and Turks clash over Cyprus.

1954

March 7. Turkey: laws inviting foreign oil companies to produce and process oil.

1957

July. Iran passes bill encouraging foreign exploration of natural resources.

1959

U.S.S.R. begins a violent campaign against Islam on its own territory.

Turkey: protests against the military accord with the Americans.

1960

Afghanistan: natural gas discovered. Construction of an oil pipeline to the U.S.S.R. and another to a chemical fertilizer factory in Mazar-i Sharif.

March 15. Iran: an agrarian reform bill passed, reducing the size of great landed properties.

1961

Turkey: violent protests in Istanbul pertaining to Cyprus; Greeks expelled from the city.

1962

Iran: program of agrarian reform

and the White Revolution; sale of state-owned factories, nationalization of forests and pastures; franchise for women; formation of a Literary Corps. Violent protests by students in Tehran; 300 students and professors arrested. Amendment limiting agrarian reform.

Afghanistan: five-year plan.

Civilization and Culture

1950

Turkey: Mahmud Makal, *A Village in Anatolia*, a novel.

Iran: poetry by Parvin E'tesami, Nima Yushij.

1951

Death of Sadegh Hedayat, Iranian, author of *The Blind Owl*.

1959

Turkey: rapid rise to fame of the poets Nazim Hikmet, Yahya Kemal Beyatli and Orhan Veli.

1962

Iran: death of Forugh Farrokhzad, poet, author of *Another Birth*.

Islam in the Far East

The Far East includes the countries with the highest Muslim populations: Indonesia and Pakistan (eastern and western). Pakistan becomes a sovereign state separate from India, and regroups around Islam. But the government adopts a Westernized political and social regime without any essential reference to the *shari'a:* the Islamist opposition seeks, unsuccessfully, to create an "Islamic" state. Involved in a latent war with India over Kashmir (Indian territory with a Muslim majority), Pakistan allies itself with the pro-American side during the Cold War through the Baghdad Pact and CENTO (Central Treaty Organization). Serious inter-ethnic difficulties and the malaise in Eastern Pakistan (which will become Bangladesh), overpopulated and under-

presented, lead to the creation of a military regime. When economic development takes hold, it is to the detriment of East Pakistan, one of the poorest
regions in the world.

Indonesia moves on to independence after a difficult struggle with the
Netherlands, which plays on the countless ethnic differences in the archipelago. The hero of independence, Sukarno, unifies the country and neutralizes
Islamic movements, since he favors the Communists and the Chinese minority
of Indonesia. Oil, with the income it provides, facilitates plans for the
development of authoritarian rule, but the *santri* encourage a large number of
abangan who are unhappy with the regime to come to their side.

Political Life and the Constitution

1945

August 18. Indonesia: Constitution
(the Jakarta Charter) of the Federal
Republic does not mention the duty
to follow the law of Islam; organization of an Indonesian Communist
Party, the PKI.

1946

Establishment of a ministry of religion in Indonesia.

1947

August 15. Birth of Pakistan (Muslim), separated from India; includes
East Pakistan (Bengal) and West Pakistan, separated by more than 1,000
miles of Indian territory.

Indonesia: Sakeret Islam splits from
the Masjumi (Muslim Unity Party).

1948

Indonesia: conflict between Sukarno
(and Hatta) and the PKI in central
Java.

1949

December 27. Independence for the
Republic of United States of Indo-

nesia (15 states) with Sukarno as president.

1950

Indonesia: Sukarno abolishes the
Federal constitution, which is replaced provisionally by one calling for
a unitary republic; reconstitution of
the PKI, growth of Muslim political
parties (Masjumi and Nahdatul
Ulama) as well as Catholic and
Catholic-Protestant (Parkindo) parties, in opposition to Sukarno's enormous National Party (PNI).

Eastern Pakistan: Mujibur Rahman
founds the Awami League.

1951

Pakistan: assassination of the president, Liaqat Ali Khan.

Malaya: opposition to the "Chinese"
Party, the Malaya Chinese Association (MCA), and to Abdul Rahman's
"Royal" party, the United Malays National Organization (UMNO).

1952

Indonesia: Nahdatul Ulama splits
from the Masjumi.

1953

Daud Beureuh, military governor of
Atjeh, declares Atjeh (Indonesia) part
of the Islamic Republic.

August. Declaration of an Islamic state in Makasar (Indonesia).

Indonesia: confirmed victory for the PNI (Sukarno) over the PKI; Muslim parties falter.

Malaya: first legislative elections.

1956

Indonesia: Sukarno, with help from the PKI, breaks with Hatta (who counts on support form the Masjumi Muslim Party and the Socialist Party); declares a policy of "guided democracy," eliminates parliamentary democracy, and rules as a dictator.

Pakistan: first constitution, secular.

1957

Independence of Malaya; Islam becomes state religion.

China: Muslims from Ningshia demand independence; arrests follow.

Indonesia: Sukarno establishes "the state of siege"; reestablishment of the presidential regime from the 1945 constitution; committee for the liberation of Irian (Dutch New Guinea).

1958

Pakistan: coup d'état and military government led by General Ayyub Khan; Mujibur Rahman incarcerated: riots in East Pakistan.

Indonesia: in Sumatra, a Muslim and Socialist revolutionary government, the PRRI, rules until 1961.

1959

July. Indonesia: beginning of a "guided democracy"; governmental accord with Daud Beureuh's rebellion in northern Sumatra (Atjeh).

1960

Indonesia: capitulation of Daud Beureuh; Atjeh maintains special status as an Islamic province.

1962

Masjumi Party is outlawed.

May 1. Pakistan: new constitution; Presidential regime with "basic democracy."

Indonesia: end of an Islamist revolt in Western Java.

1963

September 16. Creation of Malaysia: Malaya, Singapore, Sabah (north Borneo), and Sarawak (northwest Borneo); small Muslim majority.

Foreign Policy

1945

The Dutch Indies: evacuation of defeated Japanese troops.

September. British military occupation; the Dutch regain control of the rebellious regions of Java and Sumatra (Sukarno).

1946

December Indonesia: British troops retreat from Java and Sumatra; Dutch forces follow them.

1947

Indonesia: Dutch "police operations" to regain the northern coast of Java; ceasefire imposed by U.N.

August 15. India: permanent British withdrawal; the separatist Muslim state of Pakistan demands Kashmir, attached to India: Indo-Pakistani war in Kashmir.

1949

U.N. conference at The Hague demands an end to Dutch power in August: treaty of union between Holland and Indonesia; U.N. military observers.

Malaya: anti-British Communist underground.

Pakistan and India: application of the ceasefire demanded by the U.N. (January 1) in Kashmir, which remains almost entirely Indian.

1954

Indonesia: denunciation of the Dutch-Indonesian Union of 1949.

Pakistan: pro-American defense pact between Pakistan and Turkey.

Pakistan joins the anti-Communist SEATO (Southeast Asia Treaty Organization) (India not a member).

1955

February. Pakistan: Baghdad Pact (for Middle Eastern defense) with Iraq, Iran and Turkey.

April. Indonesia: organization, with India, of the African-Asian Bandung Conference: "neutralist" declarations clash with the Baghdad Pact and SEATO.

1956

Kashmir: Indian. Legislative Assembly votes to remain part of India, rather than joining Pakistan.

1957

The Malaysian Federation: independence declared from Britain. Abdul Rahman, Prime Minister.

Indonesia: state seizes Dutch wealth; expulsion of Dutch residents.

1960

Pakistan: accord with India concerning the division of water from the Indus.

Indonesia: Soviet military aid. Nationalization of oil companies.

1962

Indonesia: settlement reached with Holland over West Irian (the western half of New Guinea), provisionally administered by the U.N.

1963

Beginning of Indonesian rule over West Irian.

The Economy, Society and Religion

1947

Large-scale transfer of people between India and Pakistan for religious reasons—about 8 million Muslims flee from India to Pakistan, and about the same number of Hindus and Sikhs leave Pakistan for India.

1948

September. Indonesia: repression by the "republican government" of the Communist popular rebellion in Madium (Eastern Java). In Western Java, beginning of a rebellion by the Dar ul-Islam movement, led by Kartosuwirjo, for an Islamic state.

1954

India: Islamic Institute founded at the Aligarh Muslim University.

1957

Indonesia: secessionist movements and Islamic rebellions: state of siege.
Western Pakistan: ethnic fighting.

1960

Pakistan: second 5-year plan, foreign aid, importance of private sector.
Indonesia: agrarian law limiting very large properties.

1961

Pakistan: Personal Status Code limiting polygamy and divorce and modifying "Qur'anic" inheritance.

Civilization and Culture

1946

Death of Amir Hamzah (born 1911), Indonesia's greatest poet before WWII.

1955

Pakistan: Abul 'Ala al-Mawdudi (al-Mawdoodi, Maudoodi), *Islamic Law and Constitution* and *Toward Understanding Islam*, both translated into Urdu and Arabic.

1956

Malaysia: Takali, *The Shrimps*, a novel of social commentary in Malay.

Sub-Saharan Africa

The years from 1945 to 1962, which carry so many consequences for the rest of the Muslim world, do not constitute a major period in the history of sub-Saharan Islam, except in Sudan.

The ideologies of the period (pan-Africanism, Socialism, Unionism) find, on the contrary, an attentive audience in the rising African elite.

West Africa

1947

Chad, Abéshé: a reformist secondary school, the Ma'had al-'Ilm, opened by a former student at the Al-Azhar Islamic University in Cairo, the *faqih* (Islamic man of letters) Oulesh; he is forced to leave the country by French authorities.

1949

Mali (the French Sudan), Bamako: creation, by former students from Al-Azhar, of an organization for young reformist Muslims, al-Shubban al-Muslimin, or Subbanu.

1949–1951

November 1949–December 1951. Mali, Bamako: a *madrasa* (Arab secondary school) opened by members of the Subbanu association; closed in 1953 by the French authorities.

1957

Bamako and Sikasso: street battles between reformists (henceforth called Wahhabis by their adversaries) and Islamic traditionalists over the control of the mosques. The traditionalists prevail; the reformists move toward Wahhabism.

December 22–25. Senegal, Dakar: congress of the Muslim Cultural Union creates the federal structure that includes reformist Muslims from French West Africa. A motion to support the Algerian people's struggle is adopted.

1958

November 28. Declaration of the Islamic Republic of Mauritania, independent on November 28, 1960.

1960

June 19. Cornerstone for the Great Mosque of Dakar laid, the same day as the independence celebration for the short-lived Federation of Mali (Senegal and Mali).

Sudan

1945

Sayyed 'Abd al-Rahman, imam of the Ansar people (Mahdists), creates the Umma party, the political expression of the Mahdist movement.

1951

The Egyptian Parliament abrogates the 1899 and 1936 treaties with Great Britain, providing for a separate Sudanese constitution.

1955

Mid-August. Mutiny by soldiers

from the Equitoria Corps spreads to all the provinces in the south.

October. Repression in southern Sudan by troops from the North. Beginning of irredentism in the non-Islamicized southern provinces in regard to central power.

1956

January 1. Independence for Sudan, which joins the Arab League.

July. The Umma Party (Mahdist) participates in government.

1956–1968

Competition between religious parties: Unionists, linked to the Khatmiyya Muslim Brotherhood, and Umma, linked to Mahdism. Each group will alternatively dominate until power is seized by General Nimeiry (May 25, 1969).

1961

October. Al-Hadi al-Mahdi, grandson of the Mahdi, becomes the Ansars' (Mahdists) imam.

East Africa

1945

Agha Khan, the spiritual leader of the Isma'ilis, creates the East Africa Muslim Welfare Society in Mombasa to help Muslim communities in East Africa (primarily Sunnis): construction of schools, mosques and health clinics.

Chapter 11
1963–1989

The Muslim Affirmation

On the fringes of society in certain states, or against these states, a popular revolution develops—sometimes with surprising success—that manages to expel the Shah from Iran and to sustain an Islamic guerrilla army that ties up the Soviet army in Afghanistan. Worldwide Islamic solidarity is being created: the Islamic Pact becomes the Organization of the Islamic Conference (OIC), with a network of specialized bodies. There is communication between this official, structured Islam and "Islamism," a parallel and often clandestine movement. Several states become "Islamic": following the example of Saudi Arabia, they seek to apply the *shari'a*. But Muslim thought, either discouraged or persecuted in the previous period, is unable to provide a dynamic and modernizing message to this new slogan.

The minority ethnic and/or religious and non-Muslim communities reaffirm their presence both in the face of nation-states, which have been eroding their power, and in the face of the challenge of "Islamism," which constitutes a return to the idea of *dhimmi* that had been abolished for a century. Other problems include the interminable Lebanese civil war, the inter-ethnic conflicts in Pakistan, the questions surrounding the Kurds in Turkey, Iran and Iraq, the Sudanese in the south, and other difficulties in Black Africa.

However, often national loyalties dominate, especially in the group of wealthy countries in the region. Arrangements with Israel are established from country to country despite the Palestinian guerrilla war; OPEC is very successful despite the Iran-Iraq War; the OIC develops fully, continuing to give aid to the poorest countries and supporting Muslim minorities throughout the world, while managing to gain international respectability (for example, through the Islamic Human Rights declaration). The Sufi brotherhoods also regain some of their former grandeur, especially in central Asia. However, in Black Africa, the brotherhoods are rebuffed by fundamentalist movements and, except in Sudan, Islam's political manifestations remain limited.

Muslim societies are characterized by a constant increase in population, face high illiteracy rates, and experience a growing contrast between rich countries (income from oil) and poor ones or even very poor ones, and, in the poorest, the gulf increases between a wealthy ruling class and the impoverished masses.

1964
"Nasserist" summits held by the Arab League in Cairo (January) and Alexandria (September). Creation of the Palestine Liberation Organization (PLO) as an umbrella organization for all Palestinian societies, clubs and paramilitary organizations.

1965
Arab League summit in Casablanca: approval for a Palestinian Liberation Army (PLA). Saudi Arabia calls for the creation of an (anti-Nasser) Islamic Pact.

1967
August. Fourth Arab League summit in Khartoum (Sudan); refusal to negotiate directly with Israel.

1969
September. Islamic summit in Rabat (Morocco), creation of the Organization of the Islamic Conference (OIC), with a permanent secretariat in Jidda.

1971
February 14. OPEC announces an immediate 20% increase in the price of oil. Islamic conference in Rabat discusses family planning and contraception. OIC mediation in Yemen.

1972
The International Islamic News Agency (IINA) founded.

1973
October and December. OPEC announces a significant increase in the price of oil (to $11.65 per barrel up from $3.00; intermittently the price reaches $20 per barrel), and the embargo of certain client states, especially the U.S. Arab League summit in Algiers, ratifying Egypt and Syria's negotiations with Israel during an international summit in Geneva.

1974
February. Second OIC summit in Lahore (Pakistan) gives recognition to PLO. In just a few months, OPEC quadruples the price of oil.

August 8. The Islamic States Development Bank (ISDB founded).

October 28. The Arab League: the 7th Arab Summit in Rabat; the PLO declared "the sole legitimate representative of the Palestinian people."

1975
The Islamic States Broadcasting Organization (ISBO) founded.

1979
The Arab League excludes Egypt after Camp David agreement; secretariat moved to Tunis. The OIC excludes Egypt; creation of a model Islamic constitution. OPEC declares another increase in the price of oil following the sudden interruption in Iran's production.

1982
The Islamic Council of Europe (London), at Saudi Arabia's request, produces an "Islamic Charter of Uni-

Islamic Fundamentalism

Term designating the currents of thought and action that seek the Islamization of society. The goal of Islamic fundamentalists is to establish Islamic states where the *shari'a* is applied. Important fundamentalist movements: in the Near East, the Muslim Brothers and dissident groups in existence since 1970 (among them, Takfir wa-hijra; Jihad; Hamas); in Iraq, the Da'wa and the Mujahidin; in India and Pakistan, the Jamaat-i islami (founded by Mawdudi in 1941); in Iran, the Fedayan-e islam (since the 1950s); in Afghanistan, the Mujahidin (since 1974); in Turkey, the Party for National Salvation, the Sülaymanji group, and the Nurju group; in the Maghrib, the Islamic Movement followed by the Nahda (Tunisia), the Qiyam followed by the Da'wa, which becomes the Islamic Salvation Front (FIS) (Algeria), the Jamaat al-tabligh and the Muslim-Shabiba Youth Group (Morocco); in the Arab world, the Islamic Liberation Party (based in Jordan); in Indonesia, moderate parties such as the Nahdatul-'Ulama' and the Masjumi as well as violent groups such as the Dar ul'islam and Hizbullah followed by groups such as the Imran, the Jihad Commando; in Malaysia, the Malaysian Muslim Youth Movement (ABIM) and, in the Philippines, the Moro Front; in Black Africa, fundamentalist movements, often called "Wahhabites." These new configurations are often close to ancient Khariji and Isma'ili schismatic traditions in their aim to wage war against allegedly renegade Muslims, and their practice of tyrannicide and sacralized suicidal murder.

versal Human Rights." Extraordinary Arab League summit in Fez (Morocco) adopts the "Fahd Plan" (Saudi Arabia) for Arab-Israeli negotiations at an international conference as an alternative to the Camp David agreement; Iraq supported in its war against Iran.

1983

The Islamic Law Academy founded.

1986

OPEC fails to slow the rapid decline in oil prices after Iraq leaves the system of production quotas.

1987

January. Fifth OIC summit in Kuwait condemns Iran.

November. Arab summit in Amman, Jordan condemns Iran.

1988

December. OPEC slows rapid decline in oil prices by applying quotas.

1989

March 16. The OIC ministers in Riyadh reject an Iranian motion calling for the execution in Great Britain of "the apostate, Rushdie."

May 23–26. Arab summit in Casablanca. Reintegration of Egypt, inte-

THE ORGANIZATION OF THE ISLAMIC CONFERENCE, OIC

Member States

Afghanistan	Gabon	Morocco
(suspended Jan. 1980)	Gambia	Niger
Algeria	Guinea	Oman
Bahrain	Guinea-Bissau	Pakistan
Bangladesh	Indonesia	PLO (since 1974)
Burkina Faso	Iran	Saudi Arabia
(until 1984, Upper Volta)	Iraq	Senegal
Cameroon	Jordan	Somalia
Chad	Kuwait	Sudan
Comoros	Lebanon	Syria
Djibouti	Libya	Tunisia
Egypt	Malaysia	Turkey
(suspended May 1979	Maldives	Uganda
to January 1984)	Mauritania	United Arab Emirates
		Yemen

Observers: Nigeria, the Turkish Republic of Cyprus, the Moro Front (Philippines).

gration of the Palestinian state, approval of the PLO's recognition of Israel; designates a committee (Morocco, Algeria and Saudi Arabia) to find a permanent solution to the Lebanese problem.

The Maghrib

Independent Algeria makes its presence felt in the Maghrib by virtue of its sheer demographic weight, its Nasserist state socialism, its profits from oil supplemented by profits from natural gas, to such a degree that her two neighbors become concerned. Libya, after Qaddafi's putsch, first turns toward the Mashriq (the Arab East). Border problems flare up in Morocco, minor at first but very grave by the time of Spain's departure from the western Sahara. Beginning in 1975, a war by proxy is fought between Morocco and Algeria. Tunisia experiments unsuccessfully with a guided cooperativist system that is eventually abandoned, but Bourguiba's dictatorial power toward the end of 1987 delays multiparty political democratization, after several years of "Islamist" resistance. Algeria continues its system of state socialism, in spite of the country's declining condition (brought on by a staggering increase in population coupled with high illiteracy rates); any resistance coming from the lower echelons of society is put down by force. In Morocco, economic stagnation is practically sanctified by the fact that the monarchical regime in place (made up of controlled parties and a Chamber of Deputies with very little power) is politically stable.

The Maghrib's importance in the pan-Arab movement increases after reconciling their grave concerns about Nasserism. After several futile partial unions, the Arab Maghrib forms a serious union.

Political and Institutional Life

1963

September 20. Algeria: first constitution. "Presidential" regime with one party, the FLN.

September 23. Faced with Aït Ahmed's dissidence in the Kabylia, President Ben Bella suspends the constitution.

1964

Algiers: FLN congress produces the Algiers Charter, which gives political rule to the party.

1965

June 19. Algeria: Ben Bella removed from power and incarcerated by Houari Boumedienne and the Revolutionary Council, which takes the place of the National Assembly and mirrors the FLN's moves; armed rebellions by FLN supporters; student strikes.

Morocco: leftist politician Mehdi Ben Barka kidnapped and murdered in Paris; suspension of the constitution.

1969

September 1. Libya: Colonel Qaddafi takes power, proclaims the Libyan Arab Republic and sets up a Revolutionary Council; supports Nasser's pan-Arabism.

Tunisia: Constitution implemented, presidential democracy.

1971

July. King Hassan II of Morocco escapes an attempted coup by right-wing army officers.

1972

Morocco: failed attempt by the air force to assassinate the king; General Oufkir commits suicide.

1976

Algeria: National Charter and a constitution; Boumédienne elected president.

April. Libya: "student revolt" by Qaddafi's supporters, who dominate the universities.

1977

June. Morocco: independents win the election from the Istiqlal and the USFP.

Algeria: failed putsch by Zbiri against Boumédienne; elections (the first since 1964) for a Popular National Assembly.

Libya: proclamation of the Socialist Arab Libyan Peoples Jamahiriyya (plural of jumhuriyya = republic); "direct democracy" announced.

1978

Libya: opposition of religious authorities to Qaddafi's interpretation of Islam; many are dismissed.

September 7. Mauritania: bloodless coup d'état by the army against President Ould Daddah; suspension of the constitution.

December 17. Algeria: death of Boumédienne: Colonel Chadli Benjedid is his successor.

1979

November. Tunisia: the Islamic Movement (MTI) (former Islamic Action) holds its first congress led by Rashid Ghannoushi.

1980

Tunisia: an "Islamist" Gafsa commando on trial; 15 executions.

Algeria: special FLN congress modifies status; frees Ben Bella; pardons Zbiri.

1981

November. Tunisia: creation of new parties; legislative elections, the first in 25 years.

1982

November and December. Algeria: violence perpetrated by Islamist movements.

1984

Tunisia: 22 leaders of the MTI who had been sentenced are given pardons.

Algeria: 7 of the accused in the events of 1982 convicted; clemency for the pro-Islamists.

January. Algeria: Chadli Benjedid reelected president.

Morocco: electoral victory by the Constitutional Union (centrist) over the Istiqlal.

1986

Algeria: new National Charter. Islam serves as the reference point for "Algerian Socialism."

1987

September. Tunisia: two "Islamists" sentenced and two are executed.

October 2. Zayn al-'Abidin Ben 'Ali Tunisian prime minister.

November 7. Bourguiba dismissed.

1988

Algeria: devastating riots (especially by youths); constitutional reform; reelection of Chadli Benjedid, the only candidate.

November. Tunisia: National Pact, which recognizes all parties except the MTI.

1989

February 23. Algeria: new constitution by referendum; multiparty system made official in July.

March. Legal recognition of the Islamic Salvation Front (FIS), formerly Da'wa.

April. Tunisia: landslide victory for Ibn 'Ali in presidential election; legislative elections: seats in the Chamber of Deputies held only by members of the president's party (the Democratic Constitutional Coalition) since the Nahda Party (formerly the Islamic Movement) is not allowed to participate.

Foreign Policy

1963

October. Brief border war between Algeria and Morocco.

1964

Tunisia: French evacuate the naval base at Bizerte.

1965

Accords concerning oil between France and Algeria; trade agreements between Algeria and Egypt and the communist countries of Europe. The Ben Barka affair; the leader of the UNFP (Morocco) assassinated in Paris.

1968

Cultural and economic conventions between Tunisia and France. Franco-Libyan oil protocol. Franco-Algerian agreement allows unrestricted immigration from Algeria to France.

1969

Accords linking Morocco and Tunisia with the European Economic Community (EEC). Ifni given back to Morocco
by Spain. Libyan-Egyptian-Sudanese Confederation.

1970

Relations between Morocco and Mauritania normalize.
Libya: foreign banks nationalized; closure of British and U.S. military bases and withdrawal of troops; French contract for the delivery of combat planes; confiscation of the property of Italians and Jews; expulsion of 30,000 Italians.

1971

Libya: nationalization of B.P. (British Petroleum).
Algeria: nationalization of the natural gas industry and control over French oil companies.

1972

Cooperation agreement between Libya and the U.S.S.R.

1973

Qaddafi sends 40,000 soldiers to the Egyptian border in a failed attempt to forge a political union; invasion of Chad.

1974

January. Failure of a Libyan attempt to form a union with Tunisia.

1975

Western Sahara is relinquished by Spain to Morocco and Mauritania; proclamation of the Democratic Sahrawi Arab Republic (RASD) by the Polisario Front (supported by the Algerians); Morocco responds with "the Green March" of 350,000 unarmed Moroccans to the "Moroccan" Sahara.
Libya: nationalization of foreign trade.

1976

February and March. Morocco: military maneuvers by the Polisario in Amalga.
April. Moroccan-Mauritanian accords; they split the western Sahara. New accords between the EEC and Algeria, Morocco and Tunisia. Algerian-Libyan treaties of Hassi Masud.

1979

Rupture between Arafat and Libya, which from now on supports radical Palestinian factions. Annexation of the southern part of West Sahara by Morocco.

December 2. Destruction of the U.S. embassy in Tripoli (Libya).

1980

Libyan military intervention in Chad; "socialization" of Libyan internal trade; union with Syria.

1981

Agreement between Libya, South Yemen, and Ethiopia; attempted union of Libya and Chad fails. Two Libyan fighter jets downed by U.S.

1982

French-Algerian accord on natural gas. Morocco allows the U.S. to establish military bases on its territory.

1984

August 14. Libya-Morocco Union treaty.

November. The RASD admitted to the OAU, from which Morocco resigns immediately.

1985

Libyan-Sudanese military accord; rupture between Libya and Tunisia.

September. Libya expels 30,000 Tunisian workers.

October. Israeli bombardment of the PLO headquarters in Tunis.

December. Anti-American terrorist attacks in Rome and Vienna (possibly Libyan).

1986

April 15. American raid on Qaddafi's residence in retaliation for involvement in terrorist acts at the Vienna and Rome airports.

July 21–23. King of Morocco receives the Israeli Prime Minister, Shimon Peres. Libya violates the conditions of its union treaty with Morocco. Second Libyan military offensive in Chad.

1987

September 16. Libyan-Chadian ceasefire.

1988

Relations between Algeria and Morocco resume. Accords with the U.N. concerning Sahrawi self-determination by referendum. Relations between Libya and Chad normalize.

1989

January. Military tension between Libya and the U.S.

Algeria: Agreement with France (and with Belgium in June) on a compromise price for natural gas after two contentious years.

January 4. First direct negotiations between the king of Morocco and the ruler of Western Sahara in Marrakesh.

February 17. Treaty creating the Arab Maghrib Union (AMU) between Algeria, Morocco, Mauritania, Libya and Tunisia, signed in Marrakesh.

October–November. Fighting between the Polisario and Morocco resumes.

The Economy, Society and Religion

1963

Algeria: capital transfers regulated.

March. Decrees announcing self-administration (already in existence) or state control of lands belonging to colonizers. Permanent agrarian private sector, mostly in Orania.

1964

Algeria: petrochemical plant in Arzew for the liquification of natural gas; state-run organizations operating mines (mostly iron and phosphate).

Tunisia: nationalization of lands still belonging to former settlers.

1965

Morocco: three-year plan for 1965–1967 (guaranteeing the status quo).

March. Student riots in Casablanca, bloody suppression.

1966

Mauritania: ethnic clashes between black Africans and Maurs in Tabu.

1967

Algeria: more nationalizations.

Morocco: arrest and conviction of the Moroccan Workers' Union's (UMT) secretary and the leaders of the Moroccan National Students' Union (UNEM).

1969

January. Tunisia: generalization of state cooperatives.

September. Rapid return to economic liberalism; Ahmed b. Salah is expelled, then condemned; agricultural production stagnating since 1950.

1970

Tunisia: first significant oil production.

Libya: in Tripoli, first conference held by the Organization of the Islamic Calling (Da'wa); prohibition of Latin characters.

Algeria: Islamic movement Qiyam is outlawed.

Mauritania: drought in the Sahel (lasts until 1974).

1971

Algeria: nationalization of French oil companies in the Sahara.

1973

Algeria decrees the end to unrestricted immigration to France.

Morocco: foreign property converted to Moroccan owners.

1974

Mauritania: nationalization of French and British iron and copper mining companies.

1978

January. Tunisia: about 50 die after strikes by the UGTT and a general strike. Habib Achour, former secretary-general of the UGTT, sentenced, along with 29 other permanent members.

1980

January. Morocco: unrest in Gafsa; week-long battle between demonstrators and army.

Algeria: riots by the Kabyles. 21 sentenced. Chadli Benjedid assumes full power.

October 10. Earthquake in al-Asnam kills 2,500.

Libya: third volume of Qaddafi's Green Book appears.

1981

May 19. Algeria: "student day" with rioting in the universities.

Tunisia: UGTT congress, Destourian Socialist Party congress; the two disassociate from each other.

Morocco: riots and strikes in Casablanca; "Letter to the King" by 'Abd al-Salam Yasin, an independent militant Islamist; punishment of 1,000 USFP (Union Socialiste des Forces Populaires) militants.

Libya: the World Center for the Study of the Green Book founded.

1982

Mauritania: drought in the Sahel (lasts until 1984); the University of Nouakchott opened.

1984

Morocco and Tunisia: increase in bread prices leads to hunger revolts in Morocco, Casablanca and Tunis.

May. Algeria: the Family Code; co-existence of repudiation and legal divorce, legal status of polygamy, marriage of daughters by tutors.

Libya: industrial output is 50% of the GNP, the other 50% is based on petroleum; 16% of the work force in agriculture.

1986

November. Algeria: student protests in Constantine.

Libya: state measures to counter the appearance of Islam and the "Islamists."

Culture

1967

Fadala M'Rabet, lawyer: *The Algerians,* a plea.

1972 and 1975

Kateb Yacine (Katib Yasin), *Mohammad, Take Your Suitcase* and *The Two-Thousand-Year War,* plays written in Algerian Arabic.

1976

Publication of part one of Qaddafi's Green Book; parts 2 and 3 appear in 1977 and 1980; elaboration on the "Third Universal Theory."

1983

Algerian cinema: *The Wind of Sand* by M. Lakhdar Hamina.

The Arab Near East

The Arab Near East is first witness to the apogee of Nasserism: the ambition to develop economically above all else. During the "Arab Cold War," the Israeli army is engaged repeatedly against Syria and Egypt; against the Arab States (a weak coalition formed in 1973), and against the PLO, which launches a limited offensive against Israel. The PLO, following the Six Day War (1967), builds a certain amount of momentum. However, the disciplining of Palestinians by armies and police forces of the Arab States is a constant throughout the period: in Jordan in 1970 to 1971, in Lebanon by the Lebanese state, then by Syria and its Lebanese allies, beginning in 1973 and especially in 1976 and 1985 to 1988. The peace treaty between Egypt and Israel (1979), prepared at Camp David (1978), is the central event in a move toward solidarity among the Arab states, a move that excludes the PLO and its revolutionary propaganda.

The tenacity of the Palestinians, who practically annex southern Lebanon and attempt to dominate the government of the entire country, is evident. They also launch, in 1987, a resistance movement in the territories occupied by Israel since 1967, which greatly complicates the possibility of a Jordanian-Israeli peace plan and provokes a strong and protracted Israeli military offensive against Lebanon in 1982 to 1985. Another front develops between Iran and Iraq, stressing in a dangerous fashion an old enmity between Iraq and Syria (which supports Iran and plays the Shi'i card). This war leads to an institutional alliance centered on Saudi Arabia and composed of Arab Gulf states: the Gulf Cooperation Council (GCC). With its financial might alone, this coalition mediates between the Arab and non-Arab Near East.

Political and Institutional Life

1963

January. Kuwait: first National Assembly.

February. Iraq: military coup eliminates Qasim (Kassem), who is subsequently executed; 'Abd al-Salam 'Arif (Aref) president; the Ba'ath Party participates until November 18.

March 8. Syria: military coup. Baa'th Party holds sole power.

July 18. Syria: bungled and bloody Nasserist putsch.

Oman: tribal uprising leading to a protracted rebellion in Dhofar, led by the Dhofar Liberation Front.

South Yemen: tribal disturbances in Radfan; suppressed by the British.

1964

Iraq: provisional constitution of a democratic Socialist state; dissolution of all political parties.

Jordan: in East Jerusalem, the first Palestinian National Congress meets. This meeting leads to the creation of the Palestinian Liberation Organization (PLO). National charter and constitution, establishing a Palestine National Council, and an executive committee; first chairman: Ahmad Shuqayri; formation of the Palestine Liberation Army (PLA) from Palestine units of the Iraqi army.

Saudi Arabia: Prince Faisal, prime minister, becomes king in his brother Sa'ud's place.

Lebanon: Charles Helou elected president.

1965

Egypt: declaration of a plot by the Muslim Brothers, led by Sayyid Qutb; arrests, military trials. The Egyptian Communist Party voluntarily disbands and joins the only party allowed in the one-party system, the Arab Socialist Union.

Oman: beginning of a Marxist-Leninist revolt by the Dhofar Liberation Front.

1966

February. Syria: bloody putsch aimed at the "old guard" of the Ba'ath Party; victory claimed by the "Salah Jadid clan," known as "neo-Ba'ath" (quasi-Marxist); participation of the Communist Party.

North Yemen: civil war resumes.

April 13. Iraq: president 'Abd al-Salam 'Arif killed in a plane crash; his brother, 'Abd al-Rahman 'Arif, succeeds.

June. Iraq: armistice armstice agreed to by the Kurdish leader Mustafa al-Barzani and President 'Arif.

August 29. Egypt: three leaders from the Muslim Brothers executed, among them Sayyid Qutb.

1967

June 8. Egypt: at the end of the Israeli war, Nasser announces his intention to resign. After massive popular demonstrations, he rescinds his decision. Purges in the army: Commander-in-chief, 'Abd al-Hakim 'Amir (Amer) arrested, commits suicide in prison (September 15).

November. Jordan and Lebanon: creation of the Popular Front for the Liberation of Palestine (PFLP) by George Habash.

November 30. South Yemen: after British withdrawal, independence under the leadership of the militant Marxist-Leninist NLF (National Liberation Front).

December–February. North Yemen: following the fall of Sallal (November), unsuccessful siege on San'a by "royalists."

December. Palestine: resignation of Shurqayri.

1968

July. Jordan: in Amman, the Palestine National Council (PNC) writes a new National Charter; the army and the *fedayin* clash.

July 17. Iraq: military coup by the Ba'ath Party and the army.

July 30. coup by the Ba'ath against the army; Hasan al-Bakr, anti-Syrian; anti-Communist repression.

November. the Amman accord between the PLO and Jordan, mediated by Egypt.

Syria: the Ba'ath Party creates the Palestinian guerrilla organization, led by Zuhayr Muhsin, known as the "al-Sa'iqa (Saika) — Avant Garde of the Palestinian Revolution," whose command is integrated with that of the military. Ahmad Jibril founds the PFLP-GC (General Command).

Oman: the Dhofar Liberation Front becomes the Popular Front for the Liberation of the Occupied Arab Gulf (PFLOAG), supported by South Yemen.

1969

In Cairo, the Palestinian guerrilla organization Fatah takes over the PNC: Yasir Arafat becomes chairman of the PLO.

September and October. Lebanon: clashes between the army and the Palestinian *fedayin.*

November 3. The Cairo Accord, favorable to the *fedayin.*

1970

Iraq: new interim constitution states Iraq is a Peoples Democratic Republic committed to Arab socialism and Islam; autonomy granted to provinces with large Kurdish majorities (Kirkuk and Mosul excluded) is not honored.

March. North Yemen: national reconciliation.

July. Oman: Qabus takes his father's (Sa'id) place in a coup. Start of social and political modernization.

September 17–27. Jordan: following the incidents in Amman in February, June and August, murderous confrontation between the army and the *fedayin* (4,000 dead), cease-fire signed with Nasser's mediation in Cairo; mass expulsions of *fedayin*.

September 28. Egypt: death of Nasser; interim period secured by vice-president Anwar al-Sadat.

October 15. Sadat elected president.

November 14. Syria: General Hafez al-Assad takes power over the "Salah Jadid clan" and becomes prime minister and head of the Ba'ath party.

Lebanon: Sulayman Franjiyeh succeeds Charles Helou in the presidency.

1971

Oman: decisive military and political offensive against the Dhofar rebellion.

May 14. Egypt: Sadat eliminates the 'Ali Sabri group (pro-Soviet; in league with the military police), in the so-called "corrective revolution."

July. Jordan: the last *fedayin* are expelled; the "Black September" secret organization formed among the ranks of the Fatah.

Bahrain, Qatar and the United Arab Emirates claim their independence.

1972

March 7. Syria: establishment of the National Front as the highest authority in the country.

1974

Jordan: suspension of parliament until 1984; plan for a federation between the West Bank and Jordan.

Iraq: formation of the National Progressive Front, an umbrella organization of political parties, dominated by the Ba'ath.

North Yemen: suspension of the 1971

constitution after the dismissal of President Iryani; new ruler Lt. Colonel Ibrahim Muhammad al-Hamdi.

1975

Iraq: campaign to pacify Kurdistan; collapse of the Kurdish resistance after withdrawal of Iranian support.

March 25. Saudi Arabia: King Faisal assassinated; his brother Khalid succeeds.

April 13. Lebanon: beginning of civil war; clashes between the Phalanges (Kata'ib) and Palestinians.

Bahrain: National Assembly is suspended.

1976

Lebanon: fights between the National Movement (left-wing coalition led by the Druze Kamal Jumblat) and the *fedayin*; siege on Palestinian camps in Beirut by the Kata'ib and the Syrians; the entire Lebanese army dissolves (March); Lebanese forces brought together by Bashir Gemayyel; Elias Sarkis elected President of the Republic in September.

Oman: cease-fire and end to the Dhofar rebellion.

Kuwait: National Assembly suspended.

September. Egypt: Sadat re-elected.

Three "platforms" (left, right and center) founded after they convert into parties following parliamentary elections.

1977

March. Lebanon: Murder of Kamal Jumblat; his son Walid succeeds.

October 11. North Yemen: assassination of al-Hamdi.

1978

North Yemen: the NLF transformed into the Yemeni Socialist Party; military coup.

1979

July 16. Iraq: Saddam Husayn (Hussein) replaces the ailing President Ahmad Hasan al-Bakr; might of political police increased.

November 20. Saudi Arabia: religious fundamentalists and 'Utayba tribesmen occupy the Great Mosque of Mecca during the pilgrimage. Assault by the police after a prolonged siege.

1980

March. Syria: turmoil in Aleppo and Hama attributed to the Muslim Brothers.

Egypt: constitutional reform grants greater importance to the *shari'a.*

1981

Kuwait: a National Assembly is elected once again.

September 2. Egypt: 1,536 people ("Islamists" and Muslim Brothers for the most part) arrested for "denominational sedition."

October 6. Assassination of President Sadat by a soldier who claims to be "Islamist."

October 19. Vice president Hosni Mubarak elected; release of many of those who were detained on September 2.

Bahrain: attempted pro-Iranian coup d'état in December.

1982

Syria: in Hama, the army suppresses a riot by the National Front (led by the Muslim Brothers).

June 13. Saudi Arabia: death of King Khalid; his brother, the emir Fahd, succeeds him.

Lebanon: schism between the Amal Shi'i movement and a pro-Iranian activist movement, the Amal Islami (becomes Hezbollah in 1983), in Baalbek.

September 14. Assassination of Bashir Gemayyel (Jumayyil), elected president August 23; as a reprisal, massacres in the Palestinian refugee camps Sabra and Shatila in West Beirut by Lebanese Christian forces with Israeli consent.

September 21. Amin Gemayyel elected president.

North Yemen: establishment of representative bodies.

1983

Lebanon: the war in the Shuf (troops withdrawn by Israel) between Druze militiamen from Walid Jumblat's P.S.P. and Maronite residents; Druze victory.

November. Failure of the Lebanese National Reconciliation Congress in Geneva. Schisms in the PLO and Fatah: Abu Musa's group creates the Palestinian National Salvation Front (PNSF) in Damascus — it beseiges Arafat in Tripoli.

1984

March. Lebanon: failure of a second National Reconciliation Council in Lausanne.

May. Egypt: legislative elections. Deputies from the neo-Wafd (now legal) in the Parliament face the president's party (the National Democratic Party).

1985

May and June. Lebanon: beginning of

the Palestinian "War of the Camps" waged by Amal Shi'i militias, who take control of West Beirut.

December 28. Damascus Accord between the leaders of the three principal militias, the Shi'is, Druze and Maronites.

1986

South Yemen: bloody civil war between two clans from the only party (Communist) in power; al-'Attas is successor to 'Ali Nasir Mohammad.

Lebanon: Damascus Accord fails and civil war resumes.

March. The West Bank: the mayor of Nablus, named by Israel, is assassinated.

1987

Egypt: beginning of the repression of Muslim fundamentalism with appointment of the new interior minister, Zaki Badr.

1988

August–September. Lebanon: failure to elect a president at the end of Amin Gemayyel's mandate (September 23); establishment of two parallel, concurrent prime ministers: Michel Aoun (Maronite) and Salim Hoss (Muslim).

November 15–20. In Algiers, an extraordinary Palestinian National Congress: declaration of an independent Palestinian state ready to negotiate with Israel on the basis of U.N. resolutions 181 (1947), 242 (1967) and 338 (1973), all previously rejected.

Egypt: militants from the "Egyptian Revolution" (led by the exiled son of Nasser) convicted, accused of assassination attempts in 1984 and 1987.

1989

March 14–September 22. Lebanon: "War of Liberation" (General Michel Aoun) against Syrian forces and pro-Syrian militias — nearly 1,000 dead.

November. René Mu'awwad elected president the 5th; assassinated the 22nd; Elias Hrawi (Hirawi) elected the 24th; government of Selim Hoss. Armed opposition from General Aoun.

Jordan: first legislative elections since 1967 (not in the West Bank) on the 10th: of 80 seats, 30 taken by Muslim Brothers or other "Islamists."

Foreign Policy

1963

April 17. Accord for an Egyptian-Syrian-Iraqi Federal Union; canceled by Egypt in July.

1964

May. Egypt-U.S.S.R. association: Khrushchev in Cairo.

1965

January 1. First guerrilla activity in Israel by the Fatah. The E.E.C. grants Lebanon "favored nation" status.

1966

Increasing Soviet economic and military support of Syria.

April. Israeli aircraft down six Syrian jets.

May 12–13. The U.S.S.R. informs Syria and Egypt that Israel is preparing an attack on Syria on May 16–17.

May 22. Egypt occupies the Strait of Tiran, and closes it to Israeli shipping.

1967

May 30. Common defense pact signed by Egypt, Jordan, Iraq and Syria.

June 6-10. Israel takes Gaza on the 6th, East Jerusalem and all of the West Bank on the 7th, the Sinai as far as the Suez Canal on the 8th, the Golan Heights (Syria) on the 9th; cease-fire on the 10th.

June 6. Ten Arab states stop oil deliveries to Britain and the U.S.

June 27. Israel annexes East Jerusalem, an action that is declared invalid by the U.N. on July 14.

November 22. U.N. resolution 242 demanding Israeli withdrawal and the establishment of "secure and recognized boundaries" is accepted by Egypt, Jordan, Israel and Lebanon, refused by Syria and the PLO. The Faisal (Saudi Arabia)–Nasser (Egypt) Accord on South Yemen.

Syria: new agreement with the IPC (Iraq Petroleum Company) and Tapline (Saudi Arabian oil). Drilling resumes in Banyas and Tripoli (Lebanon) after having been interrupted in 1966.

Egypt withdraws from North Yemen.

November 29. Britain withdraws from South Yemen.

1968

February. Federation of the United Arab Emirates established.

March 21. Jordan: battle of Karameh pitting an attacking Israeli army against the Fatah and an associated Jordanian army; in spite of Israeli victory, the incident is a great propaganda success for the Palestinians. First Palestinian (PFLP) international hijacking incidents.

End of December. Israeli reprisal raid on Beirut Airport, destruction of 13 Arab aircraft.

1969

March. Egypt: the "war of attrition" on the Suez Canal (beginning in Spring 1968); intensive Israeli raids.

1970

January. Secret agreement in Moscow between the U.S.S.R. and Egypt; Soviet military advisers in Egypt at plane and missile bases.

July. Israel, Jordan and Egypt accept the American Rogers Plan for the immediate start of negotiations concerning U.N. resolution 242.

August 7. Cease-fire along the Suez Canal.

September. Syrian intervention in the Jordanian civil war; retreat of a Syrian tank brigade after attack by the Jordanian air force.

1971

April. Loose Federation of the Arab Republics of Libya, Egypt and Syria.

May 27. Treaty of friendship and cooperation between the U.S.S.R. and Egypt. Britain withdraws from the Gulf.

1972

Jordanian plan for the United Arab Kingdom of the Occupied West Bank and Transjordan.

April 9. Treaty of friendship and cooperation between the U.S.S.R. and Iraq; IPC nationalized.

June. Israeli raids into southern Lebanon. At the Munich (Germany) Olympic Games, Palestinian terrorists from the "Black September" group take hostages, then execute 11 Israeli athletes.

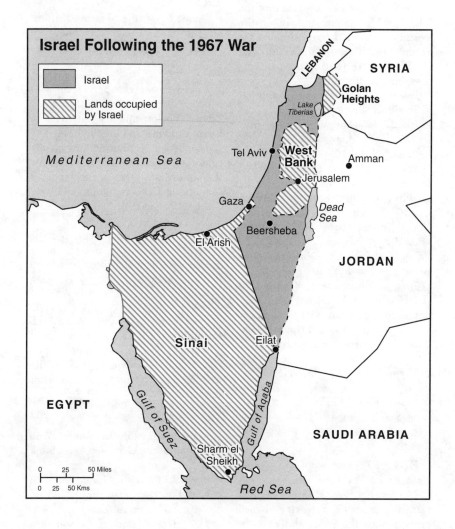

Israel Following the 1967 War

Israel
Lands occupied by Israel

Mediterranean Sea

LEBANON

SYRIA

Golan Heights

Lake Tiberias

Tel Aviv • **West Bank**

• Amman

• Jerusalem

Gaza •

Dead Sea

• Beersheba

El Arish •

JORDAN

Sinai

Eilat •

EGYPT

Gulf of Suez

Gulf of Aqaba

SAUDI ARABIA

Sharm el Sheikh •

0   25   50 Miles

0   25   50 Kms

Red Sea

Syria: nationalization of the assets of the Iraq Petroleum Company.

July 18. Egypt: Soviet military experts sent home after pressure from anti-Soviet officers.

1973

August. Egypt and Libya defer their union.

October 6. Egypt crosses the Suez Canal by surprise at the same time that Syria mounts an offensive on the Golan Heights.

October 25. Cease-fire in Syria and the Sinai (U.N. resolution 338).

November. Egyptian-Israeli military negotiations.

December 21. U.N. conference in Geneva, co-chaired by the U.S.S.R. and the U.S., boycotted by Syria.

1974

In the Arab Gulf states, majority shares (total in Qatar and Kuwait) are acquired in oil companies operating in their territories.

January 18. Agreement on mutual military "disengagement" between Israel and Egypt, and later Syria (May 31) with American mediation (Kissinger).

May 31. "Separation of Forces Agreement" (Geneva) between Israel and Syria.

November 13. Arafat, leader of the PLO, received by the U.N. General Assembly. PLO granted observer status; resolution on Palestine's right to self-determination.

1975

Border agreement between Iran and Iraq in Algiers; the deep water channel of the Shatt al-'Arab, not the Iranian shore, is now the frontier

with Iraq. Iran's support for the Kurdish rebellion in Iraq ceases. Second "disengagement" accord between Israel and Egypt, which reclaims the oil in the Sinai. Creation of an Arab Armaments Industry Organization by Egypt, Saudi Arabia, the UAE, Kuwait and Qatar.

UAR: complete control over oil production.

1976

Beginning on May 31. Syria: military intervention in Lebanon guaranteed by the Riyadh and Cairo accords, under the name of the Arab Deterrent Force (ADF) in the non-Christian zone; Beirut divided in two.

Saudi Arabia: government assumes control of ARAMCO; relations with South Yemen resumed; military and economic cooperation agreement with Egypt and Sudan (July).

Egypt: abrogation of the treaty of friendship and cooperation with the Soviets.

1977

February 22. Jordan and the PLO normalize relations.

November 19. Egypt: Sadat speaks to the Israeli Parliament.

December 25. Meeting between Begin (Israel) and Sadat in Ismailia with the aim of total resolution of the crisis. Egypt suspends the repayment of debts to Czechoslovakia and the U.S.S.R.

1978

March–June. Israeli operations in southern Lebanon; a U.N. force (UNIFIL) and a Lebanese militia headed by the Greek Catholic Major Sa'd Haddad, control the area.

September 17. Camp David accords between Egypt, Israel and the U.S. as a framework for permanent peace treaties between Israel, Egypt, Jordan, Palestine and Syria.

October. Syrian bombardment (ADF) of East Beirut (the Christian zone). U.S. sells combat planes to Egypt, Saudi Arabia and Israel.

1979

March 26. Washington Peace Treaty between Israel and Egypt stipulates self-determination for the Palestinians in the West Bank and Gaza after a period of self-government under Israeli authority; Egypt expelled from the Arab League.

Treaty of friendship and cooperation between the U.S.S.R. and South Yemen.

The armed conflict between the two Yemens resumes.

Cooperation between France and Iraq increased.

1980–1988

The Iran-Iraq War. See also: The Turkish and Iranian Middle East, Foreign Policy, page 330 onward.

1980

May. Egyptian-Israeli-U.S. negotiations on Palestinian autonomy fail.

June 13. The E.E.C. "Venice Declaration" insists on Palestinian right to self-determination, supports U.N. resolution 242, urges Israeli withdrawal and an end to the settlement policy.

September 17. Iran attacks Iraq; first Iraqi victories.

October. U.S.S.R. and Syria: treaty of friendship and cooperation. Beginning of terrorist activities in Europe

perpetrated by the Abu Nidal group under Syria's control.

1981

February. Creation of the Gulf Cooperation Council (GCC), without Iraq.

Lebanon: Israeli bombing of Syrian lines; Soviet and Syrian "missile crisis" in the Beka'a.

July. Israeli-Palestinian confrontation in southern Lebanon. On the 24th, cease-fire mediated by the U.S.

August. The Fahd peace plan proposes recognition of Israel in return for withdrawal to the 1949 frontier, an independent Palestinian state and compensation for refugees.

December 14. Syria: Israel formally announces its annexation of the Golan Heights, which had been occupied since 1967.

1982

April 26. Egypt: end of Israeli withdrawal from the Sinai.

June 6. Lebanon: Israeli invasion ("Peace for Galilee"). Syrian missiles and the Palestinian military infrastructure destroyed.

August 21. A multinational force (American, French and Italian) in Lebanon.

West Bank and Israel: strikes and riots.

September. Reagan peace plan proposes autonomous Palestinian entity confederated with Jordan.

1983

April and October. Lebanon: car bomb suicide attacks by the Hezbollah against the multinational force; 241 American and 58 French soldiers die.

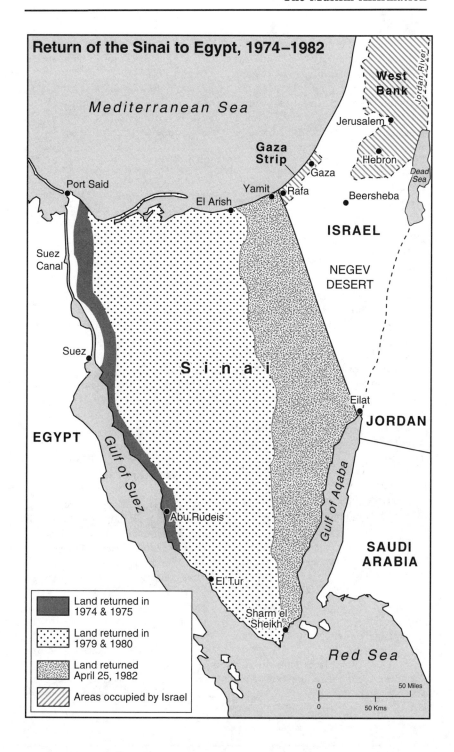

Return of the Sinai to Egypt, 1974–1982

Mediterranean Sea

West Bank

Jordan River

Jerusalem •

Hebron •

Dead Sea

Gaza Strip

• Gaza

Yamit • Rafa

• Beersheba

Port Said •

El Arish •

ISRAEL

Suez Canal

NEGEV DESERT

Suez •

S i n a i

Eilat •

JORDAN

EGYPT

Gulf of Suez

Abu Rudeis △

Gulf of Aqaba

SAUDI ARABIA

El Tur •

Sharm el Sheikh •

Red Sea

Land returned in 1974 & 1975

Land returned in 1979 & 1980

Land returned April 25, 1982

Areas occupied by Israel

0   50 Miles

0   50 Kms

May 17. Peace accord between Israel and Lebanon signed but not ratified; establishment of a security zone in southern Lebanon. Armed confrontation between Arafat and Syria.

December. Expulsion of Palestinian liberation fighters from Lebanon; new PLO headquarters set up in Tunis.

1984

Lebanon: peace treaty with Israel declared invalid under Syrian pressure. The multinational force withdraws.

1985

January. Israeli and Lebanese discussions on border security falter.

End of June. Lebanon: total Israeli withdrawal, except for a "security zone" on the border; the South Lebanese Army, headed by Major Antoine Lahad, protects the border with Israeli support. Activities of the Lebanese National Resistance Front.

September. Hijacking of the Italian cruiseliner *Achille Lauro* by Palestinian terrorists.

October 1. Israeli attack on the PLO headquarters near Tunis as reprisal.

December. Palestinian terrorist attacks at Rome and Vienna airports.

1986

Syrian troops return to West Beirut.

1987

February. Lebanon: Syria occupies West Beirut.

Egypt: agreement with the IMF to stagger its debt.

May. The U.S. places Kuwaiti vessels under American flag after Iranian attacks.

July 31. Saudi Arabia: 400 victims in Mecca after a skirmish with armed Iranian pilgrims.

December 9. Palestine: First in Gaza, then in the Israeli-occupied West Bank: beginning of a general unarmed uprising (the Intifada).

1988

March. American Shultz plan for the accelerated application of Palestinian self-rule to be followed by self-determination, refused by Israel and the PLO as well as by the leadership of the uprising. The U.S. agrees to talk to the PLO.

July 20. End of the Iran-Iraq war, with Iran's acceptance of U.N. resolution 598.

July 31. Jordan surrenders its claims to the West Bank; the PLO proclaims the State of Palestine (November 15).

December 13. Arafat, leader of the PLO, is received at the U.N. General Assembly.

1989

Official meetings of the PLO with the United States in Tunis in January, March, June and November.

February. Iraq, Egypt, Jordan and North Yemen establish the Arab Cooperation Council (ACC).

May. Palestine: Israeli plan seeking political elections in the occupied territories is partly rejected by uprising's leadership and the PLO.

September. Lebanon: the Arab League Committee obtains a cease-fire in Beirut.

October. Inter-Lebanese accord agreed to by deputies gathered in Ta'if (Saudi Arabia) calls for an egalitarian political system to replace the

6:5 majority rule in favor of Christians in effect since 1943; gradual Syrian retreat planned. Accord rejected by Aoun.

November. The West Bank and Gaza: after two years of uprisings and repression nearly 600 Palestinians and 21 Israelis are dead, 6,000 to 40,000 injured, 5,000 to 8,000 permanently incarcerated, around 60 declared expulsions, 1,000 houses destroyed or sealed off, and 100 "collaborators" assassinated.

The Economy, Society and Religion

1963

Saudi Arabia: the state opens girls' schools.

Syria: a permanent state of emergency is imposed; statist economy; violent religious demonstrations against the Ba'ath (April 15 in Hama); Muslim Brotherhood is banned.

Lebanon: social security; a central bank; code concerning money and credit.

1964

Egypt: Islam is declared to be the state religion in the constitution.

1965

January 26. Syria: violent religious demonstrations against the Ba'ath (in Damascus); large-scale nationalizations.

Iraq: large-scale nationalizations.

1967

Jordan and Syria: U.N. estimates the number of Palestinian refugees having fled the West Bank at 350,000.

1967–1973

Disastrous drought in North Yemen.

1969

North Yemen: nationalization of all foreign-owned companies, except BP.

1971

Egypt: amendment to the constitution, making the *shari'a* the main source of legislation.

1972

Lebanon: Shi'i populations south of Beirut displaced as a result of the Israeli-Palestinian conflict; Imam Musa al-Sadr forms the "Movement of the Deprived" as a mutual aid group for the Shi'is.

1974

Egypt: inauguration of Sadat's politics of *infitah*, economic opening to the West.

1975

Lebanon: Shi'i militia Amal is founded.

1976

Saudi Arabia: creation of SABIC for the petrochemical industry.

The West Bank and Galilee (Israel): "Earth Day," against acts of expropriation and confiscation.

Egypt: Muslim Brothers publish books and magazines legally.

Syria: Muslim Brotherhood launches a *jihad* against the regime.

1977

January. Egypt: worker riots in the cities set off by the high cost of living and the government decision to reduce food subsidies. Armed repression: 79 killed, 49 of whom in Cairo. The neo-Muslim Brothers begin to fill positions in universities.

Iraq: religious riots in Najaf and Karbala (again in 1979).

1978

Lebanon: Musa al-Sadr disappears while on a visit to Libya. The radical Shi'i militia Hezbollah ("Party of God") founded.

Gaza (occupied Palestine): Islamic university funded by Saudi Arabia and Jordan; 3,000 students.

1980

Syria: Formation of the oppositional Islamic Front, which includes among other groups, the Muslim Brotherhood.

1982

February. Syria: uprisings; military repression in Hama (4,000 to 15,000 dead).

Iraq: The Shi'i Supreme Assembly of the Islamic Revolution in Iraq (led by Sayyid Muhammad Baqir al-Hakim) founded in Teheran; repression.

1988

Lebanon: 130,000 dead and 4,000 hostages or M.I.A.'s, probable figures, as a result of 13 years of war; steep drop in the value of the Lebanese pound since 1987.

Iraq: Kurdish villages gassed by the government: over 5,000 killed and 100,000 displaced into Turkey.

1989

Beginning in March. Lebanon: economic blockade of East Beirut and the "Christian enclave" (pop. one million).

April. Lebanon: Syrian bombing and attack by pro-Syrian militias on East Beirut. Lebanese forces (General Aoun) bomb West Beirut (1,000 killed on both sides on September 15).

April 18–21. Jordan: riots against the high cost of living.

May 16. West Beirut: assassination of the Sunni Grand Mufti Hassan Khalid.

Iraq: after eight years of war with Iran, half a million are dead. Beginning of the reconstruction, especially in Basra and Fao.

Civilization and Culture

1966

Israel: Mahmud Darwish, *A Man In Love with Palestine*, poems.

1967

Egypt: Naguib Mahfouz, *The Children of Gebelawi* and *Miramar*, novels.

Lebanon: songs by Fairuz, among them *Al-Quds* (Jerusalem).

1968

Egypt: Kamil Husayn: *The Sacred Valley*, essay.

Lebanon: the Syrian Sadiq Jalal al-'Azm publishes *Self-Critique after the Catastrophe*, and the Syrian playwright Sa'd Wannus, *Vigil of the 5th of June*. Cinema: *The Sparrows* by Yusuf Shahin (Chahine), *Journal of a Replacement from the Country* by Tawfiq Salah.

1969

Tayyib Salih, Sudanese novelist: *The Marriage of Zayn*.

1971

Lebanon: The Complete Works of Adonis, poet.

Iraq: The Complete Works of the poet Bayati.

1974

Muslim Dogma and Human Rights, the proceedings from colloquia held by legal scholars from Saudi Arabia and Europe in Riyadh, Geneva, Rome and Paris (published in Beirut).

1975

Israel: Emil Habiby, *The Secret Life of Saeed, the Ill-fated Pessoptimist*, absurdist short stories about Palestinian life in Israel.

1980

Egypt: moderate feminism in Nawal al-Saadawi *The Hidden Face of Eve*.

1983

Egypt: modernist and liberal Muslim thought in Sa'id al-Ashmawi's *The Foundations of the Shari'a*. Cinema: *So Long, Bonaparte*, by Yusuf Shahin.

The Turkish and Iranian Middle East*

The entire territory becomes Islamic by three different paths. Turkey is the site of violent conflicts between hard-line Kemalists and "Islamists." The military intervenes and, for a while, democratic life is put on hold. A moderate Islamist movement emerges. A new corps of civil servants from this moderate group guides the country toward domestic stability, with new concessions to religious traditions, while establishing closer ties with Europe and the E.E.C.

In Iran, after the far-reaching "white revolution" (agrarian, industrial and military reform) developed and put into action by the shah, then highlighted in the 1970s by the arrival of American companies (multinationals) and by the emergence of a class of businessmen and intermediaries, there emerges an insurrectional and, eventually, revolutionary movement that gains a foothold among the Bazaar (commerce) class, led by the Shi'i "clergy." Sweeping and persistent repression intensifies this development, which eventually leads to the exile of the Shah and the election by acclamation of Ayatollah Khomeini, a recognized religious leader exiled since 1963. More repression, exercised this time against the old regime as well as its allies, the Mujahidin and the Tudeh. Assassinations are followed by repression. The "Islamic Revolution" is exported to Lebanon, but not to Iraq or the Arab Gulf in spite of the protracted war against Iraq.

Afghanistan finally follows a Marxist (though hardly native) path in its overthrow of the monarchy; against a largely popular Islamist guerrilla force, Soviet occupation comes to a close at the end of 1988.

---

*This region also includes the Muslim states of southeastern Europe that had belonged to the Ottoman Empire.

Political and Institutional Life

1964

February 27. Iran: decree concerning electoral equality gives women the vote and the right to run for office.

Afghanistan: approval of a constitution by the Grand Assembly; constitution sets up traditionally structured parliamentary regime.

1965

Turkey: electoral victory for the Justice Party (the reincarnation of the banned Democrat Party); Minister Suleyman Demirel.

January. Iran: Prime Minister Hasan Ali Mansur assassinated by the Fedayan (opposed to agarian reform); Amir Abbas Hoveyda is his successor; repression of both left-wing and right-wing extremists.

Afghanistan: first legislative elections and creation of the Afghan People's Democratic Party (Communist).

1971

March 12. Turkey: after urban violence, the army, led by General Memduh Tağmaç, forces Demirel to step down, replaces him with "populist" ministers; actions endorsed by the executive branch's amendment to the constitution.

1973

October. Turkey: elections; Minister Bülent Ecevit from the Republican Peoples Party (RPP) wins; 48 seats held by the NSP (National Salvation Party).

Afghanistan: putsch by Prince Daud (July 17); he abolishes the monarchy and establishes a republic of which he becomes president: King Zaher Shah in exile.

1974

January. Turkey: RPP/NSP coalition government.

1975

Iran: the Resurgence Party replaces all other parties.

1976

Albania: new constitution outlaws "all organizations of a religious nature."

1977

February 14. Afghanistan: new constitution passed in the Grand Assembly. Daud re-elected interim president for two years.

1978

January. Turkey: RPP victorious in elections. Ecevit, prime minister, steps down in June after pressure from the right; minority Justice Party government (October 1979).

April 27. Afghanistan: Communist coup d'état; Daud is killed, Muhammad Taraki, leader of the Marxist Khalq party, assumes full power of a Democratic Socialist Republic.

November. Iran: popular opposition movements; Azhari's military ministership.

December. Mutinies in the army; Shapur Bakhtiar appointed prime minister.

1979

January 16. Iran: Shah goes into exile.

February 1. Iran: Khomeini returns from exile in Paris and declares an Islamic republic; provisional government under Mehdi Bazargan; new constitution drafted by the Assembly of Experts (November), led by Ayatollah Beheshti; creation of new revolutionary institutions, especially the Revolutionary Guards (*pasdaran*).

November. Iran: fall of the Bazargan government.

Afghanistan: the Mujahidin alliance.

September. Amin overthrows Taraki; Amin subsequently overthrown and executed by Karmal in December.

Turkey: Minister Demirel in power once again.

1980

January 25. Iran: Bani-Sadr, Khomeini's candidate, becomes the republic's president; legislative elections in March and May, favorable to the Islamic Republican Party (IRP).

September 12. Turkey: military coup by General Kenan Evren; arrest of leading politicians; a five-man National Security Council takes control; provisional constitution (October).

1981

June. Iran: rupture within the Mujahidin; Bani-Sadr steps down (June 21); headquarters of the IRP bombed, 120 killed (June 28); prime minister's office bombed, 30 killed, among them President Raja'i.

Turkey: National Security Council dissolves all political parties, dissolves parliament, establishes martial law; installation of a new civilian government under Bülent Ulusu.

1982

November 7. Turkey: new constitu-

tion approved by referendum; features a strong president; Evren becomes president for seven years.

1983

Turkey: political life resumes. Electoral victory for the new Motherland Party (MP) (a coalition of liberal and Islamic groups); Prime Minister: Turgut Özal.

Iran: the Tudeh Communist Party outlawed and repressed.

1985

Turkey: trial against the PKK (Marxist-Kurdish group) for its armed rebellion; 22 executed.

1987

November. Afghanistan: Najibullah elected president; attempts to compromise with the Mujahidin rejected.

Turkey: lifting of the ban on the old politicians: Demirel, Ecevit, Erkaban and Türkeş, resume their activities.

1988

Afghanistan: Mujahidin Alliance rejects compromise and continues guerilla war.

May. Iran: legislative elections. Rafsanjani named president of the Parliament with broad support.

1989

February. Afghanistan: provisional government led by the Mujahidin, who make a futile attempt to take Jalalabad.

June 3. Iran: death of Khomeini. President 'Ali Khamenei takes his place as "Spiritual Guide of the Islamic Republic."

July 28. Iran: Rafsanjani elected president. Constitution is amended: presidential executive established.

October. Turkey: electoral defeat of the MP; Prime Minister Turgut Özal elected President of the Republic, takes General Evren's place on November 9.

Foreign Policy

1963

Turkey: support for the Turkish-speaking minority of Cyprus.

December. The president of Cyprus, Archbishop Makarios, announces his intention to revise the constitution, restricting the rights of the Turkish minority.

Afghanistan: Pakistani border recognized.

1964

June 4. U.S. President Johnson warns Inönü not to invade Cyprus.

1965

Turkish–U.S.S.R. trade agreement; Soviet economic aid to Turkey.

1967

U.S.-Turkey negotiations: reduction of the American military presence.

February. Iran–U.S.S.R. accords covering military equipment, railroads and oil.

1971

Iran seizes the Tunb islands and Abu Musa in the Gulf in a dispute with Iraq.

1974

After coup d'état, and the intention to implement union with Greece, new civil conflict in Cyprus; Turkey begins armed intervention (July 20),

settles 50,000 Turks in the Turkish Republic of Cyprus (in the north).

1975

February. U.S. military aid to Turkey officially suspended; in retaliation, Turkey halts work operations at U.S. military installations.

Iranian-Afghan agreement for major Iranian foreign aid.

1975

Iraq gives in to Iran's demand that the deep-water channel of the Shatt al-'Arab, and not the Iranian shore, constitute the border between both countries.

1976

Reopening of U.S. military bases in Turkey.

1977

Soviet–Afghan economic cooperation agreement.

1978

August. End of the arms embargo on Turkey. Turkish–U.S.S.R. document of friendship.

1979

Iran (Islamic Republic): breaks with Israel and opens talks with the PLO; breaks with the U.S. by storming the embassy and taking hostages.

End of December. Afghanistan: at Karmal's request, armed Soviet intervention.

1980

January 14. Afghanistan: U.N. demands Soviet withdrawal.

May. E.E.C. suspends all contracts

with Iran entered into after November 4, 1979.

June. Violent clashes with the Islamic resistance around Kabul.

September 21. Beginning of the Iran-Iraq war: Iraqi offensive in Arabic-speaking Khuzistan; capture of Khorramshahr.

1981

Iraqis advance into Iranian territory.

January 20. Iran frees American hostages who have been held in the Embassy.

March. Afghanistan: first American military support to the Islamic resistance.

1982

April and June. Iranian advances push the front back to the original border.

1983

Iran: Soviet diplomats expelled; offensives against Iraq continue in the center, the south and the north (Kurdistan).

1984

Military stalemate in the Iran-Iraq War; Iraqi offer of a cease-fire rejected.

1985

September. Iran: Iraq attacks with Mirage fighter planes on loan from France.

1986

In the Iran-Iraq War, Iran has the upper hand in the Iraqi Gulf and at Basra; capture of Fao; first Iranian attacks on foreign (especially Ku-

---

The Shatt al-'Arab, the Arab Coast

The eastern bank of this large estuary of the conjoined Tigris and Euphrates rivers is given to Iran by the 1847 Treaty of Erzerum between the Ottoman Empire (of which Iraq was a province) and Iran. Abadan and the port of Khorramshahr in Arabic-speaking Khuzistan are also given to Iran. A conflict ensues and lasts until the Teheran (1911) and Constantinople (1913) protocols, which in 1914 draw permanent borders, recognized only by the treaty of 1937. A new crisis results, on the borders in general and in the Shatt al-'Arab specifically, in 1958 and 1968. In 1969, Iran repeals the treaty of 1937, and Iraq claims all of Khuzistan, also known as Arabistan, in the name of the "Arab Nation."

An agreement is finally reached in Algiers on March 6, 1975 in which the boundaries drawn in 1914 are applied but the waters are split down the middle (the *thalweg* line), benefiting Iran. Iraq publicly contests this decision and, claiming Khuzistan once again, launches an attack against Iran in September of 1980. This war results neither in the conquest of Khuzistan nor the control of the Shatt al-'Arab, but it does damage many Gulf ports. Peace negotiations undertaken on August 25, 1988 review this question, with Iran seeking the perpetuation of the Algiers accord and Iraq its revision.

waiti) oil tankers; Iraqi chemical weapons discovered in Iran; U.N. condemnation; Iran supports terrorist acts committed in Paris; American, French, British and Italian warships in the Gulf to protect their tankers.

1987

January. Afghanistan: Islamic Resistance rejects offers from the government and the Soviets.

May. The U.S. places Kuwaiti vessels under U.S. flag.

July 20. In the Iran-Iraq War, U.N. resolution 598 demands a cease-fire and peace negotiations between both countries. Iran refuses, war of positions follows.

July 31. Saudi Arabia: 400 victims in Mecca after a conflict with armed Iranian pilgrims. Turkey submits a formal application to join the E.E.C.; fails to fulfill the necessary requirements.

1988

April 14. In Geneva, the Pakistan–Afghanistan and U.S.-U.S.S.R. agreements call for complete Soviet withdrawal prior to mid-February 1989. Progressive retreat, under continuous fire from the Islamic Resistance (absent from negotiations).

August 20. End of the Iran-Iraq War, after Iraqi advances (recovery of Fao).

August 25. Peace negotiations in Geneva between Iran and Iraq.

1989

January. Afghanistan–U.S.S.R.: Soviet negotiations with the Mujahidin in Islamabad (Pakistan) falter.

February. End of the Soviet military withdrawal; the Afghan Islamic Provisional Government recognized most notably by Pakistan and Saudi Arabia.

February. Iran: the Rushdie affair; Salman Rushdie publishes his novel *The Satanic Verses*, which some Muslims consider derogatory toward Islam and the Prophet Muhammad. Massive demonstrations in many Islamic countries against Rushdie. Khomeini issues a *fatwa*, offering a large sum of money to anyone who assassinates Rushdie. Rushdie has to go underground. Rupture with Great Britain.

June. Iran: Rafsanjani in Moscow; 10-year economic and military cooperation accords.

The Economy, Society and Religion

1963

January. Iran: laws concerning agrarian reform and the emancipation of women; disturbances in Teheran under the leadership of Ayatollah Ruhollah Khomeini; military intervention.

June. Religious uprising against these laws.

Turkey: trade unions granted right to strike.

1964

Turkey: anti-American sentiments after the crisis in Cyprus.

Afghanistan: sizable highway projects; refurbishing of the University of Kabul.

October. Iran: Khomeini exiled to Turkey.

1965

Afghanistan: student protests.

Iran: second phase of agrarian reform; plots of land of no more than 300 acres distributed to 11.5 million people.

Turkey: Khomeini moves to Najaf (Iraq).

1966

Iran: Mujahedin-e Khalq formed; oppositional group, Marxist and radical modernist religious thought.

1967

Iran: Family Protection Law, modest emancipation of women; women's right in divorce increased.

Albania: all places of worship closed.

1968

Iran: success of agrarian reform: 8,000 cooperatives for 20,000 villages. First steelworks constructed with Soviet aid. Catastrophic earthquake: 20,000 dead.

Turkey: student protests (mostly anti-American); assassination attempts by the leftist group, "Dev Genç."

1970

Iran: annual growth in G.N.P. of 8.6 percent, with an investment rate of 20 percent of G.N.P. since 1965. Success of the "white revolution."

1971

Turkey: state of siege; special tribunals; continuation of assassination attempts and social unrest.

Iran: beginning of armed revolt against government by the Mujahedin-e Khalq, and the Fedayan-e Khalq.

1973-1976

Accelerated economic growth in the region after the oil boom comes to an abrupt end in 1976.

1974

Turkey: new land reform act, reducing the size of landholdings.

1975

Iran: all publications with a circulation of less than 3,000 closed.

1977

Turkey: a bloody 1st of May. The 1974 land reform act is annulled by the constitutional court.

1978

January. Iran: popular riots in Qom after an attack on Khomeini in a government-controlled newspaper; spread of riots.

August. Conciliation toward the religious rebels — Islamic calender reinstated; casinos and night clubs closed.

September. Demonstrations in Teheran; imposition of martial law; casualties among the demonstrators.

1979

February. Iran: work resumes, numerous executions.

Popular rebellions in Kurdistan, Turkmenistan, Baluchistan and Arabic-speaking Khuzistan; armed militias set up to maintain the Islamic moral order.

March. Iran: protests by women against the chador obligation.

Soviet Muslim republics: many mosques reopened after having been closed since 1959. According to sociological studies on religion, only 20 percent of Muslims consider themselves to be atheist and religious marriages remain popular.

June–July. Iran: nationalization of banks and large manufacturing enterprises.

1980

April. Iran: radical land reform reduces size of landholdings.

1981

Iran: repression aimed at the Mujahidin Party (now illegal).

1982

January. Iran: executions; Amnesty International estimates over 4,000 executed since February 1979.

August. Turkey: assassination attempts by Armenian activists; mandatory teaching of the Qur'an in primary and secondary schools (the new constitution).

1983

May. Turkey: massive repression of the Kurds.

Iran: massive repression of the Tudeh Party (Communist).

1988

Turkey: after four years of repression of the Kurds (who joined the PKK rebels), more than 1,500 dead; around 100,000 Kurdish refugees in Iraq; positive governmental declarations toward the Kurds.

February and November. In Soviet Azerbaijan and Armenia, pogroms by the Azeris (Muslims) against the Armenians.

July. Iran: after eight years of war with Iraq, about 500,000 dead.

Afghanistan: after eight years of war, one million dead, five million refugees (three million in Pakistan, two million in Iran).

December. Iran: thousands of political prisoners executed (according to Amnesty International).

1989

February. Yugoslavia: "extreme measures" in Kosovo after a general strike by the population of Muslim-Albanian descent (90%) and Serbian protests in Belgrade against "Albanian" separatism.

February 14. Iran: Khomeini declares in a *fatwa* that the Muslim British author, Rushdie, of the *Satanic Verses* deserves to die for his public apostasy.

February 18. Afghanistan: state of emergency in Kabul and in the countryside controlled by the Najibullah government.

June and October. Turkey: influx of almost 300,000 Turkish refugees from Bulgaria.

Civilization and Culture

1963

Turkey: novels by Yakub Kadri; peasant novels by Yashar Kemal.

Iran: The Qur'anic Commentary by Muhammad Husayn Tabataba'i, with modernist tendencies, appears in Arabic. Mohammad Ali Jamal-Zadeh: *Sky and String*, a popular novel. Cinema: *The Cow* and *The Cycle* by Daryush Mehrjui.

1970

Iran: Morteza Mottahari, cleric, dies in 1979, *The Foundations of Islamic Thought* and *Man-God-Universe; Islamology*, a modernist catechism by Ali

Shariati, a lay priest who dies in 1977.

1973

Turkey: death of Ashik Veysel; his last poems published. Films by Yilmaz Güney: *Yol* and *The Wall.*

1980

Albania: Ismail Kadare, *The H File* (Homeric), novel; *Broken April,* poems.

1989

February. Iran: The Rushdie affair.

Islam in the Far East

The Federation of Malaysia moves toward independence, even though its territory is claimed by Indonesia, which enters into an era of confrontation with Malaysia until being shaken by the murderous rise to power of the pro-Muslim and anti-Communist opposition: massive massacres of Chinese Communists evoke memories of genocides. The new military regime and the Indonesian "new order" bring economic growth to their countries, even if they have to face occasionally violent Islamist movements. Malaysia establishes itself as the richest country in the region. Indonesian society seems to have evolved towards a *santri* (devout Muslim) civilization, eliminating the old cleavage between *santri* and *abangan* (nominal Muslims).

In Pakistan, a civil but strong regime continues the process of Westernization and, without much resistance, allows the secessionist state of Bangladesh to form. Bangladesh adopts a more Islamic system, based on "Islamic Social Justice." This diminished Pakistan is then taken over by an Islamist colonel who, at least in form, institutes the *shari'a* as the basis for social, economic and legal life. After his allegedly accidental death, a certain Islamic compromise is established. Pakistan's direct support of the neighboring Afghan Islamic Resistance forces it to accept an enormous number of resistance fighters who become refugees, and to negotiate a peace agreement with the Afghan regime and the U.S.S.R., without being able to put an end to the guerrilla war.

In the Organization of the Islamic Conference and in international congresses on Islam, Pakistani and Indian contributions are quite noticeable; the conferences and congresses sketch out the future of Muslim thought in politics and economics.

Political and Institutional Life

1963

Indonesia: Sukarno named president for life: the Federation of Malaysia established, including Malaya, Singapore, Sabah (North Borneo), and Sarawak (Northwest Borneo).

1965

August 9. Singapore withdraws from the Federation of Malaysia in order to lessen tensions between the Chinese majority in Singapore and the Malays who control the Malaysian government.

October. Indonesia: following an aborted coup by the Indonesian Communist Party, the army massacres over 300,000 Communists, imprisons and deports millions more.

Pakistan: General Muhammad Ayyub Khan re-elected president.

1968

Indonesia: General Suharto named president.

1969

Referendum in Irian (originally scheduled for 1963) results in Irian joining Indonesia.

March. Pakistan: after months of violent unrest in East Pakistan, Ayyub Khan steps down, succeeded by General Muhammad Yahya Khan; martial law. Concessions to the Bengalis, workers and political parties.

1970

Pakistan: first elections (December) for a constitutive assembly; in the East, victory for the Awami League (led by Mujibur Rahman, Bengali separatist); in the West, for the Pakistan People's Party (led by Zulfikar Ali Bhutto). Crisis in Bengal leads to repression.

Malaysia: end of Abdul Rahman's government.

1971

March. Pakistan: Mujibur Rahman seeks autonomy; postpones the Assembly; rioting and strikes in the East.

March 25. Government troops launch attacks in the East.

December. Separate state of Bangladesh formed in Pakistan; Yahya Khan steps down; Ali Bhutto is his successor.

Indonesia: gains by the Muslim parties in the elections (29%).

1973

Pakistan: new constitution.

1976

December 16. Surrender of Pakistani troops in the East; cease-fire one day later.

December 24. The Philippines: cease-fire agreed to with the "Moro" Muslim Separatist Front, the MNLF, which is based in southern Mindanao.

1977

July. Pakistan: General Zia ul-Haq takes power in a military coup. Martial law, political parties dissolved, Bhutto convicted and executed (April 4, 1979).

1978

The Philippines: activities by the Moro Front (MNLF) resume.

1979

Discovery and repression of a "Jihad Commando" in northern Sumatra and Java and of the "Islamic Republic of Indonesia" in Bandung.

1981

May 30. Bangladesh: assassination of Mujibur Rahman in an unsuccessful coup attempt by army rivals.

November 15. Abbas Satar becomes vice president.

Malaysia: Mahatir Mohammad succeeds Hussein Oun as prime minister.

1982

March 24. Bangladesh: military coup led by General Ershad.

1983

March 10. Indonesia: Suharto re-elected.

December 31. Brunei: independence from Malaysia; Muslim sultanate.

1986

Benazir Bhutto, Zulfikar Ali Bhutto's daughter, returns from exile in Europe; attempts to relaunch the Pakistan People's Party (PPP); violence and anti-government riots.

1987

April. Indonesia: Suharto's party victorious.

December. Bangladesh: political protests against Ershad.

1988

August 17. Pakistan: death of President Zia ul-Haq when his plane explodes.

November. Benazir Bhutto (leader of the PPP) wins the election against the Islamic Alliance (AID). Ershad declares Bangladesh an Islamic Republic.

Foreign Policy

1963

Irian granted to Indonesia by Holland; relations resume. Great Britain pulls out of Malaysia.

Indonesia: seen to be hostile to the Federation of Malaysia and judged to be pro-American and pro-British; policy of "confrontation"; raids into Malaysian territory.

1966

January. End of the war in the Punjab; Indian-Pakistani accord signed in Tashkent with Soviet mediation. Indonesian-Malaysian agreement ends hostilities.

1969

December. Philippine-Indonesian agreement over Sabah (Muslims).

1970

Suharto in Holland; results in reconciliation.

1971

December. Armed Indian intervention on the side of Bengali secessionists.

1972

July 3. Pakistan-India pact provides for withdrawal of troops from their borders.

1975

Indonesia: annexation of East Timor (formerly a Portuguese territory).

1980

Pakistan: political and military support for Afghan popular resistance.

1987

Sultan of Brunei donates $10 million to the Nicaraguan Contras.

1988

April 14. Pakistan participates in agreement on Soviet withdrawal from Afghanistan.

1989

March and May. Bangladesh: agreement with France for the construction of an anti-flood sewer system.

The Economy, Society and Religion

1963

Indonesia: peasant protests.

Federation of Malaysia: rapid economic growth.

1971

Beginning on March 28. Seven to ten million Bengali refugees in India.

Malaysia: Anwar Ibrahim establishes the "Malaysian Muslim Youth Movement," the ABIM.

China: anti-Muslim persecution begun in 1966 comes to an end.

1973

Indonesia: the Marriage Bill replaced by a law acceptable to all Islamists.

1974

January. Indonesia: student protests, riots in Jakarta.

1977

Indonesia: student protests in Bandung; many are detained.

March. Pakistan: motivated by the ANP, general strike against Ali Bhutto; 55 killed in riots.

1980

Pakistan: close to 500,000 Afghan refugees from the Islamic Resistance.

1984

Pakistan: plebiscite in favor of increased Islamization.

September. Indonesia: revolt led by Tanjung Priok, with participation from the "Pop Muslims."

1988

Pakistan: new inter-ethnic conflicts.

Bangladesh: over 4,000 dead, 30 million homeless, as a result of natural disasters.

1989

February. India: protests (12 deaths) in Bombay against Salman Rushdie's text, following Khomeini's pronouncement of the *fatwa*.

Pakistan: British Cultural Center attacked (1 dead), in protest over Rushdie.

Civilization and Culture

1980

Indonesia: P. Ananta Taer: *The Land of Men*, a saga.

1984

Pakistan: death of Faiz Ahmad Faiz, poet.

Sub-Saharan Africa

Islam does not represent one of the dominant ideologies in the independent African states, except in the Sudan and, to a certain extent, in northern Nigeria. Islam's return to prominence after 1967 is strictly linked to closer ties with the Arab world. The two Israeli-Arab wars (1967 and 1973) led to the rupture of diplomatic relations between the African continent and Israel. Throughout this period, the development of political and economic African-Arab relations, bilateral as well as multilateral, is mirrored by the development of similar religious ties (e.g., the Islamic World League).

Three sub-Saharan states dominate the scene in the Islamic domain: Senegal, Nigeria and the Sudan. In these three states, brotherhoods rooted in local history witness the rise of antagonistic fundamentalist movements (often referred to as "Wahhabis"). Nevertheless, with the exception of the Sudan, political manifestations of Islam remain limited. African Muslims today are looking for ways to escape the relative isolation and provincialism that still characterize parts of their communities.

1962–1963

Ethiopia: annexation of Eritrea. The Unionists and Muslims make up the membership of the opposition (the Eritrean Liberation Front, created in 1960), with support from Arab states.

Sudan: Missionary Societies Act, limits the activities of Christian missionaries. Missionaries expelled in 1962 and 1963. An insurrection rises in the south against measures encouraging Arabization and Islamization; the SANU (Sudan African National Union) party and an army, dubbed Anyanya, formed.

1964

January 12. Zanzibar: revolution supported by the African population ("African-Shirazi"); the sultanate of Zanzibar and its Arab rulers are overthrown.

October 29. Creation of Tanzania (Tanganyika and Zanzibar).

1966

January 15. Nigeria: coup d'état organized by Ibo officers. Sir Ahmadu Bello, a descendant of Usman dan Fodio, *sardauna* (governor) of Sokoto, and prime minister of northern Nigeria, is killed. The cycle of violence will ultimately lead to the Biafra war.

Chad: birth in Sudan of the Chadian National Liberation Front. Officially non-Islamic, the group in fact recruits Muslims from north and central Chad.

1967

January 4. Tanzania: English replaced by Swahili as government language.

March 22. Senegal: Mustafa Lo attempts to assassinate President Senghor at the Great Mosque of Dakar on the day of Tabaski (also called 'Id al-Kabir); he is condemned to death.

May 19. Mauritania: Arabic-French bilingualism made official.

May 30. Nigeria: secession of Biafra. Political conflict with the Federation of Nigeria, which favors expressions of denominational solidarity (Muslims in Nigeria, Christians in Biafra). General Gowon, the Nigerian chief of state, is Christian.

June 5. Guinea: breaks off diplomatic relations with Israel.

Sudan: state of war with Israel; a military contingent sent to Egypt.

August 29. Sudan: fourth Arab summit opens in Khartoum.

1969

Sudan: Tayyib Salih's novel, *Migration to the North*, published.

Sudan: a Revolutionary Council takes power; appointment of a civilian premier and cabinet; the 12 Northern Arab-Muslim provinces dominate government.

1970

January 12. Nigeria: capitulation of the Biafran secessionists; over one million casualties.

March 26. Sudan: the Ansars (Mahdists) attempt to assassinate General Nimeiry. The movement's imam, al-Hadi al-Mahdi, the Mahdi's grandson, is killed on the Ethiopian border (March 31).

1971-1972

Senegal: debate over the Family Code. Religious dignitaries oppose a Western-type code for the status of women, marriage, divorce and inheritance. Although officially adopted, it is poorly applied.

1972

Uganda, Chad, Congo and Niger break off diplomatic relations with Israel.

February 28. Sudan: Addis Ababa accord between the Sudanese government and rebels from the south, regional autonomy for the south.

March. Third Islamic conference in Jidda: 30 Muslim states from Africa and Asia take part; six states from sub-Saharan Africa—Mauritania, Niger, Senegal, Sierra Leone, Somalia and Chad—participate for the first time.

1973

Successive ruptures of diplomatic ties to Israel: Mali (January), Burundi (May), Togo (September), Botswana, Cameroon, Central African Republic, Dahomey, Ethiopia, Gambia, Ghana, Equitorial Guinea, Upper Volta, Kenya, Madagascar, Nigeria, Rwanda, Senegal, Sierra Leone, Tanzania, Zaire and Zambia (October), the Ivory Coast and Libya (November). Gabon "suspends" relations (November).

1973

A series of delegations sent to sub-Saharan Africa by the Islamic World League: Mali, Uganda and Senegal (May), Cameroon, Dahomey, Ghana, Upper Volta, Niger, Nigeria, Chad and Togo (June).

September. Gabon: President Albert-Bernard Bongo converts to Islam; assumes the name of Omar Bongo.

November 26-28. Algeria: ninth summit of Arab leaders in Algiers; reinforcement of African-Arab cooperation; creation of the Arab Bank for the Economic Development of Africa.

November. Mauritania joins the Arab League.

1974

February 14. Somalia joins the Arab League.

February 22-24. Islamic summit in Lahore (Pakistan). Ten sub-Saharan African states join the OIC (a coalition of Muslim and partially Muslim states): Gabon, Guinea, Guinea-Bissau, Upper Volta, Mauritania, Niger, Uganda, Senegal, Somalia and Chad.

1975

July 26. Death, in London, of al-Haj-Ibrahim Niasse, leader of the Tijani branch of Kaolack (Senegal), vice president of the Islamic World League for several years, member of other international Muslim institutions.

1976

April 19-22. Dakar: first two-party conference of African and Arab Foreign ministers adopts a declaration that condemns imperialism, Zionism and apartheid.

May. Nouakchott: first African Islamic conference, based on the initiative of the Islamic World League.

December 26. End of the work by the African Council of Islamic Coordination, a section of the Islamic World League. The organization's seat, with diplomatic immunity, is in Dakar.

1977

Djibouti joins the Arab League.

March 7–9. African-Arab summit in Cairo. Declaration on African-Arab cooperation signed by the 59 members of the Organization for African Unity and the Arab League.

1979

August. Senegal: El Haj Ahmed Khalifa Niasse attempts to create a Hezbollahi Islamic party based on the Iranian model. The movement is outlawed; its founder seeks refuge in Libya (December).

1980

December 12–28. Nigeria: test of strength between a Mahdist neo-Islamic sect known as Mai Tatsiné, founded by a convert of Cameroonian descent, Muhammad Marwa, and the Nigerian authorities. The sect's "prophet" is killed; more than 4,000 dead according to government figures.

1981

Libya and Chad announce intention to unite; Libyan troops that had entered Chad in December 1980 withdraw after French protests.

1982

June 7. Chad: Hissène Habré arrives in N'Djamena. The National Union and Transition Government led by Goukouni Oueddei falls apart after attacks by rebel forces; he seeks refuge in Libya. The regime, a branch of the Chadian National Liberation Front, is emblematic of the Islamic north's domination over the south, but the state remains secular.

October 26. Nigeria: new riots provoked by the Mai Tatsiné sect leave 450 dead; on the 28th, lesser confrontations in Kaduna.

1983

September. Sudan: General Nimeiry proclaims the *shari'a* (Islamic law), which sets off an armed insurrection in the south.

Senegal: birth of two militant Islamic journals, hostile to the secular state: *Wal Fajri* and *Jamra.*

Chad: France sends 3,000 troops to assist Habré in opposing Libyan-backed rebels.

1984

February 24. Nigeria: confrontations with the Mai Tatsiné sect; seven days of fighting in the streets leaves 700 dead.

1986

August. Sudan: following the overthrow of General Nimeiry's regime, Sadiq al-Mahdi, great-grandson of the Mahdi, becomes prime minister.

October. Niger: an Islamic university opened in Say for regional vocational training. Its creation had been decided at the Islamic summit in Lahore (1974).

1987

Chad forces drive Libyan forces out of the country.

1989

June 30. Sudan: bloodless military coup by General Omar al-Beshir, supported by the Muslim Brothers. Constitution suspended, Parliament dissolved, political parties and unions outlawed.

After the Cold War

The fragmentation of the Soviet Union gives rise to a new world order. Regional and local conflicts, which so far had been dormant under the umbrella of American-Soviet competition, become internationalized. Islamic movements fill the void left by the disappearance of the global struggle between Communism and capitalism. While most Middle Eastern states support U.S. intervention in Iraq on behalf of occupied Kuwait, Islamic fundamentalist groups condemn the deployment of foreign forces on Arab soil. In Algeria, the Islamic Salvation Front (FIS) wins democratic elections. But the government, fearing the establishment of an Islamic state, declares the elections null and void. Egyptian fundamentalists continue to battle the government in the south, causing the billion-dollar tourist industry to come to almost a complete standstill. Serbs in the former Yugoslavia wage a relentless war against their Muslim countrymen, practicing a policy of "ethnic cleansing." Neither arms shipments from Islamic states (foremost Iran), nor peacekeeping missions by the U.N. and NATO can put an end to this war. The Islamic Republic of Iran faces serious internal pressure from parts of the population dissatisfied with the reign of the Mullahs. In addition, the United States keeps trying to marginalize Iran because of its sponsorship of Islamic terrorist organizations. Turkey and Iran compete for influence in the now-independent Islamic republics of the former Soviet Union. The Kurds strive for an independent state, repeatedly provoked by Turkish intervention in northern Iraq, in spite of an American-imposed no-fly zone.

Israeli occupation of the West Bank, Gaza, the Golan Heights and southern Lebanon further strengthens Islamic opposition. During the Cold War, Israel had supported fundamentalist groups to balance the secular Palestinian struggle for independence, led by the PLO. Now it changes its policy, evoking an "Islamic menace" similar to the former "Communist threat." In this way, Israel intends to remain indispensable to the West. As a fortress against a rising tide of Islamic fundamentalism, it hopes to attract Western support. Fundamentalists in the region want the liberation of Israeli-occupied territories. In Lebanon, Hezbollah's aim is to liberate the southern "security zone" from Israel. In occupied Palestine and Gaza, Hamas fights for the establishment of an independent Palestinian state.

Among the positive developments are the Palestinian-Israeli peace agreement, the end of the civil war in Lebanon and the integration of Islamic fundamentalists into the Jordanian parliamentary system.

It seems inevitable that Islamic movements will become serious players in regional and international politics. As the great powers no longer have the will to pacify such movements for the sake of regional stability, Islamic groupings will become competitors for political influence in their countries of origin. Moreover, they will become instruments in the foreign policy of states that aspire to regional hegemony.

1989

August 29. PLO denied admission to the World Tourism Organization of the U.N. as representative of Palestine and as a state observer.

October 3. Assassination of the Belgian Jewish leader Joseph Wybran in Brussels. The Shi'i Soldiers for the Right (a.k.a. Soldiers of Justice) claim responsibility.

October 4. Amal commander Fawaz Yunis is sentenced to 55 years in prison in Washington, D.C., for hijacking a Jordanian jet (June 1985) with two American passengers on board.

December 6. U.S. State Department releases the official version of the Baker Plan for Israeli-Palestinian peace.

1990

January 21. Soviet Union allows PLO to upgrade its Moscow mission to an embassy.

August 2. U.N. Security Council resolution 660 condemns the Iraqi invasion of Kuwait, threatens sanctions. The U.S., Great Britain, Italy, the Netherlands, Norway and West Germany freeze Kuwaiti and Iraqi assets.

August 4. The European Community imposes an oil embargo on Iraq and Kuwait.

August 9. U.N. Security Council resolution 662 declares Iraq's annexation of Kuwait null and void.

August 10. 12 of 20 Arab states decide to send troops to Saudi Arabia and other Gulf states to prevent Iraqi aggression.

August 19. East Germany announces that it will end its military training of PLO members.

August 23. Oil prices rise close to $32 per barrel.

September 12. The Muslim World League supports Saudi Arabia's decision to let non-Muslim forces defend the country against Iraq.

September 16. U.S. President Bush addresses Iraq in a eight-minute speech on Iraqi television. Saddam-Hussein responds in a 76-minute speech on U.S. television on September 25.

October 12. U.N. Security Council resolution 617 condemns the Israeli

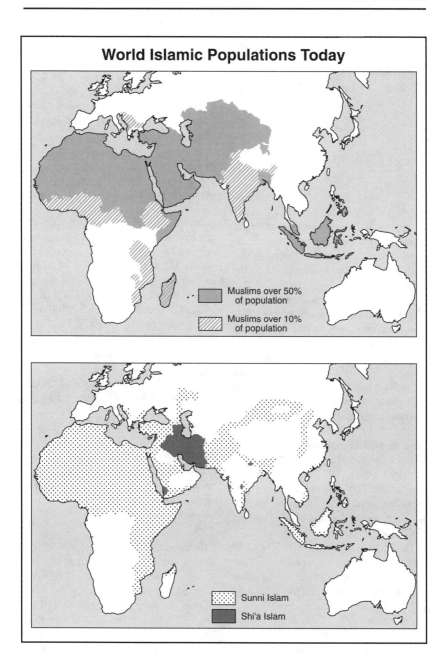

World Islamic Populations Today

Muslims over 50% of population

Muslims over 10% of population

Sunni Islam

Shi'a Islam

killing of 18 Palestinians on October 8.

November 29. U.N. Security Council resolution 678 gives Iraq until January 15, 1991 to comply with previous resolutions. Yemen and Cuba vote against the resolution.

December 5. For the first time in two years, Salman Rushdie emerges from hiding in London.

1991

January 4. France proposes a seven-point plan to settle the crisis in the Gulf, including an international peace conference. U.S. objects to the proposal.

January 12. U.S. Congress grants President Bush the authority to wage war against Iraq to force a troop withdrawal from Kuwait.

April 3. U.N. Security Council resolution 687 calls for a permanent cease-fire, concessions of Iraq, and the destruction of Iraqi biological, chemical and ballistic weapons.

April 5. U.N. Security Council resolution 688 condemns Iraqi oppression of the Kurds.

August 15. U.N. Security Council resolution 706 permits Iraq to sell some oil and establishes an escrow account for settlement of war-related claims against Iraq.

October 30–November 4. Madrid peace conference; Israel, Jordan, Lebanon, Syria, and representatives of Palestine participate; the U.S. and the Soviets are sponsors.

November 21. Egyptian deputy prime minister Boutros Boutros-Ghali is nominated U.N. Secretary-General.

December 10–18. Bilateral peace talks between Israel and Syria, Israel and Lebanon, and Israel, Jordan and Palestine in Washington, D.C.

1992

January 14–16. Third round of bilateral peace talks in Washington, D.C.

January 28. Multilateral peace talks in Moscow.

February 26–March 4. Fourth round of bilateral peace talks in Washington, D.C.

March 31. U.N. Security Council resolution 748 calls for sanctions against Libya unless Libya extradites six of its citizens accused of being involved in the bombings of Pan Am Flight 103 and UTA Flight 772.

April 27–30. Fifth round of bilateral peace talks in Washington, D.C.

August 24–September 24. Sixth round of bilateral peace talks in Washington, D.C.

October 21–November 19. Seventh round of bilateral peace talks in Washington, D.C.

December 7–December 18. Eighth round of bilateral peace talks in Washington, D.C.

December 18. U.N. Security Council resolution 799 condemns Israel's expulsion of 417 Palestinians.

1993

February 26. Bombing of the World Trade Center in New York by followers of the Egyptian cleric Shaykh 'Umar 'Abd al-Rahman.

April 27–May 13. Ninth round of bilateral peace talks in Washington, D.C.

June 15–July 1. Tenth round of bilateral peace talks in Washington.

July 2. Shaykh 'Umar 'Abd al-Rahman turns himself in to authorities in New York. The shaykh is suspected of being involved in the February 26 bombing of the World Trade Center.

August 16. A U.S. district court rejects an appeal of the deportation order against Shaykh 'Abd al-Rahman.

August 31. Eleventh round of bilateral peace talks in Washington, D.C.

September 13. In Washington, D.C., the PLO and Israel sign a Declaration of Principles on Palestinian self-rule in Gaza and Jericho.

1994

January 18. Independent counsel

Walsh's final report on the Iran-Contra affair states that President Reagan and Vice President Bush did not break the law.

January 24–February 3. Twelfth round of bilateral peace talks in Washington, D.C.

March 18. U.N. unanimously passes a resolution condemning the Hebron massacre. The U.S. insists on a paragraph-by-paragraph vote, abstaining on a paragraph that implies that Jerusalem is part of Israeli-occupied territory.

March 20. 6,000 Kurds riot in Augsburg, Germany, throw firebombs, set fire to a train in Wiesbaden, and demonstrate in Berlin.

The Maghrib

Political and Institutional Life

1989

July 19. Algeria: new electoral laws adopted by the National Assembly.

September 10. Algeria: resignation of Prime Minister Merbah; Hamrouche succeeds him.

September 14. Algeria: government recognizes the Islamic Salvation Front (FIS).

December 15. Tunisia: several days of student demonstrations at secondary schools and colleges.

1990

January 24. Tunisia: about 800 fundamentalists attack the building housing the governate in Sidi Bu-Zayd.

April 20. Algeria: a demonstration

by the FIS in Algiers draws tens of thousands. They demand presidential commitment to the *shari'a.*

May 10. A peaceful anti-Islamist march in Algiers.

June 9. Aborted coup attempt by army officers against President Bendjedid.

June 12. Municipal and provincial elections. The FIS wins 32 of 48 provinces, controls 853 of 1,535 municipal councils.

July 24. Libya: Fatah Revolutionary Council leader Abu Nidal is allegedly imprisoned.

August 30. Tunisia: the weeklies *al-Watan,* and *Les Annonces* are banned for publishing libelous material about Saudi Arabia.

November 6. Algeria: as an austerity measure, Algeria plans to close 14 embassies and 10 constituencies around the world.

December 14. Morocco: general strike by state employees.

December 27. Algeria: demonstrations by more than 100,000 after the approval of a law to make Arabic the official language.

1991

January 14. Tunisia: Salah Khalaf, a.k.a. Abu Iyad, assassinated by his bodyguard. Abu Iyad was second-in-command of the PLO, and one of the three founders of Fatah.

May 25. Algeria: nationwide strike called by the FIS; disturbances follow.

June 5. Declaration of a four-month state of emergency after 12 days of FIS-incited disturbances.

June 30–July 1. 700–2,500 demonstrators arrested.

November 17. Report that the government had deported al-Nahda leader Rashid al-Ghannoushi to Sudan several weeks earlier.

December 17. President Asad pardons 1,070 people celebrating the November 7 coup.

December 22. Over 100,000 participate in FIS rally.

December 26. Parliamentary elections. FIS gains 188 out of 430 possible seats.

1992

January 2. Algeria: 135,000 demonstrate against takeover by the FIS.

January 4. Tunisia: President Ben Ali urges Arab countries to repress Islamic movements and their leaders.

January 11. Algeria: President Benjedid resigns.

January 12. Newly formed "High Security Council" declares the first round of the parliamentary elections

null and void, and cancels runoff elections.

January 16. Muhammad Boudiaf returns from 28 years exile in Morocco after being appointed head of the Higher State Council.

February 9. Higher State Council declares a one-year state of emergency and dissolves the FIS.

February 20. FIS report says 14,000 people arrested between February 6–13.

March 12. Interior Ministry reports shows 9,000 people arrested since the beginning of the year.

April 2. Libya: demonstrations in Tripoli against U.N. Security Council resolution 748.

April 14. Libya cuts international telephone and postal lines, blocks air, land, and sea travel for 24 hours in protest against U.N. Security Council resolution 748.

June 15. Tunisia: Tunisian League for the Defense of Human Rights, the oldest and most influential human rights monitoring organization in the Middle East, dissolves itself, after the government attempts to infiltrate it.

June 29. Algeria: Higher State Council head Boudiaf assassinated.

September 4. Morocco: referendum on the revision of the Constitution; 97% of the electorate participates.

December 13. Algeria: activities of six Islamic organizations suspended.

December 24. Destruction of all unofficial mosques ordered.

1993

March 22. Algeria: about 80,000 demonstrate in Algiers to protest growing violence.

June 25. Morocco: parliamentary

elections. Government coalition wins 116 out of 222 seats.

August 7. Algeria: 34 Islamists sentenced to death, 29 of them *in absentia.*

August 22. Assassination of former prime minister Kasdi Merbah.

October 7–14. Libya: military revolt in Misratah, Tarhua, Gharitiah, Bani Walid and Brak over the lack of salaries; about 300 casualties.

October 31–November 4. Algeria: during an nationwide army operation, 40 people killed.

1994

January 30. Algeria: Defense Minister Zeroual appointed president by the High Command Council of State.

March 12. About 940 inmates escape from the Tazoult security prison.

March 20. Tunisia: presidential and legislative elections. President Zeine al-Abidine Ben Ali wins 99% of the vote.

Foreign Policy

1989

August 31. Agreement between Libya and Chad to settle the Aouzou Strip dispute.

December 14. Libya: suspension of air, sea and other communication links with France, because France withheld delivery of weapons previously purchased by Libya.

1990

May 18. Libya: suspension of economic ties with Turkey because Turkey agreed to sell water to Israel.

Turkey denies existence of such agreement.

1991

April 25. China admits to providing Algeria with nuclear technology for civilian use.

August 24. Morocco: army attacks Polisario bases.

1992

February 28. Morocco: suspension of fishing accord with the E.E.C. after the European Parliament cancels half billion dollars in credit and aid due to human rights violations.

October 26. Libya demands compensation from Italy for its 32-year occupation.

1993

May 12. Libya: after a meeting between British prime minister Major and Salman Rushdie on May 11, the government calls for an Islamic boycott of Britain.

June 17. Western Sahara: peace talks between Morocco and a Sahrawi delegation.

1994

February 3. Libya: agreement between Libya and Chad over withdrawal of Libyan forces from the Aouzou strip after the International Court of Justice rules that the region belongs to Chad.

Economy, Society, Religion

1989

July 26. Algeria: the Information Law ratified by the National Assembly stipulates that Arabic is the only language for general publications; reaffirms the state's monopoly on radio and television.

October 29. Algeria: end of government monopoly over foreign trade announced.

1990

March 14. Libya: Rabta plant, which is capable of producing mustard gas, burns. Libya accuses the U.S., Israel and West Germany of sabotage.

March 28. Algeria: adoption of a banking and investment law that permits 100% foreign ownership of certain companies.

August 8. Tunisia: subsidies on wheat products, oil and milk decreased.

1991

July 26. Algeria: program of economic reform announced, eliminating many subsidies and encouraging foreign investment.

October 18. Algeria: government announces plans to increase the price of milk, cooking oil, sugar and corn by up to 200%.

1992

June 20. Algeria: government decides to remove subsidies on all foodstuffs, except bread, wheat and milk, in order to meet the demands of the International Monetary Fund (IMF).

November 6. Algeria: import of luxury goods suspended.

1994

January 5. Libya: adoption of Islamic lunar calendar.

January 26. Libya announces that unnamed foreign countries owe it $1.353 billion.

March 23. Algeria: 25 percent to 100 percent increase of retail prices for basic foods, following IMF recommendations.

April 10. Currency devalued by 40%; IMF pledges $1 billion loan.

Civilization and Culture

1992

October 22. Algeria: publication of the French-language *L'Observateur* suspended, after it published an interview with a fundamentalist.

The Arab Near East

Political and Institutional Life

1989

September 9. Iraq: elections for the Legislative Council in Kurdistan.

September 16. Iraq: accusation and arrest of more than 80 senior Iraqi offices in alleged coup plot.

September 23. Lebanon: cease-fire goes into effect.

September 28. Palestine: Israeli Defense Force (IDF) outlaws Hamas.

September 30. Lebanon: deputies meet in Ta'if, Saudi Arabia, to discuss future of country.

September 21. Saudi Arabia: 16 Kuwaiti Shi'is of Saudi and Iranian origin are beheaded after being charged with terrorist acts.

October 12. Lebanon: agreement in Ta'if to implement balanced Christian-Muslim representation in parliament.

October 18. Gaza: Israeli Defense Force raids UNRWA headquarters, arrests three staff members and confiscates documents.

October 22. Lebanon: deputies agree in Ta'if on a new constitution.

October 24. Islamic Jihad calls the Ta'if agreement an "unforgivable treachery."

November 4. Parliament dissolved; René Mu'awwad elected president (November 5).

November 8. Jordan: parliamentary elections; Muslim Brotherhood wins 32 of the 80 contested seats.

November 22. Lebanon: assassination of President Mu'awwad in a bomb explosion.

November 24. Ilyas al-Hrawi elected president.

December 11. Egypt: 40 wounded, 300 arrested in battle between Islamists and police in Asyut, protesting mixed-sex parties.

December 12. Yemen: political parties legalized.

1990

March 9. Lebanon: General Aoun declares war over and that he is ready to negotiate with Syria and the Lebanese Muslims. Later he renounces his statement.

March 10. Iraq: general amnesty for Iraqi Kurds announced.

March 22. South Yemen: student demonstration against co-education, for more religious instruction and for the end of compulsory teaching of Marxism (in Mukalla).

April 2. Iraq: President Hussein says that Iraq has advanced chemical weapons that can destroy half of Israel.

April 10. Lebanon: release of the imprisoned French couple Jacqueline Valente and Fernand Houtekins, and their daughter who was born in captivity. Saudi Arabia announces that the quota system for pilgrims will remain in effect.

April 22. American hostage Robert Pohill released by Islamic Jihad for the Liberation of Palestine.

April 30. American hostage Frank Herbert Reed released by the Islamic Dawn Organization.

May 22. Yemen: unification of North and South Yemen. San'a becomes capital.

May 26. Iraq: about 60 officers hanged or arrested for plotting a coup.

June 10. Kuwait: National Council elections.

July 2. Saudi Arabia: 1,426 pilgrims die from suffocation in an overcrowded pedestrian tunnel in Mecca.

July 19. Iraq: legislation approved calling for the election of Saddam Hussein as president for life.

August 2. Iraq invades Kuwait.

August 7. Iraq/Kuwait: Iraqi-installed Kuwaiti government declares Kuwait a republic.

August 10. Iraq: Saddam Hussein calls for a *jihad* to save Mecca and Medina from foreigners.

August 28. Kuwait proclaimed the 19th governate of Iraq.

September 19. Saudi Arabia: Saudis withdraw employment and resident privileges of Palestinians and Yemenis because of their support for Iraq.

September 23. Iraq: the Revolutionary Command Council refers to the annexation of Kuwait as an "eternal decision."

October 7. United Arab Emirates: Shaykh Rashid bin Sa'id al-Maktum, leader of Dubai, and vice-president of the UAE, dies after an illness. He is succeeded by Maktum bin Rashid al-Maktum.

October 8. Palestine: Israeli police kill 18 Palestinians in Jerusalem after a crowd refuses to disperse.

October 12. Egypt: President Mubarak dismisses the People's Assembly.

October 13. Lebanon: Michel Aoun ousted by Syrian and Lebanese forces; seeks refuge in French embassy.

October 29. Palestine: Israel outlaws Islamic Jihad.

November 6. Saudi Arabia: 70 veiled women drive in a convoy to protest the barring of women from driving. They are detained by police and released after signing a pledge that they will not do it again.

November 8. Lebanon: all private and unlicensed radio stations closed.

November 25. Iraq: arrest of 2,500 opposition Islamists.

November 29. Egypt: elections for the People's Assembly. Ruling National Democratic Party (NDP) gains 79.6% of the seats.

December 2. Lebanon: for the first time in 15 years, the Lebanese Army is able to unite Beirut after the withdrawal of the Lebanese Forces.

December 24. presentation of a reconciliation government headed by Prime Minister Umar al-Karami.

December 7. Iraq: execution of former Iraqi chief of staff and other officers; they were charged with planning a coup.

1991

February 6. Jordan: King Hussein declares that the U.S.-led coalition intended to "destroy and reorganize the area in a manner far more dangerous . . . than the Sykes-Picot agreement."

February 11. Iraq: announcement of a boycott against the *hajj.*

February 24. Egypt: about 2,000 students demonstrate against the Gulf War at Cairo University, which is subsequently closed.

March 4. Iraq: civil uprising against Saddam Hussein in Basra, in the south, and in the Kurdish regions in the north.

March 20. Iraq: the 94-year-old Shi'i cleric Ayatollah Abu al-Kasim al-Khoui expresses his support for Saddam Hussein. Iran later accuses Iraq of kidnapping and pressuring him to make this statement.

March 28. Iraqi forces launch a massive attack against Kurdish forces in Kirkuk.

May 28. Greenpeace report notes that up to 200,000 people died in the Gulf War and 5–6 million were displaced. 343 allied soldiers died.

June 8. Saudi Arabia: seven people beheaded in first public executions since July 1990.

June 9. Jordan: promulgation of the "National Charter," reinstating multiparty democracy.

July 6. Iraq: Iraq destroys the last of its 61 known Scud missiles, 28 warheads and 10 mobile launchers.

July 28. execution of 90 officers of the Republican Guard for trying to overthrow the government.

August 5. Iraq admits to possessing enough plutonium to make an atomic bomb.

August 8. Lebanon: Islamic Jihad releases British citizen John McCarthy.

August 11. U.S. citizen Edward Austin Tracy released.

August 29. Michel Aoun leaves the French embassy in Beirut and travels to southern France. He is forbidden to return to Lebanon for five years and permanently banned from political activities.

September 9. Iraq: clashes in northern Iraq between government forces and Kurds.

September 18. Palestine: Edward Said and Ibrahim Abu-Lughod resign from the Palestine National Council.

September 23. Lebanon: British citizen Jack Mann released.

September 24. Iraq: team of U.N. inspectors, who copied sensitive material related to Iraq's nuclear and chemical program, detained in a parking lot in Baghdad.

September 30. U.N. inspection team detained in a Baghdad parking lot permitted to leave Iraq.

October 7. Kurdish guerrillas shoot and kill more than 60 unarmed Iraqi government soldiers in Sulaymaniyya. Execution of former Iraqi Prime Minister Hammadi for planning to overthrow the government.

October 16. Israel: Ahmad Yasin, one of the founders of Hamas, sentenced to life in prison by an Israeli military court.

October 21. Lebanon: U.S. citizen Jesse Turner released.

October 28. Egypt: security forces arrest 185 persons who protest against the Madrid peace conference.

October 29. Lebanon: Israeli antiaircraft guns down three gliders approaching Israel from the Beka'a Valley.

November 11. Israel: Israeli Labor Party proposes repealing the law banning contacts with the PLO.

November 12. Iraq: lifting of a nine-month blockade of Kurdish-controlled areas; rebels agree to withdraw.

November 18. Lebanon: British citizen Terry Waite and U.S. citizen Thomas Sutherland released.

November 25. Jordan: eight members of Muhammad's Army sentenced to death.

December 2. Lebanon: U.S. citizen Joseph J. Cicippio released.

Syria: President Assad re-elected for a seven-year term in a plebiscite.

December 3. Lebanon: U.S. citizen Alann Steen released.

December 4. U.S. citizen Terry Anderson released.

December 7. Iraq: massive offensive by government forces against Kurdish-controlled Najef.

December 11. Saudi Arabia: 200 Somali gunmen hijack a Saudi oil tanker in Mogadishu, force it to sail to Port Sudan, and then to Saudi Arabia.

December 22. Lebanon: body of U.S. Lt. Col. William R. Higgins found in a Beirut street.

December 27. Body of former U.S. CIA bureau chief William Buckley returned to U.S. after it was found in south Beirut.

1992

March 1. Saudi Arabia: King Fahd issues set of royal decrees establishing a Consultative Council.

March 29. King Fahd declares that

there will not be free elections, and that Islam will be the guideline for social and political laws.

April 21. Iraq: large-scale attack against Shi'i dissidents in the southern marshes near Amara, Basra and Nasiriyya.

May 12. Saudi Arabia: King Fahd proposes donating $90 million to repair the Islamic holy sites in Jerusalem.

May 19. Iraq: elections for a 105-seat Kurdish National Assembly in the Kurdish-controlled north; both the Kurdish Democratic Party (KDP) and the Patriotic Union of Kurdistan (PUK) get 50 seats.

June 17. Lebanon: German hostages Strübig and Kemptner released.

June 29. Iraq: explosion at the police headquarters in Kirkuk kills 400.

July. Saudi Arabia: 107 religious scholars submit a memorandum to King Fahd, criticizing his foreign policy, human rights, his failure to implement the *shari'a*.

July 2. Iraq: U.S. newspapers report that Iraq had started to drain the southern swamplands in order to control dissident Shi'is.

July 8. Syria: Syria destroys the opium and cannabis crops in the Beka'a Valley.

July 17. Egypt: new law ordering the death penalty for members of "terrorist groups" is passed.

July 31. Israel: for the first time in 10 years, PLO Chairman Arafat agrees to be interviewed by an Israeli newspaper.

September 17. Iraq: execution of 25 people for illegal currency transactions.

August 20. Jordan: King Hussein has one kidney and one ureter removed at the Mayo Clinic in the U.S.

August 23–September 6. Lebanon: parliamentary elections boycotted by Christians in protest of Syrian presence.

October 5. Kuwait: first parliamentary elections since 1986. Opposition candidates win more than 35 seats in the National Assembly.

October 13. Crown Prince Saad al-Abdallah appointed prime minister by Shaykh Jabir al-Ahmad.

November 11. Egypt: all mosques placed under the direct control of the Ministry of Religious Affairs.

December 10. Yemen: demonstration by thousands in San'a to protest falling living standards.

December 18. Israel: 417 Palestinians expelled; believed to be involved in Hamas activities in southern Lebanon.

1993

January 2. Egypt: the Islamic Group threatens to kill all tourists unless they leave the country.

January 19. Israel: Israeli Knesset repeals a 1986 law banning contacts between Israelis and the PLO.

February 1. Iraq: the Revolutionary Command Council amends the constitution to permit the president to issue resolutions carrying the force of law.

March 30. Israel: Knesset seals off the West Bank and Gaza Strip indefinitely.

Egypt: The Islamic Group issues a last call for all foreigners to leave the country.

May 3. Kuwait: Parliament approves the construction of a 120-mile,

9-feet-deep, and 16-feet-wide ditch along the entire border with Iraq.

June 19. Egypt: a bomb explosion in Cairo kills seven and wounds 15.

July 8. Execution of seven members of the Islamic Group for plotting to overthrow the government.

July 10. Saudi Arabia: King Fahd decrees the formation of a Ministry of Islamic Affairs.

July 22. Egypt: al-Azhar Shaykh Muhammad Ghazali states that it is legitimate to kill apostates.

Lebanon: heavy artillery exchanges between Hezbollah and PFLP-GC forces and Israeli forces. According to Lebanese sources, 300,000 persons displaced and 128 killed during the ensuing eleven days.

July 25. Israel launches air, naval and artillery attacks across the country. Israeli Prime Minister Yitzhak Rabin threatens to make southern Lebanon uninhabitable unless rocket attacks cease.

July 27. Rabin vows to create a wave of refugees in Beirut.

August 12. Kuwait: "unlicensed popular committees" banned.

August 17. Jordan: change in electoral process creates a one-person, one vote system.

August 18. Egypt: four people die in a bomb explosion near al-Tahrir Square in Cairo.

August 19. Syria: former assistant secretary general of the Arab Socialist Ba'ath Party and Armed forces chief-of-staff (1963–1965), Salah 'Izz al-Din Jadid dies in a Damascus jail.

August 20. Saudi Arabia: King Fahd announces the creation of a Majlis al-Shura, an advisory body.

August 26. Lebanon: Israeli air strikes in southern Lebanon after a bomb kills seven Israeli soldiers on August 19.

August 30. Israel: Palestinian self-rule agreement with the PLO approved.

September 4. Hamas announces that it will escalate armed resistance against Israel to defeat the peace agreement.

September 7. In Jerusalem, 50,000 Israelis demonstrate against the Israel-PLO accord.

September 21. In Jerusalem, 20,000 hold four-day vigil to protest the PLO-Israel accord.

October 4. Egypt: with 95% approval in a referendum, President Mubarak's tenure in office is extended for another six years.

November 1. The Islamic Group passes a *fatwa* calling for the assassination of eight military judges.

November 8. Jordan: first multi-party elections. Islamists win only 18 of 80 seats in the Lower House, down from 32. Tejan al-Faisal is the first woman elected to parliament.

November 14. Egypt: arrest of Ali Abd al-Hamid Hamid, the leader of the Muslim Brothers.

November 29. Newspapers forbidden to conduct interviews with Islamists.

December 8. Palestine: five days before scheduled beginning of Israeli withdrawal from the Occupied Territories, Israel increases troops to 14,000, the highest number since the outbreak of the *intifada*.

December 15. Lebanon: last of the 417 Palestinians exiled to Lebanon in December 1992 allowed to return home.

December 16. Iraq: execution of 120

army officers charged with involvement in coup attempt.

1994

January 4. Israel: Likud leader Benjamin Netanyahu announces that his party does not feel bound to honor the PLO-Israel accord, should the Likud come to power.

January 10. PLO-Israel accord endorsed.

January 21. Basil al-Assad, President Hafiz al-Assad's oldest son and potential successor, dies in a car crash near Damascus.

February 25. Hebron Massacre — U.S.-born Israeli settler Baruch Goldstein opens fire on Muslim worshippers in the Cave of the Patriarchs, killing 29 people, and wounding about 100. Widespread rioting.

March 28. Gaza Strip: undercover Israeli agents kill six alleged members of the Fatah Hawks in the Jabalyah refugee camp.

February 27. Lebanon: bomb explodes in a Maronite church in Junieh, killing nine and wounding 60.

Foreign Policy

1989

July 27. Lebanon: rocket duels between Prime Minister General Michel Aoun's forces and Syrian forces and their allies. 125,000 people flee Beirut before the fighting.

July 28. Israel captures the Shi'i leader Shaykh 'Abd al-Karim 'Ubayd, who was allegedly involved in the kidnapping of U.S. Lt. Col. William Higgins (February 1988).

July 31. The Organization for the Oppressed on Earth releases a video-tape showing the hanged Col. Higgins. Threat to kill Joseph Cicippio (kidnapped September 1986) if 'Ubayd is not released.

September 6. U.S. closes embassy in Beirut.

September 30. Palestine: The Philippines recognize the State of Palestine.

November 16. South Yemen: restrictions on travel to South Yemen lifted.

1990

January 21. Oman: decision to open an embassy for Palestine in the sultanate.

March 15. Iraq: Iranian-born British national Farzad Bazoft hanged for espionage. Britain recalls its ambassador.

March 21. Border treaty between Oman and Saudi Arabia signed.

April. Iraq: steel tubes manufactured in Britain are intercepted; tubes are intended to build a supergun.

May 23. Palestine: U.S. denies PLO Chairman Arafat a visa to attend a U.N. Security Council meeting on the Occupied Territories.

May 29. Yemen: becomes a member of the Arab Cooperation Council.

May 30. Palestine: Palestinians attempt to land six speedboats at Nitsanim and Gaash. IDF forces kill four. The PLO claims responsibility.

June 20. U.S. suspends dialogue with the PLO because the organization fails to condemn the May 30 incident.

June 26. Iraq: President Hussein warns that Kuwaiti oil overproduction will have negative effects on OPEC.

July 1. Palestine: Israel releases 416 Palestinian prisoners on the occasion of 'Id al-Adha.

July 16. Iraq: Foreign Minister Tariq 'Aziz accuses Kuwait of stealing oil from the Rumayla oil fields and of cooperating with the "imperialist-Zionist plan" of keeping oil prices low.

August 2. Iraqi forces invade Kuwait.

August 8. Saudi Arabia: thousands of U.S. forces in the country.

August 21. Iraq: withdrawal of forces from Iran is complete.

August 29. OPEC agrees to temporary production increases to compensate for Kuwaiti and Iraqi losses.

September 2. Over 550 American, European and Japanese women and children and 30 ill or elderly American men are allowed to leave Iraq.

September 14. Saudi Arabia: U.S. agrees to sell advanced military equipment worth about $20 million to Saudi Arabia during the next few years.

October 7. Qatar cancels the debts of 10 Arab and African countries.

October 29. Iraq: 263 Frenchmen, 700 Bulgarians and 16 other foreigners allowed to leave Baghdad. U.S. President Bush declares that U.S. will increase troops in the Gulf because the embargo did not have desired results.

November 8. Release of 243 Polish nationals.

November 15. Saudi Arabia: first joint U.S.-Saudi military exercise.

November 29. Gulf states agree on a $6 billion loan package for the Soviet Union. The U.S. cuts all aid to Yemen because of its vote against U.N. resolution 578.

December 3. Iraq: 1,000 Soviets allowed to leave the country.

December 8. 440 Vietnamese and 41 Japanese leave the country.

December 9. Jordan: King Hussein proposes and international peace conference and an Iraqi-Saudi dialogue. More than 900 foreigners leave the country.

December 13. Iraq: U.S. embassy staff vacates embassy.

December 28. Over 250 Soviets leave the country.

1991

January 16. British, Saudi, Kuwaiti and U.S. forces under U.N. flag launch an air campaign against Iraq.

January 17. Iraq fires at least seven Scud missiles into Tel Aviv and Haifa. About 15 people die.

January 22. Iraq launches a Scud missile at Tel Aviv killing three and wounding 90.

January 31. Israel announces a five-point Middle East peace plan, based on a series of bilateral talks.

February 15. U.S. President Bush encourages the Iraqi people to overthrow Saddam Hussein.

February 23. After the U.N. deadline, over 700,000 allied soldiers invade Kuwait.

February 24. Scud missile kills 27 U.S. soldiers in their barracks in Saudi Arabia.

February 28. Truce is implemented.

March 6. Egypt, Syria and the GCC states issue the "Damascus Declaration," calling for regional security, economic cooperation and more Syrian and Egyptian troops in the Gulf.

April 17. U.S. military takes control of an area extending up to 60 miles inside Iraq in order to build camps for Kurdish refugees.

May 8. Last U.S. forces withdraw from southern Iraq.

May 15–16. Yemen: ratification of the Republic of Yemen.

May 22. Lebanon: Treaty of Brotherhood, Cooperation, and Coordination with Syria, calls for joint government institutions.

June 29. After being threatened by Iraqi soldiers, U.N. inspectors suspend efforts to inspect Iraqi nuclear facilities.

September 4. Kuwait approves of a 10-year defense pact with the U.S., but does not agree to permanent U.S. bases in the country.

November 13. Israeli Knesset declares the Golan Heights an inseparable part of Israel.

1992

January 22. Saudi Arabia: delegation from the American Jewish Congress concludes four-day visit.

February 19. Lebanon: after an Israeli bombardment of about 30 villages in the south, 75,000–100,000 people flee toward Beirut.

April 7. PLO Chairman Arafat's plane crashes in the Libyan desert. Three crew members are killed, but all passengers survive.

April 16. U.N. Border Demarcation Committee shifts the Kuwaiti border 570 yards north into Iraq to include the Rumayla oil field.

June 23. Qatar: defense agreement with U.S. signed.

June 24. Yemen: rescue of about 3,300 Somali refugees whose boat had run into a sand bank in the Red Sea.

July 23. Lebanon: U.S. Secretary of State Baker visits President Hrawi in Zahla, reiterating that Syria should withdraw troops from the Beirut region.

August 26. Iraq: U.S. and its allies establish a "no-fly" zone in Southern Iraq to protect Shi'i dissidents.

December 20. Qatar and Saudi Arabia settle their dispute over mutual border.

December 27. Iraq: U.S. aircraft shoots down two Iraqi planes in the southern "no-fly" zone.

1993

January 3. Egypt and Tunisia agree to cooperate in religious affairs, especially in controlling Islamist movements.

January 13. Iraq: about 110 U.S., British and French planes attack radar and mobile missile sites near al-Amara, Basra, Najef, Samawa and the Tallil airbase.

January 17. U.S. ships fire about 40 cruise missiles at the Jillah industrial park in Zafaraniyya. One missile strikes the Rashid Hotel in Baghdad. In the northern "no-fly" zone, a U.S. plane bombs an antiaircraft battery.

January 29. In the first meeting between Arafat and a Knesset member since 1968, PLO Chairman Arafat meets with Israeli Knesset member Yael Dayan (in Tunis).

April 14–16. Kuwait: visit by former U.S. President Bush.

April 30. U.S. State Department annual report on terrorism lists Hamas as a terrorist organization.

June 1. Saudi Arabia: King Fahd promises to support efforts to end the state of war between the Arabs and Israel.

June 26. Iraq: U.S. ships fire 23 missiles at the intelligence service headquarters in Baghdad in retaliation for a plot by the intelligence service to assassinate former President Bush during his April 14–16 visit to Kuwait.

July 2. Egypt: leader of the Islamic Group said his group will launch terrorist attacks against U.S. targets in Egypt in retaliation for the arrest of 'Abd al-Rahman.

August 30. Norwegian Foreign Minister Holst reveals that Norway has hosted 14 rounds of secret talks between Israel and the Palestinians.

September 6. Bahrain, Kuwait, Oman, Qatar, Saudi Arabia and the UAE announce their support for the Israel-PLO agreement.

Jordan: Gaza Strip residents are forbidden to enter the country.

September 10. U.S. President Clinton announces that the U.S. will resume a dialogue with the PLO.

November 15. Iraq: 150 soldiers in civilian clothes enter Kuwaiti territory and open fire on a police post; no casualties.

November 20. About 500 demonstrators against the U.N. border demarcation enter Kuwait.

1994

January 16. Syrian President Assad and U.S. President Clinton meet in Geneva to discuss Middle East peace process. After the meeting, Assad states that Syria is ready to sign peace agreement with Israel.

February 9. PLO Chairman Arafat and Israeli Foreign Minister Peres initial the "Cairo Agreement," which calls for shared responsibility for border crossings and security arrangements for Jewish settlers in Gaza.

March 3. Jordan and the Vatican announce the establishment of diplomatic ties.

April 7. Yemen: southern troops bomb the town of Dhamar.

April 14. Northern Iraq: U.S. aircraft shoot down two U.S. helicopters, killing all 26 people on board.

Economy, Society, Religion

1989

July 23. Kuwait: government announces that non-Kuwaitis will be permitted full ownership of business in Kuwait.

August 4. Jordan: Saudi Arabia agrees to deposit $1 billion in Jordan Central Bank to support the dinar.

September 27. Egypt: investment companies banned from speculation in gold, precious metals and foreign currencies; reason: "lack of expertise."

December 5. Iraq: launch of a rocket capable of carrying satellites.

December 25. Egypt: 19 new newspapers and magazines approved by the Higher Press Council.

1990

February 20. Iraq: Arab nationals allowed to form joint ventures with Iraqi businesses as long as their share is below 50%.

June 18. Egypt: government raises the price of sugar by 60%.

September 6. Jordan: government reports that about 605,000 persons had entered the country from Iraq since August 2.

September 9. International Red Cross and the Jordanian Red Crescent set up two migrant villages in al-Zarqa for 20,000–30,000 refugees.

November 1. Yemen: Partnership agreements with BP Petroleum Development Ltd. approved.

December 19. Jordan: UNICEF report states that over one million Jordanians live below the poverty level.

December 26. Promulgation of the Fixed Asset Law, regulating the transfer of private lands to heirs. The law supersedes an old Ottoman law.

December 30. Iraq: age of mandatory conscription is lowered to include all males born in 1973.

1991

Except for Air France, all foreign airlines have canceled flights to Jordan, due to increased risks.

January 16. Crude oil prices reach $35 per barrel.

February 22. Crude oil prices drop to $17.91 per barrel.

June 10. Israel announces that it will suspend income and property taxes in the West Bank and the Gaza Strip for three years.

July 1. Bank regulators in Britain, the U.S., and five other nations seize control of the Bank of Credit and Commerce International (BCCI), which was founded by the Pakistani financier Aga Hassan Abedi and controlled by the emir of Abu Dhabi. Bank is charged with laundering drug money.

August 13. Kuwait suspends Arab boycott on companies that deal with Israel in order to speed up reconstruction.

November 6. Kuwait: last of 650 oil field fires extinguished.

December 11. Jordan: seven-year economic restructuring plan announced; includes increased dependence on Western financial aid.

December 15. Egypt: up to 389 of 649 people die when an Egyptian ferryboat sinks in the Red Sea.

December 19. BCCI pleads guilty to criminal charges in the U.S.; ordered to pay $550 million penalty.

1992

January 1. Egypt: the Suez Canal Authority raises transit fees by 11% and 18%.

January 19. Government cancels a 30% price increase on butane gas after a series of strikes.

February 21. Abu Dhabi: government of Abu Dhabi agrees to pay $2 billion to creditors of BCCI.

March 9. Lebanon: according to police officials, 144,000 people killed between 1975–1990.

March 10. Iraq: according to a report by the Health Ministry, more than 21,000 people died in January and February due to the blockade.

March 24. Saudi Arabia: domestic gas prices cut by 37%; other items by 29% to 87%.

April 23. Iraq: import duties lifted on meat and potatoes.

May 5. Lebanon: 300 demonstrate and set fire to the house of Finance Minister Ali al-Khalil to protest the collapse of the Lebanese pound.

May 18. Kuwait: plans to privatize gas stations announced.

October 11. Egypt, Iraq, Jordan, Syria, and Turkey approve plan to connect the electrical grids of their countries.

October 20. Iraq bans the import of luxury goods.

October 12. Egypt: earthquake measuring 5.9 kills at least 552 people and injures 9,929.

December 7. Iraq: completion of the "Saddam River," a 565-kilometer long and 100-meter-wide canal.

1993

March 18. Lebanon: introduction of $10 billion reconstruction plan.

August 17. Saudi Arabia agrees to buy up to $6-billion-worth of passenger planes from Boeing and McDonnell Douglas.

October 1. 43 Western countries pledge about $2 billion in aid over the next five years for the West Bank and Gaza.

November 9. Iraq conducts its first ground-to-ground missile test since 1991.

November 23. Qatar Oil Minister Abdallah bin Hamad al-Atiyah is named president of OPEC.

December 4. Oil prices plunge to $13.65 per barrel after rumors that the U.N. might lift ban on Iraqi oil.

1994

January 1. Saudi Arabia cuts budget by 20% due to falling oil prices.

February 1. Saudi Arabia signs contract with France worth over $1.5 billion, to modernize Saudi frigates, tanker supply ships and ground-to-ground air missiles.

February 10. Financial Times reports that Lebanon's economy grew 7% in 1993 and was expected to grow 8–10% in 1994.

February 24. Syria issues exit visas to all remaining 1,000 Jews in Syria.

February 16. Saudi Arabia announces purchase of $6-billion-worth of U.S. commercial aircraft.

March 13. Saudi Arabia: ban on TV satellite dishes.

Civilization and Culture

1989

July 20. Iraq: Kurdish journalist and poet licensed to publish the Kurdish-language newspaper *Naso.*

1991

December 25. Egypt: Ala Hamid, author of *Distance in a Man's Mind,* fined and sentenced to eight years in prison on blasphemy charges.

1992

January 15. Lebanon: author Mustafa Jiha, who criticized fundamentalists and Khomeini in his writings, is assassinated.

April 29. Egypt: Ala Hamid is acquitted of blasphemy charges.

June 9. Author Faraj Fuda, an outspoken critic of militant Islam, dies after being gunned down on June 8.

Central Asia and Eastern Europe

Political and Institutional Life

1991

October 13. Bulgaria: The Movement for Rights and Freedom, representing the country's one million Muslim Kurds, wins 24 of 240 seats in parliamentary elections.

1992

April 3. Yugoslavia: fighting spreads to Bosnia and Herzegovina, after the country had fragmented in mid-1991. The Serbs shell the Bosnian capital, Sarajevo, round up Muslims and launch a campaign of "ethnic cleansing."

April 30. Tajikistan: in Dushanbe,

demonstrations for and against the government with about 100,000 participants.

May 5. State of emergency declared after clashes between supporters and opponents of the government.

May 9. Armenia: capture of Shusha in Nagorno-Karabakh from Azerbaijan by Armenian forces. Armenia now controls all of the enclave.

May 17. Azerbaijan: President Mutalibov is forced to resign by the public protest at his appointment.

June 17. First ever multiparty presidential elections. Abulfez Elchibey, leader of the Popular Front, wins.

July 5. Armenia: Azerbaijani troops recapture most of the northern parts of Nagorno-Karabakh.

August 31. Tajikistan: opposition members take control of the presidential palace in Dushanbe, take government officials hostage.

October 24. Military units supporting former president Nabiyev enter Dushanbe.

October 26. Government forces, with the help of Russian forces, drive out the supporters of Nabiyev.

November 27. The Supreme Soviet replaces presidential rule with a parliamentary republic system.

1993

May 5. Kyrgyzstan: ratification of a new constitution.

June 18. Azerbaijan: President Elchibey flees Baku as rebel commander Huseynov advances on the city.

August 29. Referendum has 97.5% vote against President Elchibey.

December 13. Kazakhstan signs the Nuclear Non-Proliferation Treaty. Parliament dissolves.

1994

March 7. Parliamentary elections in Kazakhstan. President Nazarbayev wins two-thirds of the 177 seats.

Foreign Policy

1992

June 25. Black Sea economic cooperation declaration signed by Albania, Armenia, Azerbaijan, Bulgaria, Georgia, Greece, Moldova, Turkey and Ukraine.

November 28. Afghanistan, Azerbaijan, Iran, Kazakhstan, Kyrgyzstan, Pakistan, Turkey, Turkmenistan, and Uzbekistan found the Economic Cooperation Organization.

1993

January 24. The Commonwealth of Independent States decides to send another 2,000 troops to Tajikistan to control the border with Afghanistan.

February 5. Armenian offensive in Nagorno-Karabakh.

May 10. Uzbekistan cuts off telephone lines and reduces gas supply to Kyrgyzstan to protest the introduction of new currency.

May 26. Armenia and Azerbaijan agree to a cease-fire in the Nagorno-Karabakh conflict.

June 17. Armenia captures the last Azeri-held town in Nagorno-Karabakh (Maradakert).

August 8. Heavy fighting between Azerbaijan and Armenia for control of Nagorno-Karabakh. During the next two weeks about 200,000 flee from southwest Azerbaijan.

October 8. Clash between Afghan and Tajik rebels and Russian troops.

1994

January 12. Uzbekistan and Kazakhstan agree to form a common market by the year 2000.

February 20. Armenia and Azerbaijan agree to a cease-fire in Nagorno-Karabakh and withdrawal of forces for both sides.

Economy, Society, Religion

1992

August 19. Earthquake measuring about 10 on the Richter scale in Kyrgyzstan.

1993

May 5. Kyrgyzstan: introduction of a new currency, the *som*, to replace the ruble.

June 15. Azerbaijan: introduction of a new currency, the *manat*, to replace the ruble.

September 6. Armenia, Belarus, Kazakhstan, Tajikistan, and Uzbekistan sign an agreement with Russia to maintain the ruble as their common currency.

September 9. Kazakhstan reports a serious increase in cholera since June 1993.

November 1. Turkmenistan replaces the ruble with the *monat*. Azerbaijan signs a $6-billion agreement with Western oil companies to develop oil fields in the Caspian Sea.

November 15. Kazakhstan replaces the ruble with the *tenge*.

1994

April 12. Uzbekistan bars the use of the Russian ruble.

Civilization and Culture

September 3. Uzbekistan: government decides to adopt the Latin script.

The Turkish and Iranian Middle East

Political and Institutional Life

1989

July 28. Iran: presidential elections; Hashemi Rafsanjani elected. Voters also approve amendments to the constitution (e.g., transfer of all powers to the president).

August 22. Rafsanjani releases 18-page policy document that outlines Iran's future internal and external aims.

October 25. Turkey: 500 students at Ankara University protest against the ban on female students wearing the *hijab*.

October 31. Turgut Özal elected president.

December 28. Ban on wearing the *hijab* on campuses lifted.

1990

March 6. Afghanistan: offensive to overthrow President Najibullah by Defense Minister Shanawaz Tanay.

363

January 22. Iran: the Soviet Union seals its border with Iran in the Azerbaijan region.

May 2. Afghanistan: Islamic parties allowed to operate openly.

April 24. Iran: death penalty for "black marketeers, profiteers and hoarders" introduced.

June 12. Turkey: ban on overland travel to Mecca in order to stay within the quota of pilgrims set by Saudi Arabia.

October 18. Iran: unauthorized demonstrations banned.

December 26. Turkey: 150,000 coal, steel and automobile workers on strike.

December 31. Iran: severe water shortages cause frequent power outages in Tehran.

1991

March 22. Iran announces that it will confiscate about 150 Iraqi warplanes whose pilots had sought asylum there during the war.

August 24. Iran: widespread antigovernment demonstrations in Tehran.

September 19. Unrest and demonstrations in Chalius, Gorgan, Hamadan, Isfahan, Khorassan, Mashhad, Nowshahr, Shiraz and Tehran.

October 20. Turkey: parliamentary elections; of 450 seats, the True Path Party wins 178 seats, the Motherland Party 115 seats.

November 4. Iran: 15,000 demonstrators participate in celebrations marking the 12th anniversary of the seizure of the U.S. embassy in Tehran.

November 19. Turkey: the True Path Party and the Social Democratic Populist Party form a coalition.

1992

January 8. Beginning of three-day offensive against Kurdish Worker's Party (PKK) camps near Sirnak and Tunceli.

April 15. Afghanistan: President Najibullah appoints a military council to take control of government.

April 16. President Najibullah resigns, attempts to flee, but is stopped at the airport by members of the dissident army.

April 19. Former Vice President Abdul Rahim Hatif takes over the presidency.

April 28. Rebel leader Mujadeddi installed as interim president; announces a general amnesty for members of the former government (except for Najibullah).

May 30. Iran: riot by thousands of residents of a squatter community in Mashhad, following orders to vacate the houses.

June 28. Afghanistan: President Mujadeddi hands over government to a 10-member Supreme Council, which elects Jamiat-e-Islami leader Rabbani president.

July 30. Iran confiscates about 132 Iraqi planes that had sought shelter there during the Gulf war.

September 29. Turkey: more than 82 people killed when PKK guerrillas attack a Turkish outpost in Semdinli along the Iraqi border. In subsequent fighting more than 210 people die.

November 2. Iran: The Khoradad Foundation increases the reward for the murder of Rushdie to over $2 million.

1993

February 14. Iran: religious leaders reiterate the *fatwa* calling for the death of Rushdie.

April 17. Turkey: death of President Özal at the age of 66.

May 16. Prime Minister Suleyman Demirel elected president.

June 11. Iran: presidential elections. President Rafsanjani wins with 63%.

June 13. Turkey: The True Path Party elects Tansu Ciller prime minister.

November 5. During the preceding 10 days, the PKK kills 130 people, 77 of them civilians in "pro-government villages."

1994

February 11. Iran: at the 15th anniversary of the revolution, 300,000 attend a speech by President Rafsanjani.

February 17. Turkey: deaths of 57 police and three PKK members in clash in the Silvan district of Diyar Bakr.

March 26–27. Deaths of 68 PKK members in clashes with security forces in Dingol, Diyar Bakr, Icel, Kahramanmaras and Mus.

Foreign Policy

1989

September 3. Afghanistan: U.S. and Pakistan decide to give military and financial assistance directly to rebel commanders and tribal elders, bypassing the rebel parties.

August 7. Iran: Interior Minister Ali Akbar Mohtashemi calls for a new anti-American offensive.

August 22. Turkey: closure of borders with Bulgaria after more than 179,000 Bulgarians of Turkish origin arrive in Turkey.

December 17. Iran: Rumanian Presi-

dent Nicolae Ceausescu arrives for a three-day official visit.

1990

February 15. Afghanistan: U.S. suspends a $30-million food program for the rebels, because food is being stolen or sold by the government.

March 23. Turkey: establishment of a joint Soviet-Turkish airline company, Greenair.

April 8. Iran: after a 10-year interruption, Iran resumes natural gas sales to the Soviet Union.

August 8. Bodies of former Prime Minister Bakhtiar, 75, and his aide are found in Paris. Bakhtiar opposed the 1979 revolution and founded the National Resistance Movement in Paris.

1991

July 29. Turkey forbids allied forces to launch punitive air strikes against Iraq from its bases.

August 7. Turkey: Attack on Kurdish rebel forces inside Iraq by air and artillery forces.

October 12. More than 3,000 troops sent into northern Iraq to attack Kurdish guerrillas.

December 29. Iran: France agrees to pay $1 billion for money Iran had loaned to France in 1974.

1992

March 9. Iran: North Korean ship carrying Scud missiles docks at Bandar Abbas.

March 21. All non-Iranian Red Cross employees forced to leave the country.

May 5. Turkey: Germany lifts ban on military aid to Turkey.

May 26. Air Force bombards PKK bases in Iraq, killing at least 20.

October 1. Missiles from the U.S. aircraft carrier *Saratoga* accidently hit the Turkish destroyer *Muavenet*, killing at least five.

October 23. Major ground and air attacks involving more than 20,000 troops against Kurdish rebels in northern Iraq.

1993

March 5. U.S. State Department calls Iran the world's "most dangerous state sponsor of terrorism."

March 30. U.S. Secretary of State Christopher calls the Iranian government an "international outlaw."

August 4. Iran: second of two Russian submarines arrives in Bandar Abbas.

September 14. Iran denounces PLO-Israel accord.

November 4. Kurdish separatists attack 25 Turkish embassies and offices in Germany, three in Switzerland, one in Copenhagen London, and Vienna.

Economy, Society, Religion

1989

July 21. Iran: government announces that more than 55,000 drug addicts have been detained and will be deported to labor camps.

October 8. Rafsanjani announces that hard currency will be provided to industries to increase production.

1990

January 22. Iran: money-changing no longer considered illegal.

January 27. Afghanistan: residents of Badghis Province threatened with starvation due to locusts and the destruction of winter crops.

March 14. Iran: subcritical mass reactors at the Isfahan nuclear reactor become operational.

June 21. Earthquake in the Caspian Sea region (7.3–7.7 on the Richter scale) causes about 40,000 deaths and 100,000 injuries. Rafsanjani accepts U.S. relief.

June 30. Rafsanjani escapes assassination attempt.

November 6. Earthquake measuring 7.0 on the Richter scale hits the Darab area.

1991

February 1. More than 1,200 Afghans and Pakistanis die in an earthquake measuring 6.8 on the Richter scale.

June 2. Iran: all legal obstacles to foreign investment canceled.

December 31. Turkey: vehicle and fuel taxes raised between 40% and 75%.

1992

January 17. Iran: government plans to raise the minimum wage by 36% to $1.60 a day.

March 13. Turkey: earthquake measuring at least 6.2 on the Richter scale in the eastern province of Erzincan; more than 570 dead.

March 15. earthquake measuring 6.0 on Richter scale in the southeast.

September 3. Afghanistan: more than 450 people are killed by flash floods in the Hindu Kush mountains.

September 8. Iran: earthquake measuring 5.6 on Richter scale strikes Firuzabad.

November 15. Turkey and Iran agree to link their electrical power grids.

December 1. Agreement between Turkey and Kazakhstan allows Turkey to buy all of its oil from Kazakhstan after the year 2000.

December 16. Iran: passage of a bill that allows divorced women to receive compensation for their work from their former husbands.

1993

July 4. Iran: government agrees to buy a 300-megawatt nuclear power station from China.

October 15. Turkey: after a series of attacks by the PKK, Mobil Oil suspends its operations in the southeast.

1994

March 28. Turkey: The Central Bank announces that the country's account deficit is $6.38 billion, up 577 percent from 1992.

April 5. Iran: government bans television satellite dishes because they infringe on national and religious culture.

Turkey: economic program, involving new taxes and closing state-owned firms; price increases, 28 percent devaluation of the lira, another 24.5 percent devaluation one day later.

Civilization and Culture

1990

October 18. Iran: The Tehran Combatant Clergy Association begins publishing the newspaper *Salem.*

Islam in the Far East

Political and Institutional Life

1989

October 7. Pakistan: the Baluchistan Assembly calls for more autonomy.

October 21. Malaysia: Mahatir Mohamad elected prime minister for third time.

November 17. Pakistan: Kashmiris decide to create the Kashmiri Liberation Movement to fight for the liberation of India's Muslims.

December 4. Bangladesh: after seven weeks of demonstrations by opposition parties, president Mohammad Ershad resigns.

1990

August 7. Pakistan: President Khan dismisses Prime Minister Bhutto, declares a state of emergency and dissolves parliament. A caretaker parliament is sworn in.

1991

January 26. Bangladesh: the Bangladesh National Party, headed by Khaleda Zia, widow of Ziawr Rahman, the first president, wins 138 of 300 seats in elections; forms government with the help of a smaller Islamic religious party.

1992

January 28. The Association of Southeast Asian Nations (ASEAN) agrees to create a six-nation common market including Brunei, Indonesia, Malaysia, the Philippines and Thailand.

August 1. Pakistan: Prime Minister Sharif says that Pakistan plans to free the Himalayan region of Kashmir from Indian rule.

December 6. India: a mob of thousands of Hindi militants attack and destroy a mosque in Ayaodhya, Northern India. As a result, Hindu-Muslim riots break out all over India.

November 18. Pakistan: arrest of PPP leader Bhutto.

1993

March 10. Indonesia: General Suharto (age 71) elected president for the sixth consecutive five-year term.

June 29. Pakistan: imposition of direct federal rule on the Punjab province.

July 18. Dissolution of Parliament after Prime Minister Sharif and President Ishaq Khan resign. Caretaker cabinet sworn in on July 23.

October 6. National elections. Benazir Bhutto's party wins 86 of 200 seats.

October 19. Benazir Bhutto elected prime minister.

November 23. Benazir Bhutto declares that Pakistan will not curtail its nuclear program.

November 25. Malaysia: state assembly in the northeastern state of Kelentan passes a law to introduce the *shari'a* penal system.

Foreign Policy

1989

August 10. Pakistan: agreement with India not to attack each other's nuclear installations.

1990

February 21. Pakistan: France announces that it will provide a nuclear power plant to Pakistan.

May 15. Prime Minister Bhutto on eight-nation tour in the Middle East, seeking financial and military support.

October 1. U.S. halts foreign aid, when President Bush fails to ascertain that Pakistan does not have a nuclear device.

1991

August 28. Pakistani and Indian troops clash in the Kashmir region.

September 17. Pakistan: clash with Indian troops on the Kashmir border.

1993

January 31. Pakistan: Peace Corps banned.

Economy, Society, Religion

1989

August 8. Pakistan: discovery of oil near Hyderabad.

1991

February 7. Pakistan: removal of all controls on foreign currencies for individuals.

1992

January 1. Pakistan: China announces that it wants to build a nuclear power plant for peaceful purposes in Chasma.

May 20. Earthquake measuring 5.5 on Richter scale in the Northwest Frontier Province; at least 36 dead.

August 20. Brunei: Fortune Magazine ranks the Sultan of Brunei at the top of its list of billionaires, with an estimated fortune of $37 billion.

September 16. Pakistan: more than 2,000 people are killed in torrential flooding in the northwest.

December 12. Indonesia: earthquake registering between 6.8–7.5 on Richter scale kills about 2,500.

December. Government reveals that Germany has recently sold Indonesia three naval vessels including a diesel-powered submarine, worth $120 million.

December 26. Pakistan: construction of a second nuclear power plant begins at Chasma.

1993

March 1. Pakistan: discovery of 80 billion tons of coal reserves in Sind.

August 19. Announcement of economic reforms in order to reduce the budget deficit.

October 6. Bangladesh: court order for police protection of author Taslima Nasreen after she receives death threats by Muslim extremist groups, protesting her novel *Lajja*.

1994

January 25. Pakistan: Prime Minister Bhutto opens the country's first all-female police station in Rawalpindi.

February 20. Schoolbus carrying 73 children and teachers hijacked by three Afghan gunmen. Incident resolved without bloodshed.

June 7. Malaysia: agreement with Russia to buy 18 Mig-29 fighters.

Sub-Saharan Africa

Political and Institutional Life

1989

Sudan: General Umar al-Bashir, leader of the Revolutionary Command Council, decrees the formation of paramilitary popular defense forces.

1990

March 3. Sudan: agreement for political, economic, and security integration with Libya within four years.

April 22–23. Abortive coup attempt by retired officers.

June 30. March of approximately one million in Khartoum, demanding implementation of Islamic law.

July 16. Land bill prohibiting foreigners to own land, unless approved by the Council of Ministers.

November 15. Large-scale arrests after a coup attempt.

December 1. Chad: rebel forces under Idris Deby capture N'Djamena, the capital, and president Habré flees. Dissolution of parliament, suspension of the Constitution (December 3). Deby declares himself president.

1991

January 26. Somalia: President Mohammad Siad Barre is forced to resign by forces of the United Somali Congress.

March 7. Sudan: government announces that in the northern regions the *shari'a* will take effect on March 22.

November 17. Somalia: factional fighting among the rebel groups centered around Ali Mahdi and Mohammad Farah Aidid.

December 24. Sudan: government revokes the passport it had granted to the Algerian al-Ghannoushi.

1992

December 9. Somalia: U.S. forces land in Somalia to begin a relief operation delivering food.

1993

May 24. Independence of Eritrea, following the referendum in favor of independence (April 23–25).

July 5. Djibouti: government launches a major offensive against the rebel Front for the Restoration of Unity and Democracy (FRUD).

October 16. Sudan: Lieutenant General Umar Hasan al-Bashir assumes the post of president after the Revolutionary Command Council disbands.

December 8. Hasan al-Turabi appointed Secretary General of the Popular Arab and Islamic Conference.

1994

June 11–12. Djibouti: agreement between the government and the Front for the Restoration of Unity and Democracy to end the 30-month-old civil war.

Foreign Policy

1989

September 20. Niger: bomb explodes on board a plane of the French airline Union des Transports Aériens

(UTA), killing 171 people. Islamic Jihad claims responsibility.

October 31. French investigators believe a Hezbollah affiliate was responsible for the September UTA bombing.

1990

March 8. Sudan: U.S. refrains from granting new aid because of government failure to implement a democratic regime.

March 26. Chad accuses Libya of attacking its forces along the border with Sudan's Darfur province. International opinion holds Chad guilty of complicity.

1991

June 22. Nigerian plane returning from the *hajj* crashes near Jidda, killing 261 passengers.

1993

January 21–28. Sudan: Egyptian military officials issue birth certificates and identity cards to tribes in the Hala'ib region, to advance Egyptian claims to this area.

August 18. Sudan officially added to U.S. list of nations sponsoring terrorism.

1994

February 5. Sudan: air and ground offensive against rebels along the Ugandan border; 100,000 refugees.

Economy, Society, Religion

1989

September 12. Sudan: import of sugar stopped; concentration entirely on domestic production.

September 19. Subsidies on basic consumer commodities cease.

November 10. Arab militia kill about 100 Nubians in Kodafan Province at Logowa as police stand by.

December 28. Armed Asaba Arabs kill between 500–2,000 Shilluk tribesmen at Jabalayn.

1991

October 7. Sudan: currency devalued by 70%; subsidies on sugar and petroleum products lifted.

1992

May 18. Sudan: government introduces the dinar.

August 12. OXFAM reports that 300,000 people in Juba are threatened by starvation.

August 20. U.N. airlifts about 50 tons of food and medicine to Juba.

December 30. Decision to merge all primary and preparatory schools of Egyptian educational missions into the Sudanese educational system.

1993

January 4. Sudan: decision to privatize the cotton sector.

March 9. License of Cairo University's Khartoum branch revoked. Branch renamed University of the Two Niles.

GLOSSARY

The following letters, which appear in parentheses after some glossary terms, designate linguistic origin, as follows:

A = Arabic
F = Farsi
T = Turkish

Words in small capital letters indicate cross-references within the glossary.

abangan (Sanskrit)   Literally, "the red ones," i.e., dark and godless. Peasant masses in Indonesia, adhering to animistic popular culture; opposed to the SANTRI.

'abid (A)   Black and mulatto slaves who made up the ranks of the army of the sultan of Morocco Mawlay Isma'il (2nd half of the 17th century).

Abna' al-dawla (A)   Descendants of the Khurasanians; members of the 'Abbasid DAWA; a hereditary state aristocracy.

adab (A)   Literally, "good morals, good life"; Arab prose literature for the "cultivated individual," the *adib*.

'ahd al-aman (A)   "The Fundamental Pact" (September 10, 1857) promulgated in Tunisia between the BEY and the notables, introducing reforms to that country; ensured the safety and equality of all Tunisians.

ahl al-kitab (A)   Literally, "People of the Book" (Bible); members of the monotheistic religions; they were put under the special protection of Islam; sometimes Mazdeism and Sabeans were included; DHIMMI.

Ahmadiyya (A)   Sect evolving out of SHI'ISM in 19th-century India.

'ajemi oghlan (T)   Literally, "foreign children." Children and adolescents drafted in the Christian provinces of the Ottoman Empire by the DEVSHIRME system to become JANISSARIES, or the sultan's servants.

akhi (A)   Turkish religious brotherhood whose members came primarily from the artisan class.

'Alawis   Devotees of a sect evolving out of SHI'ISM in 19th-century Syria; dynastic family of the kings of Morocco since the 18th century.

almamy (A)   Contraction of AL-IMAM. Often the title of the leader of an Islamic state in West Africa.

Almoravid (A)   From *al-murabitun* ("the people from a fortified convent [RIBAT]"). An Islamic reform movement founded in Mauritania in the middle of the 11th century by Ibn Yasin; later a dynasty in Morocco and then Spain. Almoravid intervention in Spain, which began in the late 11th century, ended in the middle of the 12th century.

Amal (A)   "Hope." Name of a present-day Shi'i party in Lebanon. Also SHI'ISM.

amil (A)   Literally, "agent." During the Prophet's time, collector of taxes from Muslims and of the tribute from non-Muslims; until the 10th century/3rd century, governor of a province, later a tax collector, under the Ottomans; in general, farmer and tax collector in the provinces.

amir (A)   Also *"emir."* "Commander." Military leader, governor of a province, autonomous prince. The CALIPH is the "commander of the faithful," *amir al-mu'minin;* the term occurs in many compounds; e.g., *amir al-bahr* = admiral.

amir akhur (F)   Title of Persian origin (*mir akhur*); literally, "great constable." Under the Mamluks, he was the commander in chief.

al-amir al-kabir (A)   "Great amir"; literally, title granted by the Mamluk sultan to "all those who had grown old in the service of the state." In the 14th century/8th century, the title was reserved for the *'ATABEG AL'ASAKIR.*

amir al-umara' (A)   Literally, "the amir of the amirs" (T = *emir ül-ümera;* T-F = *mir-i miran/mirmiran*). Under the 'Abbasids for some time, a title for the commander-in-chief of the army; in the Ottoman Empire, the governor of a large province (*eyalet*).

amsar (A)   (pl. of *misr*) Garrison towns founded by Muslim conquerors; peopled by Arabs registered with the DIWAN who were given a pension.

ansar (A)   Literally, "helpers." Designated the inhabitants of Medina who supported Muhammad, as distinct from the MUHAJIRUN, "emigrants" from Mecca to Medina.

'Ashura' (A)   Tenth day of both the month of Muharram and of the year; day of voluntary fasting for Shi'is and Sunnis (SHI'ISM; SUNNISM); day of mourning of Husayn's death for the Shi'is. Performance of passion plays; carnival-like festival in the Maghrib today.

Assassins   See box on page 62.

'ata' (A)   Pension paid to soldiers and other individuals affected by war.

atabeg (T)   Highly placed dignitary among the Seljuqs, often a prince's military leader, tutor and counselor. Title was in use in the Mamluk state.

atabeg al-'asakir (T-A)   Commander in chief of the Mamluk army, first emir of the sultanate.

a'yan (A)   Notables with prestige and influence in the towns. Exercised political influence in the Ottoman Empire beginning in the 18th century.

'ayyarun (A)   Vagabonds, outlaws; often composed of jobless or those employed in menial jobs, who sometimes formed organized groups challenging local and state authority.

Ba'ath (A)   Literally, "resurrection" (word from the Qur'an). Arab nationalist and socialist parties ruling Iraq and Syria.

Baha'i (A-F)   Ecumenical Muslim sect founded at the end of the 19th century, in Iran and Palestine; still in existence.

Bambara   Ethnic group and language from central Mali. In the 19th century, the Bambara formed two powerful states, Segu and Karta, notable for their attachment to pagan traditions.

bara'a (A; T = *berat*)   Immunity; absence of obligation; exemption from border duties, administrative fees, fiscal fees, the carrying of permits and certificates.

Ibarid (A)   Postal and informational service (serving the state exclusively), inherited from the Roman and Sassanid empires. Used by the police for spying. *sahib al-barid* (A)   Postmaster, subordinate to the director of the Postal Service (*sahib diwan al-barid*).

bay'a (A)   Pledge of allegiance to the CALIPH and the UMMA.

bayt al-mal (A)   Literally, "treasure house." Designated the treasury of the Islamic state.

bedesten (bezistan, bezzazistan) (F)   Great market; a covered bazaar where precious goods are sold.

bey (beg) (T)   Prince, leader; among the Ottomans, governor of a small province, and later an honorific term.

beylerbey (T)   Governor of a large province in the Ottoman Empire.

beylik (T)   A bey's territory.

Bilad al-Sham (A)   Area to the west of the Euphrates and to the south of the Taurus; the Greater Syria region.

bimaristan (F)   Hospital that offers consultations, healing, hospitalization and the teaching of medicine.

burj (A) (pl. *abraj*)   Tower, adjoining a rampart or standing alone, that served as a bastion or a dungeon. *Burj al-haman:* dovecote.

caliph   See box on page 8.

casbah, qasbah (A)   Town; later, the fortified part of a town.

Copts   Monophysite Christian denomination in Egypt and Ethiopia; split from the main church in 451 A.D.

dahir (A)   In Morocco, a sultan's decree.

daman (A)   Legal term: civil responsibility; sometimes means "caution." In the financial sense, place where taxes are collected. *Daman al-nahar*, in Damascus: duty collected on running water.

damin (A)   A debtor's guarantee.

dara'ib hilali (A) (sing. *dariba*)   Extra-canonical taxes, collected according to the lunar calendar.

dar al-hadith (A)   Institution where the HADITH was taught, beginning at the end of the 10th century/4th century. Introduced in Syria in the 12th century/6th century by Nur al-Din within the framework of his anti-Shi'i (SHI'ISM) politics.

dar al-harb, dar al-islam (A)   See box on page 8.

darb al-hajj (A)   See PILGRIMAGE ROUTE.

darvish (F), **dervish**   See SUFI.

da'wa (A)   "Calling." Preaching, doctrine, mission; a clandestine propaganda organization with hopes of taking power; its members are the *da'i*.

al-dawadar (F)   Literally, "he who guards the royal inkwell." Position of chancellor, created under the Seljuqs and held by civilians. Under the Bahrid Mamluks, it was attributed to an emir from Dix; under the Circassians, the position became more important ("*dawadar al-kabir*" = the great *dawadar*). In the Ottoman Empire, civil servant holding the position of secretary to the Chancellory.

day'a (A)   Large domain distributed by the CALIPH and liable for the USHR tithe).

derebey (T)   Literally, "lord of the valley." Local chieftains in 18th-century Anatolia, virtually independent of the Ottoman sultan.

dervish (F)   See SUFI.

devshirme (T)   See box on page 127.

dey (dayi) (T)   Literally, "maternal uncle." Designated, in the Maghrib provinces of the Ottoman Empire, the holders of important official positions and, most notably in Algiers, beginning in the 17th century, the ruler of the province.

dhimmi (A)   "Protected subject." Devotee of one of the religions of the Book (AHL AL-KITAB). The protection is called *dhimma*.

dihqan (F)   In Iran, the agents of the Sassanid treasury; recruited among landowners, they were rural notables who enriched themselves by the collection of taxes and the usury that this collection allowed.

dinar (A)   Monetary unit made of gold in ancient Islam. The name *dinar* disappeared from coins in the 12th century/6th century in the West, in the 13th century/7th century in the East and India, and in the 14th century/8th century in Egypt. Today, monetary unit in some Arab countries.

diwan (A-F)   Administrative institution, registry, office or its chief officer; by extension, collection of texts; collected works of a poet. A distinction is established between the *diwan al-jund*, a registry of soldiers indicating salaries and rations, the *diwan al-kharaj*, which monitors the assessment and collection of property taxes, and the *diwan al-nafaqat*, for the recording of expenses. Entered into European languages via the French "douane" = customs (house).

diwan al-insha (A-F)   Chancellory of the Mamluk state with three departments: the leadership or control services; the service responsible for informing people of the CALIPH's decisions on complaints brought before him in a public forum; and a service for recording these decisions. Added to these services were the office of correspondence and a service to keep track of names.

Druze.   Esoteric Isma'ili (see ISMA'ILISM) sect from the 11th century, in Syria, Lebanon and Palestine; still in existence in Lebanon.

Dyula (Dioula)   Ethnic group and language from West Africa (Mali, Guinea, Burkina Faso and Ivory Coast). More commonly used to refer to a group specializing in trade.

emir   See AMIR.

falsafa (A-Greek)   "Philosophy." Neo-platonic and gnostic synthesis that integrates medicine, astronomy and numerical science in view of one's union with God; the *faylasuf*, pl. *falasifa*, is an exponent of *falsafa*.

faqir (A)   See SUFI.

fatah (A)   "Opening, conquest" (word from the Qur'an). Name of the leading Palestinian guerrilla organization founded in 1965 (leader Yasir Arafat).

fatwa (A)   Authorized legal decision delivered by a *faqih* (see FIQH), an *'alim* ('ULAMA') or a MUFTI.

IIfay' (A)   Immovable booty (land revenues etc.); not divided up among the

375

soldiers at the moment of conquest, but doled out among the conquerors and their descendants, to whom one fifth was sent immediately.

fida'i, (A) pl.: **fida'iyyun, fida'iyyin, fida'yin, fedayin** (F)   Literally, "One who sacrifices his life." Guerrilla soldiers.

fiqh (A)   Jurisprudence; elucidates the *SHARI'A*. Specialist in this field is the *faqih*, pl. *fuqaha'*.

fitna (A)   "Scission." Political crisis that is perceived as having religious and moral causes.

Fulbe   See *PEUHL*.

funduq   In the Maghrib, a resting place analogous to the *KHAN* (caravanserai) in the Muslim East. They are usually found within the city walls, near the gates.

futuwwa (A)   Brotherhood of "youths" (*fityan*), bachelors or outlaws. Their militant members imposed their paid protection on the *suqs* (markets); they were also easily integrated into the *shurta*, the urban police, or in the volunteer army.

ghazi (A) (pl. *ghuzat*)   Volunteer soldier on the borders of Islam; anyone carrying out *JIHAD*.

ghulam (A) (pl. *ghilman*)   "Young man," "young boy," later coming to mean slave, servant, guard; they rose, in certain Muslim countries, to high positions in the civil service or military.

Hashishiyya (A)   See box on page 62.

hadith (A) (pl. *ahadith*)   Saying of the Prophet, report of an action or an opinion attributed to him; the collection of such reports. See *ISNAD*.

hajib (A)   Chamberlain, officer of the court in charge of audiences; he raises the veil, *hijab*, that hides the caliph.

hajj (A)   Annual pilgrimage to Mecca, 'Arafat and Mina; the fifth of the five *PILLARS OF ISLAM*; every Muslim is required to perform it once in his lifetime. See also *PILGRIMAGE ROUTE*.

hakimiyya (A)   The exclusive sovereignty of God.

Hanafi (A)   Sunni (*SUNNISM*) Muslim school of law, dominant in the Ottoman Empire; attributed high value to jurists' individual judgment in cases of legal ambiguity. See also *MALIKISM, MADHHAB, SHAFI'I*.

Hanbali (A)   Sunni school of law, dominant in the Arabian peninsula; traditionalist in dogmatic issues, progressive in issues concerning treaties. See also *MALIKISM, MADHHAB, SHAFI'I*.

haram (A)   Site whose access is limited; sacred section of a mosque; an illicit thing.

Hashimids (A)   The family to which Muhammad belonged. In Jordan the family is still in power (hence the official name: "The Hashimid Kingdom of Jordan").

hatt-i hümayun (khatt-i humayun) of Gülhane (November 3, 1839)   "Majestic writing"; imperial decree, edict from the Ottoman sultan; inaugurated internal reforms and Westernization.

Hausa   Ethnic group and language in West Africa (Niger, Nigeria). Second to *SWAHILI* in number of speakers in Black Africa.

hijra (A) "Retreat, exodus" (word from the Qur'an); the flight of Muhammad from Mecca to Medina in 622.

Hizb Allah (A), **Hezbollah** (F) "The party of God" (Qur'anic expression). Name of Shi'i (*SHI'ISM*) political groups in present-day Iran and Lebanon.

'Ibadism One of the moderate forms of *KHARIJISM*, and the only one still in existence in North Africa [Mzab, Jerba and Nafusa] and in the sultanate of Oman.

ijma' (A) Unanimity, agreement of the Muslim community.

imam (A) Literally, "the one in front." Leader in prayer; above all, the caliph. For the Shi'is (*SHI'ISM*): 'Ali and his descendants, who are the rightful leaders of the Muslim community, acting as Muhammad's successors. For Shi'is and the Abbasid *DA'WA*, the imamate is loaded with mystical significance.

imdad-i seferiye (T) Exceptional Ottoman tax for the financing of a military expedition.

iqta' (A) "Lot." A temporary land grant by the government to an individual. After 950, refered to the lands of the *KHARAJ*, the tax of which provided a fixed revenue. Often incorrectly translated as "fief."

islah (A) Muslim reformism from the end of the 19th century and throughout the 20th.

Isma'ilism (A) Extremist Shi'i (*SHI'ISM*) sect in the 8th century, pacifist today, in India, Pakistan, Syria and Yemen. See also *DRUZE, HASHISHIYYA*.

isnad (A) (also *sanad*) Series of transmitters of a *HADITH*; guarantees the validity of a *hadith*.

Istiqlal (A) "Independence." Name of a Moroccan political party (in existence since 1930).

Ja'fari (A) Adept of twelver *SHI'ISM*, which recognizes the descendants of Musa, one of Ja'far al-Sadiq's sons and the sixth *IMAM*, as their *imam*.

jahiliyya (A) Literally, "the age of ignorance." Era of pre-Islamic paganism.

jalali (ta'rikh-i) (F) Persian solar calendar, its use was implemented in 1075/467 by the Seljuq sultan Malik Shah. It was used for the timing of tax collection.

jama'a (A) (**jamaat** in Urdu) Association, community.

Janissary (from T: **yeñi-çeri** = "new army") Soldier in the Ottoman infantry originally recruited from among prisoners, later through the *DEVSHIRME* system. See also *'AJEMI OGHLAN*.

jihad (A) "Effort." Asceticism; by extension, holy war, right or duty, collective or individual, according to the schools of law.

jizya (A) Originally, a tribute paid by all defeated peoples. Beginning in the 8th century, distinguished from the *KHARAJ*. A property tax, the *jizya* was a tax levied only on the *DHIMMI*.

jund (A) "Army." Military and fiscal district in Syria and Spain.

Ka'ba (A) See box on page 3.

kalam (A) "Scholastic theology" based on the tenets of Islam, dealing with questions of theology and cosmology.

kalima (A)   Declaration of divine unity. ("There is no god other than God. He is alone and has no companion.").

Kataeb (Kata'ib) (A)   "Phalanges." Name of a MARONITE political party in modern Lebanon.

katib (A)   "Scribe." Secretary to the DIWANS, specialist in calligraphy and crafted language.

Kemalism   Secular authoritarian doctrine of Mustafa Kemal in Turkey.

khan   1. Caravanserai or large building serving as a warehouse for goods and as lodging for merchants. 2. Turkish title. Under the Seljuqs and the Khwarizm-Shahs, a more elevated title of nobility, just below those of *malik* (king) and AMIR. In Safavid Persia, the *khan* was the governor of a province.

khanaqah or **khangah**. (F)   Building for SUFI activities; derived from Iranian mysticism. The word first appeared in the 10th century/4th century in Khurasan and Transoxiana. See also RIBAT, ZAWIYA.

kharaj (A)   Canonical property tax levied on conquered lands kept by the old owners.

Kharijism (A)   Along with SHI'ISM, one of the two great schisms in the Muslim world. The movement appeared after the battle of Siffin (655/37) as 'Ali was consenting to a compromise with the Ummayyads. Kharijism moved away from the central caliphates and adopted rigorous sectarian views. In its 'Ibadi (IBADISM) form, this movement still exists in certain parts of North Africa and Oman.

khums (A)   A fifth of the spoils from a war, after the deduction of the portion that goes to the spoils administration. The fifth was then divided into five parts, one attributed to God and his Prophet, another to the Prophet's close relatives (Banu Hashim and Banu al-Muttalib), one to poor orphans, one to the poor, and another to foreigners passing through the country.

Khurramiya (F)   Literally, "joyous." Iranian incarnationist sect that insists on purity.

khutba (A)   "Sermon." Political speech preceding the special Friday midday prayer; it mentions the name of the ruler, serving as an affirmation of sovereignty.

Koran   See QUR'AN.

Kunta   Arabic-speaking group from the southern Sahara (Mali, Mauritania). Originally from Touat, the Kunta were, beginning in the 18th century, a religious and commercial force whose influence was felt throughout most of West Africa. They introduced the QADIRIYYA to the southern Sahara.

lala (T)   Tax collector, governor in the service of a prince.

madhhab (A) (pl. *madhahib*)   School of law (*fiqh*). Four *madhhabs* were established during the first 'Abbasid century: the school in Medina of Malik, based on consensus (IJMA') and personal judgment (RA'Y); Abu Hanifa's school in Iraq, which stressed analogical judgment (*qiyas*); Shafi'i's Egyptian school, based on communitarian consensus; the traditionalist school led by Ibn Hanbal, extra-judiciary, against the liberty of reason, for the TAQLID. Compare also JA'FARI, 'IBADISM and ZAYDI.

madrasa (A), (**medresa, medersa**) A juridico-religious teaching facility, usually attached to an endowed mosque, often with dormitories. The first *madrasas* appeared in Nishapur, Merv and Bukhara.

mahdi (A) "The nightly guided one." Epithet of the divinely inspired prince who appears at the end of times, restores religion to its previous glory and brings justice to bear. He will carry the name Muhammad b. 'Abdallah. For the Shi'i, the hidden *IMAM* whose arrival is awaited.

majba (A) Tax on harvests collected in Tunisia; the sudden increase of this tax in 1864, led to a revolt.

makhzan (A) Literally, "a site for preservation," "warehouse." In Morocco, originally treasury, then financial organization, and finally the Moroccan government.

Malikism (A) One of the four great schools of Sunni Muslim law, inaugurated by Malik Ibn Anas (died in 796/179) of Medina. His rigor was stricter than that of other equally "orthodox" schools. Dominates in the Maghrib and in Western black Africa. See also *MADHHAB*.

marabout (A-French) From the Arabic *murabitun* (literally, "the people of the *RIBAT*"). The term took two meanings in French: in North Africa, the tomb of a saint, generally with a white cupola (*qubba*); in sub-Saharan Africa, any religious person. Often, the word has a pejorative nuance, in which case the marabout is someone who engages in "marabouting" (i.e., the sale of talismans and predictions).

Maronites Arab Christians from Mount Lebanon; since 1182 attached to Rome; traditionally maintained close relations with France.

masjid (A) Mosque.

mawla (A) (pl. *mawali*) Person associated with an Arab tribe, a freed slave; a recent convert to Islam.

mazalim (A) "Abuse." Appeals court instituted by the 'Abbasids.

Melkites (Syriac-A) Christians from the East and Sicily of Orthodox faith in communion with the patriarchy of Constantinople and the Byzantine "King."

mellah (A) Part of a town where Jews live, especially in Morocco.

millet (T) One of the recognized religious communities in the Ottoman Empire.

mollah (F), **mulla** (A) In Iran, a minor cleric, a religious man at the bottom of the hierarchy.

Mozarabs (A) The "Arabized" people. Christians from Spain, of Visigothic liturgy and Arabic language.

mufti (A) Expert in the *SHARIA*; supplies the *FATWA.*

muhajirun (A, same root as *HIJRA*) "Emigrés" from Mecca who followed Muhammad to Medina. See also *ANSAR*.

mujahidin (A, same root as *JIHAD*) Soldiers for God.

mukus (A) Taxes not foreseen by Islamic law, eliminated by Saladin, re-established by the Mamluks. See *DARA'IB*.

mulk (A) Private property, subject to taxes paid to the state.

muqatila (A) Tribal army.

Muridiyya (A)   See box, page 246.

Murji'a (A)   See box on page 17.

murshid (A)   Guide, spiritual leader.

Muslim Brothers   See box on page 260.

Mu'tazilis (A)   Opposition group in early Islam; stressed free will/ responsibility and divine justice.

müsellem (T)   One who is exempt from taxes; among the Ottomans, a cavalryman exempt from taxes.

na'ib al-saltana (A)   Viceroy, in command of the delegation of royal power, substitute for the ruler.

Ngindo   Ethnic group from Tanzania (near Kilwa, in the back-country). The Ngindo led the Maji-Maji anti-colonial insurrection from 1905–1907, then converted to Islam.

nizam al-mulk (A)   Title for a high functionary: "regent of the kingdom." Surnames in *al-mulk* ("of the kingdom") are not used by the Egyptian emirs.

nizam-i jedid (T)   "New organization" set up by sultan Selim III as a way of modernizing the Ottoman army.

nizamiye (T)   New organization of the army, instituted by Muhammad 'Ali in Egypt

Nusayris   See box on page 38..

pancasila   Sukarno's secular political doctrine known as the "five principles": one God, nation, humanism, democracy and social justice.

Pasha (T)   Turkish title, often equivalent to governor.

penjyek (penjik)   "Fifth." The fifth of the spoils of war kept for a Muslim chief of state following a conquest.

Peuhl (sing. *pullo*, pl. *fulbe*).   West African ethnic group of nomadic origin, who, after successive migrations, spread from southern Mauritania throughout the savanna, from Senegal to the Nile and from the Sahara to Cameroon. The Peuhl world has certain historical markers: Ferlo in Senegal, Futa Jallon in Guinea, Masina in Mali, Adamaoua in Nigeria and Cameroon. Educated Muslims from the Peuhl culture called for a series of *jihads* in different parts of West Africa during the 18th and 19th centuries.

Pillars of Islam (A = *arkan al-Islam*)   The five duties demanded of every Muslim: (1) declaration of faith in God, and Muhammad's position as a prophet (*SHAHADA*); (2) prayer three times a day (*SALAT*); (3) the giving of alms (*zakat*); (4) fasting during the month of Ramadan (*sawm*); (5) the pilgrimage to Mecca (*hajj*).

Pilgrimage Route (A = *darb al-hajj*)   There are three land routes to Mecca: the "Iraqi" way (*darb Zubayd*), crossing Arabia diagonally; the "Syrian" way, in a north-south direction; and the "Egyptian" way, for pilgrims coming from the Maghrib and Egypt. The upkeep of inns and cisterns with drinking water is assumed by the public treasury and the *WAFQS*.

qadi (A) also: **cadi, kadi**.   Judge. *Qadi al-qudat* = grand qadi; there is one for each *MADHHAB*.

qadi al-'asker   In the Ottoman Empire, first juridico-religious position filled in a conquered province.

Qadiriyya (A)   A Muslim brotherhood spread throughout the Muslim world. It takes its name from 'Abd al-Qadir al-Jilani (died in Baghdad in 1166/561).

qal'a (A)   In the East, a fortress or citadel.

qanunname (A-F)   Specific set of rules for each province in the Ottoman Empire.

qibla (A)   The direction of Mecca, indicated in mosques by a grotto toward which the faithful turn during prayer.

Qizilbash   Adept of *SHI'ISM* in Central Anatolia and in Iran during the 15th and 16th centuries. Given this name because of red cap worn.

Qur'an (A)   See box on page 2.

Ra'aya (A) (pl. of **ra'iyya**)   Originally, "herds," then came to mean the subjects of an empire or prince. During the Ottoman Empire, non-Ottoman subjects.

Ra'y (A)   Personal judgment.

ribat (A)   Originally, fortified town on the border that sheltered soldiers in the volunteer army, the *murabitun*; comes to mean *KHANAQAH* with the development of spiritual life. See *ALMORAVIDS, SUFI, ZAWIYA.*

ridda (A)   Apostasy, secessionist movement.

sadr-i a'zam (A-T)   Grand vizier.

sahib al-khabar (A)   In district headquarters, the civil servant in charge of informing the ruler of everything that happens in the district. He is often aided by the *sahib al-BARID.*

Sa'iqa, saika (A)   "Lightning." Name of a Palestinian-Syrian organization in existence since 1968.

Salafiyya (A)   "The Path of Forefathers." 19th-century movement of return to the sources of the Muslim community in reaction to the ossification of Muslim thought. Principal theoreticians: Jamal al-Din al-Afghani, died in 1897, and Mohammad 'Abduh, died in 1905.

salat (A)   Canonical prayer, three times a day. See *PILLARS OF ISLAM.*

sanjak (T)   Standard, flag; in the Ottoman Empire: territorial writ, province.

Santri (Sanskrit)   Practicing Muslim believers in Indonesia, as opposed to the *ABANGAN*; middle-class culture with strong influences from Arabic culture.

Sanusiyya (A)   Reformist and missionary Muslim brotherhood formed in the middle of the 19th century, founded by the Algerian Muhammad al-Sanusi (died in 1859). The group took hold in the Cyrenaica (eastern Libya) beginning in the 1840s and acquired a dominant position in the eastern Sahara. It fought all the colonial powers: France, Great Britain and Italy. When Libya gained independence (1951), the brotherhood's leader, Idris, became the king of Libya.

Saqaliba (A)   "Slavs." Under the Ottomans, contingent of slaves of Slavic descent, bought in Frankish territory, to be used as elite soldiers or faithful palace servants.

sawm (A)   The fast; especially the fast during the month of Ramadan. See PILLARS OF ISLAM.

Sayyid (A)   Title given to the Prophet's descendants, especially Husayn's descendants, who established Zaydi principalities in Yemen and in the southern Caspian provinces of Iran.

Shafi'i (A)   School for Sunni Muslim law (and ritual); predominant in Asia and in eastern Black Africa. See also MADHHAB, HANAFI, HANBALI, MALIKISM.

shahada (A)   "Testimony." The profession of Muslim faith. ("There is no God but God and Muhammad is his prophet.") See PILLARS OF ISLAM.

shahid (A)   "One who professes his faith."

shari'a (A)   Muslim law derived through the discipline of FIQH from the Qur'an, the SUNNA, the IJMA', HADITH and other forms of reason.

sharif (A)   Descendant of Muhammad, especially Hasan's descendants.

shaykh ül-islam (A), **sheikh al-islam** (T)   Leader of all juridico-religious individuals in a Muslim state; appointed by the caliph.

shihna (A)   Military government, with a police superintendent in every important town, by sovereign decree. High urban civil servant who has received certain awards from the *ra'is*. He controls the *sahib al-shurta* (chief of the police) and can incarcerate whomever he wishes.

Shi'ism (A) (derived from *shi'a* = party, faction)   See boxes on pages 2 and 28.

shirazi (F)   A myth about the founding Muslim groups on the east coast of Africa, according to which the first Muslims in this region came from the Persian city of Shiraz. More likely, they were from the Arabian Peninsula or from the Arab (Persian) Gulf.

shu'ubiyya (A)   Literary movement among Iranian scribes and scholars. Exalted the values of Sassanid "courtly" literature integrated into the ADAB; opposed to the dominance of Arab culture.

sipahi (T) also: *sepoy* (in India)   Member of the Ottoman cavalry.

Sufi (A)   Ascetic who wears wool clothing (*suf*) and is devoted to spiritual life. In the 12th century/6th century, the Sufis, defenders of Sunni doctrine, were grouped together in the KHANAQAH and the RIBAT. Both the Persian *darvish* and the Arabic FAQIR (both meaning "poor") are used to describe Sufis, referring to their style of life.

sultan (A)   Literally, "power." Title given by the caliph to the Seljuq AMIR AL-UMARA', at first without political significance. The first to have the title was Toğrïl-Beg. Following the fall of the caliphate of Baghdad, title indicating the political independence of a prince.

suluk (A)   Observance of spiritual and contemplative life.

sunna (A)   Collection of traditions (HADITH) linked to the Prophet.

Sunnism (A)   See box on page 2.

Swahili (A) (*sahil* = "coast" pl. *sawahil*)   Generic term covering all the Islamic populations of the eastern coast of Black Africa and the islands of the Indian Ocean, from southern Somalia to the Comores. Swahili, the most spoken language in Black Africa, is a Bantu (African) language with at least a third of its vocabulary consisting of Arabic words. See also HAUSA.

tabligh (A)   Preaching; eloquence.

ta'ifa (pl. *tawa'if*). (A)   "Group," "faction." Following the fall of the Umayyad caliphate in Cordoba, Muslim Spain split up into rival factions, *tawa'if*

(Berbers, Arabs, Slavs, etc.), who founded independent principalities; their princes are called the kings of the *ta'ifa* (*muluk al-tawa'if*).

takfir (A)   Anathema, excommunication.

tanzimat (T) (pl. of *tanzim*)   Reforms. In the Ottoman Empire, the period from 1839 to 1876, which witnessed many reforms in government.

taqiyya (A)   Especially among the Shi'is (*SHI'ISM*) and the *DRUZE*, the practice of dissimulating one's religion in a potentially dangerous situation.

taqlid (A)   "Acquiescence." Literal acceptance of the content of a lesson.

tariqa (A) (pl. *turuq*)   Religious brotherhood.

tekalif-i divaniye (T)   Exceptional taxes in the Ottoman Empire.

Tijaniyya, Tijani (A)   African Muslim brotherhood, founded by the Algerian Ahmad al-Tijani (died in Morocco in 1815). Was very popular in Algeria, Tunisia (led by al-Haj 'Umar) and sub-Saharan Africa. Divided into several branches, today the brotherhood is one of the most dynamic in the sub-Saharan region.

timar (T)   Grant of revenues from a plot of land to a civil servant or a soldier instead of wages; the holder of a *timar* was responsible for the management of this land and had to provide *SIPAHIS* for the army of the *SULTAN*.

tiraz (A)   Workshop for the weaving of wool and silk, a caliphian monopoly. Production eventually destined for the official dress and honorary robes that were the outer signs of power.

torodbe (sing. *torodo*)   Originally applied to those who live from begging (characteristic of Islamic students): designated the educated Islamic *TUKU-LOR*, promoters of a victorious Islamic *JIHAD* and a new regime in Futa Toro (the middle valley of Senegal) at the end of the 18th century. Name reserved for the cleric class in Futa Toro, but sometimes used, to signify other groups of clerics of *PEUHL* culture in West Africa.

Tukulor   Probably derived from the name Takrur, a town in ancient middle-Senegal. The French adopted this term to refer to sedentary peoples who speak *PEUHL*, but who are of multiple ethnic origins, who settled in the middle valley of the Senegal river (Futa Toro). The Tukulor call themselves the Futanke (pl. Futankobe): "the people of Futa," or the Hal-Pularen: "those who speak Peuhl."

türbe (T)   Mausoleum, funerary monument for an important figure.

türkoman (türkmen) (T)   Term designating Turkish tribes, nomadic or semi-nomadic, and later the dynasties created by some of these tribes.

'ulama' (A) (plural of *'alim*)   Learned man of Muslim legal and religious science: see *FIQH*, *FAQIH* and *MUFTI*.

umma (A)   The community of Muslim believers.

'umra (A)   The "lesser pilgrimage" to Mecca; can be performed any time. Also part of the "greater pilgrimage" (*HAJJ*). See also *PILGRIMAGE ROUTE*.

Urdu   Language used by most Muslims on the Indian continent; the language of Pakistan.

'ushr (A)   "Tithe." Originally, a canonical property tax levied on Muslims. It later became extra-canonical and was levied on the goods of foreign merchants; a reciprocal measure conforming to international standards during the Middle Ages. In ports, a border duty, paid in currency, according to an official estimate of the goods and following set guidelines on border tariffs.

Wahhabism (A) This movement gets its name from Muhammad 'Abd al-Wahhab, an Islamic reformer from the 18th century, born in Arabia. His education was influenced by Ibn Hanbal and Ibn Taymiyya. Having provoked negative reactions among his entourage, 'Abd al-Wahhab sought refuge with Muhammad b. Su'ud, ruler of 'Anaza from 1735 to 1765. The Saudi family, after taking power in Arabia, made Wahhabism the official state doctrine. Wahhabism is a fundamentalism that rejects all innovations, especially the brotherhoods and the cult of saints. The term *wahhabi* has been used in West Africa to refer to a militant anti-Western and anti-brotherhood movements, but it has no official tie to the Saudi doctrine. See also box on page 213.

waqf (A) (pl. **awqaf**) "Pious endowment." The giving of property, villages, shops, baths etc. to the Islamic state for pious works or for the public good. Such property usually cannot be regained and is managed by a ministery of *awqaf*.

wazir (A), **vizier** Civil administrative chief who leads the various DIWANS, also controls the revenues and expenses of the state. Beginning with the Seljuqs, he received 10% of the revenues of the state as his annual salary.

wilaya (a), **velayat** (T) Spiritual and/or political authority.

Wolof Ethnic group and language of Senegal that became the principal national language of Senegal.

yaya (T) Infantryman in the Ottoman army.

Zaydi (A) A branch of SHI'ISM, in Yemen; most moderate group of Shi'is.

zakat (A) Canonical tax in the name of solidarity that all free Muslims must pay. Levied on land or homes, merchandise put on the market, agricultural and mineral products. See PILLARS OF ISLAM.

zawiya (A) Literally "corner." In the Ottoman Empire, especially in North Africa, refered to a religious building of a brotherhood (a small mosque, an oratory etc.). The *zawiya* serveed as the residence for a religious figure and his family, as a teaching site, as a site of prayer and devotion, and as an inn for travelers and visitors. Also refers to the botherhood itself. Synonymous with *RIBAT* and *KHANAQAH*.

INDEX

The index headings are filed letter by letter. Tables are indicated by *t* following the page number and glossary items by *g*.

Great Dates in Islamic History

diwan al-insha 44, 375g
Diwan (Egyptian literary group) 259
Diwan (Hafiz) 136
Diyaf, Ibn Abi al- 225
Diyar Bakr (Turkey) 35, 126, 132, 134–35, 166–67, 207, 365
Djibouti 307t, 341, 370
Dobruja 125, 195, 200
Dodecanese Islands 197
Doghu Bayezid 202
Dolmabahçe palace (Constantinople) 218
Dome of the Rock (Jerusalem) 18
Don Cossacks 155
Dongola (Sudan) 139
Don Juan of Austria 100, 154
Dorylaeum 72
Dost Muhammad 234–35
double power, theory of 36
DP *see* Democratic Party
Dra 54
Dragut (Turghud) (pirate) 100
Drame, Muhammad al-Amin (Mamadu Lamine) 244
drought 325
drug addicts 366
Druze 204–5, 261, 263, 317–18, 375g
Dual Control 210
Dubai 352
Dulles, John Foster 291
Dumlupinar 268
Dunama Dibale (Muhammad ibn Jil) 84
Dunkas, Amara 190
Duqaq (ruler of Damascus) 61–62
Duquesne, Abraham 156
Durand Agreement (1893) 235
Durand Line 296
Durazzo 124
Durr, Shajar al- 68, 101
Durrani *see* Abdali Afghans
Durrani, Ahmad Shah 173, 181
Dursun Bey 128
Dushanbe (Tajikistan) 362
Düsturname (Enveri) 128
Dutch East India Company 186–87, 239
Dutch Indies 300
Dutch Trading Company 240
Dyula (Dioula) (ethnic group) 375g

E

earthquakes 102, 312, 333, 360, 363, 366, 368–69
East Africa 84–85, 140, 188, 191–92, 249, 303
East Africa Muslim Welfare Society 303
Eastern Pakistan 299
"Eastern Question" 193–94
East Germany 344
East India Company 237–38
East Pakistan 300, 336
East Timor 337
Ecevit, Bülent 328–29
Echmiadzin (Russia) 203
Economic Cooperation Organization 362
economy
  'Abbasids and the Muslim Empire 29–30
  Arab Near East 292–93, 325–26, 359–61
  Beyliks and Ottomans 127–28
  Central Asia and Eastern Europe 363
  Fatimids 46
  Islam in the Far East 301–2, 337–38, 368–69

Maghrib 285–86, 311–13, 349–50
  Mamluks in Egypt and Syria 111–12
  Near and Middle East 41
  Seljuqs of Rum 74–75
  Sub-Saharan Africa 370–71
  Turkish and Iranian Middle East 297–98, 332–34, 366–67
Ecuador 280t
Eddé, Emile 263–64
Edessa (al-Ruha) 61, 64, 66, 72, 105, 108
Edirne (Adrianople) 116, 120, 122, 161, 195, 197–99, 202, 269–70
EEC *see* European Economic Community
Efendi, Abu al-Su'ud 161, 163
Efendi, Mehmed Sa'id Halet 206
Efendi, Sa'd al-Din 163
Efendi, Tashköprüzade Ahmed Husam al-Din 163
Egridir 116
Egypt
  civilization and culture 293–94, 326–27, 361
  colonization and imperialism 194, 196, 200, 207–12, 219, 247–48, 257–59
  conquest and Islamization 3, 6–9, 26, 42–43, 45, 102, 105–9, 111–13
  domestic events 158–61
  economy, society and religion 8–9, 14, 17, 29, 46, 111, 113, 219, 257–59, 292–93, 325, 359–60
  foreign policy, diplomacy and war 150, 286–87, 290–92, 303, 310, 313, 318–19, 321–22, 324, 339, 357–59
  internal affairs and institutions 25, 43
  international organizations 287t, 307t
  political and institutional life 23, 25, 43, 61, 64–68, 130, 257–59, 279–80, 288–90, 305, 314–18, 351–52, 354–55
Egyptian Campaigns (639-646) 6–7
Egyptian Communist Party 314
Egyptian Earth ('Abd al-Rahman Sharqawi) 294
Eisenburg, Peace of *see* Vasvár, Peace of
Eisenhower Doctrine 291, 296
Elbistan (Asia Minor) 73, 131, 158
Elchibey, Abulfez 362
electrical power grids 360, 367
elephants 3, 36
Elizabeth I (queen of England) 147–48
Emergency Force, U.N. (UNEF) 291
Emre, Yunus 76
engineering schools 163
England *see* Great Britain
English language 238, 339
Enna *see* Castrogiovanni
Enos-Media line 202
Entente Cordiale (1904) 222
Enveri (writer) 128
Enver Pasha 217–18
Epidaura 200
Epira 122
Equitoria Corps 303
Equitorial Guinea 340
Eretna (Anatolia) 119
Eritrea 339, 370
Eritrean Liberation Front 339
Ermenak (Anatolia) 116
Ermenak, Great Mosque of 129

Ershad, Mohammad 336–37, 367
Erzerum 73, 77, 126, 159, 198
Erzerum, Accord of (1823) 195
Erzerum, Congress of (1919) 218
Erzincan (Turkey) 366
Erzinjan 73, 80
eschatology 16
Eshref (Anatolia) 116
Essence of Current Events, The (Mustafa 'Ali) 163
E'tesami, Parvin 298
Ethiopia 4, 137, 139–40, 188, 190–91, 248–49, 284, 311, 339–40
ethnic cleansing 361
Eti Bank (Turkey) 270
Eugene of Savoy 157
Eulogius (historian and priest) 27
Euphemius (Byzantine governor) 26
Euphrates and Tigris Steam Navigation Company 206
Europe *see specific country* (*e.g.,* France)
European Community (EC) 344
European Economic Community (EEC) 310, 318, 322, 327, 330, 332, 349
European Parliament 349
Eutychius (Sa'id ibn al-Batriq) 45
Evian Accord (1962) 284
Evora 55
Evren, Kenan 329–30
existential monism 114
Exmouth, Lord 222
Exposé on the Ottomans' Laws (Husayn Hezarfen) 165
ezan (call to prayer) 269

F

Fadak oasis 5
Fadlallah, Rabih (Rabih Zubayr) 246
Fahd (king of Saudi Arabia) 317, 353–55, 358
Fahd peace plan (1981) 306, 322
Faience Pavillion (Istanbul) 129
Fairuz (Lebanese composer) 326
Faisal (king of Saudi Arabia) 314, 316
Faisal II (king of Iraq) *see* Faysal
Faisal, Tejan al- 355
Faisal-Nasser Accord (1967) 319
Falkenhayn, General von 198
falsafa 39, 375g
Famagusta 154
Family Code (Algeria, 1984) 313
Family Code (Senegal, 1972) 340
Family Protection Law (Iran, 1967) 333
famines 46, 106, 109, 176, 226, 232
Fansuri, Hamza 187
Fao (Iraq) 207, 326, 331–32
Farabi, al- 40
Fara'izi movement 238
Faraj (sultan of Egypt) 105–6, 111, 133
Faramiya 6
Far East 298–302, 335–38, 367–69
Farewell Pilgrimage 5
Farid, Ibn al- 70
Farigh of Ghilan 170
Faris, Abu al- 98
Farrokhzad, Forugh 298
Farrukhsiyar (Indian ruler) 181
Fars 34, 41, 133, 135
Faruq (king of Egypt) 258–60, 288
Faruqi dynasty 176
Fassi, Allal al- 251–52, 282
fatah 375g

Fatah (Palestinian group) 315–19, 347–48, 356
Fath 'Ali Shah 228
Fath al-qussi fi al-fath al-qudsi, al- ('Imad al-Din al-Isfahani) 69
Fath Khan 234
Fathpur Sikri (India) 183
Fatima (daughter of Muhammad) 4
Fatimids 28, 38–39, 42–46, 60–71
fatwa 37g, 332, 334, 355, 364
Fayd, Mullah Muhsin-i 171
Fayd al-'ubab (Ibn al-Hajj al-Numayri) 98
Faysal (king of Syria) 206, 261
Faysal (Sa'udi leader) 212
Faysal I (king of Iraq) 265
Faysal II (king of Iraq) 288
Fayz, Abu al- 175
Fazaz, plateau of 52
Fazl, Abu al- 182
FDIC *see* Front for the Defense of Constitutional Institutions
Fedayan (Iranian group) 328
Fedayan-e Islam (Iranian group) 297
Fedayan-e Khalq (Iranian group) 333
Federation of Arab Emirates of the South 292
Federation of Arab Labor Unions 291
Federation of Elected Muslims (Algeria) 254
feminism 327
Ferdinand of Aragon 91
Ferdinand I of Castile 49
Ferdinand III of Castile 57, 88
Ferghana 16, 174–75, 178, 236
Ferid Pasha, Damad 218
Ferraoun, Mouloud 286
Fertile Crescent project 266
Fez (Morocco)
  art and architecture 58, 149–50
  conquest and Islamization 29, 42, 52, 54, 91, 94–100
  economy, society and religion 93–100, 149–50
  foreign policy, diplomacy and war 221–22, 252–53
  internal affairs and institutions 145
  political and institutional life 306
Fez, Treaty of (1912) 222
Fez al-Bali 143
Fez al-Jadid 95
Fezzan (Libya) 190, 257
Fida, Abu al- (writer) 101, 115
fida'i 376g
Fifth Crusade 67
Filada madrasa (Meknes) 149
Filibe *see* Philippopoli
fiqh 376g
Firdawsi (poet) 78
fires 43, 46, 162
First Crusade 61, 72
First Zionist Congress (Basel, 1897) 205
Firuzabad (Iran) 366
Firuzkuh *see* Jam
FIS *see* Islamic Salvation Front
fiscal reform 16, 44
fitna 376g
Fitzgerald, Edward 82
five pillars of Islam 9
Five Years' War 133
FLN *see* National Liberation Front
flooding 369
"Fly Whisk Incident" (1827) 223
Fodio, Usman dan 242–43, 245
Fonduq al-Sultan (Qasr al-Kabir building) 150

Index